Praise For
Taking the Rap

"*Taking the Rap* is a gripping personal story of the prison system's political priorities and institutional violence. It is a must-read for anyone who wants to know more about the social world of prisoners, the complexities of resistance in the face of incarceration, and the impact of colonialism, capitalism, patriarchy, and racism in Canada."

—Eryk Martin, Department of History, Kwantlen Polytechnic University

"In narrating her truth about women's incarceration in Canada's prisons and jails, Ann Hansen gives us a heartbreaking account of what the imprisoning of women really means—and the troubles it engenders. Violence, misery, and corruption are rife in these carceral spaces, but so too is the enduring resilience of so many of the women confined within them."

—Elizabeth Comack, professor of sociology and criminology, University of Manitoba

"Courageous in its vulnerability, Hansen's gripping memoir speaks to both the spirit of dignity and solidarity among those who have shared extreme degradation and the manner in which the all-pervasive injustice of prison culture is corrosive to the psyche of jailer and jailed alike. Ultimately, *Taking the Rap* advances that most urgent and compelling argument for prison abolition: the story of the imprisoned."

—Paul Quick, barrister and solicitor, Queen's Prison Law Clinic

"In this intellectually engaging, politically radical, and emotionally evocative memoir, Ann Hansen recounts her experiences in Canada's correctional system. For too long, political and legal conversations about the criminalization and incarceration of women have ignored the voices of the women prisoners themselves—Hansen's bold and raw telling of her own stories is a must-read for academics, lawyers, and policy-makers alike."

—Rebecca Bromwich, author of *Looking for Ashley: Re-Reading What the Smith Case Reveals about the Governance of Girls, Mothers and Families in Canada*

"Ann Hansen is an honest, powerful, self-aware storyteller who combines sharp political analysis with compelling dialogue and characterization. In *Taking the Rap,* she shows how a life lived in struggle can also be a life of joy, compassion, humour, and intimacy. This book is a must-read for those who are fighting against, or simply want to better understand, the deleterious effects of the prison industrial complex upon the most marginal and vulnerable people in our society."

—Richard Day, author of *Gramsci is Dead: Anarchist Currents in the Newest Social Movements*

"*Taking the Rap* reveals in sometimes excruciatingly vivid detail the injustices and inequalities heaped on women as a result of social, economic, and legal systems that privilege those in power, particularly those who are what a Maori friend refers to as the "male, pale, and stale" crowd. Her passionate alliance with the women whose struggles she shares provides readers with a rare vantage point from which to examine the impoverishment of a legal system that is too often devoid of justice."

—Kim Pate, independent senator of Canada and former executive director of the Canadian Association of Elizabeth Fry Societies

"*Taking the Rap* will change the way you think about the necessity of prisons."

—Vicki Chartrand, Department of Sociology, Bishop's University

"*Taking the Rap* is an intimate combination of memoir and critical analysis. Through a thirty-year lens, Hansen flavours her personal narrative with introspection and political insight. Anyone who wants to understand the human impact and political context of Canada's prison and parole system, needs to read this extraordinary book."

—Allan Manson, professor emeritus, Queen's University

"Taking us into the belly of the beast that is the Canadian carceral state as only a political prisoner with first-hand experience of incarceration can, *Taking the Rap* is a must-read for organizers and scholars seeking to make sense of and resist the persistence of imprisonment and its intensification."

—Justin Piché, co-managing editor, *Journal of Prisoners on Prisons*, and associate professor of criminology, University of Ottawa

TAKING
THE
RAP

WOMEN DOING TIME FOR SOCIETY'S CRIMES

ANN HANSEN

Between the Lines
Toronto

Taking the Rap
© 2018 Ann Hansen

First published in 2018 by
Between the Lines
401 Richmond Street West, Studio 281
Toronto, Ontario M5V 3A8
Canada
1-800-718-7201
www.btlbooks.com

Every reasonable effort has been made to identify copyright holders. Between the Lines would be pleased to have any errors or omissions brought to its attention.

Library and Archives Canada Cataloguing in Publication

Hansen, Ann, 1953-, author
    Taking the rap : women doing time for society's crimes / Ann Hansen.

Issued in print and electronic formats.
ISBN 978-1-77113-355-5 (softcover).--ISBN 978-1-77113-356-2 (EPUB).--
ISBN 978-1-77113-357-9 (PDF)

    1. Women prisoners. 2. Women--Effect of imprisonment on.
3. Women prisoners--Social conditions. 4. Imprisonment--Psychological
aspects. 5. Women prisoners--Anecdotes. I. Title.

HV8738.H367 2018   365'.6082   C2017-907776-7
                                                         C2017-907777-5

Cover illustration, cover and text design by Maggie Earle
Printed in Canada

We acknowledge for their financial support of our publishing activities: the Government of Canada; the Canada Council for the Arts, which last year invested $153 million to bring the arts to Canadians throughout the country; and the Government of Ontario through the Ontario Arts Council, the Ontario Book Publishers Tax Credit program, and the Ontario Media Development Corporation.

   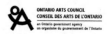

To all the women who have died in Canadian prisons. They are survivors of residential schools, abusive relationships, addictions, and other mental health issues, and of punishing prison sentences for acts of economic survival.

Contents

Introduction

This book takes off from where my previous memoir, *Direct Action: Memoirs of an Urban Guerrilla*, ends, which is on the day of our arrests, January 20, 1983. Considering what we know about memory, what is the point of writing a book that begins thirty years ago, in 1983? What is the point of writing a book about prison conditions when thirty years of change have drastically altered their landscape, not just in terms of the physical buildings, but also in terms of policy?

When I was first arrested in British Columbia in January 1983, I was remanded to Oakalla—or as it was officially known, the Lower Mainland Regional Correctional Centre—until I was finally convicted in the summer of 1984 and sent to the Prison for Women (P4W) in Kingston, Ontario. In 2014, Oakalla is no more, and P4W was closed in 2000. Today, women serving federal time in Ontario are sent to the Grand Valley Institution for Women in Kitchener. How relevant are my observations and analysis going to be?

Federally sentenced prisoners still can only make a maximum of $6.90 a day, the same maximum daily wage as thirty years ago, despite the increased rate of inflation (if this wage had been adjusted for inflation, it would be $13.28 a day today, according to the Bank of Canada calculator) and the increased number of items that prisoners must purchase on canteen. The police-reported crime rate has been on a steady decline over the past two decades, although the percentage of prisoners per capita has been exponentially increasing. In 2012, 20 percent of all federally sentenced prisoners in Canada are double bunked, a practice that contravenes the United Nations Standard Minimum Rules on the Treatment of Prisoners.[1] Writing a prison memoir that goes back thirty years is very relevant, in light of the fact that so many aspects of prison conditions have stayed the same, and those that have not have been on a steady decline since that time.

If there's one aspect of the prison system that has struck me over the past thirty years, it would be how little has changed: different buildings, same power dynamics; different policies, same MO. To be succinct, my prison memories from the last two decades of the twentieth century are just as relevant as my memories from the first decade of the twenty-first century.

I use the words *prisoners*, *prisons*, and *imprison*, instead of the more commonly used terms *inmates*, *institutions*, and *incarcerate*, quite consciously, because they more accurately describe the people and place. As radical linguists such as Noam Chomsky have pointed out, words are not neutral in terms of political or social values.[2] Language plays a role in shaping our consciousness.

Our consciousness of reality is influenced by the dialectic conflict between our objective reality and the words our culture uses to describe it. For example, there is a real animal we commonly refer to as a *pig*, and then there is the word used by the agricultural business community—*product*—to describe the same animal. The dialectical conflict between a person seeing a *pig*, but hearing it repeatedly described as a *product* by agri-business, changes a person's consciousness so they begin to view the animal as an inanimate consumer product.

Over time the Western media, which is owned by Western ruling elites, have adopted the language that reflects the values and assumptions of the status quo. As a result, words such as *inmate*, *offender*, *institution*, and *penitentiary* are commonly used to describe what I refer to in this book as *prisoners* and *prisons*. The benign terms the Western media use have the effect of depoliticizing the involuntary nature of confining another human being.

Historically, *inmate* was commonly used to refer to someone who is voluntarily and temporarily residing in some form of institution, such as a mental hospital. According to the Oxford Modern English Dictionary, *institution* is defined as "1) the act or an instance of instituting 2a) a society or organization founded esp. for charitable, religious, educational, or social purposes b) a building used by an institution 3) an established law, practice or custom."[3] None of these definitions includes imprisonment, and yet most modern prisons are officially labelled *institutions*, as in Grand Valley Institution for Women, Millhaven Institution, Kent Institution, and so on. The words *inmate* and *institution* have the overall effect of creating a subliminal image of the prisoner as someone who is voluntarily institutionalized for both their own and society's benefit. These words strip the prisoner of the involuntary, violent, and conflicted nature of their relationship with society once they have been confined within a prison.

Unlike my first memoir, the events in this book have not been previously published in newspaper articles or court transcripts. In order to protect the identities of real people, I have created composites by changing their physical traits as well as their names. There are exceptions to this rule. My Direct Action co-accused, Brent Taylor, Julie Belmas, Gerry Hannah, and Doug Stewart, are not composites, because their stories are already a part of the public record through media publications and court transcripts. I do mention the wardens of P4W, George Caron and Mary Cassidy, as well as the psychiatrists Dr. George and Dr. Duncan Scott, by name, because they were public servants whose decisions were open to public scrutiny.

I would like to claim that the events replicate reality accurately, but I can only claim that these events occurred, even though many of the timelines, conversations, emotions, and other details are not accurate. There are many culprits responsible for tainting my memory, but time has taken the greatest toll. Yet despite the fact that the descriptions of the events do not precisely mirror reality, these events did happen. If each chapter were a human body, the skeletal structure, organs, and muscle tissue are real, but the height of the body, the colour of the eyes, and structure of the nose, ears, and appendages are not.

Unfortunately, the memory is not reliable, and so two people describing the same event will more than likely describe two very different situations. If I have said things that anyone who believes they are one of the characters in this book does not agree with, my intentions were good, but my memory may not be. I have no axe to grind or dish of revenge to serve up cold. I am describing prison life as I remember it. But memory is an evil prankster that is unreliable at best, and at its worst, it turns facts into illusions that change shape or disappear entirely depending on the day and state of mind of the writer. Memory is responsible for more wrongful convictions than any other type of evidence presented in trials: "The Innocence Project has determined that 75% of the 239 DNA exoneration cases had occurred due to inaccurate eye witness testimony."[4]

My point here is that I am not immune to the frailties and trickery of my memory any more than the next person. I have tried to the best of my abilities to write a memoir that is based on events I believe are accurate, but I am sure that some of my disguised characters will swear that my version of reality is not accurate. The paradox is that neither of us is lying. However, despite any discrepancies over facts, in the tradition of Farley Mowat, I did not want to let "the facts get in the way of truth." I can honestly say that this memoir speaks the truth.

I have also tried to use the "show not tell" method of storytelling, in that I have tried to hold up a mirror to my reality in prison to make the reader feel as though they were actually there. I did not want the reflection distorted by my conscious effort to inject political correctness, or my values or analysis, or by attempts to make it more exciting.

When I first walked into a jail cell on January 20, 1983, my experiences were heavily influenced by my political analysis. Everyone's perceptions of reality are skewed, as though they are wearing sunglasses that distort everything to fit their own unique set of values, assumptions, and political perspective. In the spirit of truth-telling and the "show not tell" story format, I am going to give you my sunglasses for a moment, to reveal the prism through which I perceived the prison reality.

Throughout history, there have always been wealthy elites who have chosen, whether consciously or not, to target the most vulnerable people in their society as convenient scapegoats to be blamed for the fallout from their economic and political policies. These scapegoats are the addicted, the mentally ill, the poor, the marginalized, and are disproportionately any colour but white. In our relatively wealthy, Western society, these scapegoats are often criminalized and imprisoned.

Before the advent of prisons, what did European societies do with their scapegoats? For centuries, Europe was ruled by monarchies or theocracies that did not want to waste their tax dollars on confining or caring for "criminals." The best way for kings and queens or religious leaders to get the most bang for their buck was by using a form of punishment that would deter others, generating as much fear as possible for as little money as possible. This fear factor or deterrent to committing crimes was best achieved through must-see public spectacles in town squares, where criminals were hung, quartered, burned, or crucified. Watching a live human being attached to four horses pulling them apart in four different directions was a very effective deterrent from stealing, murdering, or committing adultery.

This very public spectacle is a far cry from today's obscure, nondescript institutional prisons, which are designed to blend in with their surroundings. The monarchies and theocracies of the Middle Ages did not have to worry about elections or unfriendly media campaigns. The goal of today's prisons is to remain invisible so as not to attract the attention of those pesky human rights organizations and media hordes that might illuminate the quiet torture going on inside.

If anything has changed over the past three decades, it would be that the class of people globally that are considered disposable is growing. Ever since the industrial revolution, there has been a systemic need for surplus labour in order to keep wages low. But in the twenty-first century, with labour being replaced by technology and computers, and free trade deals creating ever-larger surplus labour pools in North America and Europe, millions of people have become obsolete in this post-industrial era.[5] This is the disposable class, who, like "the pig" mentioned earlier, are being rebranded from people into a "product" for the burgeoning prison industry of the future.

In the twenty-first century, there is a grave danger that this growing disposable class will become restless, maybe even angry and organized, and therefore become a big problem for that shrinking but ever-richer class of people, commonly referred to as either the 1 percent or "the elites." They may be rich and powerful, but they aren't stupid. They have been increasingly using the private prison industry to utilize this disposable class of people as a source of revenue on both the supply and demand side of the capitalist market equation. Thus, the private prison industry makes money on the supply side by being paid subsidies from the government for every prisoner they control, and on the demand side, they farm these same prisoners out as very cheap wage slaves to other private industries. For Black people, this has historically been a seamless transition, from cotton slave in the pre-industrial period to prison slave in the post-industrial period. And for Indigenous people, this has been a seamless transition from residential school to prison compound. Finally, in a win-win-win situation, the rich and powerful continue to use these prisoners in their age-old role as scapegoats for all the social injustices and inequities that are a result of their own government or private industry policies and practices.

As this disposable class gets bigger and bigger, there is a grave danger of their restlessness and anger becoming a threat to the ruling elites. If there is no revolution, I predict that the ruling elites will legislate guaranteed annual incomes, which will be just enough to meet peoples' needs so they can continue to buy the reams of useless junk that allows the 1 percent to continue accumulating wealth. Despite the many legal drugs that will become available to keep the obsolete pacified, many people will still stray outside the legal boundaries. They will be arrested and shipped off to the many prison industrial complexes on the Colonies, just as their ancestors were shipped off to the Colonies before. Only this time they will be shipped off in one of Elon Musk's Big Falcon Rockets—or as they are more commonly known, Big Fucking Rockets—to the Colonies on the moon or Mars to work in the massive resource extraction industry that will no doubt be operational, if we do not go extinct first.

This is the perspective through which I viewed my reality from the day of my arrest in 1983, right up until now, 2017: a perspective that has only become more clear, bright, and colourful over the past thirty years of prison and parole.

PART I
THROUGH THE LOOKING GLASS, 1983

"Some political prisoners are arrested for staging public demonstrations that address poverty, and some are arrested for living in poverty. Some actively protest social inequality, while others turn to drugs or alcohol because they can no longer bear the brunt of this inequality. Some choose to draw attention to injustice by their words and actions, while others are swept off the streets because their very presence is a public exposure of this injustice. Every prisoner is a political prisoner."

Kelly Pflug-Back, in a letter from
Vanier Prison, Milton, Ontario, 2012

One

When the smoke finally settled, the cop car slowly turned around and headed down the Squamish highway, leaving behind the remnants of what looked like a battle scene. Looking back through the foggy rearview window, I saw our pickup truck for the last time, sitting in a semicircle of shattered glass where its canopy window had been blown out. A dozen men in camouflage army fatigues carrying rifles were milling about the unmarked cop cars parked askew on both sides of the highway. The rancid smell of tear gas filled the cop car, and left the men still on the scene wiping stinging tears off their faces as they went about preparing to leave.

The suspense was over for the time being. The Plexiglas barrier that separated Julie and me from the cops in the front seat gave us the feeling that we could relax for a little while, even though we didn't dare talk or even look at one another. I felt lucky to be alive.

A fine drizzle covered the windshield, so the cops turned on their defroster and windshield wipers, making it difficult to hear conversations. If we had decided to talk, there was no doubt they would be listening. That much we knew for sure.

I looked over at Julie once the car had settled down to a cruising speed. This sudden turn of events only strengthened my feelings of loyalty toward my friend. She always looked beautiful, no matter what. Her long black hair was dishevelled and tangled with bits of gravel. Her winter parka was covered in dirty slush, and her black mascara traced long dark lines down her face where her tears had flowed. She sat resolutely facing the window with her arms folded protectively across her chest, giving me the impression she did not want to be consoled. I stifled an impulse to put my arm around her.

Instead, I concentrated on the black asphalt highway disappearing rapidly under the car as we sped around the steep winding curves along the coastal highway. I peered out the window, trying to catch glimpses of the grey ocean through the gnarled pine trees that managed to survive among the rocky cliffs below us. On the other side, the steep sides of the mountains disappeared above the passenger window. I figured I had better take advantage of the opportunity to admire this coastal region of British Columbia, because it would probably be my last.

One of the cops turned halfway around and pushed apart the barrier window, just a little. "So what were you gals doing up here today?" His eyes contradicted his friendly voice. They looked cold, yet nervous, like we were the ones carrying the guns. I wondered why he thought we would engage in some casual banter with him after such a violent takedown.

After we ignored him for a few minutes, he nodded his head toward the road up ahead. "You don't have any friends up here waiting for you, eh?"

It occurred to me that they really did think we had people waiting to ambush them around every corner. I started noticing that each time we rounded a curve in the highway, it seemed as though they were peering ahead to see the ambush before it was too late. The light rain and cold winter air had created a fog that grew thicker as we made our way toward sea level. Their mood was infectious; before long, Julie and I found ourselves trying to make out the silhouettes of nonexistent parked cars in the fog, just out of reach of their headlights—wishful thinking on our part, paranoia on theirs.

When the fog became so dense we could only see what appeared in the beams of the headlights, I started to worry more about the speed we were driving, and washed-out bridges. The winter rains had caused mudslides in areas where the forests had been clear cut off the mountain sides. In the past couple of years, the Squamish highway had been the scene of several disasters when bridges had been washed away in those mudslides, and unsuspecting motorists had fallen like dominoes into the river chasm below.

"So where do you think they're taking us?" whispered Julie, forcing me back to the situation at hand.

"I don't know."

"I'm so scared that the boys are dead." Her eyes welled up with tears.

"Dead! No, Jules. I thought the same thing when I heard the gunshots go off, but I'm sure I saw them sitting in another cop car when we were waiting to leave."

"Are you sure?" She finally turned to look at me head on. Her pale blue eyes had that kind of energy that was almost physical.

"Unless they have twins who were coincidentally handcuffed in a police car at the same remote spot we were at today," I reassured her.

She smiled faintly. "Remember not to say anything other than you want to see your lawyer," I reminded her in a low whisper. She nodded her head vigorously.

The same cop turned around and gave us a venomous stare. "Listen up. I don't want you whispering at all!"

We settled into watching the wet, black highway snaking along in front of us and listening to the mesmerizing slap of the windshield wipers and whir of the tires racing along on the slick asphalt. I was still in a state of shock from the massive bust. Was this going to be the last time we would be outside? Was it possible that they knew everything, or were we just being busted for the stolen weapons and vehicle? I clung desperately to the hope that this was just about the guns and the truck, even though all the cops in army fatigues, and the way we had been taken down, testified to so much more.

Finally we rounded our last curve, and the lights from the outskirts of Squamish twinkled in the dusk. As we caught up to several other unmarked cars waiting at the first intersection for the lights to turn green, we realized we were actually part of a small convoy. The convoy cruised smoothly through the last few blocks before we reached the Squamish RCMP building.

The police car braked so abruptly in front of the entranceway that we lurched forward in our seat from the momentum. We got the distinct impression they were still anticipating an ambush from our mysterious comrades. No sooner had the car stopped moving than the cops in the front seat jumped out and scanned the horizon suspiciously, keeping their hands loosely resting on their gun holsters. Once again their fear was palpable, causing us to squint into the grey mist that had settled down, softly obliterating everything outside of the RCMP parking lot. Was it possible that someone was actually out there waiting to rescue us? If so, who knows what the cops would be capable of, with all that fear motivating their every move? If there was one thing I was sure of, after all those months of robbery preparation, fear is the root cause of most "accidents."

We were so busy trying to see if there were some unexpected saviours hidden in the far reaches of the RCMP parking lot that we looked right through Brent and Doug, sitting in the police car parked directly in front of us. By the time my eyes began to focus on objects other than potential rescuers, they were turned around in their seats, staring at us through the rearview window.

"Look!" gasped Julie, bouncing up and down in her seat like a little girl who had just spotted Santa Claus. Brent looked back at me with sad, longing eyes. He looked pretty rough. In the dim overhead lights of the car's interior, I could still make out how red and swollen his eyes were. Doug looked pretty much the same way.

"Where's Gerry?" Julie's emotions had swung from delight to despair again. I scoured the other cars parked behind and in front of us as best I could in the fading light.

Then we saw a cop open the back door of the car in front of Brent and Doug. Out came Gerry, his parka covered in slush and gravel. The cop escorting him motioned toward the door, but Gerry still managed to turn around and look for us. When he saw us, his face broke into a big smile. It occurred to me that if the three of them had been cleaned up, they would have looked a lot more like undercover cops than any of our marginalized friends. Brent, with his athletic six-foot-two physique, had taken to wearing his once long, curly black hair very short and sported a neatly trimmed beard in an attempt to blend in with people in suburbia. Even though Doug's camouflaged jacket was also covered in slush, his clean-cut, chiselled face and broad shoulders reminded me of a young soldier.

The cops took Julie and me into the RCMP lockup together and placed us in open barred cells beside one another in what appeared to be a small cellblock. All we could see was a cinderblock wall across from our cells, and from the way the sounds echoed off the walls, we assumed there were no other women in our block.

"Hello!" Julie called out. Gerry returned a muffled greeting through a solid metal fire door that separated us from the men.

"I miss you so much! Are you all right?"

"Yeah," he laughed. "We're all in one piece, if that's what you mean. So they got us all beside each other. How convenient, eh?"

"Yeah," Julie yelled. "What happened to you?" We knew better than to say anything to each other that the police didn't already know.

Doug chuckled. "We were just sitting there in the back of the truck freezing our butts off when suddenly all hell breaks loose. I thought we were going to die for sure. They smashed in the back window of the canopy and shot a couple of rounds of tear gas in so we couldn't see or breathe. If they hadn't dragged us out of there as fast as they did, we probably would have asphyxiated. But somehow I don't think they dragged us out to save our lives or nothin'. What about you two? Are you okay?"

"Yeah," Julie said. "It was kind of funny, 'cause there was this sign that said there was rock blasting going on up ahead on the highway. So we come to this long lineup of cars waiting for them to clear the rock off the highway. They're letting cars go through one at a time. So when it's our turn, we drive along until we come to this flag man standing in front of this big dump truck parked right across the highway. This flag man motions for Alice to roll down her window so he can talk to her." Julie was using my alias in case our cells were bugged. "Alice says to us that he reminds her of the cartoon guy, Dudley Do-Right, the RCMP guy. So we're laughing at that when sure enough, right out of a nightmare, this guy transforms into Dudley Do-Right, and puts his one hand in the window and grabs Alice, and opens the door with the other. I barely had time to figure out what's happening when some cop grabs me by the hair and drags me out of the truck onto the ground. That's when I heard the shotgun blast, and I thought for sure you guys had been shot!"

It was hard yelling through the door.

"When I was lying on the ground with that cop on my back pressing his gun to my head, I was facing you. I could see you under the truck, facedown in the gravel with a cop lying on top of you, but I couldn't see your face. I thought you were dead."

There was a long silence as we reflected on the seriousness of our situation. It made me tired, so tired. I sat down on the cot that was fastened into the grey cinderblock wall and wished I could turn off the shimmering fluorescent lights.

A cop suddenly strode in and handed everyone a roll of toilet paper, a facecloth, and a comb through the bars. Then he asked if anyone wanted a shower to wash off the tear gas. I was way too paranoid to get naked in a shower stall in an RCMP lockup, so I declined. It struck me as strange that they should be concerned about our comfort. This experience certainly conflicted with my expectations of police brutality.

I took a minute to scrub the dirt and tear gas off my face, and ran the comb briefly through the tangles in my hair. After I was done, the tiredness was unbearable, so I curled up in a fetal position to succumb to a few minutes' rest.

I must have just dozed off when I was startled into wakefulness by the sound of keys jangling in the cell door. Two uniformed cops stood in front of my cell, staring at me disdainfully. Whatever happened to that hospitality cop with the comb and facecloth? The old adage "If it's too good to be true, it probably is" can be applied to the experience of hospitality cops; the offer to use a comb is actually a sneaky way for the cops to get a hair sample for possible DNA testing.

There were no sounds coming from the other cells. I had been in the constant company of Brent, Julie, Gerry, or Doug for so long now that I felt a sense of security in their presence, as though we were family. This was the first time in years I had the feeling of being alone, and it filled me with fear.

"What's up?" I asked.

"We have a few questions." Without asking, they picked up the comb and facecloth from the sink and led the way down the hall. As I expected, the others were not in their cells.

I followed them out of the cellblock area almost immediately into a small, empty office with only a chair, a large wooden desk, and a cop with an expressionless face sitting behind it, engrossed in a sheath of papers lying in front of him. I glanced around for a thick telephone book, an electronic device, or anything else that could be used as an instrument of torture, but there was nothing but the desk, the chair, and the man.

Even though I had been very tired only a few minutes before, it's amazing how a police interrogation room can wake a person up. I repeated the mantra "I want to speak to my lawyer. I want to speak to my lawyer" over and over to myself. But when he opened up the questioning with my alias—"Miss Lillycropp, take a seat"—I decided it might be best to go along with this charade. Maybe, just maybe, this was only about the guns and the truck.

"So, Miss Lillycropp, what were you and your friends doing up in the mountains?" He gave me a piercing look.

Without hesitation I said, "Camping. Winter camping."

"That is your name, isn't it?"

"Yes," I said firmly.

There was a long silence, during which he stared at me with open contempt. Then for dramatic effect he slammed the open sheaf of papers shut. "Quit with the bullshit, Hansen. You are in very deep trouble. We know perfectly well that you are not Alice Ann Lillycropp, and if you don't start telling us the truth, you will never see the light of day outside a prison cell again."

It wasn't difficult to look bummed out as he listed the number of offences I was facing: possession of stolen weapons, a stolen truck, and false identification. But when he stopped at that, my feeling of hope remained intact, although I still felt depressed. I maintained a look of despair.

He waited for me to say something, but when I didn't, he rather quickly aborted his tactics of intimidation and decided to try flattery instead.

"You strike me as an intelligent person, Miss Hansen, and no doubt played a significant role in acquiring all those weapons, the truck, and the ID, but I assure you, it is in your best interests to cooperate with us if you ever want to be free again." He sat motionless, waiting for my response.

"I want to speak to my lawyer," I said in a voice I didn't recognize as my own. For years I had mentally prepared for this moment, picturing myself as strong and defiant in the face of the inevitable torture. Despite the pounding of the thick telephone book against my diaphragm, legs, and face, I would still muster the courage to stand tall and repeat, "I want to speak to my lawyer." Sitting on the wooden chair, balanced precariously on the brink of the concrete stairwell, I would repeat, "I want to speak to my lawyer." No matter how powerful the electric shock, I would focus on the phrase, "I want to speak to my lawyer." But here I was without any torture whatsoever, and the voice I heard was so much weaker and unsteadier than my own.

I can only assume they had higher expectations for myself than I did, because instead of playing good cop/bad cop or, worse yet, resorting to torture, he asked for the name of my lawyer.

"Stan Guenther," I said with the same sense of relief I might have felt if Jesus was about to intervene.

"We'll give him a call, and you'll see him when we get you down to Vancouver." And that was the end of that.

When they escorted me back to my cellblock, the guys weren't back yet, but I squeezed Julie's hand through the bars as I passed. The affinity I felt toward her could not have been stronger. For a few minutes we sat in silence, until we heard the laughter of the guys bouncing off the walls. I wondered how different it would be to be arrested by yourself.

I also wondered how different it would be to be Indigenous or Black or a white sex worker arrested on the streets of the Downtown Eastside. As these scenes unfolded, it began to dawn on me that all the brutality and torture I had anticipated would have unfolded if I had been any of the above, but the fact I was a young white woman who presented as middle class cemented an unconscious bond with the cops and probably the future judge and jury, who would identify with me as "just like their sister or cousin" as opposed to an "other."

"Hey, Alice," Julie whispered loudly through her bars. "They didn't ask me anything. They just started yelling at me, and basically told me I was a dupe. They've got us profiled, all right. Once they got me crying, they changed tactics and said I would walk out of here tomorrow if I would testify against you guys. It sounds like they think we're up to a lot more than camping."

I could hear the strain in her voice. Obviously they had been much harder on her, basing their interrogation on the theory that she was the weak link, maybe even the innocent victim. Like me, they had assured her she wouldn't be getting out of prison until she was old and grey if she didn't cooperate. Then they'd played the Rex card. Somehow they knew she had her old dog, Rex, who she'd played with since childhood, living with us. They reminded her that Rex would be dead long before she got out. As soon as they had her crying, they feigned sympathy and started in on the paternal, brotherly act, offering to help her if she would help them. But they had underestimated Julie. Despite her fears and sadness, she had remained silent. She was only twenty years old … almost a decade younger than me.

I guessed from TV cop shows that they probably had us pegged as a stereotypical gang with a few ringleaders, and a whole lot of foot soldiers and dupes. It seemed they saw me as a ringleader. Maybe that's why they had cut my interrogation short.

After a time, we heard the keys jangling through the metal fire door. Gerry called out, "Bye, love," in a voice filled with warmth and affection.

"Bye! I love you!" Julie cried out, like some modern-day Juliet.

Brent and I had never been as outwardly expressive of our relationship. Maybe we were subconsciously modelling ourselves after the stereotypical revolutionary couple who placed their feelings for one another second to the needs of the revolution. Maybe it's just the way we were. Regardless, I did have feelings. I pressed myself up against the bars in an effort to see the guys one last time, but without success. By now there must have been a number of cops in their unit, because I could hear metal jangling and keys turning and any number of feet shuffling out the door.

After they had left, a male and a female cop came into our unit and told us to kneel on the cots while they fastened the leg irons and chains to our legs and handcuffs to our wrists. Slowly we shuffled out to the parking lot, which was so dark by now we could only see objects silhouetted in the conical circles of light created by the overhead parking lot lamps. After struggling to get into the car in leg irons and handcuffs, we sat morosely in the dim lighting of the interior. Our skin took on a greenish hue in the eerie lighting, and our faces aged as the shadows highlighted the lines and circles under our eyes. I looked up at the car ahead and saw Brent staring at us through the back window again, but this time he looked like he was crying. He lifted his hand to his lips and blew me a kiss.

Once again a number of unmarked cars fell into line in front of and behind our car, creating a long, silent convoy that cruised serenely down highway 99 into the outskirts of Vancouver. It wasn't until we were pulling up in front of the downtown Vancouver lockup that the cop in the front seat turned to his partner and showed us his hand. I don't think he realized we were still ignorant of the extent to which they were onto us.

"Those two look more like my younger sisters than they do terrorists," he said, turning and smiling at us. He looked more like a hungry wolf than a brother.

Two

I'm pretty sure we were all building a flimsy case around the hope that this was all based on the guns in the back of the stolen truck and the phony ID, and had nothing to do with Direct Action, the urban guerrilla group we had formed a few years ago. But by the next morning, when they drove us to the federal courthouse in Vancouver from the downtown RCMP lockup, that hope was history. After speaking to our lawyers, we had learned that the list of charges against us reached well over a hundred, ranging in seriousness from stealing cars to a multimillion-dollar bombing of the Litton plant where the guidance system for the cruise missile was being manufactured.

Who knows when it all really began, but the seed began to germinate when I first met Brent in the summer of 1980. Even though we had grown up on the opposite sides of Canada, we had both come of age during the late sixties and seventies, with a remarkably similar attitude toward current events. This was a time when Marxist guerrilla groups were rampant in Europe and North America. Of course, this was not a new phenomenon. Armed national liberation movements had been active for decades throughout most of the colonized world—Africa, Asia, and Latin America. But it had taken years before white and Black North Americans applied this prototype to their own struggles within the belly of the beast.

Travelling on opposite sides of the Atlantic Ocean, Brent and I were drawn, respectively, into the support networks of the Weather Underground in California and the Red Army Faction in Germany, as though attached to the same web. Despite my coming of age in the east and Brent's in the west, our mutual attraction to militancy had evolved in synchronicity through our involvement with the prison abolition, anarchist, environmental, women's, and Indigenous movements that dominated the Canadian left during that time.

I first met Brent on Prisoners' Justice Day on August 10, 1980. A small group of prison abolitionists had organized a twenty-four-hour fast and vigil at Toronto City Hall to commemorate all the prisoners who had died in prison and distribute information about prisons. Brent was en route to a gathering in the Black Hills of South Dakota but had stayed overnight to participate in the all-night vigil. During his stay, we talked about the need for a more militant, strategic campaign against capitalism in Canada.

As prison abolitionists, we believed that prisons were the most important social control mechanism, other than executions, of any political economic system, whether communist, socialist, or capitalist. Prisons are the main mechanism ruling elites use to scapegoat and victimize those they do not want or need. With this analysis in hand, we saw prison abolition and a strategic campaign against capitalism as one and the same. My position on prison abolition and capitalism has never wavered.

A few short months later, we reunited in Vancouver, where we began to develop our own unique brand of urban guerrilla warfare. Doug Stewart joined our fledgling collective, contributing his extensive knowledge of physics and electronics, and soon after, Julie Belmas and Gerry Hannah added their critique of capitalism from a punk-rock perspective. In the end, we married the high-tech, clandestine actions of the classic urban guerrilla group with anarchist, environmental, feminist politics and Indigenous solidarity to create Direct Action.

The militant campaign of Direct Action came to an abrupt end on that remote section of the Squamish highway on January 20, 1983. It was a time when electric transmission lines crisscrossed British Columbia, like fishnet across a beached whale, bringing electricity to pulp and paper mills all over the province. Forests were buzzing with chainsaws as lumber companies clear-cut mountainsides just out of sight of the tourists travelling across the Trans-Canada Highway. The eighties were the dawning of the age of mega-projects. These resource-hungry mega-projects were the economic engine driving the provincial economy, and every virgin river, stream, and lake was dammed up to supply the insatiable thirst of the mining companies for electricity.

Globally, the Berlin Wall still symbolized the division between East and West, the respective spoils of the two superpowers, the Soviet Union and the United States. The Cold War was a term used to justify the unrelenting buildup of these superpowers' military industrial complexes, even in so-called peacetime. Canada's role in this imaginary war was to be a site for military branch plants from the United States, such as Litton Systems

Canada, where guidance systems for the untested cruise missile were manufactured. But it did not remain untested for long. In 1983, Canada became the testing ground for the cruise missile, despite vocal public opposition and the passive resistance of opposition parliamentarians.

Pierre Trudeau, Canada's Liberal prime minister, played a particularly duplicitous role in the years leading up to Canada accepting its role as the test pilot for the cruise missile. All the outward signs indicated that he would not act the silent patsy in America's dangerous game of brinkmanship with nuclear missiles. In a 1978 speech to the UN conference on Disarmament, he advocated a "strategy of suffocation" based partly on a proposal to desist from or suffocate the testing of the planes that would have to carry the nuclear missiles.[6] However, after winning a majority in the 1980 election, Trudeau began the slow but steady transformation from an outspoken critic of nuclear missiles to the usual complicit Canadian puppet, not only allowing the Americans to test the cruise missile on Canadian soil, but also lying about the supposed obligations Canada had to fulfill as a partner in the NATO alliance.[7]

The eighties were a pivotal point in history on many fronts. The presidency of Ronald Reagan marked a seismic shift in the global economic paradigm. Keynesian economics had gained popularity in the wake of the "Great Depression" because it prescribed government use of tax dollars to stimulate the economy during recessions or depressions, even if this meant accumulating public debt. The success of this economic plan lay in the fact that the great masses of discontented working-class and unemployed people in North America did not successfully overthrow capitalism for the more poverty-friendly communism that was taking hold in the Soviet Union and China.

The father of Keynesian economics, John Maynard Keynes, recognized that spending money on large public work and other "make-work" projects would put money into the hands of the people, who in turn would spend it, thus stimulating the economy. Even in good times, as an antidote to communism, Keynes advocated the use of social safety nets, such as unemployment insurance, government pension plans, and social welfare. He argued that it would be safer for the government to spend some of its tax dollars on an effective social safety net than risk the working poor falling into the menacing hands of communists or socialists.

However, by the early eighties the spectre of communism was waning, and the ascendancy of neoliberal economics, as articulated by Milton Friedman, was transforming the economic landscape.[8] The eighties would become the age of neoliberalism, a more ruthless brand of economics marked by three main policies: free trade, the privatization of the public sector, and the implementation of law and order policies.

The eighties were also swept up by second-wave feminism. The main focus of the first wave had been universal suffrage—the right for women to be able to vote in their country's elections. In keeping with this implicitly bourgeois goal, this wave was dominated by white, middle-class women, whose political analysis did not question the fundamental capitalist economic system and its class struggle.

The second wave began in the 1960s and continued on into the 1990s. This phase was dominated by issues related to the guarantee of gender or sexual equality. This wave was more radical, as reflected in the slogan "women's struggle is class struggle," drawing in more women of colour and women fighting against colonialism all over the world. But it was still heavily focused on white women's issues, such as critiques of pornography, beauty pageants, and other sexist cultural rituals.

Although these issues were being hotly debated by feminists and radicals across Canada, the majority of people put topics involving mega-projects, cruise missiles, and violent pornography on the back burner. But in major cities and towns, little pockets of radicals and revolutionaries kept pushing the Sisyphean rock up the hill, undaunted as it rolled back down over them again and again. Across North America, Indigenous peoples remained at the cutting edge of political activism, as their struggle to regain their land and water rights touched on virtually every settler issue.

On May 31, 1982, the general public awoke to news of a major bombing claimed by an unknown group, Direct Action, which caused over $5 million in damage to four 500-kilovolt transformers and an oil pumping station at the Dunsmuir Hydro substation on Vancouver Island, British Columbia.[9] Communiqués sent to various news outlets pointed out that this substation had been targeted because it was part of the $1 billion Cheekeye-Dunsmuir transmission line that would provide the electricity for a sharp escalation of industrial development on Vancouver Island. Direct Action's motives were summarized in the last two sentences of the communiqué: "We must make this an insecure and uninhabitable place for capitalists and their projects. This is the best contribution we can make towards protecting the earth and struggling for a liberated society."[10]

After its dramatic entrance onto the political stage, nothing was heard again from Direct Action until October 14, 1982, when people across the country had their late-evening news interrupted by a special news bulletin about a massive bombing at Litton Systems Canada in Etobicoke, Ontario, near Toronto. This was not the first time that Litton had made the news. It had been the notorious site of ongoing protests, demonstrations, and civil disobedience ever since the public became aware that this branch plant of its American mother company, Litton Systems Inc., was manufacturing the as-yet untested guidance system for the cruise missile.

Unfortunately, a number of people were injured when the bomb squad got too close to the van containing the dynamite, at which point their radio transmissions set off the electronic timing device prematurely. The authorities had refused to acknowledge the many layers of supposedly fail-safe warnings to stay away from the dynamite-filled van and clear the Litton plant and nearby roads. Direct Action learned a fundamental lesson in carrying out militant action: never rely on the authorities to safeguard the public, or even their own kind.

Direct Action's reasons for opposing the cruise missile as a major weapon in Western imperialism's arsenal need no explanation, but the reason they chose to bomb the plant rather than participate in the popular protests was summarized in the Litton communiqué: "We will not survive if, in the final analysis, the success of our undertakings is determined by whether the nuclear enemy can be persuaded to change its sickened mind.... We believe that, if undertaken seriously and well-supported throughout the existing movement, widely practiced militant resistance and sabotage will become effective in slowing down the clock of death and inspire people to respond to the threats to our survival with urgency, vitality and clarity."[11]

Then, on November 22, 1982, the Wimmin's Fire Brigade carried out a coordinated series of arsons on three separate Red Hot Video stores, successfully burning down one and seriously damaging a second. The attempt to firebomb the third store had to be aborted when a police car drove by just as they were about to throw a Molotov cocktail through a window.

Even though Direct Action did not initiate militant actions until the popular movement's strategy had failed, none of their actions were as popular or supported as the Red Hot Video firebombings. The BC women's community had spearheaded an unsuccessful legal campaign to shut down the Red Hot Video franchise, which sold videos depicting violence against women and children, because they were trying to normalize pornography by locating their stores in family-friendly suburbs and strip malls outside of their traditionally more reclusive red-light-district locations. After the firebombings, radio phone-in shows and letters-to-the-editors sections of local newspapers reflected a popular understanding and even solidarity with the Wimmin's Fire Brigade actions, largely due to the total lack of effort by politicians to shut down Red Hot Video using legal tactics.

This was the political backdrop as the sheriff's van pulled into the underground parking lot of Vancouver's federal courthouse on January 21, 1983.

After living a life of relative seclusion for several years, it was overwhelming to step out of the van and be attacked by the national media. I don't know how they got into that parking garage; I thought the whole point of it was to protect the prisoners from reporters and other predators. We were blinded by the flash of lightbulbs and could barely make our way to the exit through the flock of photographers. Later that night in the prison, I was surprised to see myself on the six o'clock news, raising my fist to the cameras and yelling, "Be strong and resist."

Conditions were not any better in the courtroom. Cops and reporters filled up most of the seats, with the exception of a few friends and family who had managed to force their way in. We were herded into a raised prisoners' box surrounded by a bulletproof Plexiglas window. Right from the start we ignored the courtroom decorum by standing with our backs to the judge, and waving, smiling, and using primitive sign language with our friends and families.

It was easy to pick out our friends from the crowd of undercover cops and reporters. They were the ones with unnatural hair colours, piercings, tattoos, and clothing from Salvation Army stores. They stood up, waved, hooted, blew us kisses, and treated us like homecoming rock stars. It was certainly uplifting.

After we had greeted our friends, we turned to one another and hugged and kissed, despite a shoulder-height barrier in the box designed to discourage just such behaviour. Since we knew there would be no other opportunities for contact, we made the most of it. I suppose our criminal profiling must have prepared the court for our behaviour because, surprisingly, they never once tried to force us to respect any of the normal courtroom decorum.

When Judge Sam Toy made his entrance, all those who had a vested interest in the criminal justice system (or simply believed in it) dropped whatever they were doing and jumped to their feet. Whenever they had to leave the courtroom, they would bow their heads submissively toward the judge and slink out the back door. In contrast, our comrades and supporters would emphasize their hostility toward the bourgeois justice system by stubbornly remaining seated or walking in and out willy-nilly, regardless of the efforts of the courtroom's sheriffs to stop them. Granted, many of these people worked within the criminal justice system and would lose their jobs if they refused to honour courtroom decorum, while our supporters had nothing to lose by expressing their political allegiances in this manner. To be fair, for our lawyers, recognizing court decorum was not so much a barometer of their allegiance to the status quo, but rather a small sacrifice they had to make in order to defend our legal rights.

After our obligatory first appearance, we were shipped off to Lakeside Correctional Centre. In the beginning, and for many months into our trial, all our trips to and from court in the paddywagon were accompanied by a police convoy, which we came to expect. I think we would have been a little disappointed if the convoy hadn't appeared—it would have signified we weren't as much of a threat to the government as we had come to believe.

Three

Burnaby's Oakalla Prison Farm had been known by its familiar moniker, Oakalla, ever since it had first opened in 1912, despite being rebranded the Lower Mainland Regional Correction Centre in 1970. Familiar names, like old habits, die hard. It had originally been designed to hold 484 prisoners, but when we rolled up in early 1983, at least 600 men and 13 women were either doing provincial time or were awaiting trial in the two separate prisons within the sprawling complex.

Inside the men's red-brick prison were tiers of open barred cells that resembled a classic movie set. Outside, a high turret loomed over an asphalt recreation yard surrounded by a double row of high-wire mesh fencing topped with coils of razor wire. During their first visit to the yard, the guys were warned that anyone attempting to climb the fence would be brought down by guards from inside these turrets with shotguns loaded with bird pellet, which could easily penetrate clothing and knock the wind out of a person.

After our tearful goodbyes to the men as they were unloaded at the men's prison, Julie and I were driven a few hundred yards down a winding paved drive to the women's prison. All of our trips to and from court would take place inside this sheriff's van, which contained a small caged cubbyhole for the women that was separated from the larger men's section by a thick wire-mesh grill. When the back doors were finally opened, we struggled to gain our balance because our hands were cuffed and our legs shackled together by a chain just short enough that we couldn't quite reach the steps without the chain almost pulling our feet out from under us.

Even though a couple of female guards stood at the ready to escort us into the building, Julie and I stubbornly held our ground, surveying our surroundings with the feeling that this could be the last time we would get to see the outside world. We were confronted by a long, rectangular, two-storey yellow plaster building with barred windows, surrounded by high-wire mesh fence with the obligatory razor wire coiled along the top. Architecturally it was softer and less penal than the men's prison: more like a convent or a small girl's school. It was bounded in front by a small portable building parked in the middle of a grass yard with a shade tree, and out back by a small yard known as the "rock garden" for its bushes and flowers interspersed among small ornamental rocks.

After psychologically preparing myself for nothing but walls and bars, I found myself gasping at the breathtaking backdrop to Oakalla. We were perched at the upper limits of the rolling suburban hills of Burnaby, with nothing to obscure our view of the majestic mountain ranges that border Vancouver. In the dim light of dusk, we could see skiers, like fleas, running up and down the flanks of the floodlit Grouse Mountain, nestled picturesquely overlooking Vancouver.

The first time we shuffled into Oakalla, I was filled with a mixture of emotions. Considering that we could have been shot when we were busted a few days earlier, I suppose it wasn't completely weird that I would be excited about going to prison. But the real root cause of my excitement was a movie called *P4W* that had just recently done the rounds of the alternative theatres.

The directors had been given access to the ranges of the Prison for Women (P4W) in Kingston, Ontario, the only federal penitentiary in Canada for women at the time. They had decided to document prison life by following around and interviewing two young women prisoners as they went about their daily life in P4W. They just happened to be two particularly beautiful young women in love, so the impression I got was that prison was filled with a lot of interesting lesbians who appeared to live a relatively decent life, considering they were in prison. There were a lot of scenes of the women walking arm in arm around the prison yard, either laughing together or crying over their imminent separation, or hanging out in their cells, which were decorated with photographs and other personal adornments.

Granted, there were a few interviews interspersed among these scenes with women whose guarded eyes and scarred arms hinted at a more ominous world just out of the camera's reach. It was this more ominous world that I worried about. This was the world Hollywood movies and sensational media reports had captured. This was a world where the hooded eyes and physical scars were a reminder that these women were the walking wounded, who might not have empathy for people like me and Julie.

We entered the prison through a metal door and were immediately left sitting in a small metal cage for hours until supper and count were over. When we were finally released from the "holding tank," as it was commonly known, we were ordered to take off all our clothes for a strip search. This was followed by a shower with a special delousing shampoo. It felt as though we were being marinated for assimilation into the prison subculture. Within a few hours we had been thoroughly humiliated, and were well primed toward being totally alienated from anyone in a uniform.

We were escorted upstairs to the main floor, where we waited out-side a heavy metal fire door with a small grilled window until the guards were ready to take us farther. Peering in through the window, I watched a couple of women shuffle slowly down a dimly lit cement corridor with a series of solid metal fire doors on either side.

A guard opened the door with a heavy metal skeleton key. She warned us that this was a combination orientation and security ward, where women stayed until the administration had decided whether they were a security risk to either the institution or themselves. If administra-tion decided they were, then they would stay on this ward indefinitely. In time, we learned that the official title for this area was Unit 6, but the terms *Ward 6* and *Unit 6* were used interchangeably. Regardless, the way the guard looked at us gave me the distinct impression we weren't going anywhere soon.

She handed us each a small handbook that explained the rules and regulations and then escorted us to our cells. That was the extent of our orientation. Julie was given a bunk in a large cell that could hold four women, while I was fortunate enough to be on the top bunk in a cell with just one other woman.

I was left alone in my cell to put away my few belongings until a soft knock on the door announced the arrival of a middle-aged woman with a smile that I would soon learn was permanent. She introduced herself as Eva, and seemed pleasant enough. At first I thought she must be my cellmate until she began talking rapidly about the woman who would sleep below me.

"So, hon," she began, "have you met Beverley yet?" I assured her I hadn't. "Well, you'll be surprised, because even though she murdered her own lawyer in broad daylight, she is really quite the sweetheart."

Eva sat down on the bottom bunk and began filing her blood-red nails while she gave me the lowdown on my cellmate, only pausing to look up at me so she wouldn't miss seeing the look on my face every time she dropped a bombshell of information on my naïve head. I had never met a murderer before. Eva prattled on and on. People with perennial smiles have always made me wonder what they were hiding.

"Can I get a coffee around here somewhere?" I figured I better be the last one asleep in my cell after lockup.

"Sure, hon. There's always coffee perking in the day room. I'll show you." I followed her down the hall, marvelling at the shiny linoleum floors.

The day room was a large open room littered with a couple of wooden-framed couches and chairs that didn't appear designed to promote lounging. The room was empty except for a thin woman sitting poker straight, absorbed in a TV program.

Eva made her way over to the coffee percolator, chattering away to the thin woman, who did not acknowledge her presence in any way. For a few minutes I wondered if she was deaf until she interrupted Eva's prattle in a heavy Québécois accent: "Will you shut de fuck up!" Very quickly it appeared to me that these two women were a study in contrasts, not to mention each other's nemeses: one was heavy and the other thin; one talkative, the other quiet; one aggressive, the other ingratiating.

"Why, of course, Natalie. I didn't know you were concentrating. What are you watching? Is it any good? Oh, how rude of me, I haven't introduced you to…"

"What did I just say, Eva?" Natalie tore her eyes from the TV and gave Eva a menacing look. "No, don't answer me. Just get de fuck out of dis room before I silence you!"

Eva smiled at me and nodded her head knowingly at Natalie, as though in agreement, then mincingly walked out of the room. Natalie was pretty much as uptight as a person could be. At first I thought the way she spoke to Eva was in reaction to her compulsive talking, but I began to suspect it was just her way. After Eva left, I decided to stay in the day room until lockup, which was coming up all too soon. I chose a chair as far away from Natalie as possible and avoided staring at her, but out of the corner of my eye I could see a permanent scowl on her face. My image of a women's prison as a place filled with beautiful, interesting lesbians was developing a few cracks. But I was nothing if not determined: determined to identify with and adapt to the women's prison subculture, even if it wasn't quite as fascinating as portrayed in the movie *P4W*.

Eventually a guard came bustling in and breezily turned off the television as she announced, "Lockup." I found Julie trying to use the communal phone just outside the common room.

"So how do you like your cell?" I asked as we shuffled as slowly as possible down the corridor.

"There's three of us, and the other women seem fine. I miss Gerry, though."

All down the corridor women were running in and out of each other's cells, kissing and hugging each other good night. I had never seen such a display of affection.

When we got to Julie's cell, we naturally put our arms around each other and hugged and kissed each other just like everyone else, and then separated just as a guard came walking toward us with her skeleton key poised to lock the cell door.

"I'm only warning you girls once," she said, after giving us the once over with her eyes. "If you aren't in your cells, ready for lockup by 11 p.m., you will be on charge." She pulled the door shut with a bang and locked it.

. . .

I had been so preoccupied with lockup that I had completely forgotten about my cellmate. Now I turned around and saw a very normal-looking, middle-aged woman with short brown hair and polyester pants sitting up reading on the bottom bunk. She certainly didn't fit any stereotypical image of a murderer. Even though I had been involved in prison abolition activist work before we had started our guerrilla campaign, I was still somewhat affected by movie stereotypes and the social hysteria about violent women. No amount of theoretical learning could completely erase the social conditioning I had been exposed to all my life. Of course, Eva hadn't helped either.

My cellmate stopped reading to look up at me, and introduced herself. "Hi. My name is Beverley." In fact, the only thing about her that struck me as abnormal was the sheen and pallor of her skin. It looked clammy and had a rather pasty, yellow hue. And then there was this vacant look in her eyes. It wasn't the kind of vacant associated with stupidity, but rather the kind associated with vampire stories in which people's spirits have been removed. After ruling out the possibility that she was a vampire, I decided the most likely cause was psychiatric drugs of some sort. But I would save that question until I got to know Beverley a little bit better.

I introduced myself. Then the conversation came to a roaring halt. I struggled for something to say, but nothing came to mind, so I started putting away my "effects," as the prison guard in admissions had called my personal possessions.

"Have you ever called your personal stuff *effects*?" I asked Beverley.

"No," she said with that same flat look in her eyes. I had hoped for a bit of humour.

"Well, I would love to look it up in a dictionary," I said, without the slightest expectation of finding a dictionary in our cell.

"I have a dictionary," said Beverley. "I write, and so my family brought it in."She got out of the bed, opened her drawer, and pulled out a dictionary, which she handed to me.

"'Effects,'" I read. "'In plural form, it means property. How interesting. I never thought of a toothbrush as property before." I looked over to see if Beverley would smile, but her face remained blank. I decided to ask something a little more conversation-worthy. "So are you planning on going to the pen?"

I thought my question was still a little facetious, since "going to the pen" wasn't exactly something you planned to do after considering a whole roster of other possibilities. But in her seemingly emotionally numb state, Beverley took the question at face value.

"I don't want to go, but they're planning to send me anyway. My family and lawyer are appealing the decision."

Since any sentence over two years was considered under federal jurisdiction, all women sentenced to more than two years had to serve their time in Kingston unless the province in which the crime occurred agreed to a provincial exchange. It appeared that Oakalla had decided not to accept Beverley in a provincial exchange.

"Why wouldn't you want to go?" I asked, rather boldly. "From what people tell me, there's more things to do, you know, like you can take university programs, or learn a trade or how to use a computer. Plus there's other women doing a long time, and there's not such a turnover, so you could make friends that would stay for more than a month." I wondered why I was talking to her like a travel agent for the penitentiary. Maybe it was the empty look in her eyes that made me feel more on the ball, but I told myself to back off a bit, since she probably didn't appreciate the sales pitch.

"I am very close to my family, and their visits mean more to me than all the programming in the world," she said with great sincerity.

"So when will you find out if you can stay?"

"Any day now."

The topic of transferring was obviously a sensitive one. After a long silence on my part, she still stared off into the distance, leaving her book lying forlornly on her lap. I decided to change the topic, and perhaps steer her thoughts off into a more pleasant direction.

I finished putting away my "effects" and swung my leg up onto the top bunk. Even though Beverley wasn't planning on being transferred to the pen, she certainly hadn't made her cell cozy like the women in Julie's cell. The walls were devoid of posters or photographs, and no personal adornments graced the metal bureau.

"So, what are you writing?" I asked.

"Oh, I wrote a book on riding." Her voice sounded far away.

"Was it a fictional story?" I pressed on.

"No, it was a step-by-step book on how to ride. There were photographs on each page to illustrate the instructions I gave on the opposite side."

"I had a horse once," I said.

"So did I," she replied, "but it got killed."

"How?"

"It was my fault."

I wished I could see her, even if her face didn't reveal much. I was somewhat intrigued by a woman who had murdered her lawyer and her own horse.

"What happened?" I ventured. There was a long sigh from below, then a long silence. I had just about given up on hearing the story when she began telling me in a low monotone.

"I had this operation, which the doctor screwed up. It was just supposed to be minor surgery, but he botched it up and I almost bled to death. After that I began suffering from depression and feelings of suicide, not to mention blurry vision. One day after the operation, I went for a ride on my mare. Riding was my only escape. I rode along a familiar trail because my vision was still blurry. One day, somewhere along the trail, my mare suddenly stopped and wouldn't go on any farther. I should have listened to her, but I pressed her on. Being the faithful creature that she was, she stepped forward and then fell into a hole. She was struggling to get back her footing, so I managed to get off her and realized, too late, that we had gone down a different trail, and I had forced her to step out onto a railway bridge made of ties with spaces just large enough for her hoofs to go through. She had broken her leg. There was nothing I could do, so I ran back to the farm and got my father. He came back with a rifle and shot her. I still feel guilty for forcing my poor, faithful mare out onto that railway bridge."[12]

There was a long silence between us as we both agonized over the gruesome mental images of Beverley's poor mare struggling with her broken leg on the bridge. Then Beverley broke the silence with the end of her story.

"I immediately got even more depressed. Counselling and drugs didn't help. I decided to sue the doctor who had started this whole thing with his botched-up surgery. You see, before the surgery I had been at the top of my class in school. I had a successful business and lots of riding awards.

"Unfortunately, the lawyer I hired ended up having an affair with the lawyer defending the doctor. To make a long story short, he lost the case, and tried to take every penny I had saved to boot.

"I planned to commit suicide, but decided to take my psychiatrist's advice and went to the hospital for sleep therapy. I woke up after three days of drug-induced sleep. They discharged me as soon as I was able to walk. That same afternoon I received a letter from my lawyer's lover, saying they were suing me for court costs. I phoned my lawyer, and he agreed that I should pay the lawyer he was having an affair with.

"I got in the car with a shotgun and somehow drove to his office. I didn't have a plan. I just felt numb. It's like I was on autopilot. When I got to his building, I marched right past his secretary into his office and looked at him for a few seconds. He was sitting in his chair, slightly tipped back with his hands behind his head and his feet on the desk, smirking at me. When he called out to his secretary to call the police to get 'this' out of his office, I just pulled the trigger a couple of times, and shot him right out of the chair. I don't remember what happened next, but apparently I marched right back out past the secretary with the shotgun still in my hand, and drove on home as though this was the most normal thing to do in the world.

"At my trial, my new lawyer tried to argue that I felt betrayed by my old lawyer, and that I had been discharged too quickly after the sleep therapy, but the judge didn't go for it. I got a life sentence with twenty years before I can see the Parole Board."

"It must have been difficult finding a lawyer after you shot your first one," I said.

"Let's just say I didn't get a good one, but as long as you are willing to pay, there is always a lawyer who will defend you from any crime." Beverley's voice was so flat. I was convinced they must have had her on one hell of a dose of medication.

I lay back in the semi-darkness mulling over Beverley's situation. I wished there was some way of turning off the nightlight, but it was a long fluorescent tube, cleverly encased by a plastic covering with no sharp edges where a person could hang a sheet or pillowcase.

Empathy had always been one of my strengths, and it came easily for Beverley's situation. It seemed only rational to me that someone would have a murderous impulse after being betrayed by their lawyer, and being victimized by the incompetence of the psychiatric profession. I just thought it was a miracle that more women didn't kill their abusive spouses or bosses or lawyers.

It seemed very possible that Beverley did not have control over her faculties at the time of her trail ride or at the time of her lawyer's murder. It also made sense that the judge would have been prejudicial to anyone who murdered someone in the legal profession. Other than the killer of a cop or a child, there is probably no one a judge would be less sympathetic toward than a lawyer killer.

Not long after Beverley's bedtime story, I awoke to the sound of metal keys jangling in keyways. I put the pillow over my head to muffle the sounds and light, but to no avail. It was morning. Peeking out, I saw Beverley slip through the door.

. . .

I should have been depressed waking up in prison, but instead I felt a sense of excitement at the prospect of this new life. I was young, rebellious, and relieved to still be alive. In fact, I had rarely considered the possibility of surviving our guerrilla years. Since I had never dreamed of having a family, career, or house in the "'burbs," spending a good part of my life in prison wasn't the worst option open to me. The thought of living among a bunch of wild and interesting women did not faze me in the least. Since I had always identified with the outlaws and outcasts of society, I felt a sense of compassion and warmth toward this segment of society that the average thirty-year-old woman probably would not.

With a certain amount of macho in my step, I walked toward the day room, taking care only that I didn't slip on the unnaturally slippery floors. Before I reached the day room, I heard Julie's unmistakable laughter coming from the so-called dining room. Judging from the sounds of it, she was also feeling fairly comfortable and glad to be alive. Besides her laughter, the smell of eggs and toast caught my attention. We hadn't eaten a decent meal in days, and I wasn't known for my bird-like appetite.

Julie was standing in the dining room with Eva, loading a pile of food on her plate. I could tell by her face that she was not very depressed.

There were piles of scrambled eggs, and white and brown buttered toast in separate stainless steel serving bowls on a metal cart on wheels, and a large commercial coffee percolator sitting on a long Arborite table against the wall.

I piled the eggs and toast on my plate and sat down to stuff as much food into my stomach as possible. It wasn't bad after eating cold, soggy hamburgers in the RCMP lockup all weekend.

"So, who makes the food?" I asked Eva.

"They send it up from the men's joint below," she explained. "After breakfast I'll show you the activity chart so you'll know what you're supposed to do this morning."

When Julie and I had finished eating, Eva took us into the day room, where a chart on a bulletin board indicated the different jobs available and who was doing them: the laundry room, washing and buffing floors, and cleaning the day room, the dining room, and the washrooms.

"That's it?" I asked Eva. Instead of replying, she ran her finger down the chart and pointed to washing and buffing floors. This was our task.

"That's it?" I repeated. Eva gave me a puzzled look. "Is that all there is to do in this joint?" This time I raised my voice in case she had a hearing problem.

"What did you expect?" she asked, looking surprised. "A course on mechanical engineering?"

"Well, I knew it would be bad, but this is from the dark ages," I said. "I mean, have there been no women other than the guards and warden on this unit in the past twenty years?" Eva smiled at me. She seemed somewhat quieter this morning.

"The only people from the community that come here are religious and AA," said Eva, "and they meet us in the gym." I didn't get the impression that she was particularly upset about the work schedule.

"Don't you think it's kind of outrageous that the only work available is the most mundane housekeeping work on the planet?" I continued, trying to contain my anger. "You would think the administration would want to teach us some skills so we can find legitimate work when we get out of here."

Eva snorted. "You have got to be kidding. They spend as little money on us as possible. You are some naïve." Then Eva laughed long and deep, from the bottom of her belly. She opened a hallway door and pulled out a large plastic institutional bucket on wheels and a traditional mop with long, white cotton cords, and then dragged out a heavy buffer with a padded round head.

"You know how to wash and wax a floor, I take it?" She looked at us like an amused kindergarten teacher. We rolled our eyes at her. "Okay, then, go for it. Call me when you're done and I'll show you how the buffer works. You'll have to get the cleaners and wax from the screws."

An hour later, Julie and I stood back, admiring our newly washed and waxed floor. The only thing left to do was buff it. I figured you didn't need to be a mechanical engineer to figure out how to use the buffer, and smiled at my own joke. I plugged it in and flicked on the switch. We were amazed at how quickly such a heavy, awkward machine could move from a stationary position to a high-speed crash against the baseboards. At least now I knew why the baseboards were made of thick black rubber. If we could have sat on top of the buffer, these contraptions would have made wonderful indoor bumper cars.

We pulled the plug on the wayward machine and decided to try it again, but this time with a powerful grip on the handle. The second we switched it on, the machine raced into the wall again, but this time with Julie on the end of the handle. She burst out laughing.

"You try it!" Once again the machine raced off and crashed into the wall, except this time I was on the end of the handle.

The crashing sounds had attracted Natalie's attention. She seemed to be the unofficial leader of this unit.

"From de sounds out here, I take it you ain't never got acquainted wid a buffer before?"

I hadn't noticed last night that Natalie, who didn't have an ounce of body fat, had a small, round belly. That could only mean one thing: she was pregnant. With her permanent cranky tone and look about her, she did not conjure up images of traditional motherhood.

"Here, I'll show you, or we ain't never havin' lunch." She gently raised and lowered the handle, causing a slight shift in its weight and direction. She was obviously a pro. I guessed the only people who could use these machines were people who had spent time in institutions of some sort during their lives, whether that time was voluntary or not. They certainly weren't designed for home use.

She didn't do us the favour of buffing the entire hallway, though, and left Julie and me to bungle our way through the rest of the buffing experience. By ten o'clock, we looked like we had lost the war with the buffer. Most of Julie's hair had freed itself from the confines of her ponytail, and her bangs and strands of stray black hair were matted together with sweat.

"What are you looking at?" she said irritably. She had made the effort to line her pale blue eyes with black mascara, but she had smudged the lines into raccoon-like rings with her fists from rubbing the sweat out of her eyes.

"Girls, into the day room, please." A young guard had probably saved us from a squabble. We obediently abandoned the buffer and flopped down in some chairs in the day room. There were not a lot of women on this unit. There was Natalie, Eva, two young Indigenous women who had not been introduced yet, and Julie and I, but where was Beverley? The question had barely entered my mind when I noticed the guard locking us in and then walking back into the office, a small room just off the day room.

I thought this was part of the normal routine, but the look on the other women's faces told me otherwise. By now, I had gathered that Natalie was the most outspoken on the unit.

"Hey, what de fuck is goin' on here?" Natalie banged on the glass window to the office. "Yeah, you, I'm talking to you." She was pointing her finger directly at someone in the office.

A sudden banging drew all our attention to something going on in the hallway. It didn't take long to figure out what the noise was. We could clearly hear Beverley alternately screaming and crying as they forcibly dragged her down the hall. The sound of rubber-soled shoes skidding along the linoleum and men's voices told us the story of who was taking Beverley away.

"That's a familiar trick," whispered Eva. "They did the same thing to me."

"Sounds like dey're makin' a mess of your floor," said Natalie sarcastically.

Julie and I had not been in long enough to be desensitized to injustice yet. I had found the traditional female cleaning activities outrageous, but here I was a few hours later, much more outraged over this kidnapping being carried out before the courts had even heard her appeal. My mind was racing. We couldn't let this go by without a protest. Even if it would be impossible to prevent Beverley from being transferred, at least we had to do something to let her know we cared. But what could we do? Immediate action was called for.

I looked around, but everything in the room was for the comfort of the prisoners. It would be like shooting ourselves in the foot to trash the day room. Taking a guard hostage was a bit too dramatic, even for me, but I knew something would come to mind before the day was over.

We listened to Beverley's screams disappear down the stairwell into the admissions and discharge area in the basement. Natalie was sitting poker straight in her chair, rocking her foot back and forth, staring at the television screen with no volume. Eva paced in front of the window, talking, while the two Indigenous women sat staring at the TV with Natalie. I caught Julie's eye and could see she was as pissed off as I was.

"So what are we going to do?" I directed the question at Julie, but hoped that the others would consider themselves involved. Nobody even batted an eye in my direction. Then Eva gave voice to their silence with an emphatic, "Nothing. There is absolutely nothing we can do."

"It's outrageous!" I said, hoping someone other than Julie would confirm my feelings.

"Look it," said Natalie in her fast-paced way. "I don't like de way they're doin' it, but she ain't goin' to stay, and dis sure ain't de place to do a life sentence, you know. She'll be a lot better off at de pen once she gets used to it. Nobody wants to go dere, but I have yet to see anyone come back 'cept this fuckin' rat here." She rolled her eyes in Eva's direction. It seemed that Eva had accepted her demeaning reputation as a rat. Maybe she was a rat, but then again, maybe she just didn't have the guts to stand up for herself.

It had grown quiet down below. Beverley was probably on her way to the airport. Natalie got up and turned up the volume on the television again. One of the Indigenous women had pulled out a bag of leather and was busy sewing a beaded medallion on what looked like the tongue of a moccasin. Her friend sat beside her.

I was fuming. At that moment, the perfect solution to our dilemma appeared. Down the hall came the sound of the food cart rolling in for lunch. Eva squealed with glee, "Hot dogs!" She had obviously been in prison far too long. I glanced over at Julie to see if she had read my mind. She nodded. Without conferring with the other women, we marched up to the cart and pushed it over in one dramatic move. It wasn't exactly the kind of action associated with urban guerrillas, but it satisfied our need for action at the moment. Visually it was a stunning sight: all those dull red hot dogs rolling all over the shiny linoleum floor. I don't think Julie was satisfied with the severity of the action, because she began to kick the pathetic sausages around, and then knocked the soup pot over as well. I think we had expected the other women to jump in, but I could immediately tell that they either were pissed off or thought we had lost our marbles.

Natalie immediately put her hands on her hips and yelled at us, "What de fuck are you doing? Dat's our lunch, you idiots! Who do you tink gives a flying fuck if you ruin our lunch?"

As soon as Eva saw that Natalie did not approve, she weighed the risks and benefits of siding with Natalie or us, and within seconds had put her money on Natalie. We might have been more compassionate, but Natalie had the power.

Eva glared at us. "So now what are we going to eat?" I'm sure her love for hot dogs had also weighed into the equation. She began to pick up the hot dogs off the floor and neatly pile them back up on the food cart. I'm also sure she would have eaten them if no one was looking. I wouldn't have blamed her; the floor was as clean as any plate I had eaten off in a long time.

My image of poor, downtrodden prisoners just waiting to be liberated was quickly being deflated. Julie stopped kicking around hot dogs and gave me a sullen look. Even though I was beginning to second-guess my judgment, I felt compelled to defend my actions.

"It's not right to just let them take Beverley away like that without even giving her lawyers a chance to appeal. How would you feel if you were the one kidnapped and hauled away like that?" Up until this point the guards had just been standing around, enjoying watching the prisoners condemn us, but now they saw an opening in which they could undermine my argument.

"We just got word this morning that Beverley lost her appeal. The reason we took her so quickly is because she has a history of depression and suicide attempts. If we hadn't taken her then, we would have had to lock her up in solitary for her own protection," a young guard explained, directing her comments to me with a slight smirk on her face. I shrugged.

"I don't care whether or not she lost her appeal. The fact that she didn't want to go was reason enough for me. She should have been allowed to stay if her family and friends were her main sources of strength." Defiantly, I marched down the hall to my cell, half expecting the guards to grab me from behind and haul me off to the hole. Instead I heard the guards order the rest of the women back into their cells. Eva asked them in a whining voice if they were going to serve an alternate lunch. The answer was a resounding "no."

Back in my cell, I began to seriously second-guess my judgment on the lunch debacle. I vowed that in future I would think through any prison actions more thoroughly, and certainly would not do anything that would result in negative repercussions for the other prisoners.

I looked around the cell. There were signs of a struggle everywhere. The bedsheets were draped all over the floor, as though she had clung futilely onto them for support. The metal bureau was sitting askew as though she had also tried to pry herself between it and the wall. And big, dark skid marks were all that were left of her final attempt at digging her heels in as they dragged her out. Alone in my cell with the evidence of her lonely struggle, I didn't feel as foolish for upending the hotdog cart. It might have been symbolic and a small sacrifice for the other women, but it was the least we could have done to show Beverley some support. Fuck them.

They left us all locked for the rest of the afternoon. Strategically I thought they were trying to ensure that I would have no influence on the other women in the future. Maybe I was reading too much importance into my own reputation among the administration, but it certainly seemed extreme to me to be locked down all afternoon for simply tipping over the lousy hot dog cart.

Paranoia began to set in as the thought of the other women resenting me for having ruined their lunch took on more significance than Beverley's kidnapping. My political self was already beginning to take a backseat to the self that wanted to be accepted. For the rest of the afternoon, my dual selves battled for supremacy. Most of the time I beat myself up for not conferring with the other women before acting out, but every now and then a little political voice would tell me that following the majority wasn't always right. What if the situation had been different? What if the guards took a Black woman into segregation because the rest of the prison population was bullying her for the colour of her skin? Would I have gone along with the majority of the prisoners, or would I have stood up for her because it was right? Of course the right thing to do would have been to stick up for her.

I could see that prison was going to be a tough place to maintain my political identity; it was such a small, confined population, with no human rights or any way of enforcing them, unless the prison subculture was inclined to do so. I wasn't completely sure what that prison subculture would entail. I suspected much of it was honourable, but I also guessed there would be times when it wasn't, and it was going to be scary to stand up for myself. It wasn't exactly a pacifist oasis, and you couldn't just hop onto a bus and travel to another one if you didn't like what was going on here.

The other thing I remember from that day was the taste of mental self-torture I experienced from a single afternoon of solitude. By the time four o'clock rolled around, I wondered what it would have been like if I had been hauled away into segregation for months. Certainly I had heard stories of women being held in segregation for less. Imagine how monstrous my paranoia demon would have grown in a period of months. But

I shuffled that thought away for later. Right now I had to see if there was going to be any more collateral damage from the hot dog debacle.

. . .

As soon as the screw had finished unlocking us, supper was announced. In the dining room, Julie and Natalie were already serving themselves bowls of steaming hot stew. It was hard to read Natalie's mood because her face held a permanent scowl that kept most people at bay, but I could see that she was warming up to Julie. She was serving her stew.

"Are you going up to de gym after supper?" Natalie asked Julie in her abrupt way.

"I guess," said Julie. "What do you do up there?"

"Sometimes we play volleyball or just hang out. De upstairs unit goes up dere too after supper. I got a friend up dere."

The rest of dinner was quiet, with the exception of Eva chattering away to one of the Indigenous women, whose name was Tammy. From eavesdropping, I had learned that Tammy and her friend, Sandy, were actually cousins. At first I was struck by the odds of cousins ending up in the same prison together, but as the years passed by in other prisons at other times, I encountered this situation repeatedly.

I could list a bunch of statistics in chronological order, but I can safely say that the percentage of Indigenous women in Canadian prisons hovers around 30 percent of the total prison population.[13] This is huge, considering that Indigenous people make up only 4 percent of the general Canadian population. Of course, over time these percentages have shifted by one or two percentage points, but what has not changed is the fact that Indigenous people make up an overwhelmingly disproportionate percentage of the prison population.

On October 5, 1996, Statistics Canada did a snapshot survey of adults in Canadian prisons. It revealed that "the majority of adult women prisoners were in their early thirties, single with a grade nine education or less, and unemployed." The statistics for men in the same categories were similar, although women were less likely to have committed violent crimes.[14] Three quarters of all charges laid against women by police were for shoplifting or fraud, or for violations of drug or liquor regulations.[15]

The 1996 Royal Commission on Aboriginal Peoples took these statistics at the time and concluded that "economic and social deprivation is a major underlying cause of the proportionately high rates of criminality among Aboriginal people."[16] In other words, the high percentage of Indigenous people in prison is a function not of criminal minds, but rather high unemployment, poor education, and the effects of Indigenous people being displaced from their traditional lands and ways of life through the creation of Native reserves and the residential school system, not to mention all the other traumas associated with colonization. It is within this context that I became accustomed to meeting family groups of Indigenous cousins, sisters, and even grandmothers and granddaughters within whatever prison I found myself over the years.

After dinner, we walked tentatively upstairs to the gym. It was about a quarter the size of a regulation gym, just big enough for a small volleyball court. Julie and I sat down uncomfortably in the corner, having decided to keep a low profile. There were women playing volleyball and women chatting on the sidelines, and a couple of women were doing aerobics to a tape playing on a boom box.

Natalie was sitting in a corner talking to a friend, and completely ignored us. Julie seemed oblivious to what everyone else was doing.

"So you seem to be getting along well with Natalie," I said.

"Yeah, she's all right. There's still an empty bed in our cell. Thank God. Let's do some pushups. I'm going to get fat if I don't keep working out." She stretched out on the floor and began doing pushups.

I wasn't sure if we were being ignored because we didn't know anyone, or if people just didn't like us. Paranoia led me to favour the latter possibility. Then a volleyball blew past us, smashing into the cinderblock wall just above where Julie was doing pushups.

Julie leaped to her feet and yelled, "Fuck off!" really loudly in the direction of the volleyball players. I admired her chutzpah. I noticed a few of them were giggling, but I couldn't tell if the volleyball fired in our direction was an accident or planned. Julie glared over at the players, giving the appearance that she was ready to take anyone on. I wasn't sure if it was naïveté, bad nerves, or courage playing the lead role in her outrage, or if all three were vying for the lead.

When the ball came smashing against the wall just above our heads a few minutes later, this time I knew it was premeditated. Now I was mad too. I just happened to catch the ball as it rebounded off the wall. Leaning back, I fired it at the court as hard as I could. I was definitely more angry than brave. If our reputation had not preceded us, I am sure firing the ball at them would have sparked a fight right there and then, but the women had followed the media over the weekend, and our reputation as "terrorists" left them feeling somewhat intimidated. "Terrorists" were like uncharted waters. Remember, this was the eighties. This was pre–9/11.

They had never met any before: murderers, prostitutes, drug dealers, importers, and forgers, but no "terrorists." I imagine the only "terrorists" they had ever heard of were the ones on television, and they were *bad*. Of course, we did not consider ourselves "terrorists"; both tactically and strategically, we did not believe that targeting people was either ethical or effective, unless it was necessary for defensive reasons. But the State has been smearing everyone who rebels with the same brush for as long as there have been rebels; "terrorists" in the twenty-first century, "communists" in the twentieth century, and "witches" in the fifteenth century.

In retrospect, I think the volleyball incident was a test. They were trying to get a reaction to see what we would do. They got what they wanted, and they never fired it back again.

Now I was definitely paranoid. I sat back down with my back against the wall, watching the game while Julie continued with her workout. The workout and the game went on for another half hour until a couple of women from the upstairs unit stopped playing and walked over in our direction. I smelled trouble.

The one woman appeared to be the "leader," in that all the conversations and activity seemed to revolve around her. If she missed a ball, no one said a thing, but if she ridiculed someone else for missing, the others quickly piled on. I tried not to let her appearance influence me, but she was one of those people who had a crooked smile on her face that seemed to have nothing to do with how she felt or the topic at hand. It left a creepy impression. Her face would be laughing at you, but her eyes would be ripping you apart piece by piece. It didn't help that her face was intersected by scars. I couldn't stop myself from nicknaming her "the lizard queen" in my head.

Her partner was very young. Every time there was a break in the game, she would find a reason to give the lizard queen a kiss or some other fawning gesture of her love. She sauntered over toward us with raw machismo. She was dressed like a young boy, and walked in that stilted way young teenage boys do before they have fully matured. But her large brown eyes had the soft, gentle innocence of a doe, and her face was untouched by the ravages of time or knives.

Without introduction, the lizard queen asked, "What was all the commotion about on the nut ward this afternoon?"

"They took Beverley out of her cell by force to the airport without any notice," I explained. "I thought it was outrageous, so I kicked over the lunch cart to let the screws know it wasn't right."

The lizard queen's smile disappeared for a minute as she looked me up and down.

"Well, that was some dumb. What the fuck did you think would happen when you dumped over the lunch cart? They'd stop and bring Beverley back?" She smiled sardonically. "In future, leave things to us. Believe me, I've been to the pen, and she's goin' to like it there one hell of a lot more than this joint. They've got programs and school, and rec. We got nothin' here. So leave well enough alone what you don't know fuck all about."

She never took her eyes off me. It was clearly an order. I didn't like anything about this woman, but I figured I had better keep a low profile until I knew more about what was going on around here. I didn't respond to what she had to say. I just looked at her with hooded eyes. I hadn't been in long, but it all came naturally. I didn't want her to know a thing about me: whether or not she scared me, or whether or not I would obey her.

"So Jilly, will you do my nails?" she asked her young partner, who was pulling her along like a child would her mother.

Four

As time passed, other women around us went to court, did their time, and left, while Julie and I remained on Unit 6. The rounders upstairs wouldn't accept prisoners from Unit 6 unless they had proven that they could abide by the prisoners' "code"—a word used to sum up the unique set of values and ethics that makes up the prisoners' subculture.

Not all the women who lived a life revolving around prison and the "street" carried the mantle of prestige associated with being a rounder. It had to be earned by living a life of loyalty and respect for the code. No amount of money, education, or career advancement in the outside world could guarantee a person prestige in prison.

Finally, after a year of going to court virtually every day without escaping, and after proving to the other prisoners that we weren't "rats," the administration and rounders decided we had earned the privilege of moving upstairs. One day I woke up and was told to "pack up your effects," because Julie and I were going upstairs. It felt great, like graduating from elementary school to high school. We said our goodbyes to the women on Unit 6 and carried our boxes up the stairs.

Other than the women themselves, everything else upstairs was the same—the architecture, the routine, the staff. We would wake up at seven o'clock to the sound of metal skeleton keys opening the heavy cell doors, then go to the "dining room" for breakfast, which would consist of various combinations of soggy toast, cold cereal, scrambled eggs, bacon, or pancakes, and coffee, tea, and juice. After breakfast, if we weren't going to court, we would check the schedule to see which job we had been assigned. By mid-morning we would have completed our traditional female janitorial work, either mopping or waxing floors, cleaning the bathrooms or day room, or working in the laundry room. After lunch, there would be an hour lockup while the screws had lunch and did count.

The afternoons were our own unless we were scheduled in court. Finally, we would have dinner and another hour lockup for count, after which we could go to the gym, the yard, or our cells until lockup at eleven. All and all it was very predictable, with the exception of the odd crisis.

We spent most of our time waiting to be transported to and from court, sitting in court, attending legal meetings on weekends in the men's unit of Oakalla, and visiting with our many political comrades during what little time was left. This total immersion in the trial and political discussions during visits kept our political identities intact. When you also take into consideration phone calls in the evenings, most of our time was immersed in our political community, even though we were in prison.

Despite a future with no end of prison in sight, I believe we felt strong and emotionally stable. The fact that everyone's family, except mine, lived in BC and were relatively supportive was also a contributing factor. Yet the times we did engage with the other prisoners were intense and overshadow my memories of the daily court routine. Perhaps this was because the consequences of the trial seemed so remote and intangible, whereas our interactions with the other prisoners were so intense and real.

. . .

The lizard queen, as I had continued to call her in my mind, had family visits every Sunday afternoon. It was a very small visiting room, so the warden had decided that only one family could visit at a time. That made sense to me, since I had witnessed how cramped the visiting quarters were during a visit with the family of my co-accused. My family lived thousands of miles away in Ontario.

After we had been living upstairs for about a month, the lizard queen came back one afternoon from her visit with Jilly, who had been released some time ago. She called Julie and me into her cell. I almost called it her office, because that's what it felt like. She shared a cell with a friend of hers from the street, Renee, and everyone knew that they ran the show on this unit. I couldn't understand why; the lizard queen didn't seem particularly smart, nice, or tough. I couldn't really think of anything that made her leadership material, but for some reason the other women catered to her every whim.

So Julie and I went into her cell—somewhat humbly, I must admit. She was sitting on her cot, slumped over with a cigarette dangling dangerously from her hand. The ash was longer than the cigarette and was about to fall into her lap. Her eyes were hooded and glazed. Even I, a novice in the drug world, could tell she was high. She was smiling in her usual sleazy way.

"Do you girls want to get high?" she asked, to our surprise. I looked at Julie, not knowing what to do.

"What is it?" Julie asked innocently.

"Junk," she drawled in a low, guttural voice. "Vancouver's finest. I don't usually offer it, but I like you girls. Have you ever done this before?"

"Yeah," I said, even though I had only tried it a couple of times, and both times I had had someone else fix me. I didn't know how to mix drugs or use a needle. My drug use was experimental, like so many of us coming of age during the seventies. I was quite sure Julie had never used heroin before.

"Hon, will you fix these girls up?" she asked the other woman in the washroom, without waiting to hear Julie's answer.

"Julie, you shouldn't do this," I said, feeling guilty for agreeing to use myself. I hate to admit it even now, but I had a fascination with heroin. It probably stemmed from the way rock culture glorified heavy drugs, even if it had culminated in the deaths of so many music legends.

The lizard queen piped in, "Oh, leave her alone. If she wants to do it, let her. It's not like she'll get a habit in here, and believe me, where you're goin' there's a snowball's chance in hell you'll be usin'. Did you know I was in the pen for seven years?" She didn't wait for our answer. "If you ever saw the film *P4W*, I was in that. Did you?" I nodded. "That film was bullshit. They didn't show you shit in that film. No footage of seg or what really went down in there, but at least it was solid in those days. Not like now, when every second broad's a rat. I'm tellin' you, nowadays with passes and all that other bullshit, the girls are willin' to rat you out for a song. I liked it better when we had nothin' cause then there was nothin' to lose. Now they got more so-called 'privileges' dangling in front of your head than bars." As she began to nod out, her voice also began to fade, almost as though she needed her batteries recharged.

Renee stepped out of the washroom holding a syringe, or "outfit," as it was more commonly known. She looked over at us, and then at the lizard queen, who was drooping over like a wilted flower. It appeared Julie did not want to let this opportunity slide by, and, I must admit, I shared her sentiments. She rolled up her sleeve. Renee looked as though she had been expecting us to back down as soon as the lizard queen went on the nod. She wore a scowl in such an undisguised manner it could have been classified as part of her wardrobe.

"Will you do me?" asked Julie, holding out her arm.

"I'd rather not, but I guess since Joyce said so. It's her dope," said Renee reluctantly.

She showed Julie how to clench her arm just above the inside of her elbow to make the veins stick up a bit, slid the needle in, drew it back slightly until a little blood appeared in "the fit," then slowly pressed the plunger into her vein. I watched in wide-eyed trepidation, fearful that Julie would be overdosed. Most of my drug experiences had been vicarious while watching crime dramas on television.

Within thirty seconds, I could see the drug overcome Julie. Her eyes glazed over, her lids drooped slightly, and when she spoke her voice dropped down half an octave, as though she had been injected with a little bit of Lauren Bacall.

Renee disappeared into the washroom again for a few minutes and then reappeared, holding the outfit like a dart in my direction. It had occurred to me that there was little danger of being overdosed, considering how difficult it must have been to smuggle in that dope.

After she had pressed the plunger down, sending the heroin racing toward my brain, I waited for what felt like minutes for a reaction. It was actually seconds, but when it hit, the most wonderful feeling washed over me.

Julie and I sat down on the cot facing the lizard queen, who had been nodding out, and watched her completely transform before our very eyes into a wonderful, compassionate woman we could talk to for hours, and we did. We shared stories about our arrests, our lives before prison, our fears about P4W, and what we would do if we lived to do it. Her scars melded into smile lines and her eyes twinkled with mirth as she underwent the metamorphosis from the evil lizard queen into the kindly old elf. I blamed myself for not giving her a chance because now that we were spending the time talking, she was revealing herself to be nothing less than a kind-hearted philanthropist. She told us stories of taking in homeless waifs and helping them break the vicious cycle of drug addiction and prostitution in order to become … well, the story never ended, and then it was supper.

We floated out of the cell into the dining room, where they were serving a gourmet stew. Strangely, it consisted of the same ingredients as usual, yet it tasted delicious, as though they had added some mysterious ingredient that made the flavours sing. Normally Julie and I sat together at the far end of the table, symbolic of our newcomer status, while Joyce (I couldn't for the life of me figure out why I had so unkindly branded her "the lizard queen") and the other older rounders sat at the head of the table. Tonight, however, she patted the two seats on either side of her and motioned for us to come up. With a gracious smile, she convinced her usual dinner companions to shove over one seat in order to accommodate us. It was all very exhilarating.

We felt like ladies in a court being invited to sit beside the queen. I didn't have an iota of paranoia in my brain at the moment, so I did not question her motives. I was simply in the moment, enjoying every single one of them.

I can't recall the conversation. I just remember lifting large spoonfuls of stew toward my mouth and then drifting off into another dimension in my head while the spoon of stew hovered precariously above my plate, until someone nudged me back to reality before the guards took notice. The meal went on and on until only Joyce, Julie, Renee, and I were sitting at the table, mumbling away about nothing in particular.

I remember going into the day room after dinner and watching a movie until another woman alerted me to my burning cigarette lying on the floor, where it had dropped out of my dangling hand.

"You better go to your room, hon, or the guards are going to notice," she said softly.

"Notice what?" I asked innocently. She rolled her eyes at me as though I was a fool. It had not dawned on me that I was drawing unwanted attention to myself, or, as other prisoners would say, being a heat score.

The next morning I woke up feeling somewhat groggy, but still nice. My head had cleared up somewhat. I remembered the fix of heroin and wondered how I had made it through the evening without the guards noticing. I remembered the woman in the day room suggesting I go to my room. I sat up in bed and noticed a cigarette burn in my flannel nightgown. What else had I burned?

Then I remembered that we were going to have a meeting in the day room after lunch. Julie and I were going to propose that we plan an organized protest against the way they were kidnapping women in the middle of the night who were scheduled to go to the pen and driving them out to the airport in their pajamas.

I got out of bed and cleaned up the mess I had made of my cell during my heavy smoking spree the night before. In the dining room, Julie was making a coffee and looking kind of glum. We barely spoke. As I went about my morning chores, I watched the guards out of the corner of my eye to see if they were looking at me differently. Nothing seemed out of the ordinary.

After lunch lockup, everyone drifted slowly into the dayroom for our meeting—everyone, that is, but Joyce and Renee. After waiting another fifteen minutes, we decided to start without them. One of the women had gone to the office and explained to the guards that we were having a meeting and needed privacy in order to resolve some personal issues. If the woman had explained that the "issues" involved the guards or administration, they would have either openly supervised the meeting or banned it altogether, but since it was "personal" they simply watched us through the Plexiglas, and probably listened through the intercom.

We had barely begun when Joyce and Renee came shuffling into the room in their pajamas, looking fairly grim. I vaguely remembered what she had looked like the night before, and wondered if she was the same woman. The lizard queen was back. In keeping with her status, she took a seat in the middle of the sofa at the front of the room, with Renee seated right next to her. If Joyce needed a coffee, Renee would get it for her. If Joyce had forgotten something in her cell, Renee would run and retrieve it.

Julie and I had been planning this meeting ever since the day we turned over the hot dog cart on Unit 6. Considering how little there was to do, the women usually showed up for any meeting organized by anyone, just for something to do. Over the past year, we had witnessed several more women being sentenced to federal time, then applying for the federal/provincial exchange, and then being kidnapped in the middle of the night after their application was turned down. No matter how many times administrators told these women they would be better off in Ontario, 3,500 kilometres away, the women would remain steadfast in their demand to do their time in BC. Their bonds with family and friends were more important to them than the better programming and education at P4W.

"So does anyone have any ideas of how to stop the administration from grabbing women out of their beds at night so they can ship them to P4W?" Julie began. This was an issue dear to her heart. She was planning on applying for a federal/provincial exchange, since she knew no one in Ontario and was close to her large extended family.

I glanced around the room and could see that most of the women were far from passionate about the issue. Their eyes maintained that cold, unemotional gaze they reserved for those who did not understand them and weren't a part of their world. I was even surprised that everyone had actually come to the meeting.

"What do you propose we do?" asked Renee, with a heavy note of sarcasm in her voice.

"Why don't we refuse to work?" I said, with as much confidence as I could muster.

"What'll that do?" asked Renee. "We'll just get locked with no pay or privileges."

"What privileges?" asked another woman, Lucy, who I noticed had challenged the lizard queen on a few occasions. "We ain't got no privileges, unless you consider goin' to the gym a privilege."

There were six women on the unit, and it was easy to see that the women were trying to figure out the lizard queen's position. Even though they did not look directly at her, they faced her direction and maintained their steely-eyed look, reserving their judgment until she had made her position public.

"If we don't do something, they're just going to keep hauling women off to P4W without even considering their rights to an exchange. How many women on this unit are federal?" I asked. No one budged. "Has anyone ever locked down in protest before?" No one batted an eye.

"I'm for it." Lucy looked at the others with a challenging eye. Another woman, Suzie, smiled at her, perhaps admiring her feistiness. Julie and I were not from the street, so they probably chalked up our opinions to naïveté, but Lucy was from the mean streets of east end Vancouver and knew exactly what could happen if she rebelled against Joyce inside the joint. Revenge on the street was not always sweet. Even taking such a strong stand before Joyce had expressed her opinion was considered an act of defiance.

"Well, if we go for it, I want to know that everyone on this unit's going to stay locked. Otherwise we'll lose everything for nothing." Suzie had joined the ranks of the rebels. I smiled. We had a majority: Julie, Lucy, and now Suzie, and me. That was four.

Throughout this exchange, Joyce had been sitting smoking a cigarette with her lips pursed and her eyes squinted as she looked through everyone out the window on the other side of the room. She didn't appear to be paying any attention to what the women around her were saying. She looked more haggard than usual. Her bedraggled appearance contributed to the impression that she was not aware of her immediate surroundings. But no sooner had the woman said the word "nothing" than Joyce turned her head to face the women and opened her eyes like a hawk, beady and piercing. She began talking quickly and angrily, little bits of spittle forming at the corners of her mouth.

"The first thing we're going to lose if we lock is our visits, 'cause they know how much our families mean to us, and I, for one, am not going to lose my visits with Jilly for some fucked-up reason that don't even make any sense. I have been to the pen. Has anyone else in the room?" She looked slowly around the room at each and every face.

"As I thought … no one. I am here to tell ya that it is one hell of a lot better than this joint. Sure, you don't get to see your family, but you spend so much time in there that the other girls become your family, and after a while they mean everything to ya." She paused for effect, took a deep drag on her cigarette, and continued. "They got a yard as big as a football field. They got a little house for when your family does come ta visit that ya can stay in for days. They got computers, school, a sewing and wood shop, AA, Native Sisterhood meetings, crafts, a tennis court, and a kitchen where you cook your own snacks. Believe you me, this is a dump compared to the pen, and if I had a choice I would go there in a hot minute. All these broads that don't want ta go are dumb and chickenshit. They just plain old don't know fuck all about what they're fightin.'" Then she looked at Lucy directly.

"The next time Jilly comes, I'll see ya." Then a funny thing happened. The lizard queen began to cry. I almost laughed. I had never seen her sad, only mad, mean, and moody. Tears did not become her. There was something false about them, like a bad actress overacting.

"I have no blood family. Jilly is all I got. And I am all she has. I took her in as an orphan and took care of her, and now she visits me." There were times when Joyce was on the phone with Jilly in the evenings and everyone, including the guards, could hear every word of her conversation. She would cry, scream, and threaten Jilly until she promised to come and visit her.

By the time Joyce had finished her teary-eyed role of selfless mother figure to poor orphan Jilly, her audience was on the verge of a standing ovation. Lucy had run down the hall for toilet paper so Joyce could wipe her snotty nose, and Renee had snuggled up beside her on the couch, holding her in her arms like an oversized baby. Suzie had risen to her feet and crowded up against Joyce, reassuring her that there was no way she would be so stupid as to jeopardize her visits in order to keep some misguided woman from being sent to such a wonderful place as P4W against her will. As the curtain went down, I quietly got up from my seat and shuffled down the hall to find refuge in my cell.

I was sitting with my back to the wall, my legs pulled up protectively against my chest, when Julie came in, looking as morose as I felt.

"What is wrong with this place?" she said in exasperation. "I don't care how great the pen turns out to be, the women should be allowed to stay in the province if their families are more important to them than programs. She just wants her dope. Why can't the others see that?"

"Oh, they can, all right. But most of them probably don't have families who want to visit them, and even more important, most of them aren't even going to the pen. Why would they want to risk losing visits, or the little bit of dope that Joyce gives them, to stick up for women who don't want to go to the pen?" I said.

Julie shook her head, and then gave me a determined look. "Well, I can tell you one thing. They might send me to the pen on these charges, but I sure as hell won't be there for long."

"You know what the fishiest thing about this whole thing is?" I asked Julie. She shook her head again. "The warden. You think she isn't aware that Jilly is packing in dope to Joyce every goddamn time she has a so-called family visit?"

"I have even more family visits than she does, and I've been in the same room as her and Jilly. You'd have to be deaf, dumb, and blind not to notice the play going on there," said Julie.

"And every guard in this place would have to be a complete idiot not to notice the coincidence between their visits and the fact that every time they're over, Joyce and her favourite friends for the day are as high as kites," I said, standing up indignantly. "The only thing I hate more than those women swallowing their pride for a little of Joyce's dope is the way the warden manipulates everyone to keep this place dummied up. You got to give the warden credit, though. She's pretty slick. She doesn't have to do a thing. She doesn't have to say a thing, either. That's what they call governing with the velvet glove instead of the iron fist. Everyone knows that if there is any flack, family visits will be the first thing to go. And everyone knows that family visits are code for dope. So everything stays nice and peaceful."

"I'd bet Joyce doesn't even believe in that thing she said about likin' it better when there was nothing left to lose," said Julie, smiling at me. I smiled back.

Five

After our initial court appearance and bail hearings, we spent the next six months awaiting trial in Oakalla. We were denied bail, which limited our legal communication to weekly visits with our lawyers. However, due to the public perception that we couldn't get a fair trial because of all the media hype, we were given special permission to have weekly lawyers' visits as a group in the enclosed visiting area of the Oakalla men's unit. Unlike most prisoners, we were also able to pick virtually any lawyer we wanted, despite having only legal aid, because the high-profile nature of our case was worth more money in the long run than the average legal fees during a trial. In the 1980s, legal aid was only available to those who could prove that paying for a lawyer would impair their ability to provide the necessities of life (food, shelter, and clothing) to themselves and their children.[17] If anything, the accessibility of legal aid across Canada since the eighties has only deteriorated.[18]

To be fair, this would be a very long trial, so any financial rewards for the lawyers would not materialize for a long time, if at all. It would also be fair to say that our lawyers chose to act for us because they wanted to see us get a just trial in a case that was clearly very political. The scales of justice were stacked against us.

Developing a trial strategy was complicated by the fact we were being tried as a group, even though each of us had varying amounts of evidence. So, it was inevitable that those with little evidence against them were tempted to go for a strictly legal trial, while those with mountains of evidence found it easy to choose a purely political trial. Our strong bonds of friendship and loyalty were put to the test during these potentially divisive discussions. These stresses were exacerbated by the fact that each lawyer was influenced by his (all our lawyers were men) own political guidance system in advising just how much his client should sacrifice for the collective good.

We were also very privileged in that we had both a defence and support group who helped us develop trial strategy, organized visiting schedules, raised funds for our legal campaign, and organized political awareness events. Both committees were invaluable lifelines to the community and conduits between us and the lawyers, but they also complicated matters when it came time to figure out trial strategy. There were just so many people's opinions to take into consideration.

In the end, the defence and support committees had to act autonomously to make decisions on the various issues because it was impossible to micromanage our community of support from prison. Of course, there were conflicts at times between the lawyers, and the defence or support committees, and between us, but we tried to stay neutral on divisive issues outside the prison walls because the emotional and mental energy consumed by surviving daily life in prison made it difficult to be completely immersed in these conflicts. In the midst of this maze of political, legal, and individual motivations that fuelled the trial strategy, the Crown decided to try the charges in four separate trials. They did this ostensibly to make it easier for a judge or jury to understand our charges, since there were so many of them.

They separated the charges into four different indictments related to the conspiracy to rob a Brink's guard, the Cheekeye-Dunsmuir bombing, the Litton bombing, and the Red Hot Video firebombings. By separating each of these events into different indictments, the Crown would also make it more difficult for a jury and the public to understand the political nature of the charges. We had set out in 1982 on a political campaign based on a set of anti-capitalist, anti-authoritarian principles that guided our tactics and strategy. We did not want to be identified as individuals but rather by the name Direct Action, so that when we sent out a communiqué authored by Direct Action, people would understand the principles and goals motivating that action. For example, when we bombed the Litton plant, there were injuries because the authorities did not clear the plant, despite warnings to do so. If Direct Action had not authored a communiqué after this event, the world may have mistakenly assumed the action was carried out by a terrorist group who intended to target individuals.

As an urban guerilla group, we saw ourselves as another facet of the popular resistance movement that would be capable of causing economic damage to the political/economic infrastructure, as was the case with the Cheekeye-Dunsmuir bombing, or to sabotage the structure itself, as was the case in the Red Hot Video firebombings and the Litton bombing. We did not see ourselves as leading the movement like vanguards, but rather complementing the popular movement by continuing the struggle beyond the legal boundaries the authorities set out. Unlike the aboveground movement, we could carry out illegal actions by living underground with false identification, without being vulnerable to police surveillance and arrest. But this would be impossible to do if we had to take regular jobs. So, we chose to carry out well-planned and profitable robberies that would disproportionately tilt heavily in the direction of benefits, while simultaneously creating as little risk to human life and arrest as possible. When viewed in this context, all our indictments were inextricably connected; they were all pieces within an orchestrated campaign.

A conservative estimate would see these trials going on for at least a few years. However, it was the order in which they planned to try these indictments that was upsetting. They claimed the Brink's conspiracy should be tried first because we had been in the midst of conspiring to rob the Brink's guard just before we were arrested. The Crown also had the most evidence to make the Brink's conspiracy stick, because the RCMP had wiretapped our kitchen and bedrooms for several months before our arrest. If the wire tape evidence was ruled admissible, the court would hear us preparing for the imminent Brink's robbery, in which we prepared to shoot back at the cops should they shoot at us. This potential for violence, and the car robberies and breakins to acquire weapons, would more effectively criminalize us before the rest of the trials even began, making it much more difficult for future juries to identify with our political motivations.

The rest of the indictments would proceed in order of their timeliness and the quantity of evidence involved, with the exception of the Litton trial. That would be last, because those of us charged would have to be transferred to Toronto, where that trial would take place. If we chose to go through with the Litton trial, it would be the most controversial, since a number of civilians and cops were injured when the car bomb went off prematurely. We issued a public apology with genuine regret the day after the bombing, saying that we should never have placed a bomb in a location where people's safety would be at risk, no matter how many fail-safe warnings are embedded in the plan. Murphy's law will always override "the best-laid plans of mice and men."

It would have been a lot easier to decide to take a political stance if there had been a mountain of evidence against all of us in all four trials. But there wasn't, so we vacillated between taking a purely political stance and taking a purely legal stance. A purely political stance would have meant refusing to participate in the trials, based on the fact that the bourgeois justice system functions primarily to protect the interests of the rich and powerful, and as such is never conducive to making revolutionary statements.

Over the centuries, the courtroom has evolved into a place where any opportunity the accused have to express their political motivations has been as skillfully extricated as a surgeon would a cancerous tumour. These motivations are considered not only irrelevant but also dangerous, something that could completely derail the legal course of the trial. This fact became most apparent when our lawyers tested the waters for the possibility of mounting a defence of necessity for some of our more obviously political trials, such as the Red Hot Video firebombings. The trial judge, Sam Toy, nipped the idea in the bud by warning our lawyers unequivocally that he would prevent any attempt at a defence of necessity by refusing to hear expert testimony or evidence related to motive or circumstances.

We spent the winter of 1983 working out the intricacies involved in pulling off the fine balancing act needed to accommodate five people who have conflicting trial strategies based on varying degrees of political and legal approaches. The dangers involved can't be overstated. The end result is very much like putting five people with different strategies together to cross a river on a tightrope. If they walk in single file, synchronizing their steps in rhythm and speed, chances are they will all get across. But if they don't use this approach, as in our case, in the end there are people hanging off the wire by a finger, others floating away in the whitecaps below, and some who just made it across with the help of a miracle.

Even though we eventually collectively opted for a legal trial approach for the Brink's conspiracy, our political identity sabotaged our lawyers' best efforts. They not only had to fight mountains of evidence and hours of wire tape evidence, but they also had to overcome the jury's impression that we really didn't give a damn.

Right from day one we would stand with our backs to the judge as he entered the room, laughing and using sign language to a room full of our colourful supporters. After the legal community had sat down respectfully in tandem with the judge, we would have to be coaxed back into our seats by our lawyers as we passionately kissed each other over the Plexiglas barrier separating the women from the men in the prisoners' box. Although our lawyers strongly recommended we keep our political views out of this trial, we wore T-shirts proclaiming "Free the Five" or sporting Sandinistas brandishing AK-47s in the air, or we wore earrings with a rifle in the crosshairs of a women's symbol.

At the time, the five of us did not believe that we would be acquitted no matter what kind of behaviour we exhibited in the courtroom. We had no respect for court decorum or any other aspect of the criminal justice system, but we were still willing to go through with it on the long shot that the jury might also have no respect for the legal system, and might just acquit us against all odds. In other words, we weren't about to sacrifice our identity or politics for the possibility of winning a lottery, but if given a chance, albeit remote, why not take it?

Two years before we were arrested, in February 1981, two American Indigenous men, Dino and Gary Butler, were visiting relatives in the Vancouver area and were arrested following a shootout with the local police. They were cousins who had been active in the American Indian Movement during the seventies. They were brought into the courtroom every day in handcuffs and shackles, even though they hadn't done anything to warrant this form of security. In order to protest the impression of guilt this prejudicial action would have on the jury, they refused to walk into the courtroom, so they were dragged in.

Dino and Gary Butler also applied to the Supreme Court to regain their eagle feathers, pipe, and medicine bundle, which had been confiscated by the cops. The trial judge, Allan McEachern, refused to recognize these spiritual items and also ordered the court sheriffs to stop Indigenous supporters from drumming and singing in the halls and lobby of the courthouse. The Butlers' supporters ignored this order. As a result of these prejudicial rulings, the Butlers dismissed their lawyer and refused to speak during their trial.

In contrast, we were not treated in such a discriminatory and prejudicial manner, even though we were facing many more serious charges than the Butlers. Our supporters were also not subjected to the same degree of repression as the Butlers' families and supporters, even though our supporters were more disrespectful and disrupted the courtroom constantly. The main difference between the Butlers' case and ours was that they were Indigenous and we were white. The treatment of the Butlers and their supporters, and the attitude of the court to their rights to spiritual items, is just one of the many examples of the overt racism that plagued and still plagues every aspect of the criminal justice system today.

When our first trial began, some members of the jury would glance over at us with a little conspiratorial smile. At that point, the jury probably identified with us as a bunch of misguided young idealists, much like one of their own children or maybe even themselves at our age. However, when the wire tape evidence was introduced, they carefully avoided all eye contact with us. By the time they had been exposed to hours of tapes in which we could be heard laughing hysterically while we meticulously calculated how much prison time we would get if we were convicted of all our actions, they were openly glaring at us and frowning. By then, we had lost all hope of an acquittal.

After we were found guilty in the Brink's trial, we decided there was no possibility for a fair trial on any of the other charges. In the end, we decided that people spending less time in prison was more important than using the criminal justice system as a forum for political enlightenment. That said, if the circumstances had been different, our trial strategy might have been much more political. If there had been mountains of evidence against all five of us, there would have been nothing to lose by refusing to participate. If there had been no concrete evidence, we would have had an incentive to pursue a strictly legal route seriously. Unfortunately, there is no fixed blueprint for the correct political trial strategy. As in all things political, strategy is not determined solely by ideology, but is tempered by the historical and the concrete circumstances of the time.

Rather than subject everyone to years of unfair trials, and then the inevitable long-term imprisonment that the State would demand for being forced to finance millions of dollars in legal fees, we decided to plea bargain while we still had some chips on the table. As they say, hindsight is always twenty-twenty, and so of course we made some mistakes. But taking everything into consideration, we did the best we could under the circumstances. If we had refused to participate in our trials on political grounds, attempted to mount futile defences of necessity, or forced the State to drag us through years of trials, Doug would not have received a six-year sentence, or Gerry ten.

Brent, Julie, and I did not exactly get a bargain, but then not everyone is going to be a winner in a plea-bargaining situation. Brent received a twenty-two-year sentence, Julie twenty, and I received a life sentence. A life sentence in Canada means that a person must do a minimum of seven or more years in prison, depending on the severity of their crime, before being eligible for parole. But they will be on parole for the rest of their life, until the CSC has literally seen their dead body. My life sentence had more to do with the amount of evidence they coincidentally found implicating me in every indictment than it did with my level of involvement in every action.

The week before my sentencing date, I brainstormed a short sentencing speech condemning the criminal justice system. I was frustrated by our inability to express our politics in the courtroom, and even my sentencing speech felt pointless. I wanted to feel empowered and inspire others in whatever way I could to continue the resistance. Then a light bulb went on in my head. An article surfaced in my memory about a militant woman in West Germany who had thrown a tomato at the judge during her trial. Over the next few days, I formulated a plan.

I stashed pieces of tomato from our supper salads in my cell. On the day of my sentencing, I carefully placed them in a plastic bag inside my bra. Since we had never once tried to slip contraband into the courtroom, the guards had no reason to be unusually alert on the day of my sentencing. It also helped that my comrades had already been sentenced without incident.

Somehow I managed to perform sleights of hand with my bag of tomatoes as I stripped off my prison clothes in front of the guards and changed into my court clothes. The way I saw it, the scales of justice were weighed so heavily in favour of the criminal justice system that taking advantage of the guard's sloppiness only tipped them to my side somewhat.

I sat patiently in the courtroom, listening to Sam Toy drone on about the reasons he was sentencing me to life. The words "you are a menace to Canadian society" stood out. Then he paused and asked if I had anything to say. I stood up and mustered up all the courage I had to give my sentencing speech in a tone of voice that I hoped was strong and defiant. I tried to explain the values and political analysis that were the motivation for our actions at the Cheekeye-Dunsmuir substation, the Litton plant, and the Red Hot Video stores. I tried to summarize all the things I would have preferred to have said during our trials if the judge had not made it abundantly clear that an explanation of our political motives would never have been permitted.

I had stealthily managed to transfer the bag of tomatoes from my bra to my hand before my sentencing speech. As I came to the final words, I threw the tomatoes in the direction of the judge. The tomatoes sprayed across the courtroom like birdshot from a shotgun. They hit the heavy velveteen curtains behind the judge, the court stenographer, the lawyers—everyone in their path, except the judge. The lawyers sitting in front of me and the prosecutor and his assistant ducked simultaneously. The moment my action became clear, the sheriffs jumped up and dragged me out. The next day, a courtroom artist portrayed me in the daily papers as an ugly psychotic, screaming and hurling a tomato at the judge. It was the nastiest courtroom drawing of the many I'd ever seen.

If I hadn't had such a strong political identity, I might have been shaken by the prevailing attitude that I was a raving lunatic. But in those days, our sense of political identity was reinforced by our constant contact with each other in court, as well as through a stream of political visitors to the prisons on a weekly basis. Resistance to capitalism was not just a belief; it was a way of life.

. . .

Not long after our sentencing, we were shipped off to various maximum-security prisons across Canada. Even though we had negotiated more lenient prison sentences for Doug and Gerry, we had failed to consider the terms of our imprisonment in the "bargain." The State did not play fair. Prisoners are theoretically supposed to do their time in the prisons with the security level appropriate to their crime, but the bureaucrats are also supposed to take into account the prisoner's home community. This was taken into account in our case, but not for the usual reasons. We were shipped as far away from our home community as possible in order to isolate us from our base of political support. Brent was shipped off to the Millhaven penitentiary in Ontario, even though he had spent his entire life in British Columbia. Julie's application for a provincial exchange between Ontario and BC was denied, and Doug was sent to Archambault penitentiary in Quebec. Gerry and I were transferred to prisons in our home provinces, probably because there were no other obvious options.

Brent did not contest his transfer to Millhaven because we hoped to get conjugal visits. Julie was told she could reapply for a transfer back to BC after her Litton sentence appeal and once her security level had dropped, but Doug's transfer to Archambault had no redeeming circumstances. It violated the good faith that was supposed to exist between the Crown and the defence in the plea-bargaining system. Doug's transfer was meant to punish him in a more concentrated form to make up for what the Crown saw as a lenient six-year prison sentence.

During the prosecution's countless hours of listening to the wire tapes, it is inconceivable that they could have missed Doug's frequent comments regarding his fear of leaving BC. Sending Doug, who couldn't speak French, to Archambault, where everyone, including staff, spoke French, was a transparent attempt to undermine his identity and influence.

The one thing they hadn't taken into account was just how passion-ately Doug felt about this. Within four months of arriving at Archam-bault, Doug embarked on a hunger strike, which he did not consider symbolic. Twenty-three days into his hunger strike, a group of supporters occupied the Solicitor General's office in Montreal and demanded he be transferred back to BC, where he could do time with English-speaking prisoners and have visits with his friends and family. After their arrest, a group of twenty-five people gathered outside the police station to bolster their demands. In the end, Doug became so weak that he hit his head after falling unconscious in his cell from lack of food. The authorities capitulated, and Doug was finally transferred to the maximum-security prison, Kent, back in BC.

PART II
THE LUCIFER
EFFECT, 1984

"In 1971, a psychologist, Phillip Zimbardo, set out to create an experiment, officially known as the Stanford Experiment, in which randomly selected students played the roles of guards and prisoners. Although the experiment was originally slated to last 14 days, it had to be stopped after only 6 days because the guards became abusive, and the prisoners began to show signs of extreme stress and anxiety. The results became commonly known as the 'Lucifer Effect.'"

Meredith Alexander, "Thirty Years Later,
Stanford Prison Experiment Lives On,"
The Stanford Report, August 22, 2001

Six

On July 31, 1984, the guards did not unlock our cells at the usual seven o'clock. I could hear the muffled grumblings of the women through their locked doors. After a year and a half in Oakalla, I suspected I was finally being transferred to P4W. Julie had been transferred a few months earlier, after exhausting every avenue of appeal in trying to overturn the refusal of Correctional Service Canada's refusal to grant her a provincial/federal exchange. But her fight was not over. She had merely accepted the fact that she would have to wait until after her Litton sentence appeal before resurrecting the struggle.

A guard stood in my doorway and told me to quickly pack up any paperwork and personal belongings I wanted to take to P4W, because she would be back in a few minutes to take me down to the admissions and discharge area. A rush of adrenalin coursed through my veins as I anticipated with some excitement my impending arrival at the P4W I had seen in the movie. When she returned a few minutes later, I pressed my lips up against everyone's door window as she escorted me down for my final strip search in Oakalla.

Within the hour, I was sitting in my special transfer jumpsuit in the back of a sheriff's van, speeding down the highway toward the Abbotsford airport. When I arrived at the airport, I was surprised to see a line of dejected-looking male prisoners slowly shuffling onto the plane in their leg irons and handcuffs. A female guard fastened my handcuffs to my leg irons with a chain, which made movement even more awkward. A cameraman was filming everyone as we shuffled onto the plane. I wondered why we were being filmed, since there must have already been a paper trail for every prisoner going up the staircase. Could it be they wanted visual proof that we had actually gotten on the plane in the event of a crash? Not even Houdini with a key could have survived a plane crash wearing all that hardware.

Everything about this flight spelled economy class. Since there wouldn't be an in-flight movie, I hoped there would at least be an entertaining stewardess who would go through the pantomime of putting on an oxygen mask while handcuffed and chained.

I was assigned a front-row seat, with a guard at the arm. The rest of the plane was filled to capacity with male prisoners. It was a kind of long milk run in which prisoners would be either dropped off or picked up in stopovers at Edmonton and Prince Albert en route to Kingston, Ontario, the prison capital of Canada, with its eleven federal penitentiaries. It was an uneventful flight if you didn't take into consideration washroom excursions and meals. At the best of times it is no easy feat to make your way along a narrow aisle on a moving plane to reach the washroom, and then hover above a communal toilet seat without spraying urine everywhere. Add a maze of chains tying your hands and feet together and it is damn near impossible. The prisoners looked respectfully away as we each took turns making the difficult journey to and from the washroom, but every now and then a fleeting glance of unmistakable solidarity would pass between us, a bond familiar to anyone who has shared extreme degradation with another human being. Not for a moment did I fear the men on that plane.

Eating was just as difficult. The prisoners had to ask a guard to open the aluminum foil that covered our meal trays. The chain that attached everyone's handcuffs to their leg irons made the range of arm motion very small indeed. Eating involved bending down low over the meal tray and carefully trying to get a plastic spoon of food to one's mouth without the chain yanking and spilling it first. Once again, the too-short chains between the leg irons and handcuffs had no conceivable purpose other than to humiliate and aggravate the prisoners. Almost every tray sat unopened. Hunger was preferred over humiliation.

By the time I arrived at P4W in the back of another sheriff's van, it took all the strength I had left just to press my face against the steel mesh wire of the windows to get a glimpse of my future home. The view was limited, but I saw just enough to realize that this prison could have been a stereotypical Hollywood movie prison set. We drove by a three-storey limestone fortress with the words "Prison for Women 1935" etched deep into the masonry above a set of huge wooden doors, bordered by barred windows. Its copper-plated roof and cupola had turned a pale green with time. Moments later we passed by an eighteen-foot concrete wall, over which towered the top floor of the prison ranges. In our mind's eye we could imagine the women on the ranges peering out at us from behind these two-storey high black windows, absorbing the diminishing light from the dying day.

We travelled almost a city block beside the wall before we turned through a gate leading to an area called the sally port. In time, I learned that this area, where all incoming and outgoing vehicles stopped for inspection, would normally be called a gatehouse by regular civilians. However, the penitentiary staff, with their quasi-militaristic identity, still clung to this archaic term, *sally port*, which was historically used to describe a controlled and secure entranceway to a fortress.

Architecturally, the prison resembled exactly what it had been designed for in the early twentieth century: an impenetrable fortress. In contrast, modern prisons are designed to look more benign than they actually are, like warehouses, high schools, or even suburban bungalows. Unlike its modern-day counterpart, this prison flaunted its thick walls and bars, reinforcing in citizens just how dangerous prisoners were and reminding them of what was in store for those who dared to stray outside of society's legal boundaries.

P4W had been philosophically and architecturally modelled after its neighbour, Kingston Penitentiary (KP), even though P4W had been built a century later. KP had been built in 1835, during an era in which prison reformers pioneered the idea that prisoners should spend their time seeking forgiveness for their sins from God, rather than being punished through corporal punishment, torture, or death.

These reformers were part of a seismic political shift in which the traditional monarchies that had ruled Europe for centuries were being overthrown by revolutionaries advocating for democracy. Monarchies had used corporal punishment as their preferred form of deterrence mainly because the public spectacle of burning "criminals" at the stake, quartering them with horses, or leaving them in stockades was a much cheaper method of maintaining law and order than prisons.

During the last decade of the 1700s, the simultaneous ascendency of democracy and the penitentiary over monarchies and corporal punishment in the Western world illuminated the phenomenon of democracy and prison reform moving in intersecting orbits. During this significant decade, the French Revolution unfolded, the United States entrenched the Bill of Rights into its Constitution, and the British Parliament passed the Penitentiary Act.

In the United States, the Quakers advocated for the construction of penitentiaries to reform prisoners instead of subjecting them to the usual corporal punishment of the day. The root of the word *penitentiary* is *penitent*, meaning "a repentant sinner." Penitentiaries would be places of silence, but also hard work, so that prisoners could earn their keep and earn grace in the eyes of God. However, the concept of deterrence, which the brutal public executions of a previous era had embraced, still manifested itself in the fortress-like appearance of these penitentiaries.

. . .

When the van finally came to a stop inside the compound, I stumbled out and looked around at the large, grassy prison yard. The walls of P4W might have evoked an earlier time, but inside the walls, the changes in penal philosophy during the late twentieth century had definitely made their mark. There was a tennis court, a quarter-mile track, a baseball diamond, and a quaint little bungalow just off to the side, which I later learned was for family visits. But before I could really get my bearings, I was hustled into the building by a couple of guards in olive-green uniforms.

I felt somewhat dangerous in my handcuffs, leg irons, and connecting chains. The guards I encountered either looked at me coldly, as though I had done them some grievous harm, or they looked right through me as though I were invisible. Either way, this only added to my feelings of alienation. I was subjected to the same strip search and delousing shower, in the same nondescript room, the same colour of faded nicotine, as I had had in Oakalla. These rooms, with no adornments, no plants, and no photographs, could only be described as bureaucratic.

Finally, I was escorted from the bowels of the building through a maze of windowless cement corridors and stairwells up to the second floor, where I waited for the huge barred gate to be opened electronically so I could get onto the range. I stood silently in awe, like a kid looking down at a midway for the first time.

"A" range was a huge, cavernous corridor with two tiers of fifty open barred cells that faced a series of two-storey windows overlooking the prison yard and Lake Ontario. A number of gigantic ceiling fans, whirring noisily on worn bearings that made out-of-sync ticking sounds, provided a backdrop for an eclectic blend of country and rock music wafting out of the cells from a dozen different boom boxes. The music and sounds of women laughing and yelling at each other echoed off the high cement walls. Women in street clothes strutted or shuffled up and down the corridor, as though they were heading downtown for the evening. Even though I must have piqued their interest, no one even glanced in my direction. The excitement that had infused my anticipation of life in P4W still existed, but seemed in suspended animation.

There was a whirring sound and the barred doors opened slowly along a track until they hit a metal stop with a loud crack. A guard came beetling out of the office and motioned for me to follow. She hustled me around the corner to B range, an orientation range for newcomers.

"The Inmate Chairperson will be along in a minute to give you an orientation handbook," she said brusquely, and disappeared back down the range, heading toward the guards' office again.

On my way down the range, I had noticed that each cell had a sheer curtain hanging over the bars to give the women some privacy, but the doorways were open. Each cell appeared to be decorated to reflect the personality of its inhabitant, with photographs, magazine pictures, leathercraft, beadwork, and other adornments, like a tiny apartment. There were women inside the cells watching TV, doing crafts, reading, or playing cards. It didn't look that bad.

My cell was barren. Blobs of toothpaste peppered the painted walls, where they had doubled as an adhesive for some prisoner's pictures. In some spots the paint had peeled away, revealing layers of paint over the cinderblock walls. The cell was furnished with a thin metal cot, a tall metal wardrobe and bureau, and a one-piece sink and toilet unit. I paced out the room. It was roughly nine feet by six feet.

I looked out over the prison wall at the roofs of the Portsmouth neighbourhood and the spire of the local church, which I later learned was the Church of the Good Thief.

Seven

For the first three months after arriving at P4W, I had to live on B range. This was the orientation range, where newcomers stayed while they were being assessed by the administration. The common rooms of A and B range were separated by a wall with three-foot-high Plexiglas windows through which the guards could observe us. They would sit in their office, which overlooked these areas, taking notes the administration would use to determine if we were ready for life on A range.

Julie had arrived at P4W a few months before me and had been moved to A range, so we only saw each other briefly at meals or in the evenings in the gym. As soon as I arrived at P4W our relationship was strained, but I cannot remember an exact moment or event that precipitated this estrangement. Unfortunately, it only got worse.

On the first night I walked into the B range common room, I was surprised to find myself being examined like fish in a bowl, not only by the guards in the office but also by the prisoners on A range. Although nobody actually stared at me, I could feel the women watching me from the corners of their eyes. Every new prisoner has an effect on the delicate equilibrium inside the closed hothouse environment of a prison.

I lost some of the machismo in my step when I realized I was being scrutinized by so many women all at once. There must have been about twenty women sitting around, watching TV and preparing toast for lockup. Julie was nowhere to be seen. Self-consciously, I sat down and stared quietly at the TV.

After lockup, I sat down on the edge of my cot and wrote Brent a long, romantic letter, vowing to write him at least a page a day until we were reunited again outside the walls. I ended the letter with a quote from a Led Zeppelin tune, reassuring him that I would love him until the mountains tumbled into the sea. When I fell asleep that night, I felt warm inside knowing that Brent was only a few miles away in Millhaven. We would have to remain charge free and wait a few years for our security level to drop, but we would eventually be able to look forward to conjugal visits, which would rejuvenate our love. I never doubted our relationship would last forever, since we had already risked our lives for one another on more than one occasion.

A few days later, a guard called me to the barrier and told me I had been accepted for a job placement in the wood shop. I didn't know what this entailed, but it appealed to me a lot more than the janitorial or kitchen jobs that dominated prison life. I headed down the metal stairs and through the maze of cement corridors toward the wood shop with a bounce in my step. The shop was a huge cement room filled with a couple of rows of industrial sewing machines and various woodworking machines, like the kind found in a high school woodworking shop. They would be useful for making solid wood furniture or smaller projects such as spice racks and jewellery boxes. In a far corner half a dozen women sat around a table, drinking coffee and smoking cigarettes.

An older man sat at the desk in an office with Plexiglas windows overlooking the shop area. He was peering over his half-glasses at me. I figured I had better introduce myself. He stayed seated and looked me up and down with the kind of expressionless face familiar to prisoners. Without offering his hand or a smile, he immediately launched into a stern overview of the rules in "his" shop.

"I'm Joseph, the shop instructor," he began. "If you are interested in learning woodwork or industrial sewing, just ask me, and I'll put you to work. Otherwise all I ask of you is to keep out of trouble and don't use the machines unless I have taught you how to use them." He paused for a few minutes while he finished ticking off names on a list for attendance purposes, then nodded his head in the direction of the women sitting at the coffee table.

"If you want a coffee, you can go over there with the other girls, and let me know if you need any help." I got the distinct impression he didn't want me to bother him anymore, so I walked out of his office toward the group of women at the table.

It felt like high school all over again. No one looked up to greet me. Instead, a couple of the women got up slowly and meandered over to the sewing machines with coffees in their hands. Another couple of women were playing a game of rummy and scraped their metal chairs over a little so I would have room to sit down. I pulled a chair over to the table and lit a cigarette.

Across from me, two young women were giggling and joking with each other like a couple of kids. They couldn't have been more than twenty years old. From their conversation, I gathered the chubby one was named Lisa and the skinny one was called Sammy. They were both short and appeared to be Indigenous, but otherwise did not resemble one another at all.

"So what are you goin' to do when you get out, sis?" Lisa asked Sammy while glancing shyly in my direction.

"I'm goin' to get a pony." Sammy sat with her body angled away from me.

"A pony!"

"Yeah, just a tiny little pony. A miniature pony, like the kind you see at the fair."

"Where are you going to put a pony? Aren't you going to live with Lauren?"

"They're only about three feet high. If you can live with a dog in an apartment, why not a pony?"

"What about when it shits?"

"You teach it to go outside like a dog."

While Sammy was talking, Lisa lowered her cigarette as though she was going to butt it in the ashtray, but instead carefully began singeing some hair off Sammy's arm. Instead of reacting, Sammy's eyes went as big as saucers. I followed her gaze to the wall just above Lisa's head, where a long centipede covered in lint rippled down the wall toward her head. When Lisa saw the expressions on our faces, she whirled around and thrust herself so violently backwards that her chair catapulted across the concrete floor behind her. In one motion, the two young women turned to each other and started screaming.

The old man was standing in his office, peering at us over his half-glasses. "It's okay, Pops!" yelled Sammy. He shook his head in exasperation and motioned toward the woodworking section.

In my short time in prison, I had noticed a pattern in which guards tended to treat the under-twenty-something prisoners like grown-up children. Like so many young prisoners, Sammy and Lisa seemed to have learned the adaptive behaviour of acting very childlike around guards and even some of the older prisoners whenever this behaviour served their best interests. The lack of control over their lives had the effect of infantilizing many young women who had spent most of their youth in some form of correctional institution. They had learned at an early age how to manipulate authority figures with their innocence, charm, and cuteness.

For a few seconds, Sammy looked through me toward Pops, her eyes squinted like Clint Eastwood in a Dirty Harry movie, but as she turned to leave her eyes locked with mine for a mere second. I think that was the moment my infatuation began. Two tattooed teardrops dripping out of the corner of one of her eyes left a permanent impression of profound sadness, while an upside-down crucifix tattooed in the middle of her forehead added a sinister edge to what was otherwise an innocent beauty. She had huge dark eyes, round cheeks, and the kind of full lips that come with youth.

She sauntered lazily over toward the woodworking machines in her cowboy boots like someone in a bad spaghetti western. The old man came scurrying out of his office after her, wearing a leather apron with a woodworking tape clipped to a pocket and a seamstress tape wrapped around the back of his neck. His short, stout physique and habit of peering out at the world over his half-glasses reminded me of a stereotypical tailor from some bygone era.

I kept Sammy in my peripheral vision as I finished my cigarette. She moved about the shop in slow motion, following the instructor, maintaining a guarded expression on her face. Even though she never actually looked my way, I got the distinct impression that she was watching me from the corner of her eye.

Lisa was sitting across from me, scribbling away at a crossword puzzle, while the other two women continued to play rummy. Perhaps her youth and unrestrained exuberance made me feel I could ask a question that would normally be considered too direct, particularly in a prison environment.

"Is she your sister?" I said, rolling my eyes in Sammy's direction. Lisa squirmed uncomfortably in her seat, then smiled. "Yeah, we're both from Saskatoon. We've been runnin' together for years." She got up and ran over to Sammy and the shop instructor.

I passed the morning finishing up crossword puzzles, waiting for the instructor to make some sign that he was ready for me, but he never did. Just before it was time to go back to the range for noon count, the women left the sewing machines and Sammy and Lisa returned to the coffee table. Sammy sat across from me and worked on a letter.

"Is Cheryl getting out with you?" one of the women playing cards asked.

"About a week later," said Sammy, without looking up. She took long, slow drags on her cigarette, letting the smoke drift slowly from her parted lips up into her nostrils.

"She stayin' with you at Lauren's?"

"Yeah, we'll be stayin' with my sisters 'til we got our own place." She squinted at the clock in the office.

"She'll love having a pony," the woman said sarcastically.

"I don't care what she loves," said Sammy in a quiet voice.

At exactly eleven, everybody got up and shuffled out of the woodworking shop. Sammy and Lisa were in front, pushing and shoving each other back and forth playfully. I could hear their laughter echoing down the stairwell as we made our way up toward the ranges. When we reached the main corridor where the women living in the wing (a separate area of the prison for minimum-security women) separated from the women on the range, I saw a thick, muscular woman, much older than Sammy, put her arm around her waist. Sammy reached up and draped her arm around the shoulders of the woman I assumed must be Cheryl. They were surrounded by a group of Indigenous women who were obviously their friends. I watched them walking in step, glued at the hip, down the long corridor toward the wing. I could hear the sound of the women's shouts and laughter long after they had disappeared from view. I climbed up the flight of stairs to the range two steps at a time.

Over the next few days I found myself hyper-aware of Sammy's presence in the shop, even though she painstakingly managed to somehow remain at the opposite end from where I was working. Even when I wasn't in the shop, I would always be looking to catch a glimpse of her leaving the cafeteria after the wing's shift or out in the yard or in the gym in the evening. Once in a while I would see her, but she was always with Cheryl, attached as though they were one.

Sometimes I would overhear tidbits of information about Sammy that I would absorb like a sponge. I learned that she was active in the Native Sisterhood and had been adopted as a young child by German Methodists in Saskatoon. She had also been the youngest person to be admitted to P4W in the early eighties, at the age of sixteen. I wondered if her blood family had also been from Saskatoon, since it seemed she had many sisters and aunties in the area.

There were very few Black women in P4W in the eighties, but, as in Oakalla, there was a high percentage of Indigenous women. Although the different races did intermingle, it was clear that the Indigenous women shared a history and common cultural traditions that bound them together with a level of solidarity that did not exist among the white women. The most powerful group in P4W was the Native Sisterhood.

After a few days I got up the nerve to ask our instructor for a project. "Just call me Joseph," he said. "Joseph Bodi. I'll teach you to make a jewellery box. Would you like that?" I nodded.

He unlocked a little storage room and brought out a couple of red and yellow cedar planks for me. He gave me basic instructions for using the planer, then left me on my own. "If you need help, ask Sammy. She's an old pro," he said, winking at Sammy, who was working within earshot of us. She smirked at him with a twinkle in her eye. He seemed to have a fatherly kind of attitude toward her that he didn't have for anyone else.

At one point, I lowered the planer a little too much and the machine laboured noisily through the wood, leaving a rippled effect in its wake. Sammy glanced in my direction, then came over and reset the machine back so it wouldn't plane so much all at once—all this without a word.

When we gathered around the coffee table waiting for the clock to mark exactly eleven o'clock, one of the women who played cards all day commented, "How'd you get Joseph to cough up the wood?" I shrugged. She smiled. "We never see half the materials that get ordered in this shop." She folded up her cards and placed them neatly in the corner. "I've seen a whole truck full of wood arrive, but if you ever get a peek in that storage room, there's only a few planks in there."

"He's an old con, no better than the rest of us," said her partner.

"Don't be cuttin' up Pops," Sammy said defensively.

After lunch, Joseph called me into his office and handed me a blueprint of a simple jewellery box. In the shop, he took my planks and showed me how to use the mitre saw, marking the side I wanted cut with an "X" so I wouldn't make the cut off the wrong end. While he was demonstrating this to me, we were startled by the sound of glass smashing. We turned around to see a broken cup lying in pieces near the concrete wall. One of the women who had been working at the sewing machines was pacing back and forth in an agitated fashion. Without a word, Joseph went over to her. She threw her arms in the air as though to warn him away. He scuttled back into the office. I expected to see guards come swarming into the shop any minute to take her away, but it never happened.

He watched her periodically over his half-glasses, but she eventually stopped pacing and went back over to the coffee table to talk to the other women. Nobody interfered, as was the usual prison protocol.

After I had finished cutting all the pieces, I leaned over the blueprint to see what the next step was. Sammy was clamping some pieces of wood together a table over. I decided to ask her for help.

She leaned over my blueprint and examined it for some time.

"I'm amazed Joseph didn't call the guards," I ventured.

"He wouldn't do that," she said without looking up. "Pops is like us. If we mind our own business, he minds his. As long as there's no blood and nobody's noddin' out on the machines, he don't see nothin'."

I had never stood so close to her. Her energy made me aware of every hair on my body, and my stomach churned in anticipation of something. It was as though my body was being drawn toward her by some powerful magnetic force.

"You got to clamp and glue those twelve-inch-long pieces together for the top and bottom of your box and then do the same for the shorter pieces for the sides," she said, looking directly at me. I felt sick.

I went over to clamp up the pieces of cut cedar for my box. As I tightened the clamps, I felt her presence behind me. I could feel her breath on my neck. When I turned around, she stepped up beside me and pushed down hard on one of the pieces that had warped up from the surface. I placed my hand down beside hers for added pressure, and for a second they touched. Without thinking, we turned, and she pressed her body up against mine and began kissing me so gently, her lips were like butterfly wings. I pressed hungrily against her and felt her thick tongue wrap around mine. We pulled apart after only a minute, but I could see Joseph shaking his head slowly as he watched us over his half-glasses.

I had vowed to write Brent a short letter that evening, since I hadn't written him in days, but once again felt I distracted. The same old pronouncements of love and loyalty sounded forced and stale. I couldn't conjure up the passion to inspire me. Instead I kept envisioning Sammy examining the blueprints, standing so close to me that I could hardly breathe. I sat back in my cell to try to think of something to say, but instead drifted off into a fantasy world of politically incorrect Harlequin romance. Sometimes in my daydreams I would storm into the crowded cafeteria, where Sammy was being held captive by her abusive girlfriend, and I would grab Cheryl by the throat, toss her aside like a rag, and swagger back out again with Sammy by my side, while everyone in the cafeteria looked on in awe. The main storylines would always paint a picture of me as the underdog hero, rescuing Sammy from Cheryl. In real life, there was not a shred of evidence that Cheryl was abusive. My unedited imagination seemed untouched by my staunch revolutionary values.

On the way back down to the shop the next day, I gave my head a shake. She was thirteen years younger than me. We were like oil and water, fire and rain. If we were ever to have a relationship, surely it would be the worst thing for both of us. She was completely submerged in the prison subculture. What could a white woman have in common with a young Indigenous woman from Saskatchewan? She was obviously gay, and I had never been with a woman before. I couldn't imagine being able to get conjugal visits with Brent if I was involved with Sammy. Yet my passions drove me on despite my rational objections.

Our kissing in the shop was like an addiction. Her girlfriend's tough reputation led me to believe there was a certain element of danger involved, yet still I could not stop myself. Apparently she felt the same way, because every day she would find a way to push herself against me and give me these kisses that were every bit as powerful as any drug I could imagine. Everyone must have seen us; it often happened right out in the open, but no one ever said anything, except Joseph.

"You're going to get killed if you're not careful," he said one day when he walked in on us in the storage room, where we were supposed to be getting some wood.

"Don't worry, Pops," Sammy said, ruffling my hair.

Miraculously, the day came for Sammy's release without incident between Cheryl and me. If she ever learned about our affair, she didn't let on. At that point I was more in lust than love, so I felt a mixture of sadness and relief on the day Sammy would be leaving. I didn't expect any goodbyes, but just before eleven, she burst into the shop. Her first stop was Joseph. After what appeared to be a lot of joking and laughter, she came running over to me in the woodworking section and wrapped her arms fiercely around me.

"I'll be back, Pooks," she said, using an endearment from a comic strip. Pooky was Garfield's teddy bear. Then she ran out of the shop as fast as she had come in.

Eight

Sure enough, Sammy was back sooner than I could have imagined. She was a woman of few words, but she did explain to me briefly that she had been staying with a girlfriend, who had a young daughter. Like so many of Sammy's relationships, she would periodically describe her friend as her sister, particularly if she was Indigenous. Sammy had tried to shoplift a Pocahontas doll for the child for either her birthday or Christmas, I can't remember which. She had been too wasted and was caught outside the store, where she put up a fight with one of the store "dicks," during which she ended up pulling out a pocketknife—a violation of her parole. Based on the joy she expressed at seeing everyone in P4W again, I figured she didn't regret being back.

Even though over a year had passed since she had left P4W, in prison time, it felt like barely a month. Time was a paradox. On the one hand, each day was structured exactly like the next, so that the memory of a month often felt like one day. Yet life within that predictable daily structure was so intense that some days felt like a year. Every day was marked by rigid routines determined and controlled by forces completely out of our control. Like products on a factory conveyor belt, we moved from one station to the next, until a year had passed as though it was just one long day. But our relationships on that conveyor belt were anything but dull and predictable. We made up for the lack of control, the repression and joyless routine, through the intensity of our relationships.

Some days we had to make life-or-death decisions. Should we back down from an argument with a woman we knew would use a shank? Should we bring up contraband oranges from the cafeteria for our sick friend and risk losing our parole and years off our lives? Should we go back in our cells when ordered so the guards could take our suicidal friend to segregation, or should we stand by our friend and end up in segregation as well? The concentration and awareness involved in our every action, and the extreme consequences of these decisions, made each hour feel like an entire day. Not to mention the toll it took on our psyches to witness the overwhelming amount of injustice that went on around us on a daily basis.

When Sammy came racing down A range, we started off exactly where we had left off, except this time Cheryl was out and gone from Sammy's life, never to return. She leapt into my arms, kissing me and whispering "Pooks" in my ear, even as the guards yelled from the barrier, threatening to charge her for being on the wrong range. However, she was quickly transferred over to A range and back to the wood shop, because she had only been "out" for a prison "minute." Even though my rational side argued against the relationship, my primal instincts got the better of me. I fell hopelessly in love and became addicted to a woman thirteen years younger than me.

A few months after Sammy's return I had to visit Helen, our Inmate Chairperson, about a grievance I was writing. I climbed the stairs to the narrow tier above the main range and let out a sigh of frustration when I heard voices coming from behind her closed shams. I decided to wait a few cells down until her visitor was gone. I stared out the windows that overlooked Lake Ontario and the Portsmouth Harbour Yacht Club. The lake shone dark blue in the midafternoon sun, in sharp contrast to the white sailboats that cut through the glistening whitecaps. I often wondered if the hundreds of women who had stood in this same spot had also found the beauty of this scene painful.

I was just about to head back to my cell when a young woman exited Helen's cell and headed off down the tier. I hesitated, thinking Helen was probably tired of visitors, when she stepped out and opened her shams again.

"Ann, how are you?" She smiled at me warmly. "Come on in. What's up?" Her lean figure moved smoothly in the cramped quarters of her cell. She sat down at her desk, where a Chinese book of horoscopes lay open beside a neatly stacked deck of tarot cards, and poured me a cup of herbal tea from a small teapot. I sat down on the edge of her cot. If I hadn't known any better, I would have sworn I was sitting in her small bedroom, not a prison cell. Her eye for detail was obvious in every nook and cranny of the cell. A silk headscarf had been transformed into a tablecloth for her metal bureau, and a climbing green vine wound itself up the bars toward the light above the shams. Shiny bits of granite and quartz, picked from the yard, had been cleaned and mixed in a bowl with shells and beads from her craft supplies to create a soothing display of colour and texture. The atmosphere of her space and the fragrance of the herbal tea calmed my jangled nerves. I took a sip of the warm tea and felt the tension leave my body. She sat quietly sipping her tea, patiently waiting for me to explain my visit.

"I was wondering if you would look over my grievance and see if I've missed anything." I handed her the grievance. She read it over carefully. "I don't even know why I'm bothering. They are totally useless," I explained. "I mean, what are the odds of the warden reversing a decision by V&C? He's the one who suggested I be placed on closed visits in the first place." V&C is the Visiting and Correspondence Committee, made up of staff who review visitors' applications. I was furious over the decision that all my visits would be limited to one hour inside a closed visiting room in which I would be separated from my visitors by a glass screen. It was recommended that these visits last until my security level dropped, which could be years. Other high-security women did not have closed visits unless they had done something inside the prison to warrant them. Closed visits were normally reserved for those in segregation.

"I know," she agreed, "but if they don't drop your closed visits and you decide to challenge it in court, you'll have to exhaust the grievance procedure first."

"How long will that take, three years?" My tone of voice had gone back to frustrated. "First I have to grieve the warden, and no doubt he'll take months to respond, and then if he rejects my grievance, I have to send it to regional, and that'll take another few months, and if they reject it too, then I have to send it to national headquarters, and if they reject it, then it'll be another few months. By then, I'll probably have regular visits anyway, because my security level will have been dropped to medium. Fuckers." I pulled out a smoke from a plastic case in my pocket and lit it. Taking a deep drag, I blew the smoke out in a long forceful sigh of exasperation before continuing on with my rant.

"I'm just sick and tired of sending useless grievances to the same cops who investigate themselves. There must be some other way of protesting the crap that goes on around here. I mean, my visiting situation isn't that important, but what about all the other shit that goes on around here?" Helen nodded her head in agreement.

I continued venting until she abruptly changed the subject. "Have you ever had your Chinese horoscope done?" She probably realized that I had crossed the line from useful analysis into an endless loop of ranting. I shook my head. "Would you like me to do yours?"

"Sure."

"I can't do a very accurate one without a lot of information, but I'll do a simple one if you tell me where and when you were born." Helen picked up a thick book on horoscopes.

I told her. While she leafed through the book and studied a few pages, I noticed many of the TVs and boom boxes on the range had been turned off, since most of the women were snoozing before our lunch shift started.

The range was like a huge amorphous being made up of the sum total of the fifty women who lived here. In such close quarters, each individual's emotions affected the others, creating an overall atmosphere that was almost palpable. I had overheard guards say that some days when they came to work on the range, they would know within minutes what kind of day it was going to be. Some days the tension could be cut with a knife, while on others the laughter was contagious. I often wondered if my mood was rooted in events surrounding my own personal life or if it was something I picked up from the overall atmosphere around me.

My reflections were interrupted when Helen let out a loud chuckle. She was studying my horoscope. I began watching her face intently. As she read, her brow became furrowed, until she came to the end and looked up at me with twinkling eyes.

I must admit that I do not put much store in astrology. I am sure that astrology has some impact on each of us, but I can't imagine it can be any greater than the infinite number of other events that happen to us in our daily lives. And if I were to concede that astrology does have a tiny influence on the outcome of our daily lives, this could only be determined by someone who has studied astrology and has taken considerable time to prepare an astrological chart and reading.

However, there was something about Helen that made me suspend my usual cynicism about astrology. For one thing, she was not just very intelligent in the intellectual sense of the word, but she was also wise. She was one of those people that made you feel that she understood what you were thinking and feeling and why. She had this way of listening to you as though you were the most important person in the world, whether you were a sex worker or a white-collar fraud artist. Despite my reservations, I waited with some anticipation for my Chinese horoscope.

"You are born in the year of the snake, according to the Chinese calendar, and are the sign of the fire horse. Ann, this is really amazing. Your reading shows that you have the ability to inspire people. If you continue on this path, you will become a great leader."

"It doesn't really say that," I interrupted her. I needed some reassurance that this was really true.

"Why, of course it does," she said incredulously. "See?" She pointed to my fire sign. "This is the sign that deals with the future, and it shows that you are a leader and engaged with many people. If your sun had been under a water sign, it would have meant you were more of a loner. I don't make this stuff up."

She went on at great length to describe me as a strong person with an important future. When I thought she must be finished, she shuffled the tarot cards and asked me to lay them out in a pattern that she dictated. Then she asked me to turn over certain cards. As I slowly flipped them over, her face broke into a wide smile.

"See, I was right. These cards confirm my reading of your horoscope. See, this horse indicates that you have an important future. I have never seen so many cards that point to a positive future."

"I hope it starts tomorrow," I said. She chuckled.

I do not generally like to describe myself as a follower of a particular ideology, like a Marxist, anarchist, conservative, or liberal, because then I feel as though I will be prejudged and defined before people even get to know me. However, if a gun were held to my head, I would readily describe myself as an anarchist. I share with anarchists the general analysis that societies with structured hierarchies and leaders are destined to become oppressive for those who are not in the upper echelons of power. Without getting into a long-winded monologue on anarchism, becoming a "great leader" was not one of my goals, but I was as vulnerable to someone else's notion of flattery as the next person. This was particularly true when the flattery was coming from someone I respected as much as Helen.

Our tarot card reading was interrupted by a guard's voice announcing lunch over the intercom system. I thanked Helen profusely, both for reading my grievance and for doing my Chinese horoscope.

As I walked down the range, merging with all the other women heading toward the barrier, I felt as though there were springs on my feet. How could I possibly feel depressed with a future like mine? No matter how much I reminded myself that she was not a mystic but had simply read a chapter from a horoscope book, followed by a formulaic reading of the tarot cards, I still felt like a butterfly about to emerge from its cocoon.

The electronic barrier cracked open as I arrived, and we flowed like a river down the stairwells and cement corridors leading to the cafeteria. Everyone I spoke to seemed to laugh at my jokes and take my conversation seriously. I felt like today was a turning point in my life. From now on, I could rise above any insults, administrative setbacks, and injustices, because my future looked bright, even though I genuinely did not aspire to become a leader of anything.

Of course, this feeling did not last very long. By the next evening I found myself seething with jealousy and insecurity when Sammy went outside with a new friend who just happened to be quite beautiful. I vowed not to humiliate myself by going outside to spy on them, but nonetheless found myself doing just that, peering discreetly from between the bars of the huge windows. By the time lockup rolled around, I had completely forgotten my horoscope reading.

. . .

But not for long. About a week later, it surfaced again. I had just come in from the yard on a beautiful Saturday afternoon when I ran into Sammy strolling down the range. Even from a distance I could see that she was in fine spirits. But when she caught my eye she became downright dramatic, running the last twenty yards and throwing her arms around me as though we hadn't seen one another in twenty years.

"Pooks!" she cried softly. Her huge black eyes were gleaming.

"What's up with you?" I asked suspiciously. I was still struggling with my jealousy over her new friend.

"Guess what?" she asked in one breath, and then answered herself in the next. "When I went up to show Helen my drawing, she did my horoscope, and she said I was going to be a champion weightlifter."

"That's great."

"I never told her I wanted to be a weightlifter, but she read it in my cards. They're real, you know." Sammy jokingly pulled up her sleeves and flexed her biceps. She did have good biceps. At times like this she reminded me of a black bear cub, her Cree nickname.

"She said I had 'unusual determination and persistence, and that these gifts, plus my natural athleticism, would make me a successful athlete.' I'm working out after supper. You comin'?"

"Sure." We often worked out in the weight room together in the evenings.

After evening count, Sammy came skidding into my cell in her stocking feet, carrying her expensive Nike Air running shoes in her hand. She was wearing her matching sweatsuit with the Nike logo emblazoned on her chest. Everyone in the prison aspired for brand-name clothes, which in this case I had arranged to have sent in for her by a friend in one of my parcels. She had insisted on the Nike logo. These garish brand-name logos were a status symbol; they showed you had someone on the street with money.

"Helen said I was a determined person who could beat the odds if I did not give in to the angry side of me," she continued enthusiastically.

"Well, that's true. Come on, let's go."

"Hey, don't forget your boom box."

I walked with my radio in one hand and hers in the other, down the cavernous range that was still relatively quiet from evening count. Outside the huge windows, the sun cast long shadows in the yard as it began its descent towards the west. Flocks of seagulls soared over the lake, diving intermittently after fish in the water.

There were a few other women waiting for the barrier to open. At exactly seven o'clock one of two guards sitting on the other side of the barrier got reluctantly up from her chair and entered the office to push the button that activated the heavy electronic doors. They whirred loudly as they slid slowly apart on their metal track until they hit the metal stop with a loud clang. As soon as the doors were open wide enough, the women began filing through while the guards scribbled down their names and destinations on passes, which each woman had to show to the guards at their final destination.

I had witnessed early on that the Indigenous women often reacted with much more outrage than the white women at having to show passes to the guards. They were aware through their elders and the Native Sisterhood of the historic relevance of this "new" pass system, which had just been introduced into P4W shortly before I arrived in 1984.

The "pass system" was one of many methods the first settlers used to achieve their ultimate goal of Indigenous assimilation.[19] The pass system was first used in Canada in the late 1800s to control the movement of Indigenous people in the Prairies. In order to leave the reserve, they had to have a pass, which would state the destination and estimated time needed for the round trip of the Indigenous traveller. Without a pass, any "Indian Agent" could put on his judge's cap and then charge and convict the Indigenous person for "trespassing." The pass system isolated Indigenous communities from one another and prevented coordinated resistance to colonization. It became a very important counter-insurgency tool in the wake of the Métis rebellion in 1885. Echoing history, the P4W prison passes would allow the guards to keep track of the prisoners' movements and prevent us from gathering in groups, which would make it difficult to organize any kind of resistance.

Even though there was no reason to hurry, we all walked briskly to the stairwell and trotted quickly down the winding flight of stairs leading to the maze of corridors on the ground floor. There were no windows from the range to the gym, just stairs and corridors made of cement and steel with no adornments to absorb the sound. Our footsteps and voices echoed all the way to the gym. For anyone with enemies, this was a long, forlorn, dangerous route.

The gym was regulation size, capable of hosting basketball and volleyball games, with a floor made of thin wooden strips that would absorb the shock of pounding feet. There was a good-sized stage at the far end with dark blue velveteen curtains. On either side of the gym was a wooden door. One opened up into a small pool room, and the other into a well-equipped weight room, packed with weightlifting equipment, mats, barbells, and a universal gym.

The other women separated from us in the middle of the gym and headed into the poolroom. I plugged in the boom box while Sammy put a thick coat of chalk on her weightlifting gloves. It was always easier to work out to some good pumping music than it was listening to the rhythmic clang of steel hitting steel in the otherwise quiet room.

We never talked when we worked out, and at least for a while, it looked like we had the room to ourselves. I had a set routine that I did night after night, adding more weight each time I mastered a series of repetitions. I wasn't very competitive with myself, or anyone else for that matter, because my goal was just to stay in shape. Sammy, on the other hand, worked her guts out night after night, whether she was alone or not. She had not articulated why, but now I figured she had this goal in mind to become a professional weightlifter. I didn't know if this was a goal she had secretly harboured before her horoscope reading or if this was a new goal, but either way, she always pushed herself to the limit.

The music was blasting as she stood there holding a small barbell in each hand, flexing them rhythmically up and down to her chest, facing the black barred windows so she could watch herself in the reflection. The upside-down cross and teardrops dripping out of her eye gave her determined expression an almost sinister look. When she had finished her reps, I told her I was done and wanted to go back. She glanced over at me out of the corner of her eye.

"Wait. I want you to spot me for a while, and then I'll finish by myself." I could never say no to her.

I helped her load the weights on the barbells and positioned myself behind the bar while she lay down on the bench, focusing intently on the ceiling. The weight trembled in the air as she held it above her head for a few seconds while she slowly exhaled through her pursed lips then slowly brought it back to rest on its cradle.

Over and over she repeated this routine, adding another few pounds each time until she had surpassed her record from a previous time. On her final rep, I almost thought she was going to collapse as the bar wavered slightly back and forth above her face, which had turned red and was glistening with sweat from the effort. When she finally let it drop into its cradle, she smiled slowly at me, revealing the black space where a molar was missing.

"Pooks, do you think I can be a woman's weightlifting champion?" Sammy was only about five foot six and 130 pounds soaking wet, but I figured if there were weight categories, she sure had the determination and work ethic to be a competitor.

"Why not?"

"The cards say I can."

"Well, then you can. Don't lift any more heavy weights though, eh? Promise?"

"Promise. I'm working out 'til lockup, though."

. . .

I was happy for Sammy, but some of the mystique of the tarot cards had left me. When I got back to the range, it was in full swing. It sounded like every TV and boom box was on full volume. Every now and then some angry words, a laugh, or a yell would break through the wall of sound, but, as always, the rhythmic ticking of the huge fan blades in the background held it all together. I strode down the range in sync with the ticking of the blades, smiling at some secret joke of my own until I ran into a friend, Punkie, coming down the stairs from the upper tier. Her eyes were swollen and red from crying. I had already passed her by a couple of stairs when I paused, turned, and asked if there was anything wrong. It wasn't always cool to interfere with someone's grief.

"Nothin'," she said, still heading down the range. I shrugged and kept on going, but then she called up and asked if I wanted to see a photo of her kids she just got. I turned around and went back down to her cell on the range, feeling slightly irritable at the idea of spending my last hour before lockup looking at family photos.

She was sitting on the edge of her cot with a crumpled-up letter and a couple of small photos of two young Indigenous girls on her lap.

"They're in foster care till I get out," she explained, "and I'm lucky if I ever hear from them. The letter's from the foster parents, and they said it's not a good idea for me to write the girls 'cause it just upsets them 'cause they don't understand why I don't come and get them." She was a rough-looking Indigenous woman with numerous scars on her face that made her look much older than her years. She picked up the photos tenderly and placed one carefully into my hand.

"This is Star," she said in a low, guttural voice that reminded me of liquor, bars, and cigarettes. "And this is Cheyanne." I admired the two young girls smiling broadly in their best dresses, sitting neatly in front of a velveteen backdrop in some portraiture studio. One girl was missing a front tooth, like her mother. In the next photo, the girls were wearing the same clothes but with a Mickey Mouse design backdrop.

"I can see why you'd be so upset. If I had kids, I know time would be so much harder to do."

"Oh, the thing with the girls bugs me, all right, but it's not that," she said, lighting a smoke. She inhaled deeply and held it in her lungs a long time before she let it out in a short blast. She flicked the ash at her ashtray, missing by a foot. "It's that damn Dr. Adams. He called me down today and said I had to do some psychological tests: stupid shit like picking out which pattern out of four doesn't match. Stuff like that."

"I think I did those. They're those IQ tests that aren't supposed to have a cultural bias," I said.

"What does that mean?"

"It's supposed to mean they are designed so people who are from cultures other than European or who haven't had much education can do them, and do as well as people who are white and educated."

"Oh." She fell silent, hunched over looking at the floor while her cigarette burned away until a long ash dropped. "He tells me the result of my IQ test is 75. So I says, 'What does that mean?' and he says the average score is 100. I ask him what the IQ stands for, and he says, 'Intelligence quotient,' or something like that. I guess that means I'm retarded, eh?" She took another deep drag off the smoke and let it out again in a short blast.

"Don't even think about it," I said. "Intelligence can mean anything. Those tests have been discredited. There's lots of proof that they don't measure different kinds of intelligence. Some people are great artists but do lousy in school. Even Einstein, who's a genius, dropped out of high school. You know, there are lots of super smart people in here who don't even have grade nine!" Still I could tell that nothing I said was going to make the numbers go away.

"Yeah," she sighed. "He's a moron."

Nine

Every Saturday morning after breakfast, there was a ritual cell cleaning. We would get our juices flowing by pouring ourselves some coffee, then we would pump up the volume of our boom boxes and drag all our belongings out into the middle of the range.

We would get down on our hands and knees, scrubbing the floors in our cells and taking breaks in little groups, whispering and laughing over the latest gossip. In some ways I imagined we were just like millions of other working-class women in the city who spend their Saturday mornings cleaning and gossiping.

I had finished cleaning and was lugging in bits and pieces of my stuff when I noticed Sammy and her best buddy, Paddy, doubled over laughing at something in Sammy's hand. From five cells down it looked like a letter or photo or note or something, but whatever it was, it made them laugh more than usual, and those two loved to laugh. They would just calm down and start working again when one of them would bring the thing over to the other, and they would burst out laughing again, with that deep-belly kind of laugh.

I had finally managed to get everything back in my cell except my tallboy, a big, metal, closet-like object, which was just too heavy to move by myself. Sammy was still laughing so hard that she had doubled over to keep herself from falling.

"Oh lay," I said, "get a grip. Do you think you can help me get my tallboy back in?"

"Okay, Pooks, let's go."

When I got her away from Paddy, I asked her what was so funny.

"Nothin'. It's just something we found that somebody accidentally left behind in the weight room last night."

On Monday morning, they were still breaking into fits of laughter whenever the topic of that thing in Sammy's hand came up. They worked together as the gym cleaners, which meant that every day they had to go to the gym and sweep, wash, and sometimes wax the huge varnished wooden floor, as well as keep the poolroom and weight room clean and organized.

They had more in common than most blood sisters. Paddy was a young Cree woman who had arrived within a year of Sammy from the Saskatoon area of Saskatchewan, and they shared the same life experiences of foster homes, juvenile detention centres, living on the street, and now living in the penitentiary. About the only thing they didn't share was Paddy's penchant for cleaning, which verged on obsessive.

Paddy went far beyond the call of duty when it came to waxing and polishing the floors of the gym. Prisoners and staff alike cringed in fear if they were unfortunate enough to be caught by Paddy scuffing her floors. Rumours alone of someone tarnishing her floors brought on a torrent of obscenities that shocked newcomers and visitors alike. But there was little the staff could do about these admonishments; it was hard to punish her for taking her job so seriously.

Now the rest of this story is based on the tidbits of information that leaked out of Sammy as the years passed. The only way to tell it is as though I were there, even though I wasn't. I should add that when it came to her comrades, Sammy was as honest as they come, so the skeleton of this story is true, but I fleshed it out with my own imagination based on my knowledge of these characters and the bare bones that Sammy gave me. This would be the story that most embodies Farley Mowat's principle of not letting the facts get in the way of telling the truth.

Anyway, on this particular Monday morning, Sammy and Paddy had pulled themselves together by the time they got to the recreation office. Bob had worked for "the service" for a long time, both in men's penitentiaries and now in the women's. He was the kind of staff person that prisoners appreciated because most of the time he was invisible, and he had a reputation for turning the other way whenever something was up. Like most non-custodial staff, he had a clean record in terms of charging people.

He was the kind of guy who seemed trapped in his defining years as a rock musician in a high school band from the sixties. He talked about it often, and still wore what was left of his wispy grey hair pulled back from his balding forehead into a ponytail that was only noticeable from behind. Since he wasn't a guard, he was allowed to wear his street clothes, which almost always consisted of a pair of faded blue jeans and Birkenstock sandals in the summer, or track shoes in the winter. He was lean and was considered somewhat cool in comparison to the guards.

He had an office with walls made of wood and Plexiglas that rose to the ceiling, so the recreation staff could survey the gym and the corridor outside the gym without leaving their office. As usual, Bob was perusing the daily paper when Sammy and Paddy arrived. He handed them the key to the cleaning supply closet without looking up. After they got their supplies, they came back into the office so Bob could take note of the various cleansers, mops, and brooms they had removed. When Paddy slid the key across the table at him, he glanced up briefly to acknowledge that he had a record of the supplies they had removed.

"Thanks," said Paddy, and then, after a pause, "Bob." Sammy almost burst out laughing again, because Paddy never used Bob's name to his face, ever. Still Bob did not look up from his paper.

As they walked out of the office, Paddy began to shut the door, but then hesitated and left it just slightly ajar. She raised a finger to Sammy to get her attention, then stopped outside the door and began fidgeting with the cleaning supplies. In a voice just loud enough for Bob to hear, she began talking to Sammy about something they both knew was of great interest to Bob. From where Sammy was standing she could see Bob raise his eyes toward them for the briefest of moments, then continue to read his paper as though he was oblivious to what they were saying.

After they had finished their conversation, Paddy plugged in her boom box, put on a Black Sabbath tape, and turned up the volume. They separated to opposite sides of the gym with their wide brooms in hand and began sweeping. They had just finished stripping and waxing it on Friday, so even though it had not been cleaned over the weekend, the floor still looked spotless and shiny. By the time they had finished washing it, there was still another half-hour left before lunch, so they pulled their buckets and mops into the weight room and pumped weights until the floor had dried.

Before heading up to the range for lunch and count, they returned to the office so Bob could count the supplies to make sure they hadn't stolen any. He had finished his newspaper and was doing some kind of paperwork, and as usual, he glanced briefly over the supplies and nodded his head. Paddy slid the key across the table at him and sat down on a chair.

"Bob," she said, looking at him directly. This time Bob stopped looking at his paper and fixed his gaze at her. "Me and Sammy was thinking it was about time we had a break. We've been bustin' our asses down here without ever taking a break. How about we take this afternoon off?

We'll come down here, okay, but we're just going to work out in the weight room."

Bob stared at her. This was highly irregular. "Hmmmm … sure." And he went back to browsing through his paperwork.

I began noticing that Sammy and Paddy were taking quite a few afternoons off after that day, but not always in the weight room. Quite often I would get home from my afternoon in the wood shop and find Sammy snoozing in her cell or reading a book.

"What's up, Sammy? How come Bob lets you guys off work so much? Doesn't custody say anything?"

She just shrugged, but as it turned out, custody had taken notice. After a few weeks of coming "home" early three afternoons out of five, a couple of guards questioned them at the barrier.

"I guess Bob figures we deserve a bit of time off," explained Paddy, "and if you don't believe us, just phone him. He'll vouch for us." Sure enough, after a few more afternoons off, the guards did not open the barrier for Sammy and Paddy to return to the range but dialled up the extension to the gym. They stood joking around with one another while the guard talked to Bob, and after a few minutes she snorted and let them through.

Bob must have been feeling the heat, because after another week of this, one Monday morning as they were about to leave his office, he said, "Whoa, partner! I think it's about time you characters clean those windows around the gym. They're filthy and they need a good cleaning. The bars, too."

Without saying a word, they got out their cleaning supplies and the twenty-foot extension ladder. Paddy was not one to complain about cleaning. She spent the whole week cleaning and shining those windows, the sills, and the bars until all you could see were a few smudges on the outside of the glass. Of course that bugged her, so she asked Bob if they could clean them on the outside as well. He arranged for a guard to supervise them. They climbed up the ladder and washed and shone those windows so clear that the birds couldn't even tell there was glass in them.

It was while they were cleaning the windows that they noticed a tall redhead named Stacey, from the wing, visiting with Bob in his office one afternoon. This wasn't unusual; prisoners often dropped in to talk to Bob about something related to his role as recreational officer. But when Bob noticed them watching him, he said something to Stacey, and she looked back over her shoulder at them for a second, then got up and walked slowly out of the office, closing the door softly behind her.

A few days after they had finished cleaning the windows, Paddy noticed a catalogue sitting on Bob's desk. He was sitting behind his desk cleaning out a drawer and barely looked up when they walked in and sat down in the two hard plastic chairs across from him. Without a word, Paddy picked up the catalogue and started leafing through it.

"You know that Stacey chick, Bob?" said Paddy without looking up from the catalogue. Bob made a non-committal "hummmmph."

"You know that hot redhead with the white, white skin, and just the right amount of freckles on her nose? She is hot, eh, Sammy?" Paddy kept leafing slowly through the catalogue while she said this, and Bob kept putting stuff from his drawer all over his desk and acting like he couldn't hear them.

"Yeah, she's hot all right." Sammy slid her chair over so she could look at the catalogue over Paddy's shoulder.

"Hot, hot, hot. Too bad she likes cock, eh, Sammy?" Sammy almost burst out laughing, but bit her lip instead. "You know what I heard, Sammy? A lot of people are complaining in the wing 'cause every night she takes a bath and just lays around in there for three or four hours. Can you believe that?" Sammy didn't dare say a word for fear the laughter might escape. "Why the fuck would anyone need to take a bath for that long? She must be trying to clean something off that just won't come off. You think, Sammy? It don't make her any less hot, though. A friend of mine in the wing says she looks just like a pickle when she gets out. She even turns kinda green and wrinkly, just like a pickle in brine. Can you believe it?" This was too much for Sammy. She burst out laughing. Bob started putting things back in his drawer in a very neat and organized fashion.

"Okay, okay, now," Bob said, a bit irritably. "Don't you two have anything to do?"

"Actually, Bob, we do." Paddy had developed this air of confidence whenever she spoke to Bob. She sat up very straight and enunciated each word very clearly. She picked up the catalogue and held it up to his face, open to a page with pictures of Jane Fonda and her workout tapes. Bob stopped putting away his stuff for a few seconds to glance up at the page, then kept on working, ignoring the fact that she continued holding the page in front of his face.

"A lot of girls would really appreciate it if you could order these three Jane Fonda tapes with the money in your spring budget. You know, Bob, ever since we got here, we haven't seen one new pool cue, one new barbell, one new anything in this damn gym. What the hell happens to all that money, Bob?"

Now Bob showed some emotion. He looked up irritably at them. "We don't get very much money in our budget, and it goes to things like the powwows, socials, cleaning supplies, and your salaries."

"That doesn't sound right, Bob," said Paddy, putting the catalogue back down on the table. "The rec budget doesn't pay for powwows or socials, and I think our six dollars a day comes out of Inmate Pay, doesn't it?" Paddy seemed to gain more confidence by the minute.

"Look," Bob said, "it's more complicated than you think." Then he pulled out some paperwork and started filling in columns of numbers.

"You'd be surprised, Bob, at just how many girls would come down here to use those Jane Fonda tapes." Paddy opened up the catalogue at the exact page on which a nice stationary exercise bike was circled in black magic marker, just like a magician who can cut a deck of cards to the exact card she wants. Sammy was impressed, although Bob didn't give any indication he even noticed.

Stabbing her finger at the bike, Paddy said, "It would also be real nice if we could get one of these too, since we got nothin' for cardio to do in the winter. There's a lot of joggers in here who could do with a cardio workout until spring ... Bob." Paddy reached over and picked up a white and red striped candy off Bob's desk, unwrapped it, and popped it into her mouth. Then she crumpled up the wrapper into a tiny little ball and flicked it effortlessly into his garbage can a good five feet across the room, not an altogether easy feat considering how light those little wrappers are. She got up with Sammy and headed out the door.

"Thanks, Bob."

A month went by in which I noticed that Sammy and Paddy stayed at work in the gym all day, and from all reports, everything was normal. Then one evening, not long after the gym had opened, one of the women came back from the gym, yelling up to anyone who would listen, "We got Jane Fonda! We got Jane Fonda!" A few women leaned out over the upper-tier railing to get confirmation that she meant the videotapes and the audiovisual equipment needed to use them. A few days later, a beautiful stationary exercise bike appeared in the weight room too.

It might not seem like much, but there were a number of women who were out of shape and took to going down to the gym every night and doing the Jane Fonda workout. It started with a few regulars, but after a few weeks the workout became a fad, and soon there were sometimes 20 women out of a total population of 120 doing the Jane Fonda workout. By the end of the winter, the regulars had transformed from hunched-over, flabby couch potatoes into edgier, less glamorous Jane

Fonda clones. They even started ordering those erotic workout outfits from the Sears catalogue.

As for the stationary bike, there was always a hardcore group of joggers who didn't do much all winter, but once the bike became available, you could hear it whirring away from the weight room all winter long.

Sammy and I didn't work out together every night, but a few times a week we would go down to the weight room together so we could spot each other for the heavier weights. It wasn't more than a week after the Jane Fonda tapes and stationary bike had arrived that we were strolling hand and hand down the corridor toward the gym when we saw Stacey coming toward us. As she passed, I noticed her eyes were red, and she was crying.

"What's that all about?" I asked Sammy.

"Who knows? Maybe one of her pen pals dumped her," Sammy said flippantly.

The next day at lunch, Sammy and Paddy came back up from the gym with long faces. "Bob's retired," announced Paddy, "and they've sent in a broad to replace him."

"What are you talking about?" I said.

"We go to work and they've got this broad working there. Too bad about Bob, he was okay."

We didn't have much time to mourn Bob's passing before Sammy came running into my cell explaining she needed her shank, not for herself, but for someone else, just in case. She had to go back to keep six, but wanted me to get it for her, and explained that Paddy would watch for the guards.

I went into her cell and leaned the heavy tallboy up against the sink while Paddy hung over the upper-tier rail, talking to someone down below. I lay down on my back on the floor, reached deep in underneath, and felt the handle all covered in masking tape to keep it from collecting fingerprints. I got as good a hold of it as I could and yanked until the tape that held it to the floor of the tallboy ripped. Underneath the shank was an envelope, still stuck to the tape.

I knew it was none of my business, but since Paddy was still talking outside the cell, my curiosity got the better of me. I opened it. Inside was a Polaroid snapshot of a man's torso, naked, with his head and feet cropped off. He had an athletic build and grey chest hairs. The photo was framed so that the first thing that caught your eye was his erection. The second thing was the backdrop of a bench with a barbell in the P4W weight room.

Ten

When Julie and I first arrived at P4W, we spent a lot of time together, but within a year we had begun to grow apart. I was not aware of any animosity between us during that first year. We simply had different friends and activities. I loved working in the shop, and Julie began to take university courses by correspondence. I lived at one end of A range and she on the opposite. In Oakalla we had shared a very strong political identity, which was reinforced by sharing the same experiences of living in the same "unit," sitting in court most days, and visiting the same people on our days off.

In P4W we naturally began to develop our own unique identities, but these identities took a hit politically because the pressures of daily life began to take centre stage. We still had visitors from the radical political community, but not as frequently, since P4W was so far from BC or even Toronto. I believe our daily decisions became more subliminally rooted in our survival instincts in P4W, as opposed to our political consciousness in BC.

One day I ran into Julie on the way back up to the range from the gym and a little argument arose.

"I always felt pressured by you guys to do things," she said, referring to Direct Action. My blood pressure immediately shot up as all our old conflicts quickly resurfaced.

"What are you talking about? Have you forgotten that you pressured us into working with you? Have you forgotten crying and telling Suzie that you were mad because we wouldn't take you target practicing? Doug had a strict policy about not working with people as young as you. If it wasn't for Brent we would never have let you come with us," I snapped back, no holds barred.

"I never wanted it to go so far, but I never had the power to make decisions." Her arms were crossed protectively across her chest, her feet slightly apart. "And you promised me that you and Brent would never let anything happen to me at Litton," she said.

"We did our best," I said. "How could we help it if they taped your voice? You know as well as I do that the cops would not drop the Litton charges on you no matter what we said."

We continued to argue over our interpretations of the past until it threatened to break out into a shouting match. As usual, we were both right. Julie was very persistent and eager to get involved in our guerrilla campaign, but she had not had the years of political experience required to make an informed choice to get involved in something so dangerous and irrevocable. Once she became involved, she also did not have the same degree of power or control over events because she was so much younger and less experienced than Brent, Doug, and me.

During our trip to Toronto to bomb the Litton plant, Julie became very lonely due to the isolation of living exclusively with Brent and me. She also began to second-guess her decision to join our campaign. Once we returned from Toronto, Brent and I had numerous arguments with Julie. Gerry was Julie's partner and very much in love with her, so he backed her up most of the time. But since he had not been involved in the Litton bombing, he was not as emotionally invested in the possible implications of getting busted as Julie was, so there was not the same degree of acrimony between Gerry and us. Doug lived in an apartment on his own, so he was cushioned from the daily stress of arguing that really began in earnest when we returned from Toronto. The growing tensions between each of us in Direct Action fuelled many thoughts of taking a long break or even retiring before the end of 1983.

When our argument had lost any semblance of reason and reached an emotional climax, Julie turned and stomped up the stairs toward the range. Not long after this I heard through the grapevine that she was seeing the shrink and the reverend on a regular basis. The reverend surprised me; Julie had always been very critical of religion.

Eventually she moved to the wing. The wing had different eating shifts for lunch and dinner in the cafeteria than the ranges. But the wing and range shared the cafeteria for breakfast because so few people ever went down for breakfast anyway. It was relatively easy to avoid being in contact with anyone from the wing because the yard and the gym were the only other places where people from the wing and ranges could mingle.

Then one Saturday afternoon I thought I saw her walking around the track talking to our mutual friend, Helen. After a double take, I realized it was indeed Julie. Despite the heat, she was walking briskly around in a pair of baggy polyester pants like the kind older ladies would wear, and a plain, light-coloured, short-sleeved shirt. She had her head down, staring intently at the ground. As long as I had known her, she had always dressed in black or brightly coloured clothes, accessorizing with layers of cheap costume jewellery like a punk rocker. Her hair was ever-changing, sometimes jet black, sometimes pink, and she always ringed her eyes with mascara. Her outspoken manner, coupled with her eccentric style, had made her a standout in any environment.

She had always talked in a very animated fashion, with her hands accompanying her voice while her head kept up a steady bebop rhythm. But today, even at a distance, I could see there was something subdued about her. Her upper body was very still while her legs kept up a steady, level walking rhythm. Her hair was still dyed black, and her eyes ringed with mascara, but otherwise I wouldn't have recognized her.

I hadn't spoken to her in months, not since our argument in the stairwell. But I wasn't concerned, considering how many blowouts we'd had in the past. She could be hot tempered, but I had to admit that some of her criticisms of me were accurate. My sisters had accused me of being "bossy" for as long as I could remember, and sometimes I think I did come off as a cold, domineering zealot. And of course, like most people, my bad qualities came out in spades whenever I was angry.

I got back to reading my book under one of the few trees, enjoying the cool shade of the hot autumn day while continuing to surreptitiously observe Julie pacing the track with Helen. Finally, Julie broke away from Helen and headed toward the building, where she would have to pass by me. When she got within hearing distance, I threw her a friendly greeting. I was hoping we might even have a conversation. I was curious about her getup. But she kept her face to the ground, and just before reaching me, she made an awkward arc toward the door. I stared at her incredulously. I hadn't known her to be the type to hold a grudge.

My curiosity got the better of me. After waiting a few discreet minutes, I angled across the yard and caught up with Helen. I knew that her standards for ethical conduct would prevent her from gossiping or revealing a confidant's secrets, but I felt compelled to try to penetrate her moral armour. I just had to solve the mystery behind Julie's complete transformation.

"I'm concerned about Julie." I had decided to broach the topic circu-itously. I was concerned about Julie, but curious would have been a more accurate word. Helen saw through me immediately, and smiled.

"I'm not asking you to tell me what you were talking about," I con-tinued, "but I was wondering if you could tell me why she's avoiding me. I'm afraid she'll blow up if I ask her directly." I glanced at her face to gauge whether or not I had crossed some kind of line. Her face was a benign mask.

"Well, all I can tell you is what everyone else seems to know. Appar-ently she says you've threatened her, and she's afraid for her life. She thinks you or one of your friends is going to beat her up. And that's all I know." She gave me a reassuring smile.

I was truly taken aback. It had never occurred to me to threaten Julie. In fact, I had not said a word to her since that day in the stairwell. Where was this coming from? None of my close friends even mentioned her. Since she had moved to the wing, we did not share the same circle of friends, and our paths rarely met.

Later that week, I decided to go down for breakfast. It wasn't my usual habit, but I was getting hungry in the shop every morning and thought a change in eating habits might help. Even though I was a little late, the cafeteria was almost empty, so Julie's profile immediately jumped out at me. She was sitting with her back to me, reading a heavy book. As I stood waiting for my eggs easy over, I examined her unabashedly. Her thick black hair had been dyed a mousy brown and cut to just above her shoulders. She sat ramrod straight, lifting each spoonful of cereal up to her mouth in a slow, mechanical rhythm. Knowing Julie from the past, I figured she was working hard to control a lot of repressed emotions that would explode if anything set her off.

I took my plate and sat down in a far corner behind her. After a little while, she carefully closed her book, placed her utensils neatly on her plate, dabbed a napkin around her mouth, and quietly placed her tray in the slot to the dishwashing area. She walked with short, even steps, as though there was a line drawn on the linoleum for her to follow. Her face remained frozen forward as though she had been ordered to do so. She had the look of an automaton. As she passed by my table I noticed that the heavy book she had been reading was the Bible, which only added to the slightly insane aura that followed her like a spotlight on an actress. Up until this moment, I would have been less surprised to see her carrying a human scalp than a Bible.

I felt a little unhinged. It was unnerving to see someone I thought I knew so well go through such a rapid transformation into someone so completely different. She had embraced a new persona who was not only the exact opposite of her previous self, but also someone she would have disrespected only a few months ago. My own sense of identity felt a little shaky. Could I fall victim to whatever forces had eroded her values and sense of identity so quickly and completely? Maybe I hadn't known her at all.

Coincidentally, when the mail arrived at noon I received a letter from Brent expressing outrage that Julie was appealing her sentence for the Litton bombing on the grounds that she had been pressured and intimidated into participating. Brent and I had also appealed our sentences, but on technical grounds, based on precedents in which others had received much lower sentences for similar offenses.

Our lawyer explained that Julie was doing her own appeal and was presenting evidence based on certain books that had been found in our house in which urban guerrillas recommended killing fellow urban guerrillas who had either renounced their militant politics or had threatened to become informants; once an urban guerilla, always an urban guerilla. The only way out was death. I wracked my brain, trying to remember any passages of this nature anywhere in our house, or anywhere at all, in fact. I could not recall reading that Western urban guerillas advocated executing their comrades for ratting out or for renouncing their politics, but that didn't mean militant writings denouncing traitors did not exist. Even if there had been writings of this nature in our house, we had never even hinted at threatening Julie, much less killing her or anyone who wanted out of our urban guerilla campaign. In fact, we had taken to discussing retiring to the country for a while, but obviously she had conveniently forgotten those discussions.

The irony of confronting her over these false accusations was not lost on me, so I decided against it. She had been moved to the wing much more quickly than most prisoners. I never saw her, not in the yard or the gym. She was always holed up in the wing doing university courses and appeared to only leave for meals, which were separate from the range.

I did not consider what I interpreted as Julie's manipulation of the past to be informing or ratting out to the authorities. I think Julie actually believed these books and writings existed in our house, and maybe they did, although I had never seen them. I believe her involuntary transfer to P4W in Ontario had isolated her from her family, her friends, and the political community in BC, which resulted in an unravelling of her political identity. Julie was not unique. Many women experienced some form of depression, anxiety, or even suicidal thoughts after being trans-ferred out of province, far away from their emotional and spiritual support systems. Some killed themselves. Most of them probably suffered from post-traumatic stress disorder, a diagnosis that is still so politically charged it eludes the marginalized and non-white segments of the population even today.

Since the day of our arrests, the cops and other authority figures had been portraying Julie as the innocent dupe whom Brent and I had manipulated for our own ends. And now that she was no longer useful to us, we were quite happy to abandon her to the sharks while we went on our own merry way. At least this was the stereotypical group profile that the cops, the media, and every other authority figure used to explain the group dynamics in any "criminal gang." Julie was particularly vulnerable to suggestions that she had been the victim of this group dynamic. She was very young, and suffering from isolation and fear in a federal prison in Ontario, far from her support network of family and friends. I became more and more convinced that the combined efforts of the shrink and reverend had convinced her that she really was an innocent dupe who was being used by these Machiavellian characters, namely Brent and me.

The last time I saw Julie, she was coming down from the "hospital" and had to walk past the barrier of the range to go back to the wing. She had really made a complete metamorphosis in a matter of months, from a flamboyant political punk rocker to a subdued, mousy Christian. Her new brown hair colour made her white skin appear sallow, and without the thick rings of black mascara surrounding her pale blue eyes, they had lost some of their intensity. She looked small and thin, in part because she had actually lost weight, but also because her polyester pants and cotton shirt were a size too big. Her frailty and weakness brought out my compassionate side. It would have been as difficult to stay angry at her as it would be someone dying of a particularly aggressive form of terminal cancer.

One of the guards wanted to see her pass, which was a prerequisite for being in the hospital area. She turned and looked back at the guard, but did not acknowledge me.

"I was just up seeing Reverend Downes," she said in a small, soft voice. She looked pained, as though uttering those words had taken a lot of effort. The guard seemed to see the same thing I did, because she nodded, giving Julie permission to carry on even though she didn't have a pass.

During lunch count most of the boom boxes went mercifully silent as quite a few women dozed off after eating. I was one of them. I dreaded the sound of the huge wheel spinning to open the doors at the end of the range. I wanted to stay in this relaxing dream world as long as possible. Despite our workweek hours being somewhat mutated by the major prison population counts at noon and the three o'clock shift change, we were as enslaved by a Monday to Friday, nine-to-five work routine as the rest of the world.

"Hey! You coming down to eat?" yelled a young Québécois woman we called ZZ, through my shams. I sighed deeply, my cheek wet from the drool that had soaked a corner of my pillow. Slowly I dragged myself into a sitting position on my cot and pulled open the shams. I could see people sailing and windsurfing on the glistening lake just past the prison walls.

Sammy and ZZ strutted past my cell in sync with the dominant music from the growing symphony of boom boxes filling the cavernous range. Pauline, who was ZZ's lover, shuffled along behind them. Even though Pauline and I weren't exactly old in years, compared to ZZ and Sammy we were certainly older, in both years and spirit. Sammy had at times even taken to calling me Baby Burnout instead of Pookie. I didn't even try to keep up with her. I assumed Pauline probably faced the same awareness of her age in the face of ZZ's boundless energy. I vowed that I would never again take up with someone so young. At nineteen, Sammy was a constant reminder that at thirty-two, I was handicapped by periodic fatigue and a need for solitude.

We headed down the range and into the common rooms, where ZZ flopped down across the arm of her chair. Sammy followed and sat next to her, staring intently at the TV screen. A half-burnt cigarette dangled between her thumb and index finger. Pauline and I also came in and sat quietly watching TV, patiently waiting for the next movement, dinner.

"Hey," said Pauline, "I got a letter from Oakalla today, and guess who's there?" I looked over at her. "Your little friend Julie," she said in a singsong voice. It had been a while now since I had last seen Julie coming out of the hospital while I had waited for a pass at the barrier.

"I hadn't even noticed she was gone," I said truthfully. "How did she get transferred there that fast?" I knew I should know the answer to this, but I wasn't sure. I hadn't heard the outcome of Julie's appeal.

"My buddy says she won her appeal and got her sentence reduced and a provincial transfer," said Pauline matter-of-factly.

"She was afraid of you," added ZZ. "One of her friends in the wing told me you were going to beat her up in the yard."

I laughed. "That's her guilty conscience talking. The thought never crossed my mind. I was pissed off at her about some things she said, but I would never have touched her or threatened her."

"Supper!" a robotic-sounding voice echoed through the intercom system. The women in the common rooms got up in one motion and began walking toward the range. The ancient, electronically controlled doors at the end of the range separating the guards from the prisoners slowly opened and came to a stop with a metallic clang. We jogged down the winding stairwells among the pockets of women flowing like molten lava to the ground-floor corridors leading to the cafeteria.

Women were lined up in front of the cafeteria's steaming cabinets, waiting for a prisoner server dressed in kitchen whites to dish up whatever was on the menu for that day. It was Friday, fish and chips day. We walked over to the same brown Arborite table in front of the long window we had occupied since I had moved over to A range.

"I can't eat fish anymore," said Pauline, picking her fish apart and neatly organizing it in a pile at the corner of her plate. "Ever since I went back and saw the body in the lake, I just can't do it."

"What the fuck are ya talkin' about?" said ZZ, looking up at her.

"After we killed that girl, we rolled her body up in a carpet, drove down to the ocean, and dumped it. Well, after a few days, my old lady starts to get curious and wants to see if it's still there or what. So we go back and there it is all white an' slimy, covered in eels and leeches and some kind of fish sucking out the blood, I guess, and eating the flesh. I've never been able to eat fish since."

"Thanks for that." ZZ wrinkled up her nose and pushed her plate away. "Hey, Rocky!" ZZ motioned across the cafeteria toward a stout young woman with a broad smile wearing blood-smeared kitchen whites. She was the butcher's apprentice. She lumbered over to our table, holding a plate with a raw steak in the middle.

"Do you want some?" she asked Sammy in a child's voice. Sammy nodded and held out her plate. Rocky held her fork in one fist and her steak knife in the other, sawed the raw steak laboriously in two, then stabbed one piece with her fork and lifted it dripping with blood onto Sammy's plate. I still managed to wolf down my fish and chips.

With great zeal the two young women picked up their steak in their hands and began ripping into it with their teeth. More than one person watched them devouring the raw steak with their bare hands, letting the blood drip out of the corner of their mouths, off their chins, and onto the table. Their eyes were gleaming as they ate without manners, utensils, or restraint, apparently relishing the primordial experience. By the time they were finished, there were trails of blood running down their forearms and their hands were covered in raw bits of fat, meat, and blood.

I knew there were guards watching this display who interpreted it as further proof that some prisoners were still primitives, ruled by their instincts, not reason, without the capacity to adopt the finer social etiquette of modern-day civilization. I, on the other hand, interpreted this display as an act of defiance against a civilization that treated some people like animals. You want to treat us like animals? Well, here I am … an animal. How do you like me now?

Pauline could not stomach any more after the fish, and got up to leave. Wanting more information on Julie, I hurriedly dropped my utensils on my tray and followed at Pauline's heels, but there was no more information coming. We huffed and puffed our way up the winding stairwell to the range.

At the top of the stairs, the guard's station was right outside the electronic barrier to the range. Usually there were two guards sitting at a desk in order to both observe the range and give out passes for women wanting to leave. Perhaps the guards were miffed because they had already heard from the guards in the cafeteria that the cook had allowed us to eat raw steak for lunch, or maybe it was just one of their random searches, but we were stopped and searched for contraband just before passing through the barrier. Contraband was so ephemeral, impossible to define or put your finger on. An orange was food in the cafeteria, but contraband at the barrier. A butcher knife was a tool in the kitchen, but a weapon at the barrier. The designation of contraband was about as random as their searches.

After the guard had run her hands lightly down Pauline's sides in a half-hearted attempt to find something, Pauline requested that she feel her breasts. The guard looked at her wryly and told her to get in before she sent her to the nursing station for an internal.

"That would be even better," quipped Pauline, turning toward the hospital area.

"Pauline," the guard said warningly.

"What?" Pauline's voice went high and whiny. I stood waiting for her to finish toying with them. Finally, she passed through the barrier and pulled out a bag of sugar from under her waistband.

We could hear ZZ, Sammy, and Rocky laughing behind us. Sure enough, the guards pulled them over as well. ZZ and Sammy had just caught up with us when we heard Rocky yelling at the guards. We turned around and saw one of the guards dangling a small bag of sugar in the air. Just about everybody brought up sugar for their tea or coffee at night. It also happened to be an essential ingredient for a brew, just like oranges or any other kind of fruit.

"It's … for … coffee!" yelled Rocky, drawing each word out slowly and with some difficulty. It was hard to tell whether she had a slight speech impediment or some kind of developmental disability. Despite her power-ful, masculine physique, her voice and behaviour were very childlike.

The barrier was still open, so when she saw us standing not twenty feet away waiting for her, she simply walked on through. As we walked together down the range, one of the guards kept yelling like a broken record, "Rocky, come back here," over and over again.

Rocky's cell was not far from the barrier. We slipped in and draped ourselves on the cot, chair, and bureau. Rocky was sitting on the edge of her cot with her head resting in her hands, her sausage-like fingers spread across her face.

"I just can't do it again," she said, referring to seg.

"They're not going to take you for a tiny bag of sugar," I said. Sammy raised her eyebrow at me skeptically.

"I'll go down to the barrier with you and talk to them," said Pauline. She often tried to help the younger women, who had less control over their emotions.

"I know they're goin' to put me in seg, Pauline," said Rocky, her brow furrowed in anger. "They never let me go."

The voices had stopped calling her. For a few minutes my naïveté got the better of me, and I actually entertained the idea that they would let it go, until we heard the barrier clang shut and the sound of soft-soled shoes marching rapidly toward us.

"Girls, get back to your cells," one of the guards warned, while another yelled up the range for the other women to get in their cells for count. It was early. It could mean only one thing. They were taking Rocky to custody. Already we could hear the sound of a guard running along the upper tier, shutting the cell handles.

"Come on, girls, get back to your cells." The guard's voice was more commanding this time.

"Go on," said Rocky quietly. "It's all right. I'll just go."

"No way," said Sammy defiantly. "I'm stayin' with you."

"Come on, Rocky, we're just taking you down to custody to see Fucillo," the other guard pleaded. Fucillo was the CX8, or head of cus-tody for the shift.

"I'm okay," said Rocky to Sammy. "Just go."

Pauline pushed open the shams and squinted at the guards. "If you keep her, I'll have my lawyer all over you."

Reluctantly, we walked back to our cells. The wheel spun at the end of the range, locking our doors for count. I had saved a letter from Brent to read in lockup when I knew Sammy could not pop in. She had taken to flying into a rage whenever I got a letter from him. Her tactics seemed to be working, because I found myself dreading the moment the guard would hand me one of his letters whenever I was walking with her. I associated his letters with threats and recriminations. She wanted me to cut off all contact with him to prove that I loved her.

I had just finished putting the letter in an envelope when I noticed the range had become eerily quiet as everyone turned off their boom boxes and TVs. Then I realized that Rocky had still not gone down to custody.

"I am not an animal!" Rocky's voice reverberated against the stone walls like the sound of thunder breaking through the lull in a storm. Her angry pronouncement was followed by sharp smacks, the muted thumps of punching flesh, and the teeth-shattering sound of rubber soles skidding on the linoleum.

I squeezed my mirror through the bars at just the right angle to witness Rocky being dragged with her arms cuffed behind her back through the open barrier. Based on the small number of guards involved, and on Rocky's physique, it was obvious she was relatively subdued. She was not the type to go down without a fight, but in this case, her heart was not in it.

A few prisoners punctuated Rocky's original cries with "Let her go," but by and large there was an air of futility about it all. Once we were locked down there was nothing we could do. Even in the short time I had been in P4W, I had become accustomed to the constant stream of injustices that numbed a person to outrage. Something had to be very extreme to get us out of bed.

I must admit that my peer group, my fellow prisoners, and the prison subculture did have a strong impact on me. It wasn't that my core beliefs and values had changed; it was the circumstances that had changed. This subculture did support resistance against injustice, but it also valued an honest appraisal of the practicality of resistance, especially in light of the disproportionate amount of punishment that would no doubt accompany resistance of any kind. Time and again, prisoners had experienced being physically, mentally, psychologically, and spiritually punished to an extreme degree for a tiny infraction: ending up in segregation for refusing to obey a direct order as trivial as not turning down the volume of your radio fast enough; having the goon squad and dogs called over from KP for refusing to be locked at eleven o'clock on New Year's Eve, despite promising to lock voluntarily at midnight, as was the perennial ritual in other years. The examples are endless. Anyone who has been in prison for any length of time knows that in the risk-benefit equation, the risks will always outweigh the benefits to an extreme degree. This does not mean that prisoners do not participate in revolts, resistance, or revolution, but rather that they weigh, using measures of practicality, whether the punishment is worth the meagre benefits that may or may not follow. In conclusion, it's not that I had abandoned my revolutionary beliefs and values, but rather that I realized in the prison environment the threshold for action had to be much higher if there was to be any chance of success.

I rolled over and flicked on the TV. When the sitcom was almost over, I pulled open my shams to watch the minute hand of the clock make its rounds toward six, the usual time our cell doors were opened after supper count. By five after six, a few young women with energy to burn were yelling at the guards to open their cells. At quarter after, Fucillo came marching down the range, glaring at the upper tier.

"That performance cost you girls your evening, so if you play your cards right, you'll be unlocked in the morning," she said in a voice that could be easily heard, since everyone had turned off their TVs and boom boxes when the doors were not unlocked at six.

"What about Rocky?" Pauline called out.

"She'll probably be out in the morning," Fucillo said. I didn't get the impression she wanted to hang around on the range too long, like a sitting duck at the midway. Women had been known to fire spitballs or cups of urine at guards as they ran the gauntlet back to the barrier. Fucillo was old-school enough to know when to make a quick exit.

I was not one to dread a lockdown, particularly a short one. The days when prisons were places of silence and solitude were long over. I had read in books about the days when prisoners were not allowed to speak, and spent the little time they weren't working in prison sweatshops alone in their cells. Now a prisoner was lucky to have their own cell, and even then there was a constant stream of visitors. It was often difficult to think your own thoughts against a loud backdrop of competing televisions and stereos. At least a short lockdown would give me some time to finish letters and a pair of moccasins I was working on, and get some much-needed downtime.

By the time the lights went out, I felt refreshed from relaxing all evening instead of working out in the weight room. I looked across at the dark window, which acted as a mirror, reflecting the black-and-white images of the television screens in shades of grey from the women's cells down below. I rolled over with a smile on my face and pulled the pillow over my head to muffle the buzz that would continue late into the night.

Hours later, I woke up to the sound of screaming making its way through the foam stuffing of my pillow.

"I am not an animal!" The voice came bellowing up through the ventilation grills at the back of each cell. The segregation unit was right behind the end of our range. Any loud sound in segregation carried through the ventilation grills into the plumbing and electrical corridor that separated the two ranges.

Rocky continued this refrain in a voice mixed with pain and sadness. Sometimes she would scream violently, at other times pitifully. Either way, it was a haunting soundtrack to the vivid images that played like a tragic movie in my mind's eye on the dimly lit ceiling. Interspersed among Rocky's refrains were the sounds of heavy objects being smashed about her cell, like a diabolical symphony building toward its climax. I could hear the faint rustling of other women waking up on the range. Then there was a paralyzing silence. Everyone knew there was nothing anyone could do at this time of night.

Every now and then, the guards could be heard yelling at her in vain. The sound of metal and glass shattering brought to mind images of Rocky ripping the metal cot right off the bolts that held it to the cement wall. I could imagine Rocky, with the kind of superhuman strength brought on by psychiatric drugs, using the cot to smash apart the porcelain toilet, flooding her cell and the segregation floor outside it. Porcelain toilets were about to become a thing of the past, replaced by the unbreakable metal sink/toilet combination. The voices of the guards had reached an excited pitch, only eclipsed by the sound of jackboots reverberating in the distance. Maybe it was the sound of batons beating rhythmically against riot shields.

The smashing sounds were still punctuated by "I am not an animal," but were growing more pitiful as Rocky grew more exhausted. Her plaintive cries resonated through me. The silence of the range was a testimony to our collective angst.

The marching jackboots grew louder and louder until they were drowned out by the sound of water gushing and splashing against the walls of the segregation area. Rocky had taken on a second wind as she raged against the firehose that was no doubt being used to subdue her. I could picture the prison nurse scurrying up the stairs from the hospital with a needle to inject Rocky with a sedative as soon as they had her handcuffed to a bed. Sure enough, after the sounds of the firehose, we could hear the faint sound of rushing bodies and then the eerie stillness that signalled Rocky's subjugation. All of us lay silently, imagining Rocky lying in her wet clothes, probably on the floor, sedated and handcuffed until morning. Even though I had never been taken down like this in segregation, I had heard enough of the events unfolding through the ventilation grill, and from enough women, to feel them as my own.

Eleven

The morning came too soon. I was surprised to find we were still locked down. I could hear the metal medication cart moving noisily down the upper tier. Right behind it rattled the food cart. I laughed at the sight of Pauline standing straight-faced in her kitchen whites, sliding a Styrofoam tray through my bars. A guard stood sternly beside her.

"I hope you find the toast and boiled egg to your satisfaction, miss," she said in a facetious falsetto. "Coffee or tea?"

"Coffee, heavy on the caffeine," I smiled.

"Come on, Pauline." The guard moved on impatiently. "We don't have all morning."

"What's up?" I asked.

"Who knows," Pauline said, ignoring the guard. "Probably a house-cleaning coming."

"How's Rocky?"

"I haven't seen her, but word is they slapped her with a shitload of charges last night. She won't be seeing the light of day for a while."

I had barely finished my soggy toast when one of the women in the cells closest to the barrier yelled up, "Cell search." I didn't have any contraband, so I just lay back, waiting for my turn. The guards moved quickly down the range in pairs, ransacking some cells, superficially searching others. Some women were being escorted to the shower rooms for a strip search. It was customary for custody to order a cell search after an incident like last night, either as group punishment or as a precautionary measure, in case we were planning some kind of retaliatory action.

"Okay, Hansen, step out here," said the guard when they came to my cell. I stepped out on the tier and watched as someone was taken to the shower rooms below. Instead of televisions and stereos, the cavernous space was filled with the sounds of women grumbling, laughing, and yelling, and a general sound of subdued mayhem. I tried not to look interested in their search, but kept a steady eye on them all the same. They dumped my boxes of letters on the bed after they had pulled back my sheets and blanket. Then they went through my leatherwork supplies, toiletries, and drawers, but overall left my cell somewhat intact.

By noon the cell search was almost over. I heard Paddy, who was next to me, hiss, "Kite." A small piece of paper attached to a piece of yarn flew in front of my bars. I took a broken coat hanger and hooked it in. "They found a shank," was all it said. I ripped it up into tiny shreds and flushed it. I figured we were down for a few days at least. Whoever had the shank had gone quietly, because there had been none of the usual commotion.

After a few days, the novelty of the lockdown wore off. Too much napping and not enough exercise made it difficult to sleep at night. My concentration was waning. It was a hot morning, leaving me feeling slimy from the heat drifting to the top of the range. The huge fan blades worked tediously to push the heat back down from the ceiling, but it still felt like we were slow-baking in an oven.

I woke up exhausted from a restless night. My legs were jumpy under the blankets, so I got up and began pacing to wear off the anxious sensation. In a six-by-nine-foot cell, much of the space is taken up by the cot, tallboy, bureau, and toilet/sink module. It became a dizzying task to pace back and forth in a two-foot-by-seven-foot aisle for half an hour twice a day. In order to take my mind off the monotony, I would often focus on meticulously planning out every detail of some future life I wished to have. I let my eyes glaze over so the walls of my cell were out of focus in an attempt to combat dizziness. Three steps down, turn, and three steps back. Sometimes the friendly banter between cells would penetrate my concentration and bring me back to the prison. As the days passed, the usual banter became increasingly angry, with less laughter.

After listening to a particularly uptight exchange between two women, an overwhelming feeling of anxiety passed over me. There was no source for this feeling other than the overall atmosphere. The anxiety made my stomach ache and my heart race. I felt as though something terrible was going to happen to me, even though I knew rationally this was unlikely. For the rest of the day I flitted from the TV, to my book, to writing letters, to napping. Nothing seemed to quell this feeling of fear and apprehension building up inside. Finally I fell into a fitful sleep, but I was jarred awake by a primal scream. There was a faint rustling as other women woke up and tossed about uncomfortably. I made a mental note to visit Helen as soon as the lockdown was over to see what we could do about Rocky.

I tried to change the channel in my head from one of Rocky lying chained to her cot to one of us having water fights out in the yard, but the periodic animalistic howling coming from seg made it difficult. I rolled over and pulled the pillow tightly over my ears. In the morning, I couldn't remember whether I had fallen asleep before or after the screaming stopped, but I was exhausted. I couldn't believe how draining being locked in a cell for a few days could be. I imagined years. I found it hard to believe that there was almost always at least one woman in segregation who had been there for one or two years at a stretch, occasionally of their own volition.

I was finding myself looking forward to *The Cosby Show* with an almost manic anticipation. I think it had something to do with the idea of escaping into the happy, stress-free world of the Cosby family. Before I went to prison I had never watched much television, but since coming to P4W, I found myself chuckling in the shop over sitcom characters that had become as much a part of my life as real people. I knew it was a sign of the deprivation and stress in my life.

Today was no exception, until the canned laughter was drowned out by the sounds of women screaming for the guards. I found myself wishing this could be happening after the show was over, and wondered at the callousness of such a thought. After a couple of long minutes, the electronic doors hummed open, allowing the guards to come onto the range. I stuck my mirror out through the bars. Two guards were walking briskly down the range toward the commotion. They stopped and leaned up against a radiator across from a cell halfway down the range.

"Put it down!" ordered one, while the other spoke into her walkie-talkie. They repeated the order.

An indignant voice came from inside another cell nearby. "So what are you waiting for? What're you goin' to do, just stand there and watch, you sick fucks?"

The guards stood with their arms crossed defensively across their chests, speaking in low tones to the prisoner inside the cell. They looked both defiant and guilty at once, glancing sheepishly at the rows of prisoners watching them from all directions, yet smirking to prove that they weren't intimidated by their hostile audience. When another couple of guards and a nurse came shuffling along toward them after what felt like hours, the pair noticeably relaxed. Finally, the spotlight was off them.

The wheel spun at the end of the range and one of the guards lifted up the handle. A pale, rail-thin girl known as Dusty, barely out of her teens, came shuffling despondently out of her cell. Her chin rested against her chest like it was too heavy to lift, and her skinny arms hung limply at her sides. Streams of bright red blood poured out of the long slash wounds, leaving small pools of blood on the linoleum. The nurse took her arm and held it up while she applied pressure with gauze bandages to a particularly deep wound. Dusty did not resist but just kept shuffling along toward the barrier, hunched over like an old lady. It was hard to get a clear picture of what was going on with a mirror made of polished stainless steel.

As soon as she had passed through with her entourage of olive-clad guards, the barrier clanged shut again, and silence filled the void. Respectfully, no one commented, and TVs and stereos were set at half volume.

Everyone knew where Dusty was going: to the prison hospital to be sewn up, and then to the hole until the administration decided she was stable enough to refrain from killing herself. Anyone who slashed or attempted suicide was automatically sent to the hole until they were happy again. Sometimes they just continued to deteriorate until they were shipped off and disappeared into the St. Thomas forensic psychiatric "hospital" in Ontario.

As the kitchen staff began to make their supper rounds, pushing the Styrofoam plates under each woman's door, the noise level began to rise. I couldn't stop my glands from secreting saliva at the sight of meatloaf, potatoes, and gravy. Boredom can do that to a person.

I sank back on my cot, fighting off a sense of irritability at having missed my TV show. The parade of injustice and tragic incidents was so constant that only newly arrived first-time prisoners could sustain a genuine sense of outrage. I had seen it time and time again. A woman from a privileged class or skin colour would arrive who had rarely personally experienced grave injustice. For a few months, maybe even years, she would agitate every time a prisoner's rights were trampled. But eventually the numbing effect of so much injustice, coupled with the deaf ears of the administration and public and a cynical prisoner population, would begin to erode that genuine sense of outrage. I had sustained my healthy sense of injustice in Oakalla, but somewhere along the way in P4W, I had felt it waning. It wasn't that I didn't feel it anymore, but I had grown tired of the terrible effort and sacrifice involved in getting just a tiny piece of justice, if anything at all. By the time I had written and addressed letters to various women's and political groups about this slashing, for instance, something else equally outrageous would have happened. This is not an excuse, just an explanation.

· · ·

Our chairperson, Helen, was one of those prisoners who had not suc-cumbed to the grind of daily injustice. I could hear her demanding griev-ance forms from the guards to officially complain about the lockdown. I admired her tireless efforts, and wondered how long it would take before she would become cynical.

One of the many problems with the grievance procedure is the length of time it takes for these complaints to work their way through the system. It often takes months for a prisoner to receive a response from each level, so it is not unusual for a year to pass before the complaint has exhausted its course through the entire hierarchy of the CSC. The correctional inves-tigator, who documents and suggests remedies to prisoner complaints, has consistently highlighted this problem in his annual report to Parliament. But even his complaints and remedies, like so much hot air from a pressure cooker, seem to be more a means to relieve pressure than a serious means of redress for the many injustices being perpetrated behind the walls. The correctional investigator's recommendations are generally ignored, because no one is legally responsible for enforcing them.

The vast majority of prisoners do not bother filing grievance forms to officially complain about abuses they suffer. On the most basic level, 50 percent of all federally sentenced women have less than a grade nine education, which means they would struggle to file grievances even if they did believe in this system.[20] But more importantly, so few women feel they have experienced justice through the legal system outside the walls that it is only logical they would hold no hope of experiencing justice inside the walls, especially when the grievance procedure is based on the principle of the perpetrator investigating the perpetrator.

When the visiting and correspondence committee decided that I should have one-hour closed security visits until my security level was dropped, I was skeptical that a grievance was worth the effort, but I was just naive enough to try it once. George Caron was still the acting war-den, but would soon be replaced by Mary Cassidy. After he had turned down my complaint, I sent my complaint on to the Citizens' Advisory Committee (CAC), which was another option in the grievance procedure.

The creation of CACs in federal penitentiaries was supposed to be a reform that would allow access and oversight by an independent group of citizens into an otherwise closed environment. Since the CAC was always appointed by correctional officials and had to be approved by the warden, these good citizens invariably shared the values and life experiences of these officials, and undoubtedly had never spent a day in prison. There was no danger that they would be mistaken for a prisoner's peer group. To no one's surprise, they backed up the warden's rejection of my complaint.

By the time my grievance had run its course of unwavering support for the V&C committee's recommendation, I was close to having my security visiting status reviewed anyway. But I did learn a valuable lesson in prison 101. Grievances create the illusion that prisoners have an institutional recourse to injustice, when in fact they don't.

But I must admit that Helen's relentless use of the grievance procedure did score the occasional victory, and was a constant burr up the administration's butt. When I first arrived at P4W there was no hot water in the cells or cable television, but on October 29, 1987, hot water flowed out of the taps in our cells for the first time, and by 1988, cable was installed. This was not a miracle. Technically the task of making hot water and cable appear in our cells was not a difficult one. The men's prisons had both ten years earlier. However, these things were never going to spring from the well of goodness in some CSC bureaucrat's heart without some serious drilling and boring from prisoners like Helen.

When a guard who was supervising the kitchen workers picking up empty trays appeared outside my cell door, I demanded a grievance form, too. The guard shot me a resentful look, to which I returned an insolent smile.

When the main lights came on the next morning, I woke up with a start at the sound of door handles cracking open, signalling the end of lockdown. I pulled the pillow back over my ears and decided to go for another fifteen minutes of sleep before coffee. I had just begun to relax enough for a bit of drool to roll out of the corner of my mouth when someone jumped on top of me. Sammy whispered, "Pooks," in a low, guttural voice, triggering a rush of adrenalin to course through my veins. I rolled over and looked up into her huge brown eyes peering through the thick hair hanging over her face. She was beaming. I could feel her hot breath on my face and was surprised at how limp with lust I felt almost immediately. The kind of intense, compelling relationship I had with Sammy could only be likened to drug addiction.

When it came to sex, she was naturally sensual and gentle. She brushed her velvety lips softly against mine, teasing me until I arched my back up toward her. She held my arms down and began to kiss me tenderly yet passionately, her thick tongue slowly exploring the inside of my mouth. She could be the sweetest, most gentle creature.

Twelve

Almost two years passed before Sammy's mandatory supervision date came up. Mandatory supervision is now known as statutory release. All federal prisoners, except those designated as dangerous offenders, must be released after completing two thirds of their sentence, but they are not free. For the remainder of their sentence they must obey whatever conditions the parole board stipulates or their mandatory supervision will be revoked and they must complete the rest of their sentence in prison.

Sammy was scheduled to be released in the fall of 1988 under mandatory supervision. She had never applied for early parole. She said it was because she did not want parole restrictions hanging over her head, but I suspected it had more to do with the fact that she had nothing and no one to go to on the street. There were many other women who also lived by this policy.

A few days before her scheduled release, she came skidding in her socks into my cell one morning, grabbed my hand, and pulled me off my cot.

"Hey, shouldn't you start packing up?" I blurted out without thinking. I wasn't quite awake yet. Her excited expression immediately transformed into a scowl. She looked at me reproachfully, reminding me this was a sore topic.

"I got somethin' to show ya," she said, dragging me out of my cell. I walked along behind her, wondering what it could be. Most of the women were either in the common rooms getting coffee or down in the cafeteria eating breakfast. I could never adjust to silence on the range. Even after everyone else was gone, the noise kept lingering like phantoms in an empty stadium after a loud concert.

Sammy handed me a letter with two pages of script, neatly printed with the same creative flair she would use when drawing. It was not every day that she wrote a letter, so I prepared myself for the worst. I sat down on her cot as though I were waiting for a death sentence.

It was addressed to an organization that helped the adopted and their natural birth mothers find one another, but both parties had to be registered as actively searching. This was known as mutual disclosure. Since 2007, adoption records in Ontario have been opened, so both parties can obtain information on the other and make contact if they wish.

Even though Sammy claimed to have confided more in me than almost anyone else in her short life, she had rarely spoken of her childhood. Little glimpses into her past had been revealed here and there, but she obviously guarded these memories carefully. Even these revelations had only occurred during times of crisis, when she had inadvertently let her guard down for a moment. Like others who had spent most of their lives behind bars, Sammy considered the ability to endure pain without complaint a sign of strength, and conversely, to ask for help a sign of weakness. So I found this letter, written in a simple voice, a measure of just how much she needed some answers. Unfortunately, the following text is not a direct transcript, but based on my recollection, and the names are fictional.

My adopted name is Samantha Newman and I am in the Prison for Women. I am nineteen years old, and came here three years ago.

I have wondered who my blood family is all my life. I know I can't change my past, but maybe you could help me find my real blood family.

What I know is what my adopted family and social workers told me. My mother got pregnant when she was fourteen in the United States, and wanted to keep me, but my grandmother didn't because she thought my mother was too young and wild to take care of a baby. I guess my grandmother was tired and had her hands full taking care of my mother and her sisters and brothers, so she went back to Saskatchewan and left me at the Children's Aid in Saskatoon.

I believe I am Cree but I don't know anything about my real mother and father. My adopted parents picked me up from the Children's Aid when I was about three. All I remember about that time was being paraded around in circles in this little room in front of people who were trying to decide if they wanted to keep me. My adopted parents are German Methodists who I later learned were trying to save their marriage by adopting a little girl after having three boys of their own. They told me this themselves.

The last time I ran away, my adopted mother told the social worker in front of me that they couldn't handle me anymore. After that I lived with foster families and training school, but as soon as I could, I always ran away. I don't think I've been outside an institution much more than six months since I was thirteen. I was shipped from Pine Grove provincial prison in Manitoba when I was sixteen to the Prison for Women here in Kingston. I think I was the youngest federal prisoner ever sent to P4W.

I have grade nine in school. I am learning woodwork in the prison shop and I am involved in the Native Sisterhood. The only hope I see for my future would be finding my real family for support.

I am enclosing a separate piece of paper with the full name of my adopted family, where we lived, and everything I can remember about them. I am getting out soon, but if you send any information to my girlfriend, she will send it to me.

Meegwetch,

Sammy

As I began refolding the carefully creased letter, a dog-eared, three-square-inch photo fluttered to the floor. I saw Sammy blush when I picked it up. A young girl of around three or four with round cheeks and huge dark eyes was propped neatly on top of a photographer's table in what appeared to be a professional studio. She was wearing a bright red velveteen dress and a wide smile, with a tiny gap between her perfectly white front teeth. The photograph looked as though it had spent many miles in Sammy's wallet.

"That's great, Sammy! It's a great idea to try to find your real mother. I didn't know you had found an agency that could help you," I said, looking up. But Sammy had already turned away from me, immersed in a pencil drawing of an eagle.

"I asked the elder at Sisterhood to find it for me. Will ya keep any letters they send for me? I'll send ya an address when I get out and ya can mail 'em to me, 'kay?" For once she seemed shy. "Let's go grab a bite, eh?"

As suddenly as she had revealed this letter, she ended the topic and pulled me off the cot. She practically dragged me down to the cafeteria for the first and only breakfast we ever had together.

I felt euphoric for the rest of the day. My anxiety melted away, just like I hoped the rage and violence inside Sammy would somehow transform into something serene and solid. As she pulled me down the corridors back toward the range, I pictured her exchanging letters with a reunited Indigenous family, flying to Saskatchewan to live with them again, and eventually living traditionally in a little log cabin on the reserve, happy finally to find her place in the world. This mental picture, albeit stereotypical, gave me some serenity. Selfishly, I was also relieved; if Sammy reunited with her family, I wouldn't be chained by my own guilt to a possibly violent, drug-addicted relationship on the street.

On our way back from breakfast, we ran into Pauline, who explained the latest buzz on the range. George Caron, who had been the warden since 1980, was being replaced by a woman. It didn't matter to me one way or another. On a personal level, he was only memorable in that he was taking such pains to keep my closed visiting status as long as possible, and had promised my mother that he would transform me from "a skunk cabbage into a rose." His floral ambitions became known after he barged in uninvited on my first visit with my mother in years. If only these were the worst accusations that could be made of the man. According to prison legend, a woman in segregation once sent him a piece of her flesh in a sealed complaint form after he refused to release her from administrative segregation.

As we waited to get in through the barrier, we noticed the first sign of the new warden. A group of painters were busy prying open cans of white paint on drop sheets they had spread around the guard's station. I knew that the colour of the prison walls was not an important issue, but I had always liked the different shades of turquoise that covered the walls and bars of the prison. Whether intentional or not, this created a water motif that enhanced the illusion we were part of the breathtaking lakefront vista just outside the walls.

Whenever anything new appeared on the prison landscape, it had to be thoroughly inspected, dissected, and analyzed, in the same way zoo animals would a new object placed in their sterile, static enclosures. Even though we were able to follow the news on television, we were so insulated from these events it was almost as though they were happening on another planet. Our interest in the news was only piqued when it involved details from the courts, such as who was charged and who was testifying and who was sentenced. Sometimes there was an interest in changes to the law, but even these rarely affected us in any real way.

By now a small group had congregated at the barrier. No one bothered to ask the painters anything. They were outsiders. There was no use asking them questions. Either they would have been warned not to speak to us if they wanted to keep their jobs, or they would talk to us like we were hookers or criminals from some cop show.

Helen came marching through our little gathering at the barrier, waving a sheath of papers in the air. "Are you coming to the Inmate Committee meeting today?" she asked. At the time, I was the A range rep, and ZZ was the French group rep.

"I guess so," I said reluctantly. I was very cynical about any political or legal mechanism set up by the administration to address prisoners' rights. As a political organization, the Inmate Committee had no power and was undemocratic, despite being elected by the prison population. Anyone with outstanding charges couldn't run, and of those left, the wardens could veto anyone from running that they didn't like. It was a puppet government at best. For all intents and purposes, it was really designed to be a social committee to organize Family Days and such. The wardens had also been known to use the Inmate Committee to help them implement unpopular policies.

The real political decisions were made on the ground, among women who had either the respect or fear, or both, of the general population. These decisions were made informally and were enforced through peer group pressure and, sometimes, force. The real leaders reflected the changing values of the general population over time. Sometimes they would be real bullies, and sometimes they were intelligent, sensitive women, but they were rarely the people the warden would have chosen.

Helen was an exception to this rule. Possibly the warden had misjudged her capacity to be controlled because she had lived a middle-class lifestyle before coming to prison, and this factor, combined with her intelligence, had led him to assume she would be open to his carrot-and-stick form of persuasion.

Helen turned out to be one of the best chairpersons P4W ever had. She knew the grievance system was a Catch-22, but she still believed enough in society's values to cling to the faint hope that working from inside the system could produce justice. This belief served her well, since her job as chairperson hinged upon her willingness to work from within.

When she had first arrived at P4W, she had holed up in the library and studied the commissioner's directives, regional instructions, and the standing orders of the warden at P4W, all of which had to be compliant with the rules and regulations in the *Corrections and Conditional Release Act*, as laid out by the federal government in accordance with the Canadian Charter of Rights and Freedoms. She used her extensive knowledge of this legal framework to be sure that our rights were not being ignored. In a few cases, this knowledge improved our living conditions. For example, before Helen's arrival it was not uncommon for the prison to be locked down for up to ten days at a time for any number of reasons, but after Helen pointed out that, according to the CSC's own regulations, prisoners had to be provided with clean bedding every three days during lockdowns, suddenly the lockdowns rarely lasted more than three days. If the reason for this sudden change were put to the bookies, no doubt their money would be on the guards' aversion to laundry.

"I'm filing a group grievance over that lockdown," Helen explained while passing around the grievance form. "It was completely outrageous to lock everyone down when the whole incident came from the abuse of power by the guards. They are the ones abusing Rocky in the hole. Did you know they laid about ten charges on her the night they called in the goon squad, including assaulting a guard? Apparently it started early in the evening when they wouldn't come around with cigarettes. I guess they missed a few rounds, so by late that night, she just blew her lid. She'll be in there forever if we don't do something."

Everyone signed the grievance form without reading it. The signatures were more a sign of trust in Helen than they were a sign of trust in the grievance procedure.

"So what happens now?" asked ZZ.

"It goes to the warden, and if he doesn't agree that we shouldn't have been locked, then it goes to the CAC. I'll be seeing Rocky later and hopefully she'll let me help her fill out a grievance about the way they treated her. It's a clear case of double jeopardy, considering how many times they charged her over the same incident. Not to mention her mental state."

"That'll really cause some waves," ZZ snickered.

"Well, it's all we got." Helen was nothing if not determined.

"You mean a big fat nothing."

"I've never seen a grievance do fuck all," added Pauline, throwing her arm around ZZ's shoulder.

"Yeah, I grieved them 'bout makin' my mother-in-law take off my baby's diaper so they could search him before a visit, and it took so long to reach national, the little rug rat was out of diapers," said ZZ bitterly.

"Well, if you ever want to take them to court, you have to exhaust the entire grievance procedure first," said Helen, with less conviction now.

"Yeah, and we all got money to pay some lawyer to take them to court. Hey, how's your transfer going?" added Pauline.

"Not good. I'll see you up there." Helen bustled off down the range to get more signatures.

Halfway down the range, Pauline disappeared into her cell for a nap. I waited for ZZ to pick up her smokes and headed back toward the barrier for the Inmate Committee meeting in the warden's office.

. . .

"Inmate Committee meeting," ZZ yelled back at the guards as she raced down the winding stairwell two at a time. ZZ was athletic. Her nightly workouts in the weight room were paying off. Her muscles were as defined and developed as any of the women in the bodybuilding magazines she collected in her cell. Her petite stature and cute features made her dream of becoming a successful bodybuilder a potential reality. The only snag in her plan lay in the tattoos winding around her legs and arms like modern-day hieroglyphics. But she was optimistic about the new laser surgery being developed in the late eighties, and reassured everyone that they could be removed without scar tissue after she got out.

After being cleared by a secretary to enter the administrative area, we tapped softly on the warden's door, and when a familiar voice said, "Come in," we opened it. We could recognize Caron's voice anywhere. ZZ and I looked at each other.

Helen was already sitting business-like in the centre of a semicircle, arranging her notes for the meeting. She was flanked on both sides by reps from the wing, B range, and the Native Sisterhood. ZZ sauntered across the room in front of me, taking her time to greet each prisoner individually. There was a definite air of defiance and machismo in her entrance. She was in no hurry to sit down, and she bristled with attitude.

When we were finally all seated, we fixed our eyes on Caron. He did not speak to us like a robotic, bureaucratic clone, nor did he use his university education to baffle us with psychological penal bullshit. He talked more like a man who has clawed his way up from the streets. At least with Caron, he said what he meant. You did not have to go through layers of artificial veneer before you finally reached the real person.

I remember the first time we met. He had called me into his office shortly after I had arrived at P4W. I suppose he wanted to establish a rapport with me. Perhaps he was curious to meet a "terrorist." Oddly, he used the same technique as the first cops who had interrogated me in the Squamish lockup. He tried to flatter me with comments about my intelligence, and how it would be obvious to someone like me that my best interests lay in cooperating with the administration during my stay at P4W. Since we had never met before, he had no idea whether I was intelligent or not. Instead of feeling flattered, I felt insulted that he would think I would fall for so cheap a ploy as charm.

"I can see you're all disappointed that I'm not the new warden," Caron said by way of an introduction to the Inmate Committee meeting, "but as you can see we are preparing for her takeover. Yes, you heard me, 'her.' Mary Cassidy will be the new warden, and I hope you treat her better than you do me."

His office had already been repainted a blinding shade of white. It was impossible to avoid making comparisons to attempts at sterilization, a new beginning, purity, and sensory deprivation. However, it did make a good backdrop for the tropical plants and the colour portraits of past wardens displayed throughout the administrative area.

The only other person in the room was the social development officer, a well-groomed young man who appeared perpetually nervous and confused. His job description involved placing women in appropriate prison jobs or in the school, overseeing Native Sisterhood, Lifer, and French group meetings, and organizing socials, sports days, and powwows.

After Caron had ruffled around his papers for a few minutes, he launched into a short speech about his legacy.[21] He reminded the women of the programs and educational opportunities that existed to "help the women" and ended with a stern reminder that they would only work if the women wanted to "improve themselves." Then, raising his voice slightly to emphasize the importance of what he was about to say, he continued, "There is a new policy about to be implemented throughout the Correctional Service of Canada to integrate all the women into the general population, and by that, I mean the women we used to call protective custody prisoners. If you think about it, I believe you will share my view that this is an enlightened policy, reflecting this administration's refusal to institutionalize discrimination. In the past, we have let a few bullies frighten the rest of the population into ganging up on certain inmates who have committed crimes that predators have judged morally wrong. Who are they to judge? You have all been sentenced to prison, and as such, have been denied your freedom. It is discriminatory for certain inmates to decide to exact an even greater punishment by judging and then threatening other inmates until they must be held in protective custody for their own protection. This administration will not tolerate this so-called prison code any longer, and will severely punish those who in any way threaten other inmates being integrated from protective custody into general population."

Protective custody prisoners have historically been people convicted of a crime against children, particularly "sexual" crimes, and those who have given incriminating information about another person to authorities such as cops and guards, or have testified against another person in court. These two categories of people are generally labelled child molesters and rats. Some rapists must also seek protective custody. But today there are many other people who seek protective custody: those with mental health issues; those with debts owing to another prisoner; or simply those who do not feel safe in the general population.

As soon as these words had left his mouth, everyone but Helen started talking at once, interrupting him mid-speech. He banged his fist on the table and shouted, "Quiet," then continued in a softer voice.

"If there are any actions taken against the protective custody women by other inmates, the administration will have no choice but to punish the perpetrators as well as the Inmate Committee for these actions, since it will be your responsibility to explain this new policy to the other girls."

Everyone's face went blank except Helen's. She stood up to make her point more forcefully. "I can't believe you're saying it's our job to enforce this new policy. I also can't believe you're saying this without our consultation." She glared at him. "And here I had prepared a list of topics for discussion, including a group grievance about Rocky's treatment in segregation and the misuse of institutional charges against her, and the lockdown, and you don't even have the decency to ask me about our agenda."

"I had every intention of discussing topics of interest to the general population," he retorted, "but I thought we should start out with the protective custody issue since I predicted it would cause some debate."

"As you could guess," said Helen, "this is not a topic open to debate. To my knowledge, in Canada, if a prisoner does not feel safe in general population, the CSC has a legal obligation to provide a place where they can be safely imprisoned. You can't just change women's attitudes overnight. You are jeopardizing the PCs and other women in general pop who have a history of sexual abuse."

"I'm sorry, Helen, but I have a job to do, and that is ultimately to maintain the good order of this institution. I don't make all the rules, but I must enforce them. I can't change this rule, but I do agree with it. How can you people, who wouldn't want to be punished twice for your crimes, believe you have the right to exact an even more extreme punishment on other women who have committed a crime you don't happen to like? I find that extremely hypocritical." He sat back with a satisfied expression on his face.

"You do?" said Helen, stepping forward. "Well, then, how do you justify punishing anyone who is convicted of killing a cop or guard with a first-degree murder conviction? They automatically have to spend at least twenty-five years behind bars before they can see the parole board. Is that crime worse than murdering a young mother? And don't tell me that society treats sex offenders just like any other criminal. What about whole communities that petition their local MPs to make sure a paroled sex offender is not located in their neighbourhood? Society does not treat all crime equally, so why should prisoners? I am not going to get into how I feel about women who have killed their children or sex offenders, but I can tell you why most prisoners do not want to do their time with protective custody prisoners. Let me remind you that we learned how to deal with people we perceive as criminals from you folks. The good citizens don't want halfway houses, treatment centres, or psychiatric outpatients in their neighborhoods. It's crazy for you to expect us to accept protective custody prisoners living and eating right next to us. The day you and your wife agree to live with some sex offender, watch TV and eat supper with him, will be the day we agree to live with protective custody prisoners. The only reason you're so-called integrating them is to save money so you don't have to pay for separate living areas for them. They should be in treatment centres where they can learn to deal with their issues."

She paused before continuing her rant. "Now if you want to get into specifics about why women have a hard time with women that have killed their kids, there are lots of reasons for this. For one, it's a gut reaction against a feeling that's too close to some women's hearts. Don't forget 80 percent of the women in here have been sexually or physically abused as kids, and that's your statistics. Anyone who's been abused can't help but identify with the victims, the children, of these women. You don't need a Ph.D. to understand why women who've been abused would feel hostile toward people who have killed or abused children.

"As for rats, or as you would call them, informants, if we let them live in population, then we can never trust one another. We have no way of getting away from a rat once they're living in population, so you're going to have to expect them to get hurt or killed. And you are responsible for those rats because you created them. You give them the incentives to rat out, so you should be responsible for their safety. If you are going to dangle carrots in front of them to get information, then you should be prepared to protect them from the consequences. You dangle open visits with their family, passes, transfers to the wing, and all kinds of shit in exchange for information about what is going down in this hellhole. There's going to be a price for that kind of information, and the price is going to be either protecting them or owning the guilt for their blood. Once you put those rats in population, you'll have more blood on your hands than the ones who shank them."

The rest of the Inmate Committee was even blunter than Helen. ZZ stood up and spat, "I quit," then marched out in the most insolent manner possible. Everyone else stood up immediately after and walked out behind her, hissing, "Fuck you," in barely audible tones as we passed his desk by the door.

Helen remained behind for a few seconds, waiting patiently for a reaction. Just before we got out the door, he yelled after us that anyone who disagreed with this new policy should resign from the Inmate Committee. On that note, Helen marched after us, marking each step with the heel of her shoe like exclamation marks at the end of a sentence.

Before the end of the day, the entire Inmate Committee resigned in protest against not only the new policy of integrating protective custody prisoners into general population, but also the threat of punishing anyone on the Inmate Committee who did not successfully convince the population to accept this policy. Resigning was easy for me; I had already found the Inmate Committee to be useless for anything other than organizing social events.

Thirteen

As her release date approached, Sammy grew increasingly quieter and more surly with each passing day. Her emotional state was perplexing to me; I could only imagine being excited about getting out, and being a woman of few words, Sammy said nothing to discourage my assumptions. One day I was cheerfully blithering on about how great it would be to get out when I noticed a tear running down her cheek. She was sitting on her cot, leaning back against the bars, writing a letter. I sat down beside her.

"What's wrong?" I asked.

"Where should I go when I get out?" she asked me quietly. It was an obvious question, but one I had never considered. She had always talked about Saskatoon with such loyalty. There was an Indigenous family she referred to, and a number of other women. She was always telling me exciting street stories about the adventures and solidarity this group of women shared.

"What about Lauren and Joannie, or Lisa?" These were her Native "sisters," even if they were not blood, in Saskatoon.

"Lauren's got some boyfriend, and Lisa is fucked up." She never raised her head from the letter.

"Don't you know other people in Saskatoon, your family, maybe?" I asked naively.

She turned on me angrily. "Haven't you heard a thing I've been saying? My family gave me up when I was thirteen. I haven't seen them since. They have never visited me here or in Pine Grove. Nothing has changed just 'cause I'm gettin' out. The only people I know are from here, and they're all fuckups. Most people I know can hardly survive as it is, let alone take care of me."

That was the closest she had ever come to admitting she was not able to survive on her own. For a few minutes I let her reprimand sink into my Pollyanna consciousness. Despite my life sentence and doomsday attitude toward human society, I still had this optimistic attitude toward my personal life and those around me, which was no doubt rooted in my privileged upbringing as a white woman from a working-class background.

"What about Morley?" I said hopefully.

"She's turning tricks," she said. "Tell me one person I could go to the day I get out."

My mind raced desperately from one person to another. The friends from prison, the Native Sisterhood volunteers, the people she referred to from her past. No one suitable came to mind. That question dealt the death blow to my cheery attitude. The longer I thought, the sadder her eyes became. In the end she just began writing again.

She was getting out on her mandatory release date, after serving two thirds of her sentence. There simply weren't enough halfway houses in Canada to meet the demand of women like Sammy, who needed a home and support the day they were released from prison. "Weren't enough" is an understatement. In fact, in the eighties there were no halfway houses for women in the Atlantic or Prairies regions. There were only a few halfway houses for women in Ontario, British Columbia, and Quebec. The vast majority of women would be released from the gates with only a modest release check, a bus ticket to the destination of their choice, and a change of clothes in a bag.

When her release date finally came, we spent the morning lying around, cuddling on her cot. Her cell was barren. Gone were her pencil drawings of eagles, feathers, and Indigenous people, and the magazine photos of female bodybuilders in bikinis. All that was left were dried-up blobs of toothpaste on the walls. The sweetgrass and clay smudge plate that had sat on the black-fringed shawl covering her bureau had been passed on to someone else. There were only a few pieces of metal furniture covered in chipped turquoise paint, a dirty stainless-steel sink/toilet module, a thin cot, and a faint whiff of sweetgrass. I was amazed at how the personal adornments had duped me into forgetting how prison-like these cells actually were.

I had taken the morning off work, which the guards had overlooked by leaving my cell unlocked. They weren't all bad. The sound of the fans ticking sounded louder than ever in the stillness of a weekday morning. If it wasn't for the faded background sound of some tragic country tune, I would have thought we were the only ones left on the range.

"Anyway, at least you'll get away from all this bullshit," I said, unable to break my addiction to positive thinking.

Sammy rolled her eyes at me then placed a soft kiss on my forehead. "Pooks." She smiled at me as though I was pathetic for being so naive.

"Samantha!" Her birth name sounded strange booming down the range. "Samantha!"

We walked arm and arm down the upper tier toward the stairwell. We stopped at the emergency door that led into segregation. Everyone yelled in messages through the crack in the doorframe. One last time Sammy called, "Later, Rocky!" We could hear Rocky's muffled voice call back.

When we got to the barrier, Sammy gave me one last kiss and made me promise to write her every day, at least as soon as she had an address.

. . .

Sammy hadn't been gone long before I got a short letter from her written in uncharacteristically scrawled handwriting. There was very little information about where she was or what she was doing, but it was filled with testimonials about her love and loneliness for me. Her tumultuous emotions were the wind beneath her wings, as a popular song at the time declared. Despite my doubts about the relationship, I read the letter over and over, much like someone playing their favourite tune, indulging in the soothing emotions of love and longing that the melody elicited. After a while I sat up and carefully folded the scrap of paper and tried to insert it back into the envelope, but it jammed on something. Holding the envelope upside down, I shook it slightly, and out dropped a narrow strip of photographs taken from a passport photo machine in some mall. I held it in front of me like a treasure and stared at the photos of a much thinner Sammy with short-cropped hair. Set against an emaciated face, her normally large brown eyes and full lips seemed huge. With no evidence other than Sammy's handwriting and dramatic weight loss, I figured she was wired.

As I stared fondly at her photograph, I forgot the difficulties of my relationship with Sammy, as so many women in long-distance relationships are prone to do, and instead was flooded with the fond memories of our good times together. I longed to hold her and drifted off into a dream world in which we lived together on the street, working, making supper, and going out to visit friends in the evening. If I stopped to think about it long enough, I knew these dreams were unrealistic. Living on the street with Sammy would probably be one series of tragic dramas after another, but for now these fantasies, like the feel-good TV sitcoms, sustained me through the turmoil of daily life in P4W.

My reverie was disrupted by the clang of cell handles being manually flipped open after the lunch count. The guard hadn't even left the upper tier before ZZ and Pauline, dressed in black, stepped through my shams. They were wearing every piece of Harley paraphernalia they could find. Not only that, they had chains draped and coiled around their pant legs. These weren't normal chains, but plastic chains that someone had sent in to me in a hobby craft parcel. Someone had had the brilliant idea of sewing these chains around their pant legs, on their T-shirts, and just about everywhere. Now they were the latest in P4W designer wear.

"Come on. How come you're not dressed?" said ZZ, trying to pull me off my cot by the arm. I held out the envelope for them. ZZ grabbed it and pulled out the letter. She read it slowly out loud in her Québécois accent.

"Ohhhh. She loves you." She looked down at me affectionately.

"There's a photo," I said. ZZ turned the envelope upside down and the photo fell out.

"She'll be back soon," said Pauline after studying the photo. "What's with the haircut?"

"You know Sammy. She hates looking like a girl. In here her long hair gave her a more traditional look, but in Toronto, it probably makes her look more like a girl," I explained.

"Come on, come on," said ZZ, hopping up and down impatiently like a young child. "Celine's going to be on our team."

It was Sports Day, an annual event organized by the recreation department. It was a kind of Sunday-school-picnic-meets-high-school-track-meet. The women divided up into teams of four and competed with other teams for points. Winners got ribbons, and at the end of the day there was usually a barbecue, and sometimes even a dunk tank where the prisoners could dunk the staff. The dunk tank seemed harmless enough, but it never took long before certain women had to choose between aiming the baseball at the target or directly at the staff member.

I didn't have any Harley paraphernalia, so I just put on my darkest summer clothes, with the plastic chains, of course. Celine appeared in my doorway wearing dark mirrored sunglasses under her black bandana. It was distracting looking at my own reflection while talking to her. She had sunglasses for all of us. We looked about as much like athletes as any bikers could.

The three of them ran ahead of me and down the upper-tier stairwell. Once out of the sight of the guards at the barrier, they stopped and turned toward me. ZZ held a pile of little light blue pills in the palm of her hand. Everyone but me took a few. I had discovered in Oakalla that I wasn't attracted to the mind-numbing effects of Valium.

We followed the small stream of women winding their way down the stairwells toward the yard. Considering the lack of options, most women were either participating in or watching Sports Day. A large number of them had congregated around a small, wooden, pentagon-shaped building in the middle of the yard, which had been constructed to protect the guards watching us from the cold of winter and the heat of summer. Today it was being used as the registration point for the various events: standing long jump, running long jump, high jump, the one-hundred-metre dash, the two-hundred- and four-hundred-metre races, and the relay races. I managed to register our team in all the events. Despite the biker garb and pills, we took winning seriously.

We separated into our different events. I had to wait for ZZ to finish competing in the running long jump, so I sat down on the baseball bleachers until their event was finished. I watched her with pride. She was a good foot shorter than any of the other competitors, but made up for what she lacked in height with pure willpower and athleticism. She strutted about with her hands on her hips, staring down anyone who dared to meet her eye. Her shoulder-length hair was pulled up in a tiny ponytail at the top of her head with a shower of loose hair falling out from around it. Just below the stray hairs on her neck, a newly tattooed Chinese symbol stood out in welts around her jugular. She generated machismo like an electrical force.

When it was her turn, she sprang out of the blocks like a cougar, her arms pumping in rhythm with her powerful legs. Hitting the board, she coiled in the air and thrust her legs out in front of her. She rebounded off her landing, pumping her arms into the air, revealing a washboard stomach that any bodybuilder would have been proud to sport. After she won her event, I came down off the bleachers and gave her a high five. She hopped up and down off the balls of her toes before sprinting off to tell Pauline the good news.

Mary Jane was up first in the standing long. Her mother was one of those flower children from the sixties who had named her child, using a code word, for her drug of choice. As one could imagine, Mary Jane's childhood had been somewhat shaped by her name, but by the time she was a teenager this shape had taken on the form of a biker rather than the hippie her mother had probably envisioned. If there were two things that Mary Jane believed in, it was the supremacy of the Harley-Davidson motorcycle and the authenticity of pro wrestling. And she was no wanna-be biker, either; she was the real deal.

She was a wall of solid muscle from her neck right down to her ankles. She was built like the proverbial brick shithouse, square and solid, except for a pair of well-endowed breasts, which tipped the balance of her equilibrium decidedly in favour of her front end. So I wasn't altogether shocked when she fell down flat on her face after the first few swings of her arms. For a few seconds she just sat there shaking her head, until she regained her composure and pulled herself together to try again. She swung her arms back and forth in slow motion while her girlfriend urged her on in a slightly slurred voice. Then, just as she was about to leave the plate, she reached her equilibrium point and fell straight forward again, but this time she didn't get up. Everyone laughed out loud, even the guard. But when her girlfriend tried to help her up and fell over on top of her, their cover was blown. Something was obviously not right. A patch was set up immediately.

"Wow, MJ," said Celine, who had been on the sidelines. "You look like you got a bit of a heatstroke. Hey, scratch her!" she ordered the guard. "She ain't well at all." Without missing a beat, about six women surrounded Mary Jane and her girlfriend and tried to get them to move away from the pit, but it was too late. They were out cold, and they were just too heavy to pull over into the shade. The guard's brow furrowed as she watched the women struggle with the heavy bodies. She turned on her radio and called for backup.

At about the same time, the crack of the starter's pistol drew everyone's attention away from the dilemma at the standing long pit to the track, where the four-hundred-metre race had just begun. One group of women burst away from the starting line while a second group stumbled off in the opposite direction. I watched as the women heading in the wrong direction staggered along as though they had been hit by shotgun pellets until they crumpled to the ground one by one in little heaps all over the track. Unlike Mary Jane and her partner, these little heaps were in plain view, and were quickly preyed upon by pairs of guards who had started to notice a pattern of impairment. From that moment on, it was less a Sports Day than it was a competition to see if the guards could get the wasted women off to segregation before their less wasted friends could get them back to their cells.

Oblivious to the chaos around them, the original group of four-hundred-metre runners continued around the track, valiantly hurdling over any bodies that might stand in the way of the finishing line. One by one they threw their arms up in the air as they passed the finish line. Women were bent over laughing all over the yard.

After the race, I joined those who were trying to convince the staggering women to go back to their cells. But as anyone familiar with Valium, Ativan, or Xanax knows, people on benzodiazepines are the last people to admit they are out of it.

ZZ and Pauline were in the staggering class of people. By the time the race was over, they could barely walk or talk, yet there was nothing I could say to convince them to go back up to their cells. Within several hours the yard had been cleared of the noticeably staggering women, leaving a small number to finish off the hot dogs and hamburgers from what was left of Sports Day. All in all, it was a relatively peaceful affair, as the women who hadn't taken any Valium knew they were outnumbered and realized there was no point putting up any real resistance on behalf of their fallen comrades.

I wasn't surprised that the administration didn't lock us down early. They wanted everyone on Valium to be wandering around in plain view so they could spot them and pick them up before locking everyone up for the night. The last thing they would want was a bunch of women on Valium in their own cells after lockup, overdosing on their stashes or slashing or something. They would save the lockdown for tomorrow.

. . .

Then as now, there was a constant ebb and flow of drugs. When it comes to accessing drugs in prison, "necessity is the mother of invention," as they say. They came in ingenious ways: hidden in parcels, over the wall, using innovative and creative ways of passing drugs through visits, and the age-old method of using guards as drug mules. Although the drug mules were not quite what the name would imply. More often than not, if the guards who doubled as eager, greedy entrepreneurs were caught, they would sell out the prisoners faster than the cops could ask questions. In every prison there are staff who are more than willing to supplement their income, and administrators who will facilitate and overlook drug transactions if they can use the drug trade to control the prison leaders and population. Of course, not all staff are corrupt, and not all prisoners are willing to go into business with staff, but there are always those who will. The black-market trade in drugs inspires such innovation and creativity that, if it could be harnessed with the proper tools, invisible cloaking devices and time machines would be reality.

Every drug comes with a parasitic personality that will inevitably consume the natural personality of its host once addicted. No matter how intelligent, loving, or stable the host normally is, they will never be able to fend off the parasitic drug's influence. The longer the drug is consumed, the more it will consume its host until there is nothing left. Cocaine addicts become psychotic and paranoid. Junkies live in a dream world, making unrealistic plans they'll never deliver. Potheads become mellow, while people on Valium black out and act out their worst primal urges, like zombies in a B-grade horror movie.

The worst drugs in prison are the benzodiazepines, the home brews, and the cocaine derivatives. Once these drugs have entered the bloodstream, every wall the host has painstakingly built up to contain their most dangerous urges will come tumbling down like a broken levee in a flood. There will be more bloodletting, whether it takes on the form of slashing or stabbing, than there is in a Quentin Tarantino film.

Earlier that summer someone had had a shipment of PCP sent in, or as it's more euphemistically known, Angel Dust. PCP is legitimately used by veterinarians as an animal tranquillizer. Although the shipment that ended up on A range was not enough to create the kind of psychosis that prolonged use would induce, it was enough to keep half the range floating around like they had snorted a good hit of acid mixed with a gram of coke.

Every morning during that week, we would get up and snort back about a teaspoon of this white powder, which we believed was Angel Dust, and go to work. Even though we were able to function and complete the normal daily routine, there was nothing normal about the way we experienced it. It was as though we were living in a Salvador Dali painting. We were not encumbered by the rules of physics that define energy and matter. Hard surfaces like floors became rubbery. Smells in the air were tangible, and water felt like silk. We didn't walk to work, we floated. At dinner, the smell alone of the meatloaf and potatoes was enough to satisfy our hunger.

Normally after dinner a small number of women would go to the gym to work out while the rest of us would hang out in our cells, socializing or watching TV, but this week everyone on Angel Dust was gravitating to the back of the common room, drawn by the magnetic force of the boom box music. It was impossible to sit still. Women who normally wouldn't be caught dead dancing were gyrating and spinning like windup toys. Not just for an hour, but from the moment we were unlocked after supper count until the last moment before lockup.

The only way the guards could *not* have noticed that women who normally lived like rocks were dancing themselves into a dripping frenzy would be if they were deaf, dumb, and blind. But guards will often follow the path of least resistance by turning a blind eye when large numbers of prisoners are intoxicated, as long as they are passive and obedient. Only the most foolish and sadistic guards would make work for themselves by trying to lock up half the population for dancing or otherwise acting harmlessly odd.

The Angel Dust had arrived at a particularly opportune time, when a group of us were approved to go out on an escorted pass to the local swimming pool during the same week that a rare dance was scheduled for Saturday night. Each of these events was rare, and to have all three occur in the same week was serendipitous.

On the morning of the swimming pass, we each snorted a small pile of PCP. The old Artillery Park pool was in a limestone building with thick glass blocks along one side of the pool instead of windowpanes. It was as though someone had designed the lighting to be appreciated particularly by those on drugs. The diamond-shaped cuts in the glass blocks fractured the sunlight into millions of sparkling stars that reflected in the soft ripples of the pool. Even twenty-five years later, I can clearly remember the sensation of drifting weightless on a fluid substance, denser and silkier than water, in which it would have been impossible to drown. I couldn't quite walk on it, but I could float as though I was buoyed by a thin layer of Styrofoam. Half awake and half dreaming, I floated around, listening to the sounds of the other swimmers' voices echo softly and infinitely off the cement walls and sucking in the intoxicating and exotic smell of chlorine that wafted off the water's surface. Although nothing outside of our altered consciousness was eventful, to my knowledge this was the last group pass approved for the Artillery Park swimming pool.

The week culminated in an orgy of dancing on the Saturday night. We were all dressed up in the latest prison fashion, as though we were going clubbing on the street. Everyone was wearing prison-altered everything, designed and sewn together in the industrial sewing shop. The most popular fashions for the more feminine women were skin-tight Spandex miniskirts and T-shirts slashed up with scissors that would have been illegal on the street on the grounds of indecent exposure. For the more "masculine," the fashionable things to wear were blue jeans or black sweats draped with plastic chains and T-shirts with Harley-Davidson logos. The younger, hipper women accessorized with a prison tattoo on their neck or face, while the old-school women clung to the standard tattoo on the arm, chest, or legs. The night could be described in three words: Saturday Night Fever.

I had just put the finishing touches on my getup when I heard ZZ yelling for me, "Hey, Pooks!" She had begun using Sammy's term of endearment for me. I walked along the upper tier to her cell and pulled back the shams. There was a pile of white powder on a mirror sitting on her bureau. She took a card and expertly cut the pile, dividing it into four. She leaned over with an empty pen casing and snorted up as much as she could. It took ten times as much powder to get high as it would cocaine. She stood up for a few minutes, her finger pressed against one nostril and then the other, sucking back as much residue as she could before going at it again. When I finally began to snort back my stash, she warned me that the party was almost over. I was relieved, because after a week the drug was starting to make everything look rubbery and out of perspective, like looking in a funhouse mirror at the carnival.

After Celine and Pauline had snorted their piles, we headed down to the gym. The guards smiled at us condescendingly as we passed through the barrier.

"Don't look at us like that. At least we'll be outta here someday," said Pauline. You could tell by their faces they didn't like to be reminded of that little fact very often.

Long before we reached the gym, the stereo beat could be heard and felt, echoing off the concrete walls of the corridor that connected the main building of P4W with the gym. The original cellblock and administrative area of P4W had been built of limestone blocks hauled from a nearby quarry in 1935. During the prison reform movement of the seventies, the Correctional Service had purchased an old army barracks and gym from the nearby Kingston military college, which had been added on to the original prison. The old army barracks were transformed into the "wing" for minimum-security women, and the gym was used for recreational activities, with a small pool room and weight room on either side. The wing allowed the women to live in small rooms with solid doors, unlike the open barred cells and tiers of A and B range in the old cellblock.

Heading down the corridor, our bodies became a conduit for the music. Our steps fell in time and our bodies began to gyrate. When we stepped into the gym, women were dancing without inhibition to the pulsating music. Their movements were captured by the bright flashes of a strobe light in slow-motion light frames, while a seventies disco ball sent prisms of rainbow lights twinkling around the room. The guards in their drab olive uniforms looked out of place, captured in slow-motion photographic stills, frozen in portraits of envy and disdain.

Someone had the bright idea of sprinkling a whole bottle of talcum powder all over the varnished wooden gymnasium floor so we could slide as we danced. Someone else had added baby oil to the mix, and we slathered it onto our hands and arms so we could rub each other without friction. It didn't take long for the talcum powder to make its way from the floor to our skin, covering our bodies in a bright white film. The rhythmic flashes of the strobe light snapped shots of our bright white faces, arms, legs, and bellies, like scenes from a midnight lightning storm. The scene vacillated between that of a New York nightclub in the disco days of the early eighties to one of a ghostly tribal dance.

Fourteen

Once the guards had finished rounding up people on the evening of Sports Day, I decided to hunker down early in anticipation of the inevitable lockdown in the morning. I lay back on my cot to read Sammy's letter again, mulling over each word, trying to decipher as much meaning from it as possible. Clearly, she was lonely and unhappy. Finally I put the letter carefully back in its crumpled envelope. The range was strangely quiet with half its occupants locked up in seg. It must be full, I thought. At least Rocky would be happy to have the company.

At eleven the bright fluorescent lights shut off, leaving only the nightlight. It gave off a pale-yellow hue that softened the sharp outlines of the tallboy and bureau and erased all the stains and ground-in dirt that were an integral part of a fifty-year-old prison. I lay back and admired the turquoise patterned cloth that I had used to fashion a matching curtain for my tallboy and tablecloth for my bureau. I stared at the photographs of my friends and family on the wall. I admired the shiny rubber leaves of the vine growing around the bars above my shams. I would have appreciated the vine more if I had known plants would soon be classified as contraband. I marvelled at how comfortable and cozy I could feel even in prison, surrounded by the familiar objects of my cell, away from the uncontrollable forces of the range.

I was surprised to hear the handles clanging open the next morning. I ran down to the segregation door and yelled in for ZZ and Pauline, and a general hello for all. Only Rocky's voice answered back. She said they were sleeping, and I figured she meant sleeping it off. I went down to the common rooms, made myself a coffee, and sat quietly in my cell, thinking how odd it felt not having someone barge in on their way to wherever.

After Sammy had left, I had requested a job placement in the Works department as a carpenter's apprentice for a change of pace. The electrician, painter, plumber, and carpenter each had a prisoner apprentice. The only other apprentice who had not been popped during Sports Day was the plumber's apprentice, Hayley. She was already sitting at the card table, sipping her morning coffee with the tradesmen, when I breezed in.

"So what's up?" I asked the carpenter, who was smirking knowingly at me as though I had somehow escaped going to seg by sheer luck. Obviously custody had briefed them about Sports Day before they had arrived in the Works department. Even though we did not treat them as the enemy, like we would a uniformed guard, tradesmen were still considered double agents who weren't to be trusted with any inside information. I wasn't about to give them the pleasure of gossiping about Sports Day. Hayley was a clam.

"We're going to segregation to visit your friend," said the carpenter.

"How so?" I looked at him skeptically. The only prisoners allowed in seg were kitchen staff and the Inmate Committee.

He pointed over to a shield made of a huge piece of Plexiglas framed by two-by-fours. It was leaning up against the wall in the woodworking section of the shop.

"Where'd you get that?" I asked.

"Storage, until the guards need it for protection from flying piss, shit, and blood." He smiled cynically. I looked at Hayley, who was rolling her eyes. I pondered the ethics of helping a staff member, even the carpenter, carry this shield into segregation. If I refused there would be no negative repercussions. I made the dubious decision to help carry it by justifying that they would get it to seg with or without me, but if I was there I could take kites back to the range and report on any abuses to the outside world. It was a lame excuse. I really just wanted to see my friends.

"Okay, let's get this over with." I glanced over to Hayley for approval, but her eyes were blank. She was too loyal to be openly critical of my actions.

It was a heavy, awkward frame, about twelve feet long by seven feet high. We grabbed it from underneath and balanced it between us. I groaned a little, both at the weight of the thing and at the image of myself carrying it into seg. I struggled along with the carpenter up the flights of stairs leading from the Works department in the basement all the way up to the segregation cells on the third floor. The carpenter banged on the heavy fire door separating the segregation and protective custody area from the rest of the prison.

We waited for a few minutes while a guard eyeballed us through a peephole in the door. Just before she let us in, we heard her yelling, "Man on the range," to the protective custody prisoners. I had never been through protective custody before. There were four women sitting around a card table in the middle of the range. There were a total of ten cells, five on the range behind them that had been converted into an eating area, a bathing/shower cell, a storage and linen cell, and a TV area, and one cell that had been converted into an office for the guards who worked in segregation. Five cells on the top tier were presumably the prisoners' personal cells, since they had shams across the bars.

They were obviously unprepared for me, because as soon as they noticed I was a general population prisoner, their eyes grew round and they watched me guardedly. I felt like a fox in the henhouse. The PC prisoners were the constant target of insults and attacks whenever they were escorted through the general population. There was nothing they could do to overcome the stigma of having killed a child. At the time, there were no women doing time for sexual assault–related charges.

My end of the shield banged on the cement floor when we had to stop to gain access to segregation at the end of the protective custody area. The women around the table were startled. They looked pale and pasty from spending so much time in such a confined space. Whenever they did go out in the yard, it would be for an hour's walk in the enclosed tennis court, just like the women in the segregation unit. I understood why the prison code demanded that general population women shun women who had killed their children, but I believed it would be more humane to give them whatever psychological treatment existed for women who had killed a child. I didn't have the stomach for placing these few small chickens into a den full of foxes, as the Correctional Service was planning to do over the next few years.

After we were let into segregation, we passed through an office area in which images of a couple of women prisoners sleeping on their cots could be seen projected live on small TV screens hanging from the ceiling. These must be the women under observation. After we passed through another fire door into the segregation unit, the first thing I noticed was the black-painted bars on the observation cells so the guards could more easily view the prisoners in the video images.

I was immediately struck by the filth and depressing atmosphere of the place. Garbage lay strewn about on the concrete floor in front of the open barred cells. I assumed it was not the guards' jobs to clean up refuse thrown out of the cells. The cells were barren except for a heavy wooden cot bolted into the cinderblock walls. With the exception of the video cameras, it could just as easily have been a prison scene from the 1800s as one from the 1980s.

All the women in the first five cells lay curled up, sleeping off the Valium, in tangles of thin blankets and dingy-looking sheets. I wasn't even sure which of them were ZZ and Pauline. But as we neared the end of the range, I heard the eager, childlike voice of Rocky calling to me from above. The effect on me was not what I expected. Instead of feeling happy to see her, I felt overwhelmed with guilt for being here with this shield and the carpenter, and for being in general population instead of segregation with the rest.

I looked up and saw her pressed as close to the bars as possible, her round face beaming. Her hair looked greasy and her skin white and pimply.

"Is there anything I can do for you?" I called up.

"Chocolate bars," she smiled.

"I'll send some up on canteen," I smiled back. It was a horrible feeling knowing she had been here for so long for so little. There must be more I could do.

"Come on," said the carpenter, pulling me along. We were almost at the end of the range. I looked up and saw Lucifer, standing looking down through a thick curtain of hair that completely covered her face. The only indication she was facing me were the pair of bumps on her chest that slightly protruded under her sweatshirt. She had been here for over two years, voluntarily. I couldn't imagine her life. How could anyone think this was the decision of a sane person? I had been told she never went out for her hour of exercise when offered, and her face was constantly shrouded in her thick veil of long brown hair. I had never met her on the range. I wished I could escape her invisible gaze. I wondered what she looked like. I had heard she had an upside-down cross on her forehead, just like Sammy.

My attention was drawn away from her by piles of human shit and food lying on the floor outside the last cell. The smell was enough to make me gag. The carpenter stepped gingerly in front of the cell, picking his way carefully in between the smeared shit and food. As I put my end down, I saw the woman inside the cell.

She had been admitted to general population a few months ago, the kind of inconspicuous woman I had barely noticed. She was a plain woman with an average build who spoke with the kind of dialect familiar to most poor white people living in the densely populated social housing projects of downtown Toronto. Yes, I remembered her, but not because there had been anything memorably insane about her. This was no longer the case.

She was completely naked and covered in what I could only assume was her own feces, pacing back and forth in her filthy cell, completely oblivious to us. Her huge breasts swung back and forth with each step, and her hair was knotted and tangled up with bits of dried bread. For a moment she stared straight at us, but, from the glazed and unfocused look of her eyes, I think she was looking right through us at something only she could see. My tenuous grip on my own sanity and reality felt shaken by the sight of her. I felt sick in the pit of my stomach and wanted to run from there. So did the carpenter.

As soon as he had the shield in place, he turned and walked quickly toward the segregation door. I scurried along after him like a mouse. When the guard opened the door for us, he asked her indignantly why "that woman" wasn't in St. Thomas, a forensic psychiatric institution for the "criminally insane."

"We're waiting to ship her out as soon as there's a bed available," said the guard. "You'd be surprised how many of them come down here and just go into some kind of psychotic trance for some unknown reason." She escorted us through protective custody and continued talking to the carpenter in a low voice I couldn't hear.

I remembered another woman I had met on the range who had been very anxious about her daughter and her life on the street. With the exception of insomnia and a case of bad nerves, she had seemed quite normal. One day she had checked herself into segregation, and about a month later they had shipped her off to St. Thomas.

When we got back to the Works department, I sat down at the card table again, unable to work. The carpenter sat down across from me.

"The guard said she stuffs her food up her vagina to feed something inside her, and then fishes her shit out of the toilet and throws it at them every time they walk by outside her cell. That's what they needed the shield for," he said with a big sigh. "I asked if there wasn't something the doctors could give her, but they've tried different meds and nothing seems to work. Hopefully they'll be able to get her into St. Thomas soon."

I thought about Rocky and Lucifer. From what I'd heard, there was always someone in segregation for a stretch of a year or two at a time. They were usually women like Rocky, who went in on a small charge and then either kept racking up more and more charges or, like Lucifer, they grew accustomed to segregation and didn't want to leave. Of course, they would get more and more mentally unstable the longer they were in there, which in turn would justify the administration keeping them there. Catch-22.

Who should I call? The administration would have a perfectly reasonable explanation for any curious reporter or Citizen's Advisory Committee member. They would point out Rocky's history of violence and the long list of charges she had racked up in segregation. They would say, "How can we maintain the good order of the institution if we don't charge and punish the girls when they act out or assault staff?" In Lucifer's case, they would say that as long as the Segregation Board reviews her case every month, it is safer to let her stay in segregation than put her back in population against her will, where she might hurt herself or someone else. As for the woman we had just seen, she would probably be shipped to St. Thomas before anyone from the outside could even see her. It seemed unlikely that any reporter or authority figure would question the whole concept of keeping people locked up in cells the size of a small bathroom for years at a time.

Fifteen

A few days after Sports Day, the administration decided to let the women out of segregation early when a few who weren't normally suicidal tried to hang themselves or slash. If Valium had a personality, it would be clinically depressed. In the glass window outside her segregation cell, Pauline saw ZZ's reflection hanging from one of the crossbars and called the guards. Luckily they reached her in time, but then Pauline slashed. There just weren't enough observation cells to keep track of everybody.

I was pleasantly surprised when I saw ZZ and Pauline come walking through the barrier a few days later as I waited for the guards to call lunch. They had recovered quickly. The only signs that they had been suicidal were a raw red bruise under ZZ's throat and white gauze bandages covering Pauline's forearm. They were laughing and talking in loud voices when they saw me.

"Hey, Pooks!" yelled ZZ, jumping up and wrapping her legs around my waist and her arms around my neck. Although she couldn't have been an ounce over a hundred pounds, I was almost collapsing from her weight.

"I hear Musqua's coming back," said Pauline, using Sammy's Cree nickname.

"Yeah," I smiled. "She's coming back with a broken paw."

"What happened?" asked ZZ after she was on her feet again.

"You know Sammy's letters, short and to the point. All I could figure out was that she wanted back in her cell at the West and the guards wouldn't let her, so she kicked a door and broke her foot."

Sammy was being held in the provincial remand jail at the time, the West Detention Centre in Toronto. According to her letter she was pissed off because she had been transferred to Toronto for sentencing on a number of charges that had taken place there. She had mistakenly believed that if she pled guilty to all her charges in Toronto and Kingston, she would then be sentenced in Kingston and transferred back to P4W pronto. There is nothing pronto about the wheels of justice.

"So is she excited about coming back?" asked ZZ with a big smile.

"She's homesick, all right. She's got some kind of partner in there with her … Renny, I think's her name. Says she seemed okay on the street, but now that she's straightened out she says this Renny is not cool."

"Guess who they're lettin' out?" ZZ's face lit up excitedly.

"Rocky?" I guessed.

"Lucifer didn't want out, but I guess they were afraid Rocky'd string up once they let the rest of us out. She'll be coming up any minute."

"What's with that shit?" I asked, pointing at ZZ's throat.

"Eh, I don't even remember doin' it. Neither does Pauline," said ZZ. Pauline nodded her head in agreement. "That shit's blackout drugs. You could kill someone and not remember you're doing it. I swear those pharmaceuticals are ten times worse than street drugs."

Pauline and ZZ left me at that point to unload their pillowcases full of clothes from segregation. I watched them walking arm in arm down the range. You would never have guessed ZZ had attempted suicide only a few days ago.

Then I heard Rocky's voice coming toward the barrier from the hospital. She was being escorted by the nurse. As soon as she saw me she beamed. Her eyes shone clear and true like a child's, without ulterior motive.

"It's so good to see you!" I wrapped my arms around her thick chest. Her dark hair looked like it had been cropped short with a pair of scissors. It also looked greasy, like it hadn't been washed for a while, so it stood up every which way in clumps. She leaned back against the radiator, still staring at me with that big, genuine smile. Her eyes looked a little glazed, but then, that was to be expected after spending six months in segregation.

"I bet you're starved," I said, thinking of Rocky's legendary appetite. Her brow furrowed a little, as though she were mildly perplexed. I made small talk until other women started gathering around, waiting for lunch. They peppered Rocky with questions, but she just stood there with that huge smile fixed on her face.

When Pauline and ZZ returned from their cells, they herded Rocky away from the crowd. She was beginning to look uncomfortable around so many people.

"So what's for …" Rocky looked down at her feet as she searched for the word.

"Lunch," said ZZ quickly. "Meatloaf, I think, but I bet John will get you some steak." Rocky looked at her with a puzzled expression. John, a muscular man with a kind, smiley face, was the noncustodial kitchen supervisor. Like the carpenter, plumber, painter, and electrician, he was not considered in the same "enemy" category as the guards and administrators. Rocky was apprenticing to become a butcher under his tutelage.

"Want to go down to the gym after supper and work out with us?" ZZ stood on her toes so she could put her arm protectively around Rocky's shoulders.

"Ummm. Yeah, we could lift …" Once again she shifted her weight uncomfortably from one foot to another as she searched for the word.

"Weights," ZZ mercifully filled in the blank for her.

One of the guards sitting at the barrier went into the office and yelled, "Lunch," through the intercom system. The door cracked open and slid noisily into the metal door jambs. ZZ guided Rocky through the crowd.

"Those motherfuckers have convinced her to get shock treatments again!" said Pauline when Rocky was out of earshot. "Yesterday afternoon I heard them come and get her. They asked her if she was ready for her treatment, and she went."

"Shock treatment!" I was genuinely shocked myself. "Do they still do that?"

"Oh yeah," said Pauline. "Rocky's had it before. Who knows how many times. The last time she was in seg, they offered it to her after about a year. They kept fucking with her. You know, not bringing her a cigarette on the hour. Only giving her a few sheets of toilet paper at a time, and every time she swore at them or threw something out of her cell they'd write up a bunch of charges, so in no time she was looking at months of segregation. She's like a kid who can't control her temper, so it looked like she might do her whole bit in seg. I wasn't there so I don't know how it happened, but it sure looked like they offered her shock treatment in return for being released. She agreed, and said she liked it."

"Liked it?" I asked.

"Yeah, liked it," Pauline said. "We asked her, and she says it makes her forget bad memories and feel calmer. The downside is she can't remember anything, not even the simplest words. It'll take her months to get her vocabulary back. Those shrinks don't have a clue what kind of damage they're doing, and with someone like Rocky who's got no one out there watching out for her, she's a perfect subject."

At that time there was an older woman, Dorothy Proctor, who was back in P4W after having done time in the sixties. She often claimed to have been subjected to both electric shock and LSD experiments. Her allegations were met with skepticism, both because the general consensus among the population was that she was a little crazy, and because even prisoners thought it was unrealistic to think the government would conduct experiments using LSD and electric shock treatment on us.

It wasn't until 1998 that I read an article in the *McGill Reporter* that confirmed Dorothy's story.[22] The article reported on an investigation by professors Norbert Gilmore and Margaret Somerville into the ethics of administering LSD and electroshock "treatment" on twenty-three prisoners in P4W during the early sixties. Apparently these women had given their consent for this treatment. Prior to the early sixties, consent had not been mandatory. But the professors concluded the treatment was unethical because this kind of government medical research benefited the institution more than it did the individual prisoners. Proctor's lawyer, James Newland, argued that prisoners cannot freely give consent because they are in prison, where their well-being depends on measuring up to the expectations of their keepers.

Electroconvulsive therapy (ECT), as the scientific community has rebranded shock treatment, is still commonly used today, both in institutions and throughout society to treat severe depression. Its use increased from 1980 to 1986, particularly on the elderly, because they are more vulnerable to the suggestions of authority figures such as psychiatrists and doctors.[23] Prisoners, like the elderly, are also vulnerable to signing off on ECT because there is a clear yet unspoken message coming from the authority figures: that their freedom is inextricably linked to their willingness to obey.

Down in the cafeteria, Rocky was greeted like a homecoming war hero. She was the kind of person who wore her heart on her sleeve, for better or for worse. As women came over to our table to welcome her back, her face would light up for some and appear confused for others. I started to wonder if she even recognized half of them.

Meanwhile ZZ had flagged down the cook, John. After a short conversation, ZZ proudly placed a raw steak in front of Rocky as though it were a birthday cake.

The raw steak drew the attention of other like-minded carnivores. Rocky may have had a sketchy memory for words, as well as the names of a few women she hadn't been close to, but her passion for raw steak had clearly not been forgotten. Picking it up in her bare hands, she ripped a couple of pieces off to share with the two vultures who had settled down at our table. They tore into it gleefully, letting the blood run out of the corners of their mouths and down their forearms onto the table. Occasionally they would glance defiantly over at the guards with big smiles on their blood-red lips. Once again the guards wisely decided to follow the path of least resistance, turning a blind eye to the carnivores.

Sixteen

Every New Year's Eve the warden would let us stay up until midnight, just like when we were kids. After a few hoots and hollers, the guards would warn us, "Lockup," and everyone would trudge off to their cells. We had become creatures of habit, and in the years I was there I can't remember anyone ever refusing to be locked after a brief New Year's Eve hurrah. As we did every year, we were saying our goodbyes to the old year, which in this case was 1988, in the back common rooms, dancing ourselves into a frenzy to the tunes of INXS, Prince, Sinead O'Connor, and Michael Jackson throbbing out of a huge boom box.

No one was drunk or high. Making brews and arranging drug transactions were crimes of opportunity that didn't usually coincide with something as clockwork as New Year's Eve. When the ingredients could be found and the brew was ready, it was consumed on the spot, New Year's Eve or not. Ditto for drugs.

Even though it's been twenty-five years, I remember that New Year's Eve celebration very well. It had been a year marked by four suicide attempts, culminating in the suicide of Marlene Moore, who was better known as Shaggy. Marlene had been in and out of prison her whole life and was well known and liked in P4W. She had hanged herself from her cot in the prison hospital on December 3, 1988, only four weeks before New Year's Eve, so the atmosphere was more like an Irish wake than a joyful celebration. The soundtrack of shouts and laughter was interspersed with the keening and bitter wailing of a funeral.

About ten minutes before our usual lockup time of eleven o'clock, some guard announced over the PA system that we would not be staying up until midnight like we had other New Years because they were "disappointed in how rude we had been over the past year." This news passed through the ranges and common rooms like an electrical current, jumping over jagged broken copper wiring with a pop, a crackle, and a puff of smoke. As the clock ticked closer and closer to eleven, conspiratorial whispers of sedition wafted from one woman to another all down the ranges, around the corners, through the fire doors leading into the back of the common rooms, and under the emergency doors that connected the two ranges.

Cries of "Fuck that shit! I ain't gettin' locked at 11! We never go in that early. I'm stayin' out 'til midnight" could be heard, like the sounds of sparks crackling as they dropped here and there along the way. There was no official meeting, just one woman conferring with another until a critical mass began to have a magnetic draw on those still remaining in their cells on the range. They began to meander to the common rooms while they still could.

There was no nefarious atmosphere, no weapons, no hate—just unbridled emotion, like a bunch of kids at a pyjama party who are defying Mom and Dad's order to go to sleep. If anything, this collective decision was naive, made without any concern for the consequences. I mean, how bad could it get? It was just a temporary refusal to go to bed at exactly eleven. No one had said we wouldn't lock at all. Just that we were going to stay up until midnight, like every other year, like the rest of the world, and then we'd get locked.

But there were some women who could feel which way the wind was blowing. They wordlessly drifted into their cells just before eleven, without defiance or animosity, just simply out of knowing that they did not want to jeopardize whatever privileges they had coming up. Maybe they had a parole hearing in the coming months, a visit with their children, a pass, or a transfer to the wing. Maybe they had nothing to lose but simply wanted to stay in the relative peace and quiet of their cells. But no one in the common rooms was concerned about what the women on the ranges did, because no one considered the decision to defy custody as serious.

I wouldn't be surprised if the warden was out partying somewhere and so was also unaware of the inclement pressure system building up in the bowels of the beast. When it comes to daily security matters, decisions are made by the CX8, or the "head screw" of the shift at the time, not the warden. If events take an unpredictable turn, the warden will be notified, but it is custody that runs the show. This is their specialty, and the last thing they want is a warden who is going to stick their nose into places it doesn't belong. The warden is there to rubber stamp whatever security decisions custody makes on the ground. The warden handles policy decisions, various administrative functions, and diplomacy between the various departments of the CSC, but when the shit hits the fan it's always the warden who gets the blowback and has to own it, because they are the head of the prison, whether or not they were responsible for the shit in the first place.

The first signs of trouble appeared in the minutes leading up to eleven, when the CX8 and the guards who usually locked up the women in the wings appeared along with the regular range guards in the Plexiglas-walled office overlooking A and B range. They were now listening in to the conversations in the common rooms through the two-way intercoms. When one of them beetled over to the microphone and announced, "Lockup," her voice had risen an octave in pitch.

Out on the range, the majority of women had obediently walked into their cells and pulled their huge metal doors shut—an action that could not be reversed without help from someone outside their cell. Another dozen women had not walked into their cells but were hanging about lazily, leaning up against the huge radiators that ran all down the corridor of the cavernous range. They were in the grey zone between the peace and security of obedience and the wild euphoria of rebellion.

When several more warnings over the intercom system became increasingly severe and loud, everyone understood that they had to make a decision: either go to their cells, where they would be safe, or head to the back of the common rooms, to the unknown. I did not have any serious privileges to lose, but even if I had, there was never any choice as far as I was concerned. I was in. I was drawn to the possibility of resistance like a drowning person to oxygen.

At eleven o'clock, the guards locked the fire doors separating the common rooms from the ranges and the cell doors on the ranges. Everyone was locked into their position: twenty in their cells, twelve hanging outside their cells on A range, and eighteen in the common rooms. The distribution was similar for B range.

I remember how fluid the situation remained in the common rooms. There were no designated leaders, and no one tried to organize the situation. I remained with some women in the back, dancing to the boom box, while others began to figure out how to disassemble the wooden chairs made by CORCAN. It only took about two seconds to figure it out: lay it sideways on the floor, lift your foot up, and smash it down on the leg of the chair as hard as you can until it breaks. Then begin trying to smash the Plexiglas window that separates the common rooms from A and B range.

As everyone began to unleash their restraints and let themselves go, the atmosphere became more and more wild and euphoric. It had been a long time—maybe even never—since the women had vented their anger, frustration, and violence against a system that had confined, punished, and, in some cases, tortured them for years and years. As some women danced to the rhythm of the bass beats of the boom box, others leaned back and drove those CORCAN chair legs as hard as they could against the Plexiglas windows, drywall, tables, and anything else they could, other than the few appliances that we treasured, like the coffee percolator, toaster, and fridge. Every now and then, women would glance back at the office, crowded with glaring guards, and throw them the finger, the fist, and laugh with glee, revelling in their portrayal of the lunatic fringe, the personification of whatever would terrify the guards the most, because this was our moment, no matter how fleeting, to turn the tables around, to make them afraid, to show our power and vent all the hate and violence back on the representatives of those who were responsible for it in the first place.

When a couple of women tried to exit the common rooms, the CX8 got on the mic again and screamed, "In a few minutes we are going to allow anyone who wants to go back to their cells to do so, and after that the rest of you will be going to segregation." This announcement only added fuel to the fire, if that were possible. It was obvious that we had not planned this little insurrection, since there were no weapons, extra chairs, or other ammunition, which would obviously have been useful if we had hoarded it in the back. This was no act of organized resistance.

I must admit that in my years in prison, I do not remember any act of organized, collective resistance other than the perennial refusal to work and eat for twenty-four hours on Prisoners' Justice Day. I must take some responsibility for this, since I did not personally initiate any organized resistance either. There were lots of individual acts of resistance, in which women trashed their cells, refused to be locked, trashed ranges and pods, refused to eat, attacked guards, and filed complaints, but no collective meetings in which the prisoners decided to act as a whole in order to either improve or protest anything.

Prison dynamics are surprisingly similar to those outside the walls. The only real difference lies in the degree of violence and the power imbalance between the prison regime and the prisoners: more exposed and raw than outside the walls; less mediated and cushioned by civil rights and public scrutiny. But ultimately the differences are just a matter of degree and race. I'm pretty sure my Indigenous and Black comrades in the common rooms that New Year's Eve were more aware of the potentially severe consequences for our actions than I was.

Ultimately, our lack of collective resistance was rooted in the same soil as the complacency of the general public. After a few years in prison, the sheer number and scope of injustices that surrounds you is so overwhelming that it creates a sense of inertia. You find yourself becoming desensitized and cynical, which are more seductive coping mechanisms than resistance. Then there is the subconscious awareness that the majority of women will not go along with any kind of action that will jeopardize their personal privileges; that you and your crew will be blamed for the consequences of resistance by those who don't want to participate; that the administration and their prisoner lackeys will turn your act of resistance into the stuff of legends that will be told over and over again as a parable about the dangers of going against the current; and you know that there are women with mental health issues who may slash or hang themselves in an act of resistance gone sideways.

Throughout this memoir I have referred to the influence that stereotypes have had on my attitudes toward other people. Sometimes this phenomenon would be reversed, in that I would sense that the stereotype of the hardcore, unbending revolutionary would be superimposed on me. I don't want to disappoint those who are looking for a stereotype to inspire them to greater revolutionary action, but I am compelled to be honest. I am a human, not a stereotype, and just as vulnerable to the social conditions in which I find myself as the next person. Any revolutionary who lives to an old age is bound to go through periods where a certain degree of complacency will take its toll. It's not a case of selling out, but rather of knowing when it's time to fight and when it's time to chill.

I had not abandoned my values or my belief in revolutionary change. There is nothing I would have wanted more than to be part of an organized collective resistance, but I was not immune to the factors that create complacency, especially in a prison setting, where everything from injustice to punishment is magnified many times over.

In P4W, Helen was one of those people who had not become complacent; instead, she had become a master at using the CSC's own rules and regulations to improve the living conditions for her fellow prisoners. She had not been a political activist before prison, but in her own words, "prison politicized me."

In Oakalla, there had been no electricity in the cells, so the women had no TV or radio unless they purchased batteries, which were very expensive. When Helen inquired into the reasons for the absence of electricity, she was told it was too expensive to put in the cells. So, she studied the usage of electric wattage and found that there was plenty of electricity as well as money in the Inmate Welfare Fund. The prisoners automatically had one dollar taken out of their pay every two weeks, which was deposited in the Inmate Welfare Fund for "social activities," but the only social activity was bingo. Plus, a 20 percent markup on canteen supplies was also supposed to go into this fund, which meant that about seven or eight thousand dollars was going into the Inmate Welfare Fund each year without any documentation or accountability.[24] So, when Helen said, "Show me the money," the administration claimed they didn't know where it was.

The end result of this saga was that the women got electricity in their cells, and Helen got the reputation of a smart, litigious prisoner whom the provincial authorities did not want in Oakalla. By New Year's Eve, 1988, Helen had been turned down for a transfer from P4W back to BC seven times, joining the good company of the many other prisoners who had embarked on the dangerous journey to get back "home."

Back on the range, Helen had decided to lock in, along with twenty other women. She favoured more organized, strategic resistance than spontaneous insurrection. It wasn't like she didn't have the moxie to rebel, but the New Year's Eve rebellion did not start with any clear objective other than refusing to be locked before midnight.

Almost a year earlier, after her husband had suffered a heart attack, she had engaged in a hunger strike in another failed attempt to be transferred back to BC. She was also waiting for her federal court case against the CSC to address Charter challenges concerning the discriminatory treatment of federally sentenced women relative to that of federally sentenced men. However, this court case would not necessarily result in Helen being transferred back to BC even if she did win.

After she had locked, she pleaded with the twelve women still lingering in the grey zone out on the range. "You know you're going to get hurt here. We'll protest this tomorrow. We'll file grievances—please lock in."[25] But they refused to be locked. Helen still believed in transforming the system from within: a reformist.

Back in the common rooms, after what felt like hours, the CX8 announced that anyone who wanted to go back to their cell could do so now. The fire doors separating the ranges from the common rooms shielded us from the sound of the goon squad marching through the tunnel from KP, banging their batons rhythmically on their shields, creating a thunderous beat to accompany each of their synchronized steps. The women who had stayed in their cells told us about this formidable sound and the paralyzing effect it had on them.

At first only a couple of women in the common rooms stepped up to the fire door, but it didn't open. They waited and waited, and finally sat down on the floor near the door. At 11:45, the guards let everyone from the common rooms through the door into the dimly lit range, where we were suddenly confronted by two Dobermans and a team of Darth Vader lookalikes. For "security reasons," custody had dimmed the range lights so that visibility was almost nonexistent.

Along with the other twelve women who had been hanging around outside their cells until now, we made a mad, panicked dash for the first cell we could get into. The dogs were released and began chasing and nipping at us as we ran around chaotically, trying to find an empty cell. Sometimes three or four women would be trapped, cowering on top of someone's cot while a Doberman snapped at them menacingly.

When it seemed as though everyone was in a cell, the goon squad marched down the range, running their batons along the bars, until they found someone who had refused to lock at eleven to "extricate from their cell." Everywhere they went water rained down on them from the women on the upper tiers. To the women's amusement and the guards' dismay, the dogs refused to go up the narrow staircase to the three-foot-wide upper-tier walkway, no doubt feeling skeptical about the capacity of a thin four-foot-high metal pole railing protecting them from a one-storey drop to the cement floor below.

By the end of that night I was double bunked in segregation, along with the other women who had refused to be locked at eleven that New Year's Eve. The next morning, the women who had not been taken to seg-regation were still locked in their cells. The warden did not deviate from the usual group punishment paradigm, which very effectively turned many of the women who had locked against those who had not. As usual, the women were given no reason for the lockdown. But that day a big investigation began into discovering who "the ringleaders" were behind what had happened on New Year's Eve. The warden threatened to keep the whole range locked down until everyone had agreed to be escorted off the range, where they would be interviewed individually and privately by the "unit manager."

Helen tried her best to organize a collective response to this illegal interrogation by sending a kite down the range suggesting that every-one refuse to be interviewed, but many women were intimidated by the administration's threats. The warden responded by keeping the whole range locked down until all the holdouts agreed to be interviewed. Five women, including Helen, went to segregation rather than submit to being interrogated. They did not want the administration to use them as the scapegoats for the other women on the ranges remaining locked.

This was the last straw for Helen. I learned later that she

> believed at the time that I couldn't do any good there, that things were not getting better even though I did everything I could. I wrote letters until they were coming out of my ears. I wrote just about every Member of Parliament, all sorts of women's groups, colleges, you name it. And nothing changed. Nobody came to help. Things were getting worse and worse there. So with all the loss of privileges, with the suicide of Shaggy (Marlene Moore) and with the attempted suicides of the 4 other women just prior to that, I thought that the best thing I could do for them is try and get myself out of there, and try to get them some help from outside. So I decided I was going to fast to the death totally.[26]

Even Helen was beginning to be affected by the unrelenting injustice and feelings of powerlessness that define prison.

Segregation was so crowded that we were double bunked, which was unheard of in those days. (I am astonished that more people are not murdered in prisons today, considering how many prisoners are double bunked, even in segregation. In 2011, 13.46 percent of federal prisoners in segregation cells were double-bunked.)[27]

Luckily I was double bunked with a good friend, but that did not prevent us from getting on each other's nerves. The sound of someone snoring, like a loud clock ticking on a sleepless night, can bring on the most vivid fantasies of murder. These fantasies began to border on reality when my cellmate, another woman, and I decided to fast in solidarity with Helen. A few days into our fast, the warden decided to end the lockdown on the ranges and ordered most of the women out of segregation, other than Helen and a few others who had outstanding charges related to the New Year's Eve "riot." At first the three of us who were fasting in solidarity with Helen refused to stop fasting and leave segregation, but Helen, in her usual honourable manner, insisted for a number of ridiculous reasons that we go back to the range, a suggestion we eventually accepted.

Helen was not fucking around. Her hunger strike, like that of my co-accused, Doug Stewart, in Archambault, was not symbolic. As soon as the CSC realized that Helen was serious, they kept her isolated in segregation. The CSC played hardball, in keeping with how they treated all the other prisoners who did not accept being imprisoned in a province far away from their families.

Helen did not try to get the rest of the population involved; she knew many women were too fragile to either hunger strike or resist, and she did not want anyone else to serve the inevitable consequences that come with resistance. But even though she had embarked on this dangerous journey alone, she had done her homework and had already garnered a large population of outside support, not only for her transfer back to BC but also for her federal Charter challenge to pressure the government to give women prisoners the same opportunities as men in terms of prison programs, education, and skills training.

After fifteen days of fasting, during the last three of which Helen had refused to drink water, the CSC doctor warned the warden that Helen's death was imminent. The warden folded.[28]

Transfers serve a number of purposes for the CSC, not the least of which is social control. It would be a grave mistake to underestimate the damage involuntary transfers inflict on prisoners in terms of being separated from their fellow prisoners, blood family, or outside support networks. In the short time I have spent in prisons, I saw women in Oakalla fight tooth and nail to stay in their home province; Doug Stewart almost died in a hunger strike in his attempts to be transferred back to his home province of BC from Quebec; Julie completely disintegrated in P4W as she fought to be returned to her home province; and a number of women in P4W committed suicide between 1989 and 1991 after being refused transfers back to their home provinces.

In January 1989 Helen was transferred to Matsqui, a men's medium-security prison in BC, where she was held in the infirmary but was able to visit with her family and attend university classes inside the prison. Then she spent three more years in a men's halfway house, because the only women's halfway house in BC would not allow her to stay there that long.

Helen did eventually win her court case against the CSC. As part of their settlement in 2002, the CSC said they were "committed to substantive equality, under section 15 of the Canadian Charter of Rights and Freedoms for all federally sentenced women offenders through the provision of facilities and services."[29] The CSC was referring to the six new regional federal prisons for women that had been opening up across Canada since 1995. However, time would tell better than words how easily this organization, like the proverbial snake, can periodically shed its skin to reveal itself as a shinier but otherwise identical version of its original self.

Seventeen

After lunch I always tried to get in a short snooze during count. I would put the pillow over my ears to muffle the noise, and almost immediately I would be in a drooling, semi-conscious state. I could feel the tension leave my body as my mind drifted randomly from one thought to another.

It was during one of these ritual snoozes in early 1989, a few months after the New Year's Eve fiasco, that I felt someone's warm breath on my face, and a familiar smell. I opened my eyes and there was Sammy's face, so close she was out of focus.

I let out a burst of laughter. "Shit, do you look ugly! What are you doing here?"

She lifted a finger to her lips so I would lower my voice. "Move over. I'm on B range."

I lifted the blanket so she could crawl in, but the situation made me uneasy. "Don't you think they might charge you?"

"What are they going to do? Put me in jail?" she said, wrapping herself around me. The only thing protruding out from under the covers was her cast-covered foot. I swear I could smell the pheromones on her breath. Her smell was so intoxicating I took it in deep breaths. But before anything could happen, the sound of the guards yelling at the barrier reached us under the blankets.

"Samantha! Come to the barrier. Samantha!" Despite the sound of her name over the intercom, Sammy brushed her lips against mine again and again. I would have lost all power to stop touching her had the shams not opened.

An unwanted head peered in and hissed, "Samantha, if you don't get out of this cell now you will be eating supper in segregation." We pulled the blankets down off our heads and saw the guard standing in the cell door with her hands on her hips. Sammy looked up with her huge doe eyes and pouted at the guard.

I got up and watched Sammy limping with her heavy cast down the range, staying a few pitiful feet behind the guard. I shook my head. Sammy was versatile. In other circumstances, she would never have let that cast hold her back.

At supper Sammy briefly explained some of her local charges. She had only been out for a prison minute, six months at the most. As was her custom, she spoke in what we would now call sound bites, and even these were only forthcoming after a lot of pressure from us. She also admired the bruises on ZZ's neck and ridiculed the size of the slashes on Pauline's forearm.

"Those are chicken scratches," she said, running her finger slowly over the stitches on Pauline's arms. "We had to sew up this chick in Pine Grove once. At least we tried. But we couldn't get them tight enough and the blood just kept pouring out. She dug deep with a piece of glass so you could see all her white fat hanging out. The guards saw the blood on her floor after lockup and made her go to the hospital. She got twenty stitches."

"Well, I don't remember a thing," said Pauline apologetically. "I've done a better job than that before." She ran her index finger gently over the many little ridges of scar tissue from old wounds along the vulnerable underside of her forearm.

Without saying a word, Sammy held out her own forearm, where the letters "POOKS" had recently been tattooed underneath a stick figure that vaguely resembled a bear. Her pink flesh was raised in a welt around the tattoo. I shook my head as though I was disappointed she would add another tattoo to her collection, but I could barely conceal the satisfaction I felt in seeing her love for me stamped irreversibly on her arm. That same week I got ZZ to tattoo a symbol of my love for Sammy on my shoulder. With a mind to my future conjugal visits with Brent, I wasn't quite so forthright, opting instead for a pair of Indigenous feathers rather than her name or term of endearment.

Prison tattoos were made by wrapping cotton thread very close to the tip of a long sewing needle. Then the tattoo artist would dip the needle and thread into a regular bottle of writing ink and puncture the skin, following the lines of the tattoo drawing with the ink-drenched needle tip. Each time the tattoo artist would plunge the needle into her subject's skin, the thread around the tip would act as both a sponge for the ink and a stopper. But the needle would still penetrate deeply enough to break small blood veins, so that between the blood and the excess ink, the artist would constantly have to be wiping this inky, bloody mess up with a rag. It was a very primitive process, but a skilled tattooist could produce some pretty amazing art. In the men's prisons, where they had access to more tools and shops, they were known to build quite sophisticated electric-powered tattoo equipment. Twenty-five years later, I still have a few prison tattoos that have not faded or lost their meaning.

The first cases of AIDS were identified in 1981, but the first test for the HIV virus was not developed until 1985, so we were not concerned about contracting HIV or full-blown AIDS from sharing either tattoo needles or syringes. Hepatitis C was not even discovered until 1989. So it was not surprising or outrageous that during my entire time in P4W during the 1980s, there was no mention of the dangers of transmitting HIV or hep C through contact with blood, semen, or vaginal fluids. Sheer luck was the only reason I did not contract either of these deadly viruses.

By the new millennium, the CSC's blindness to the need for harm reduction programs to control the spread of HIV and hep C had become not only wilful, but morally outrageous. In their own literature they acknowledge that the prevalence of HIV in prisons is ten times greater than it is in the general population.[30] In Ontario, the prevalence of hep C is twenty-two times greater in the remand prisons, where all prisoners first enter the system, than it is in the general outside population.[31]

Despite this awareness, in 2015 no Canadian prisons offered HIV or hep C prevention or harm reduction programs, such as access to sterile syringes and tattoo needles, even though these programs are legally available across Canada in outside communities. The perception that government authorities would rather be seen treating prisoners as disposable than needles is emphasized through prison policies that make the possession of syringes and tattoo equipment illegal, not to mention consensual sex in some prisons, such as the maximum-security units in women's federal prisons.

A few days after Sammy's return, she dropped a couple of newspaper articles from the front pages of the local daily paper on my cot that a staff member had discreetly given her. The articles said:

> Two young transient women, arrested Sunday night after they hijacked and terrorized a local taxi driver, appeared in provincial court yesterday in Kingston and pleaded guilty to a spree of offences, including 2 local robberies ... the first involving $60 taken at knifepoint from an Amey's cab

driver on Saturday night, and the second arising from the Sunday night knife wielding abduction of a 28-year-old cab driver. The two women were arrested in Napanee after hijacking the 28-year-old and his cab and forcing him to drive them west, menacing him with blade points in his ribs and forcing his face up against the vehicle's steering wheel. At some point between Kingston and Napanee, they took his money and let him out on Highway 401.

The cabbie said, "I got out as quick as I could and started running because I didn't know if they were going to swipe at me." He described the blade as "like a knife you see Rambo using."[32] Sammy was sentenced to seven years concurrently for all the Kingston and Toronto charges combined.

My life was as consistent and predictable as one could expect in prison. I got up, went to work in the shop, exercised in the gym or yard in the evenings, wrote letters, and did leatherwork. I had my friends and tried to remain charge free in order to be eligible for visits with Brent in Millhaven. However, now that Sammy was back for an extended period of time, my life slowly began to change in order to adapt to her. Within a week of her return I was enthusiastically doing another bit in seg— enthusiastic because until then, in the back of my mind, I felt shame and embarrassment that I had not done much time in segregation. Every self-respecting prisoner expects to do some seg time; otherwise they risk being profiled by the general prison population as one of the cowards and traitors who are complicit with the administration. It is almost impossible to be a free-spirited, independent thinker who is loyal to one's comrades for many years in prison without doing some seg time.

Days after Sammy's return, ZZ and I were waiting for the barrier to open when Sammy pressed her lips to the bars and whispered that she was coming over for a visit. It was considered illegal for any prisoner from B range to go on A range or vice versa until the administration approved the move. It was just a stroke of luck that the guards hadn't charged her when she had dropped into my cell unexpectedly on the day of her return.

As the electronic motor whirred, I saw Sammy watching the guards at the barrier out of the corner of her eye. ZZ laughed loudly. As soon as the barrier was open, the guards became preoccupied giving out passes to a couple of women going down to the gym.

Sammy slipped through the barrier with the heavy cast on her foot as though it was a bedroom slipper. Without any planning, she planted herself between ZZ and me, hissing, "Press close together so they can't see me." Like actresses in a movie, ZZ and I wrapped our arms around each other's waists and leaned in close so we could whisper sweet nothings into each other's ears, thus closing up the gap so Sammy would become invisible.

For about a hundred feet the whole charade appeared to be working, until one of the guards shouted out Sammy's legal name from the barrier. "Samantha! If you think we can't see you, think again! Get back to the barrier! You are all on charge!"

We were charged with "doing an act calculated to prejudice the discipline or good order of the institution," which resulted in five days in seg. It wasn't anywhere near enough time for the respect I wanted if I was ever to fit in seamlessly with Sammy and the hardcore prisoners that were our family, but it would do for starters. However, it didn't take long for a better opportunity to present itself.

One evening Sammy began muttering threats under her breath about some woman on B range. Naturally I began questioning her to find out more, but, on a more subconscious level, I also began to formulate a germ of a plan. As it became clear that Sammy had been threatened for some reason she would not disclose, my plan for attaining prison cred also became clear. In my own defence, I didn't consciously decide to rebrand myself as a prison tough; it was more a case of deluding myself into believing that the threat to Sammy was real, and that it was my responsibility to protect her.

Without giving my plan time to steep, I walked briskly down the range and into the common room to scout out my victim, or, as I saw it then, Sammy's enemy. Serendipitously, there she was, sitting on B range watching TV. I sat down in a chair as close to the barrier between the two ranges as I could. I had no weapon other than my need for vengeance. As any hippie would say, everything that happened that evening unfolded as though it were meant to be. Within minutes I heard the familiar crack of the barrier as it opened for a couple of women going into the gym.

Like the Flash, I leaped up and seamlessly slid through the barrier along with the women going to the gym. But instead of following them, I strode purposefully past the two guards at the barrier and into the B range common room. This was no surreptitious, well-planned attack; this was a suicide mission.

Guards will never physically restrain a prisoner without overwhelming backup, so the guards didn't grab or follow me. They just went into their office to see what I was doing in the B range common room and called custody for backup.

The poor woman had no warning. I was on top of her before she even knew what was happening. She was standing up at the time and tried to defend herself, but she didn't have a chance since I had ambushed her in mid-stride from behind. By the time we were on the floor, about four guards were standing around us, screaming for me to let her go. I had leaped onto her back and wrapped my arms around her neck, so there was little she could do but fall to the floor and use the only weapon available, her teeth. She bit into my forearm as hard as she could, leaving me with a scar as a reminder of my shameful behaviour.

For a long time the guards stood there screaming, "Hansen, let her go!" I remained locked in place by the steel trap of this young woman's teeth embedded in my arm, while she remained trapped in my headlock from behind.

I ended up in segregation with an antibiotic prescription for thirty days, and the young woman ended up being shunned for having "threatened" Sammy in the first place. Unfortunately, Sammy and I were higher up in the prison pecking order, so no matter who was right or who was wrong, the group dynamic was such that we were considered to hold the moral high ground—although within twenty-four hours I realized just how despicable my actions had really been. To make matters worse, Sammy let it be known that she felt humiliated in the stereotypical role as the damsel in distress and had not appreciated the protection.

I'll tell you one thing for sure. Solitary confinement is not a place for penitence, but it sure is a place for paranoia. Whatever useful thoughts one may have quickly become warped and mutated into paranoia and anxiety.

I spent my thirty days in the hole dwelling on the fact that my political identity and principles were becoming more and more of a background character, overshadowed by my growing prisoner identity. Unfortunately, my new role as action hero had been created by victimizing the young woman on B range. Too late, I came to see my actions that day as those of a giant asshole motivated by a medieval code of honour.

I had lots of time to wonder why the prisoner code was based on such archaic, medieval principles as defending one's honour through violence. I lay the blame mostly on the doorstep of the prison regime, which leaves us powerless and suffering an endless stream of injustices with no means of rectifying our situation. This inevitably leads us down the path of least resistance, which paradoxically is venting our outrage on one another. But I knew better.

Eventually the thirty days passed and I was let out, but not before I had experienced the overwhelming sense of anxiety and paranoia that comes with being isolated even for a relatively short period of time, as negative thoughts boomeranged around in my head without any distractions or interaction with others to help put things into perspective.

. . .

Not long after I was released from seg, I was dragging my laundry down to the common room when I decided to stop to see if Sammy wanted to come along. When I opened her shams, I found her so engrossed in a letter that she didn't even notice me. The fact she hadn't noticed me was not as odd as the fact she had received a letter.

"What's up?" I said, sitting down beside her.

With a big smile on her face, she picked up the pages and waved them in the air. "My sis, Pooks! My sis! She answered my letter." She had all but given up hope when a letter had arrived from the organization that helped link up adopted individuals with their blood families. Without prodding, she began to slowly read the letter out loud. First there was a short cover letter from the organization explaining that serendipity had played a big role. They went on to explain that Sammy's sister had already sent a letter into the system, which had eliminated any controversy regarding the willingness of both parties to be reunited.

Her sister's letter could have been a carbon copy of Sammy's. The script was neat, and the content was heavy on emotion but light on facts. The letter went on at length about her desire to find her sister before providing a skeletal portrait of their mother as a young woman who spent more time in prison than not. Sammy's sister had been raised by her maternal grandmother. No mention was made of a father. They lived in the United States but would very much like to visit Sammy. The last page was a series of questions for Sammy to answer, with a final comment regarding how uncanny the similarity was between Sammy's photo and her mother.

Sammy held up the small black-and-white photo of her mother, which resembled the photo Sammy had sent me from a passport photo machine in the Winnipeg train station. Her mother had short dark cropped hair, with black eyes and full lips that jumped out at the viewer from her thin face. She wore a pair of skinny black jeans, a baggy man's shirt, and running shoes. She looked more like a young boy than anyone's mother.

Sammy stared at the photo in my hands reverently. After a few minutes she took it delicately from me and carefully slid it back into the envelope, as though it might disintegrate any second.

"Would you do my laundry, Pooks? I got to get a visiting application form from the Inmate Committee and write my sis a letter." She looked over at me with soft, moist eyes in such a way that I felt saying "no" would be like denying her dying request. I picked up her pillowcase full of laundry and dragged it down to the laundry room along with my own.

Despite her elation over discovering her blood family, she quickly contained her emotions, as though they were a weapon that could be used against her. When I mentioned how great she must feel to have found her mother, she retorted, "What's so great? That my mom's a con like me?"

When Sammy received a confirmation letter that her family had been approved to come in on Family Day, she began to work on a special pair of moccasins for her sister. I attributed her growing moodiness to this momentous event, but as time went on I wondered if it had more to do with my impending conjugal visit with Brent, or perhaps even Lauren, one of Sammy's many "sisters" from Saskatoon whom she stayed with during her short stints outside prison. Trying to find out Sammy's feelings or thoughts was more difficult than guessing the contents of an unmarked, unopened can. I could pick it up and shake it, but other than a few vague clues, it was all guesswork.

There was no doubt that her feelings about my relationship with Brent were decidedly negative. Whenever she saw me get a letter from him, her face would instantly cloud over, and she would begin making disparaging comments about him that I couldn't counter without provoking a fight. I thought she was completely irrational, since she had never met him and had never spoken to anyone else who had. When calling him ugly and wimpy-looking didn't provoke a reaction from me, she would dig down deep and pull out the label that every prisoner dreads. She began calling him a goof.

To anyone who has been in prison, the word *goof* is synonymous with serious threats. It is difficult to define the word because it is more of a condensed threat than it is an accurate description of anything. Calling anyone a goof in prison is what people used to call "fighting words." If a person does not respond to these words, the rest of the prison population will often treat that person like a subhuman, someone who has no self-respect or honour. To this day, I still find myself involuntarily flinching whenever anyone calls someone else a goof, even though people who have never been to prison intend it as a harmless, jokey word.

The fights began in earnest. Not just verbal, emotional battles, but physical fights. They would always start during the lunch hour after I had received a letter from Brent. In short order, Sammy would call him a goof, and if I dared defend him, she would hurl herself at me, punching and kicking at every part of me but my face. I was a good six inches taller than her and probably just as strong, so I usually found a way to pin her down on the bed until her fury had subsided.

One afternoon the blood left her face and little bits of spittle flew at me as she hurled one obscenity after another at both Brent and me. When I finally managed to pin her down, I felt her fist pounding rhythmically on my back, and I couldn't help but wonder what would have happened if she had had a shank. The next day I discovered that the same thought had passed through her mind, not in retrospect, but in real time as she was pounding on my back. Uncharacteristically, she confided that she had imagined stabbing me repeatedly.

At the time I felt as though her hatred for Brent was a reflection of her insecurity around our relationship. But every now and then the nagging realization would surface of just how unfair it was for me to expect to keep up a primary, sexual relationship with Brent and Sammy at the same time. Perhaps I couldn't actually have sex with Brent, but applying for a conjugal visit and writing "love letters" amounted to the same thing. It wasn't fair to either of them. Sammy was gay and did not see our relationship as just a prison fling that could be discarded as soon as one of us got out. Brent wrote to me, explaining how painful it was for him not to know how I really felt or whether we would ever get conjugal visits. The hard, cold truth was that I loved them both, but knew in my heart that a relationship with Sammy on the street would be a nightmare. She was far too committed to drugs and the street life, or so I thought. In fact, I did want to have my cake and eat it too. I wanted Sammy in prison, but Brent when I got out. It was hard for me to accept just how selfish this scenario was.

I wasn't the only one in a relationship walking around the prison with bruises on my arms and legs. There were other relationships in which damaged individuals were strained to the breaking point by the tensions of this hothouse environment. It wasn't all bad. There were healthy relationships as well, but no matter where a relationship fell on the spectrum between good and bad, there were few women doing any significant time who didn't have a relationship with another woman. These relationships were the main antidote to the lonely and frightening daily reality of prison life.

Little by little, my love and commitment to Brent began to erode. Some of the erosion was caused by distance and time, but the greatest catalyst was the repercussions from each reminder of Brent's existence. It simply became easier to avoid getting letters from Brent by not writing him in the first place than it was to fight with Sammy. My motivation to remain charge free so we could visit evaporated. Eventually I came to the conclusion that my relationships in P4W took precedence over any relationships outside the walls. This was my here and now. The world beyond the walls seemed as far away as China, and had about the same impact on my life.

Ironically, during the months that I began to let my relationship with Brent slip away, Sammy began to drop hints that a long-distance relationship she had with Lauren back in Saskatoon might come back to haunt her. I first became aware of this relationship during our short five-day stay in segregation. My suspicions were aroused when Sammy's reassurances that Lauren was like a sister were embellished with feelings of love. Her love for Lauren became even more obvious when she began to warn me that Lauren might actually be coming to P4W, since she was awaiting sentencing on serious charges in Pine Grove.

By this time Sammy's campaign to make me dump Brent was beginning to have its desired effect. I had stopped writing him and had told my classification officer that I wasn't going to visit him for personal reasons. I gradually learned through visits with mutual friends just how devastated he was over this decision, even though he was aware of my relationship with Sammy. I had effectively sacrificed my feelings for him in order to keep my relationship with Sammy alive. I knew in my heart that even if Lauren came to P4W and Sammy dumped me, I could not resurrect my feelings for Brent.

I didn't see Brent again until I was released to the halfway house. Some friends from Kingston introduced him to a wonderful woman who visited him regularly. They were married a short time later, while he was still in prison.

There was one more aspect to my feelings that I couldn't ignore. Lauren was Cree, and I knew rationally that Sammy would be better off in a relationship with another Cree woman from her home province than she would with a white woman from Ontario. Besides, I had defeated myself in my struggle to save my relationship with Sammy by imagining Lauren as this mythical yet stereotypical Cree warrior woman to whom I could not compare. I had already prepared myself to relinquish Sammy to Lauren before she had even arrived.

Eighteen

I heard Lauren had arrived before I actually met her. There was a buzz that spread like a wildfire, from the segregation cells up to the ranges and over to the wing. I could tell by the way the women in the Native Sisterhood spoke that she was a respected leader who would probably shake up the normal pecking order more than most new arrivals. Even the non-Indigenous population picked up on this vibe and began to reassess how their relationships would stand up. When I began to detect people scanning Sammy and me out of the corner of their eye, I realized that we were at the epicentre of this social maelstrom.

By the time Lauren had arrived on the range, Sammy's reassurances that she could never be with Lauren were so frequent that I had become quite concerned. When I heard the electronic doors crack open uncharacteristically at ten, I leaned over the top rail of the upper tier and watched with a feeling of resignation a tall woman with long black hair walk confidently down the range. All the women from the Native Sisterhood and Saskatchewan came out of their cells to greet her. I watched her smiling serenely at her friends and listened to her laugh easily at their jokes. Even when I went back into my cell, her clear voice and easy laugh seemed amplified.

The effect of all the stories I had heard left me both fearful of and fascinated with Lauren. In my uncensored mind, she was like the warrior princesses depicted in children's books, someone with whom I could not compete or compare. The stories from Sammy and the other women in P4W were not entirely to blame for these feelings. My own tendency to romanticize Indigenous people, and to belittle myself, had laid the groundwork for my complete resignation to the fact Sammy would and should be with Lauren. I put up no fight.

In the beginning Sammy tried to keep both relationships alive until she could figure out what she wanted. I waited and watched painfully from a distance, hardly saying a word to Lauren. This was not particularly difficult, since our worlds did not intersect anyway.

Our importance in Sammy's world was overshadowed by only one group of people: her blood family. Not long after Sammy had received the first letter from her sister, the invitations for Family Day appeared on the range. When I asked Sammy if she was going to invite her sister and grandmother, she said, "I might," as though contemplating whether to go out to the yard after supper. But the next morning she casually showed me an eager letter addressed to her sister, along with forms for her whole family to fill out for Family Day.

Everything between that day and Family Day flew by in a blur. If Sammy was ever sent a photo of her family, she didn't show it to me. I found myself picturing her sister as a stereotypical postcard Indigenous woman with long black hair, dark eyes, and olive skin. I pictured not only her sister but also the whole reunion as stereotypical. I envisioned her grandmother shuffling in as an elder with a shawl, a long skirt, and a ribbon shirt, holding the hand of her granddaughter, who was decked out in cool street clothes with traditional accessories. They would embrace and spend the whole evening talking and laughing, cementing a solid bond that only death could destroy. I was aware of the dangers of stereotyping, but it's difficult to undo a lifetime of mainstream cultural messaging. Sammy, on the other hand, often reminded me that they probably wouldn't even come at all. She figured she would get a letter with an excuse like they were sick or too far away, or didn't have any money. A few times she said they were probably at home complaining about her being in prison, a loser, a fuckup. This was a more realistic expectation for Sammy—something she could deal with. Whenever anyone asked Sammy if her family was visiting, Sammy would gun them off and flippantly say she wasn't holding her breath. But her family did return the invitations with reassurances that they were coming.

As the day drew nearer, Sammy became moody, oscillating between manic happiness and hair-trigger anger. She began to agonize over her wardrobe, spending long hours into the night beading medallions for her moccasins and fancy beadwork for her leg wraps. How much traditional clothing should she wear? The women would spend weeks preparing traditional outfits for powwows, but for Family Day, Sammy decided on a combination of black denims, a baggy turquoise ribbon shirt, and moccasins with beaded leg wraps.

The night before Family Day she dampened her jeans and shirt with a wet cloth before piling books on top of them in order to press out the wrinkles. She swept her cell floor, cleaned her toilet and sink, and arranged everything meticulously in anticipation of the one hour in which visiting families would be allowed on the range. After lockup the range was thick with the smell of sweetgrass from Indigenous women smudging and praying to the Great Spirit.

The families began arriving by one o'clock the next day. The gym was already filled with long wooden folding tables covered with white paper masquerading as tablecloths. The wooden gym floor had been stripped and varnished by the cleaners, and a dance band, fronted by the guy who ran the prison beauty shop, was tuning up on the stage.

Little groups of women sat nervously around tables they had claimed for their family and friends. Most could not sit still and flitted back and forth between the wings, ranges, and gym as they anxiously awaited their families. Everyone was dolled up. Prison fashion was always distinct from fashion in the outside world. Since only a fortunate few received parcels from the street, most outfits were improvised from materials available inside the walls. At this time, micro-miniskirts and tiny halter tops fashioned in the industrial sewing shop from a roll of spandex material were all the rage for the more feminine women. The more masculine women, their hair slicked back with gel, wore dress pants and shirts. Cleavage, thighs, and stilettos were mixed and matched with moccasins, beaded leatherwork, and biker paraphernalia.

My family, in particular my mother, had visited me regularly in prison, but I didn't feel comfortable about inviting them in for Family Day. In making that long drive up from Toronto to Kingston on a regular basis my mother had shown more solidarity with me than most friends. But my family was one world and my prison friends were another, and I just couldn't picture myself sitting comfortably through those two worlds colliding.

Maybe I was wrong in feeling that way, because a brief encounter between my mother and Sammy through the fence during a twenty-four-hour family house visit had gone quite well. My mother, looking a little like the Queen, had smiled and waved at Sammy, who looked as much like any mother's nightmare as a person could. The night before my visit Sammy had given me a huge hickey on my neck to force me to tell my mother about our relationship. All things considered, my mother had taken the news in stride, remarking how "cute" Sammy was. Coincidentally, Sammy also used the word "cute" to describe my mother to our mutual friends on the range. But a brief encounter through the fence was one thing; a whole afternoon and evening was another.

In Sammy's case, I imagine the need to meet her blood family over-rode all other concerns. Anyway, on Family Day Sammy sat stiffly at the table with ZZ, Pauline, and me. Their families weren't coming either, although Pauline was helping greet visitors at the door and guiding them to the gym. Sammy looked sullenly at the entrance to the gym, anxious, I imagine, that her family wouldn't show, anxious that they would. By two o'clock most of the families had arrived, but still not Sammy's. But then, they did have to drive up from New York.

I was staring at the entrance to the gym, willing them to arrive, when I noticed Pauline leading a small older woman in our direction. She had a grey perm held tightly together with a thick coating of hairspray. A young teenager with white skin and straggly brown hair struggled to walk slowly enough behind them. The older lady wore a clean polyester dress, a string of pearls, and a small plastic handbag draped over her arm. The teenager wore clean blue jeans that were frayed along the hems and a pair of cheap scuffed-up running shoes. As Pauline steered them in our direction, the teenager flashed a shy smile, revealing a chipped front tooth.

I glanced over at Sammy, but she was looking right through them at the traffic moving in and out of the gym. Even when Pauline had stopped in front of our table, Sammy craned her neck in order to see around the obstruction the older lady and teenager were creating. They were obviously not who Sammy was expecting.

"Sammy!" Pauline stepped directly into Sammy's line of sight. At this point the pair smiled warmly at her. Sammy got up slowly and held out her hand.

"You must be my grandmother," she said very politely. The old lady shook Sammy's hand once, said her name was Doreen, and sat down beside her, looking forward uncomfortably. The teenager introduced herself as Karen and sat down on the opposite side. If Sammy was disappointed, she didn't show it, but her feet were bouncing up and down nervously. In keeping with my maternal role, I struck up a conversation in order to break the ice between Sammy and her family.

I struggled on valiantly while Sammy sat stiffly listening, like a casserole warming slowly in the oven, until suddenly it seemed she had reached a point where she was ready and began to bubble and spill over, talking and laughing excitedly to Karen. I felt a sigh of relief pass through my body.

Sammy wasn't a talker, so after a few quick jokes she grabbed Karen's hand and took her on a walk around the gym, introducing her to almost everyone. She had morphed into her childlike persona, expressing her joy and affection in physical play. At first Karen had seemed uncomfortable surrounded by so many people she didn't know, but when Sammy pushed her childhood buttons, she relaxed and came popping out of her shell. Even though they didn't look like sisters, they sure acted like it, running around the gym, sliding in their socks, and playing hide-and-seek with the real children.

"She is just like her mother," said Doreen. "It's too bad she is in prison because she would have loved to have met Samantha."

"Sammy hates the name Samantha," I explained. "She's more like a guy than a woman." The words "guy" and "woman" did not feel like the right words to describe Sammy.

"I can see that," Doreen smiled. "She's so much like her mother. She has never forgiven me for encouraging her to give Sammy up, but she was in no shape to raise her, and I was already struggling to keep food in our mouths as it was."

Glancing up at the clock, I knew that they would be calling us for supper soon. I would never get the chance to learn more about Sammy's past once we were all seated and eating, so I took the plunge and began digging.

"Sammy told me she was adopted in Saskatoon. Is that where you were raised?" I asked tentatively.

"Oh no," said Doreen, glancing over at me. As soon as I had turned the conversation in a snoopy direction, she immediately camouflaged her real emotions with the hooded eyes I was so familiar with in prison. Her smiling eyes turned cold. I could tell instantly that she was not the kind of woman who opened up to strangers easily. There was a stiffness to her face and posture. She wore her tight smile like a mask and sat ramrod straight, as though she had to protect herself from a hostile world. She was not your stereotypical warm, cuddly grandmother.

"I'm sorry for prying," I said quietly. Doreen straightened out a few wrinkles in her polyester dress and watched Sammy and Karen dancing with some kids to the dance band on the stage. She had offered up what she felt was appropriate, and I should not have asked for more.

"Dinner!" the voice boomed out of the gym intercom. "Will the women with guests for Family Day please go to the cafeteria first, and the rest can follow. Please let the elderly and children go to the front of the line." As soon as the instructions ended, the doors opened and the crowd filed out to make their way down the winding corridor leading to the cafeteria. Sammy came running over and slid her arm under Doreen's so she could guide her to the front of the line.

"Isn't she cute?" Sammy asked me proudly. She was not much of a conversationalist, but she had a way of disarming people with her innocent persona that never failed to bring out the maternal instinct in women. As the line made its way slowly toward the cafeteria, Sammy and Karen shifted their weight impatiently from one foot to the other, periodically hunching over in uncontrollable laughter at some unspoken joke. Their eyes were glistening and their faces were flush with excitement. The energy between them was palpable.

Karen asked Doreen if they could spend the night in Kingston so they could visit Sammy again the next day, but Doreen reminded her that she had to work. They carried their trays back to the gym and ate dinner between small talk. After dinner, the huge banks of fluorescent lights were dimmed to highlight the thousand points of light from the giant disco ball. Husbands and wives, children, and pairs of women glided about the gym, dancing to the tunes of the hairdresser's band. There was a warm and fuzzy atmosphere, much like a wedding reception but without the drinking. Even the guards had serene-looking smiles on their faces. Women without families sat comfortably at tables with their friends' families, soaking in the infectious feeling of belonging that wafted among the people on that day. On Family Day and powwows the women were no longer prisoners, murderers, drug addicts, whores, or thieves, but rather mothers, daughters, wives, and sisters.

The last dance was a slow one. Sammy came over to the table, took Doreen's hand, and pulled her persistently until she reluctantly stood up.

"Come on, Grandma," she said softly, her huge liquid eyes staring unwaveringly into Doreen's. "Let's dance."

Sammy wrapped her arms around Doreen's waist and pressed her face down into her shoulder as though she was a man dancing with her love. Doreen shifted stiffly from one foot to the other, but her facial muscles had loosened up somewhat.

As soon as the last dance was over, the guards began to herd people discreetly toward the exit doors, where the families had to say goodbye to the women left behind in the gym. Sammy hugged both Karen and Doreen for a long time. Karen shuffled backwards down the corridor outside the gym, continuously waving, while Sammy waved back at her with wet eyes. Doreen walked slowly away without looking back.

Finally, all the families had been teased from the body of prisoners. Sammy's eyes slowly lost their glisten, and her movements grew slower and more controlled as she transformed from playful kitten into enigmatic sphinx. After all the families had left the building, we slowly went back to the wing and ranges. Some were laughing and reliving the wonderful day, while others shut themselves reclusively in their cells, mourning the loss of their loved ones until the next social.

"So did you have a good day?" I asked, lying back on Sammy's cot. She leaned over and flicked on the TV. She lay back down beside me, wrapped up in her own thoughts, oblivious to the backdrop of fifty different conversations, TV shows, and music stations.

"Karen said we're gypsies," she said to the ceiling cryptically.

· · ·

Once Family Day was over, Sammy slowly began to leave me for Lauren. The fact that I had anticipated this did not make it any less painful. At first Sammy would see Lauren at Native Sisterhood meetings and during short visits to her cell on the upper tier to say goodnight before lockup. But in no time, the goodnight visits began to drag on for hours, and Sammy's description of her history with Lauren became revisionist.

"I never thought she'd actually come here, Pooks," she'd explain to me when I showed signs of jealousy. "I really don't want to be with her. I want to be with you, but I told her I'd be with her if she ever came here. I didn't think she would really come." Her cheerful explanations made my heart sink, and a painful knot would form in my stomach so I couldn't eat, relax or sleep.

"You see, Pooks," she would say, "Lauren and me are like sisters, and I just can't hurt her, but you got to believe that it's you I want to be with. I know that Lauren and I will never work out."

Her explanations were a mass of contradictions that I understood about as well as I understood Sammy. She was a complicated person. She wanted a maternal superhero who would be comforting and supportive during her times of need, but ready at any moment to transform back into her lover without the mortal human qualities of jealousy and bitterness that would normally accompany the kind of infidelity I had been experiencing. She wanted unconditional love.

At times, I found the incestuous, maternal lover relationship Sammy and I shared disturbing. But I also realized that if Sammy had been a man, ironically, our relationship would have been considered normal—that is, the expectation that I would be both Madonna and whore would have been considered normal.

Unfortunately, I was not a superhero. I lost weight and started to look a lot more like Olive Oyl than Wonder Woman. When I hadn't gone down for meals for a few days, Sammy would hunt me down, furious that I wasn't eating. She would pounce on me in my cell, admonishing me for being so skinny. When I explained how painful it was to go down and sit by myself at our table, unable to avoid seeing Lauren and her laughing and eating together, she would fly into a rage. She hated me for not having the strength of a saint. Sometimes I couldn't help feeling that the three-year-old who had been adopted in Saskatoon had never matured, and was still locked inside the body of this grown woman raging against me.

At the same time, she became insanely jealous if she thought I might begin a romantic relationship with some other woman. If she caught me hanging out with anyone else she considered a "butch broad," she would storm into my cell, accusing me of fucking around on her. Sometimes her face would drain of all colour and spittle would fly out of her mouth as she raged, and I would have to lie on top of her, holding the rails of the cot for support while she pounded my back rhythmically with her fist.

It was during one of these episodes that I decided it would be in my best interests to follow the path of least resistance by biding my time on the range rather than trying to escape from her in the wing. Any escape in prison, other than over the wall, would be an illusion. I would be judged for not having the courage to fight either Sammy or Lauren to defend my honour, while Sammy would lose face for not preventing me from making her affair and my subsequent unhappiness a public spectacle. The concept of fighting to the death to defend one's honour to prove one's love or avenge any humiliation was normal. Even if people didn't actually die, real, physical fights defending or avenging honour happened every day. The fact that we could not confide in any intermediaries, such as counsellors and psychologists, without risking ending up in segregation forced us to resolve all our domestic disputes ourselves.

Lauren was only there for "a minute," as we described a prison time period of less than a year. Within days of her leaving, Sammy popped back into my life as though she had never left. I did not want to be in a romantic relationship with her anymore, but I knew that the consequences of rejecting her would be serious. So I acted as though nothing had changed between us, despite the humiliation I felt at being treated like a Pookie toy. I was just too tired and fed up to fight Sammy, plus I knew that my time in P4W was nearing an end. Not long after Lauren left, I learned I was being transferred to the new minimum "house" across the street from P4W. Once again, the path of least resistance paved my way.

During those months before being transferred, I started noticing that I was not the only one acting. Sammy was also merely playing the role of my lover. In reality, she was starting a new relationship with another young Cree woman from Saskatchewan. It was as though we were in a play with the exact same plot, script, and characters as when Lauren had first arrived, except this time Sammy did not try as hard to disguise her interest in her new lover, and I was not as jealous.

Each evening Sammy would go to the gym to play volleyball with her new "friend," and then find an excuse at lockup to run down and say goodnight. Each evening the "goodnight" would last longer and longer until there was no doubt in anyone's mind that a lot more than "goodnight" was going on behind the shams. With Lauren, I had been consumed with anxiety and the feeling that there was no way out, but this time I was relieved to be able to focus on my transfer to the minimum.

After Family Day, Sammy continued to write to her sister, Karen, but as usual she said very little to anyone about the letters. From little scraps of conversation here and there, I gleaned that Karen and Sammy were half-sisters, sharing the same birth mother. To my knowledge neither her birth mother nor her grandmother ever wrote her a letter. This must have hurt Sammy a lot, but she never complained or articulated her feelings about her mother in the short period of time I had left at P4W. I would imagine that the pain associated with abandonment had become a normal part of Sammy's life.

Nineteen

The new minimum-security prison for women, known as the Isabel McNeill House, was situated in a nineteenth-century limestone mansion that had originally been constructed for the deputy warden of Kingston Penitentiary, which was conveniently located across the street. It was the first and only stand-alone minimum-security prison for women in Canada, compared to the twelve minimum-security prisons available for men across the country at that time. Before opening the new minimum-security prison, P4W had been designated a multi-security prison, which meant that women from all security levels lived within a maximum-security perimeter and shared the same facilities, although medium- and minimum-security women were allowed more privileges than the maximum-security women.

Separate minimum-security prisons are advantageous because they allow prisoners to interact more easily with the outside community through jobs and recreational and social events. They are constructed so that the prisoners can live more like people in outside society, with separate bedrooms that aren't locked at night and with kitchens where people can cook their own meals. It is often said that minimum-security prisons allow the prisoners to decompress from prison life. They can get used to the greater freedom and responsibilities of normal life.

I was one of the first eleven women to transfer to this long overdue minimum-security prison in 1990. We literally walked out the front doors of P4W, crossed the street, and walked into the minimum-security "house." But in that short walk we experienced a major culture shock. We left the concrete prison ranges and walked into a mansion with a white shag rug, white leather furniture, hundred-dollar tropical plants, and a solid oak dining room set. In a postmodern world where the line between film and reality is blurred, we felt like reality show contestants, auditioning for the part of Eliza Doolittle in a modern-day remake of *My Fair Lady*.

On our first day we toured about the house, touching and experiencing the furniture as though this was our first contact with civilization. We touched the huge rubber leaves of the tropical plants to see if they were real or plastic. They were real. We bounced up the broadloom-covered stairs into the bedrooms and jumped up and down on the beds in our shoes like little kids to see how much spring there was in the mattresses compared to the wire mesh supports of our cots from our previous life. We walked gingerly around the yard, daring each other to step over the invisible boundary line delineating the divide between the minimum and the paved parking lot for P4W employees. It took a supreme effort to restrain ourselves from running down the street just because we could. At the end of our tour we sat around the huge oak dining room set, talking in exaggerated accents like upper-class characters from various British sit-coms. We were hysterical.

After we had exhausted our Monty Python imitations, the warden sat down at the dining room table to explain their social transformation experiment. They figured if our standard of living was dramatically improved, in time we would internalize these standards and begin to aspire to maintain them in our own world outside the prison walls. They figured that no matter how many years we may have lived under some sort of oppressive regime, a six-month stint in a mansion-like setting would produce such a strong craving to maintain these upper-class standards that we would somehow magically figure out how to acquire them.

This quaint theory was riddled with holes that only magical thinking could conceal. One hole that appeared obvious to us was the fact that it takes a good education and career to maintain even a middle-class standard of living. A few years after the opening of the minimum house, during the 1996 Louise Arbour Inquiry, "the Survey of Federally Sentenced Women revealed that … two-thirds of federally sentenced women (fsw) are mothers, and seventy percent of these are single parents all or part of the time; sixty-eight percent of fsw were physically abused although this figure jumps to ninety percent for Aboriginal women; fifty-three percent of fsw were sexually abused and sixty-one percent of Aboriginal women were sexually abused; fewer than one-third had any formal job qualifications beyond basic education prior to sentencing, and two-thirds had never had steady employment."[33] Unless the CSC decided to provide higher education and job training, as well as addressing some of the other underlying issues that lead to crime, the only way any of us were going to live in a mansion would be by becoming high-class hookers, or through organized crime.

Another glaring hole was the one in the women's souls. In other words, you could take the woman out of prison, but you couldn't take the prison out of the woman. The imprint that prison leaves on a person is not made by the walls and bars, but rather by the institutionalized injustice that is prison. This institutionalized injustice is the result of a myriad of senseless rules and regulations that are enforced by guards with unregulated power, which leaves the prisoners powerless and in a state of perpetual angst. Physically this new environment was much improved, but the same invisible oppression remained virtually unchanged. The fact that a person could be shipped back to P4W within the hour for anything from smoking a joint to talking back to a guard made sitting on a leather couch in a white room with a shag rug irrelevant.

Of course, the transfer to the minimum did represent a slight improvement, but it was too little too late to make any significant changes in our lives. Some of the women took on janitorial work at CSC regional headquarters across the street, others cleaned and cooked inside the minimum, and a few, myself included, learned more high school–level woodworking skills on a prison farm outside the city. If there had been more emphasis on allowing the women to interact with the community through real jobs and education, instead of simply spending a lot of money on fancy furniture, rugs, and plants, this might have gone a long way toward changing our lives.

I had only been in the minimum a few months when I was called into the office one morning to be informed that I was going back to P4W to have my prison identification photo updated. Within the hour, an escort was arranged to accompany me across the street. I had a foreboding feeling looking up at the huge grey limestone facade with "Prison for Women 1935" etched into the stone header over the thick wooden front doors. Once inside, the foreboding feeling became one of vulnerability as I listened to the sound of clanging doors and voices echoing throughout the building. The powerful smell of industrial cleaning solutions stung my nostrils. Everything about the place was a reminder that my freedom to walk out again was fragile. The guards in the front office looked at me with that same cold, unemotional gaze with which prisoners gaze at guards. It is the kind of look that transmits a feeling of no feelings. In my gut, I knew these people would think nothing of locking me up in segregation for years simply because they were ordered. It didn't help that the first set of doors we walked through, within five feet of entering the building, clanged shut behind us. People without criminal records who had visited me had described the same experience.

As we made our way down the stairwells into the bowels of the building, we had to pass through a locked barrier every time we entered a new area. By the time we reached the corridor to the Admissions and Discharge area, there were a long series of locked barriers separating us from the outside world. I could hear the laughing and yelling voices of the women echoing down the cement corridors from the ranges several storeys above. It was hard to imagine there were 140 women carrying on the mundane activities of their lives in this concrete fortress for years and years. People can adjust to captivity just like animals in a cage.

As I walked past a metal barrier that separated the corridor outside the woodshop from the A&D offices, I was taken aback to see Sammy pressed up against the bars.

"Pooks," she whispered.

"How did you know I'd be here?" I asked with surprise.

"I've got my ways," she said cryptically. I looked over at the guard who had been escorting me, but she had already gone inside the A&D office to chat with the guard who worked there. All the guards were aware of our relationships with one another, so this particular guard must have been somewhat sympathetic to Sammy and me or she wouldn't have let me talk to her.

"How are you doing?" I said, pushing my hand as far as I could through the bars. Sammy took my hand and held it gently. I had been immediately struck by how pale and thin she looked. Her normally round cheeks were hollow, creating the impression that her eyes were bigger than usual. Her lips were bloodless and dry.

"I don't think I'll be here much longer, Pooks," she said softly.

"What are you talking about?" I said with some alarm.

"I just can't take it in here anymore." Tears welled up in her eyes. I had never seen her look so depressed.

"Don't be stupid," I said in my most optimistic, chipper voice. "I'm going to send you in a parcel soon, and when I get to the halfway house you'll be able to phone me. Things will get better for you." I knew we didn't have the time to really talk. The guard was already calling for me to get away from the barrier.

"That's enough, Hansen. Let's go," she said with finality.

"Write me a letter," I said. "I love you, Sammy." She remained pressed against the bars, staring after me as though she would never see me again.

I went through the motions of being photographed for my new ID card, haunted by Sammy's face. As soon as I got back to the minimum, I sought out ZZ, who had also been transferred over in this first group. She was busy making a sandwich in the kitchen.

"I saw Sammy," I said, struggling to fight back a huge lump in my throat.

"Wow. How was she?" ZZ turned to look at me. She could hear the tears in my voice.

"Not good." The tears began leaking out of my eyes. I hated it because now I couldn't talk. "I have this horrible feeling she might do something to herself," I said, not wanting to articulate exactly what I meant by "do something," in case by saying the words I would make it happen. ZZ leaned up against me, sharing my sadness.

There really wasn't anything I could do; we weren't allowed to communicate with the women in P4W, and telling the authorities was in the same vein as ratting out. Suicidal prisoners were immediately taken to segregation, where they were held in an observation cell until the authorities guessed the threat was over. The last place anyone feeling depressed wanted to be was locked up inside a barren cell twenty-four hours a day with a video camera recording their every move. Obviously, the main objective for the authorities was to ensure that the prisoner did not successfully hurt themselves or commit suicide. Helping them to feel better was not a consideration. I placated myself with the thought that Sammy would get over her depression as she had so many times before.

During the six months that we spent at the minimum, another woman and myself travelled for a couple of hours every day out to the country and back to work at the Freedom Farm, the dream child of some male prisoners in the minimum-security Frontenac prison. Despite being operated under the auspices of the CSC, this was a progressive project in which prisoners managed and worked out of a renovated barn in the country, building commercially sellable wooden products. It was a great program, run entirely by ex-prisoners, with no CSC staff onsite.

Every day, a big yellow school bus would pick us up at the minimum and then stop at Frontenac for a load of guys before resuming the hour-long drive up to Tamworth and the Freedom Farm. The bus was driven by an ex-prisoner who could easily have been typecast in any Hollywood film of either the prison or horror genre. He was a huge, burly fellow with a long, unkempt beard; a man of few words, but a reputation that kept just about everybody at bay. Rumour had it that he was a real sweetheart, but to all appearances, not a man you would want to mess with. His reputation was augmented by an axe he kept conveniently located just under his seat. There were lots of rumours floating around the bus that involved him brandishing his axe at anyone who dared to impede the momentum of his bus in any way. But in reality, every driver of a commercial bus probably had access to an axe to make an emergency exit possible.

We had been deprived of freedom, power, and adventure for so long that, like teenagers in high school and men in mid-life crisis everywhere, the vehicle had become our medium for attaining these missing ingredients. Once the bus was loaded, everyone pretty much sat ramrod straight, concentrating on the road ahead, anticipating the "joyride" that was inevitably going to happen.

Every day, as soon as we turned off the main highway onto the long, narrow, gravel country roads, this big, yellow, cumbersome bus would transform into a sleek, flexible flying machine that could reach literally breakneck speeds, accelerating toward every rise in the road until we hit the crest and became airborne for a few stomach-turning seconds. These roads were somewhere between a single and double lane, making it impossible not to stare in unadulterated terror at the fast-approaching crest of the rise, wondering if this would be the time that another car would be reaching that same crest at the same time, but coming from the opposite direction.

The bus driver would always head toward these hills with his hands clasped to the wheel, a look of supreme ecstasy on his face, ready to meet his maker anytime, the ultimate thrill of a gambling man. All or nothing. As fate would have it, our driver met his maker peacefully many years later, solo in his sleep, without any collateral damage.

Despite fearing a horrific death and knowing that we were clearly on the unethical side of the moral line, no one tried to stop the driver or report him to the authorities. The code around ratting out was a moral imperative overriding all other considerations. As luck would have it, no one ever did hit a crest at the same time as us, and the few times we did encounter another vehicle they always prudently took the well-worn path of least resistance—the shoulder of the road.

After six months at the minimum, I was transferred to the Joyce Detweiler House, a halfway house for women in Kingston. This move represented a real change because now we could leave during the day to find work and go out in the evenings to socialize. But the anxiety of imprisonment still dogged us; although we had more freedom, we could still be sent back to P4W at a moment's notice for the most trivial reasons. Our leashes were longer and less visible, but they were still there.

During this time, I was one of the fortunate few who found a real job, working for a kitchen cabinet manufacturing company. Two factors made this possible. I had remained focused on learning woodworking skills during my entire time at P4W and the minimum, so I actually did have the skills to get a job with a commercial cabinet company. And I had saved up all my money so I could buy a used car, which had increased the area of my job-hunting circle. My good fortune also had much to do with having the privilege of a supportive family and friends who sent me in supplies to earn extra money through hobby crafts and other perks that less fortunate prisoners did not have.

I bought a classic black 1980 Z28 Camaro with white leather interior and an Alpine stereo system that looked and sounded like every small-time teenage drug dealer's dream. The Batmobile had a 350 four-barrel under the hood and a dual exhaust under a spoiler in the rear, with a bass amp to challenge the sound barrier. This car, like the school bus, was the medium for attaining the freedom, power, and adventure we had been deprived of for so long. How else can I explain buying such a gas-guzzling muscle car?

The feeling of surging down low close to the pavement, with that huge engine compartment framing the vista in front of me and the deep bass pounding out the rhythm of the Rolling Stones' "Street Fighting Man," was orgasmic. At least temporarily, this car was literally the vehicle for the fix of power and freedom I needed after all those years of submission and control.

One weekend I drove my friend who lived with me at the halfway house to her mother's cottage, an hour's drive from the halfway house. After a fun day of swimming and barbecuing, we decided to leave a little early, since we had a strict curfew like everyone else at the halfway house. We started driving home down the winding unmarked gravel roads in the dark, laughing and basking in the joy of driving and being out at night. But as we travelled toward the country highway that would take us to the main freeway back to Kingston, we began to realize that it was taking a lot longer than we had anticipated. In fact, many of the gravel roads were unmarked and ended in forks and dead ends that were unfamiliar. In those days, cell phones were rare. By the time we came to the realization we were lost, we had also realized we were going to be late.

We were well aware of the strict policy at the halfway house of calling the cops to report "escaped inmates" if we did not arrive by five minutes after our curfew. Driving frantically down the dark country roads, we started turning up driveways to try to borrow a phone to call the halfway house, but unluckily the first few farm families either didn't answer the door or weren't home. Finally, we ran into a Good Samaritan who offered to escort us to the main highway leading to the freeway. At this point we decided to speed home as fast as possible, praying that we would make it before they called the cops. After breaking every speed limit on every road to the halfway house, we just made it by five after eleven. We lived with this constant fear that our invisible leashes would be used to yank us back into prison for circumstances that would normally be considered legal, but in our case were not.

Betty was not so fortunate. A friend of Betty's, who was also a prisoner living in the halfway house, forgot where she was one day and confided to a halfway house employee that Betty had given her some pills from her prescription. Although the employees, who were euphemistically called "house mothers," did not see themselves as prison guards, the effect of their decisions was often the same. The "house mothers" had a mandate to make a written report of anything of interest an "inmate" said or did, even in confidence, no matter the consequences. Despite the fact that the information from the acquaintance could have been incorrect or malicious gossip, Betty was soon back in prison because she had supposedly given away some of her medication to another "inmate."

My fondest memories of this time are of the extraordinary bonds and experiences I shared with the women in the halfway house. There were six of us who had been imprisoned in P4W and the minimum at the same time. Our experiences were so unique and intense that I think only soldiers of war could relate to them. I don't want to minimize the dangers and horrors of war, especially in light of the fact that I have never been in a war. But I believe being a prisoner cemented our bonds as though we were living through a different sort of war against a common enemy, which we only survived through solidarity, and in some cases courage. We shared a common history, language, culture, and identity that were at odds with society and made it difficult to relate to anyone who hadn't been in prison for a significant period of time. As it turns out, this feeling would stay with us for the rest of our lives, although it would fade somewhat with time. But I never could replace my prison friendships with other people.

· · ·

I had been at the halfway house a little over a month when I was called into the office one evening to find Pauline on the other end of the telephone line. I don't remember her exact words other than Sammy had hanged herself, but had survived. After those words I really didn't hear anything else.

The phone call had been very short. What did it mean? I went back into the office and asked one of the halfway house workers if they could find out more information about Sammy. Everyone, including the staff, was shocked. But I wasn't altogether surprised that Sammy had attempted suicide, because my last short visit with her in P4W a few months earlier had haunted me with a feeling of foreboding every day. The odds of Sammy committing suicide were far greater than the odds she would be released from prison and live happily ever after. If there was a God, she had stacked the deck against Sammy from day one.

I didn't want to talk to anyone. I had always felt a deep sadness for Sammy, which had played a role in my incapacity to leave her despite everything. I couldn't think of anyone so young I had ever met who had suffered so much. Even though in her short life she had victimized a few people, she was the victim the greater part of her life by far.

The next morning I was called into the office again, where Sammy's situation was explained to me by the staff to the best of their knowledge. Pauline had found Sammy hanging in her cell. While screaming for the guards to come and cut her down, Pauline had managed to hold Sammy's weight up to minimize the strangulation effect of the homemade noose. She was still alive but unconscious. They rushed her to the hospital, where she was presently in a coma. No one knew yet whether there was permanent brain damage.

Even though Sammy had been involved with other women during the past few years, our relationship had remained constant over a five-year period. Since her adopted family had never visited Sammy, the halfway house staff and prison administration accepted me as her next of kin for the time being. I immediately began the process of applying to visit Sammy. I must admit, I did not expect the prison administration to let me visit her, so I was shocked when my parole officer told me that I could visit her in Kingston General Hospital in the intensive care unit, at least until the official next-of-kin determination had been made. Apparently she had come out of the coma, and the doctors thought it might help her recovery if she had a few visitors. They didn't think there was any harm I could do anyway, since she was under constant surveillance by two guards from P4W.

Those visits with Sammy will forever be etched into my memory. I had never been in an intensive care unit before. A nurse led me past a number of beds with lumps under the blankets and shrunken heads on the pillows, attached to tubes and cords that connected them to machines with numbers and lights flashing. I don't remember seeing the guards, but they were somewhere within view. Sammy was lying on the bed with tubes protruding out of the neck of her hospital gown. There were tubes coming out of her nose, her arm, her stomach, and a hole in her throat. Her eyes were wide open with a look of fixed horror. Almost immediately a lone tear slid out of the corner of her eye and rolled down her cheek. I began to sob silently. I had cried for Sammy before, but not like this, and I was the kind of person who didn't cry at funerals. I had brought a photo album because I had been warned that she couldn't talk and that no one was sure what was going on in her head. The look on her face was a good indicator.

I was afraid that if she saw the despair in my face it would only make her feel worse, so I tried to distract her by flipping open the photo album and pointing to various photos from P4W we had taken together. My tactic didn't work. Her eyes remained focused on my face. My phony gushing over the photos faded fast as I realized how humiliating it must be for Sammy to be treated like a tiny child who could barely understand a thing. But then I began to wonder if the reason her gaze remained fixed on my face no matter what I said could be the result of brain damage. Finally, I asked her to blink her eyes if she could understand me. No blink.

Her fingers and hands lay in a cramped-up position on her belly, as though her muscles were contracted. Suddenly her hand began to shake as she moved it upwards with what appeared to be a supreme effort. Her index finger hovered painfully above the place where the tubes entered her stomach. It seemed either that she wanted me to know these tubes were hurting her or that she wanted me to pull them out. I asked her, but her face remained fixed in that expression of wide-eyed horror that I will never forget. I found a nurse in the area and asked her if she could help me for a minute. Sammy's hand had fallen back down on her gown in that paralyzed, askew position.

I asked the nurse a number of questions. She answered that Sammy was on a lot of pain medication, but they had no way of knowing for sure if she was still in pain. She explained that people with brain injuries often had tears come out of their eyes and that once again, no one could be sure if they were just tears coming out of the tear duct or tears of sadness. Finally, she said that they did not yet know the extent of Sammy's brain damage or whether she would recover at all. To all my questions, her universal answer was that they did not know what Sammy was experiencing.

The enormity of her suffering overwhelmed me. For most of her life she had been a prisoner, and now even suicide had failed to free her. She was locked in the most hideous prison of all, her own body, unable to move, talk, cry, or perhaps even think. What kind of world had we created where a person is not allowed to die with dignity, but instead is forcefully kept alive in some kind of painful purgatory?

P4W continued to allow me to visit Sammy as though I was family. Those visits are the most painful experience I have ever had. No one knew whether Sammy would improve, but we were all hopeful. The hospital did a battery of tests and came to the conclusion that Sammy would never be able to function outside of a medical institution. She would always be severely brain damaged. At first we did not accept this diagnosis and believed she would recover, but as the days turned into months, we began to succumb to the depressing prediction of the hospital. Many different Indigenous elders who came to Kingston to visit the Native Sisterhood in P4W visited Sammy and prayed for her, but her improvement was minimal.

I still remember vividly the last visit I had with Sammy. She had been transferred to a ward on one of the upper floors of the hospital. I took the elevator up, expecting to find Sammy in bed, but was surprised to see her strapped up into a sitting position in a special wheelchair, parked outside her room in view of the nursing station. Her head was supported by a headrest, but her muscles had atrophied so that she sat up tucked into a fetal position. Her legs and arms were curled up and her head hung to the side unnaturally. She did not look comfortable or relaxed, but rather as though she was being forced into this upright sitting position. I'm sure the nurses had her in this chair as a form of physical therapy and out in the hall so she would get some stimulation, but she was painful to watch. As the nurses bustled in and out of the nursing station, they would often stop and make some cheerful comment to Sammy or fluff her pillow or pat her affectionately on the head. I knew that those nurses must become somewhat desensitized to suffering, considering how much of their life is spent witnessing humans in extreme pain. Yet I felt as though their concern for Sammy was heartfelt. Even now, in her shrunken, mangled state, she had the capacity to draw out those protective, nurturing feelings in people.

Over the past few months she had made some progress, in that she was no longer hooked up to machines to breathe, but there were still feeding tubes curling down the neck of her hospital gown into her stomach. When I stepped into her line of sight, she made no sign of recognition. Once again I felt the sobs of sorrow welling up inside of me. It was all I could do to hold them back while I was with her. I must admit I spent many hours debating the possibility of injecting a fatal dose of opiates into her feeding tube to end her misery. The only thing that stopped me was the cowardly fear that I would get caught and be sentenced to life for murder. Maybe Sammy did not respond to my visits because she was angry at my betrayal. Surely she would have risked everything to save me from a similar fate of perpetual torture.

After that last visit, the CSC lawyers came to the legal conclusion that Sammy's adopted family should make all the decisions regarding her life. Maybe the authorities realized how easy it would be for me, or any of her friends, to do what would appear to be the humane thing—put her out of her misery. No one would let their dog suffer like this. Or maybe it was just the cruel fate that had followed Sammy her whole life. With the exception of a short visit to the hospital by her brother, her adopted family never visited her while she was in P4W or in the hospital. This did not stop them from ordering the hospital to aggressively keep her alive, in keeping with their religious beliefs. They also made it clear that they did not want anyone, even the Indigenous elders, visiting her until she could be transferred to a long-term care facility in Saskatchewan.

I made a few desperate phone calls to the brother who had visited her briefly, and whom Sammy had spoken of fondly, but he made it crystal clear that the family would not waver in their decision to prohibit any visitors until she was back in Saskatchewan. It was around that time that I learned of a suicide note and some of the circumstances that had preceded her suicide attempt. She had left a note expressing her wishes that Lauren arrange to have her buried in Saskatchewan.

Sometime during that period, I learned that after I had left P4W the relationship Sammy had begun with the young Cree woman from Saskatchewan had resumed. From all accounts it was a tumultuous relationship, which was inevitable given that they were both young, damaged, and trying to make their way within a prison environment. There had been a serious fight. Sammy was put in segregation and her girlfriend was sent to the psychiatric treatment centre in Kingston Penitentiary, where she was to be held until she could be released directly onto the street. I did not know the circumstances of the events other than this very skeletal account.

I don't think very many people thought Sammy would live much longer after her adopted family had cut communication off from all her friends. She was like an emaciated little plant, shrivelling up and dying from lack of moisture and nutrition. But against all odds, six months passed, then a year.

After six months in the halfway house, I was released on full parole to my own apartment a few blocks away. The first night I spent in that apartment, with no furniture, an old, raggedy carpet, layers of frayed wallpaper, and dirty paint, I sat up late into the night, wondering how I could ever be unhappy again. I was free to go out into the street and look up at the stars. I could cook whatever I wanted to eat. I could phone up whoever I wanted. I was as free as a person could be outside of prison.

How quickly we forget the taste of freedom. It didn't take very long before I began to complain about all the mundane things we complain about every day: the heat inside a sweltering apartment, the grind of a nine-to-five job, the late-night noise from the apartment upstairs. But I did not forget Sammy. She lived inside my head every day.

Finally, the phone call that I had been expecting for so long came. Sammy had stayed at Kingston General Hospital until a bed had become available in some long-term care facility her parents had chosen for her in Saskatchewan. Sammy died on the plane not long after it entered the air space over Saskatchewan.

PART III
THE MORE THINGS CHANGE, THE MORE THEY STAY THE SAME, 1990–2006

"While the settler or policeman has the right the livelong day to strike the native, to insult him and to make him crawl to him, you will see the native reaching for his knife at the slightest hostile or aggressive glance cast on him by another native, for the last resort of the native is to defend his personality vis-à-vis his brother."

Frantz Fanon

Twenty

Seven women committed suicide in P4W in the two years between December 1988 and February 1991—an astonishing number, considering P4W's population hovered around 140 women during that period; astonishing, because six of the seven women were Indigenous; astonishing enough to be referred to in prison literature as a "cluster." In contrast, only one woman had committed suicide in P4W during the fifteen years between 1959 and 1975, and then three more in the ten years between 1977 and 1988.[34] All these numbers can make a person forget that these women were mothers, daughters, and wives.

Marlene Moore, the first of the seven women in the 1988–91 cluster, was the only woman to commit suicide during this period who was not Indigenous. She was infamous for being the first Canadian woman classified as a "dangerous offender," and equally infamous for the roughly one thousand slash marks all over her body. On December 3, 1988, she hanged herself from her cot in the hospital ward of P4W.

On March 29, 1989, Pat Bear, a twenty-five-year-old Sioux woman, hanged herself from a tree with her shoelaces in a popular waterfront park a few blocks from P4W. She had just been released two months before her expiry date so she could go to a treatment centre.[35] Unfortunately, the treatment centre did not have room for her, so she had no place to go and no one to go to. She had not wanted to be released. Whenever I thought of Pat's death, the haunting metaphors from "Strange Fruit," Billie Holiday's ode to the lynching of Black people in the southern United States, would plague my mind.

On October 12, 1989, Sandra Sayer was found by a guard during cell count hanging from her bed sheet. She was a twenty-five-year-old Indigenous woman from Calgary who had wanted to do her time closer to home, but the provincial authorities declared she was "too dangerous" and refused the provincial exchange. She only had two more months of time left in P4W.

Marie Ledouxe (Custard), a twenty-seven-year-old Indigenous woman, was visiting her father in the family visiting house inside the P4W compound. She got up sometime during the night of February 16, 1990, put on a nice dress and makeup, and went into the basement and hanged herself. Her father woke up in the morning and found her. Ten days earlier she had been successfully resuscitated from a suicide attempt. She had been very distressed over her request for a provincial exchange being denied.

On Sept 15, 1990, thirty-one-year-old Careen Daigneault from Saskatchewan was found hanging in her cell. She had been in the midst of a spiritual fast along with fifteen other Indigenous women in support of the Mohawks at Oka. The Mohawks were involved in an armed standoff with the Quebec police over their unresolved land claims.

On November 16, 1990, twenty-three-year-old Janice Neudorf, who was known as Johny Bear, was found hanging in her cell. She was cut down and remained in a coma, only to revive with severe brain damage. She lingered on for almost a year and a half before she died on May 12, 1992, in the plane transporting her to a long-term care facility in Saskatchewan.

A twenty-three-year-old Indigenous woman, Lorna Jones, was found hanging in her cell on February 4, 1991. She had been suffering from muscular sclerosis. She was serving a two-year sentence and was scheduled for statutory release in two months.[36]

Within four years of the completion of P4W, the 1938 Archambault Commission had already condemned P4W as "unfit for bears." This would be the first of over fifty government commissions, inquiries, and reports that would condemn the conditions inside P4W before it was finally officially closed in 2000. Despite their repeated calls for P4W's closure, or at least changes in prison conditions, none of these government bodies had the legal authority to close or even force change on P4W.

In 1989, the Commissioner of the CSC commissioned yet another task force to review the CSC's management approach to federally sentenced women. But this time the task force took what was considered an "innovative approach" by involving federally sentenced women in examining the lives and experiences of the women prisoners through surveys, and then helping to develop a plan and guidelines for CSC management. It was considered exceptional at the time to actually consider the thoughts, experiences, and opinions of the prisoners directly. The result was an equally exceptional document, *Creating Choices*, which recognized the oppressive and abusive history faced by Indigenous people, women in particular. *Creating Choices* also recognized that this abusive history continued on into the present day in the form of systemic inequalities and injustices in Canadian society that were in large part responsible for women committing crimes. *Creating Choices* made the important connection between systemic inequality and injustice and crime.

Creating Choices spelled out the values, principles, and core beliefs that the CSC must use as the foundation for any future prisons and programming. "The CSC with the support of communities has the responsibility to create the environment that empowers federally sentenced women to make meaningful and responsible choices in order that they may live with dignity and respect."[37] The task force also recommended the closure of P4W and the construction of regional prisons for women. *Creating Choices* would become a blueprint for the future recommendations of the Louise Arbour Inquiry in 1996, but for now, the federal government was so taken by *Creating Choices* that they mandated the CSC to use it as a template for any future planning and programming in federal women's prisons. As history would confirm, the problem would not be in articulating the problems and solutions, but in their actual implementation.

If anyone truly believed in the authenticity of the CSC's will to make a sea change in women's imprisonment, the events in P4W over the next few years would prove them wrong. In 1991, a year after the decision to implement the recommendations of *Creating Choices*, B range, which had formerly been used as an orientation range, was redesignated a "separation unit" in order to separate and control the movement of the twenty-five women whom the administration had deemed a danger to "the good order of the institution." These women were only permitted security visits with their families, which meant they were separated by glass and could have no physical contact. They also had a separate yard in which they could only exercise when the rest of the population was inside. The "separation unit" was like a prototype for the maximum-security units that would be built in the new millennium.

In 1991, the CSC also began to send women, once again mainly Indigenous women, to the Regional Psychiatric Centre, a forensic mental hospital in Saskatoon, Saskatchewan.

In December 1993, all the women on B range decided to go on a hunger strike after one of the women had her private family visit unexpectedly cancelled after only a couple of hours. But the hunger strike was also about the warden refusing to meet with them, and about some staff, particularly the younger staff, harassing them by announcing dinner with calls for "kibbles and bits" and stomping, banging, and flipping up shams during the night shift. Indigenous women on the range and wings also complained of guards interfering with their prayer bundles, prayer time, and the Sisterhood's grandmother drum.

After two or three days, the prisoners decided to cancel their hunger strike so that another woman's private family visit wouldn't be terminated. Ironically, this incident occurred during a Canadian Association of Elizabeth Fry Societies (CAEFS) meeting with the administration to negotiate the right of B-range prisoners and their families to attend the December 1993 Family Day. The executive director of CAEFS, Kim Pate, encouraged the women to use the official complaints and grievance procedures rather than expressing themselves in ways the staff could use against them by laying institutional charges.[38] Rather than commending Kim Pate's attempt to channel the prisoners' rage into the official legal channels of dissent, the warden advised Kim that she was "inciting" the women. Not long after this veiled threat, when two women tried to put in a group grievance on behalf of the entire B range, they were segregated for "threatening the good order of the institution."

On April 22, 1994, the tension between the prisoners and guards erupted in a fight between a small group of guards and six prisoners. After the prisoners were taken by force to segregation, the guards were debriefed. Some were given sick leave, but all had meetings with other staff to deal with the emotional trauma of the fight on April 22.

The six prisoners were placed in segregation, where a number of women were already serving time for other infractions. They were not debriefed or given an opportunity for counselling. Once in segregation, the prisoners, including those who were already there, expressed their frustration at the guards by yelling, throwing things at them as they passed outside their cells, lighting small fires, and demanding their rights so loudly people thought the segregation unit was vibrating. In retaliation, the guards would not take the prisoners out of their cells for any reason, including lawyers' phone calls, exercise, showers, or visits. The conflict continued to escalate for four more days until finally, on April 26, 1994, the guards called in the Institutional Emergency Response Team (IERT) from Kingston Penitentiary across the road.

The IERT consisted of men dressed in black, wearing plastic helmets with dark visors, high leather boots, gloves, and bulletproof vests. They carried high Plexiglas shields and clubs and had various restraint devices hanging from their belts. They were trained to respond to prison emergencies using tactics that are potentially violent, both physically and psychologically. This was not the first time they had been called in from their home base, conveniently located across the road from P4W. Also for convenience, but even more for dramatic effect, the IERT would arrive via a tunnel running underneath King Street that connects KP to P4W. As soon as the IERT was within earshot, they would begin pounding their shields rhythmically with each step of their knee-high leather boots. The audio effect would be amplified ten times over by the round concrete walls of the long tunnel. By the time they appeared, Darth Vader clones in goose step, the fear factor would also have been amplified tenfold. This tactic clearly had no purpose other than to paralyze its targets with fear.

Once inside the segregation unit, the IERT ordered the women to strip, and when they did not respond, they began systematically going from cell to cell, handcuffing all the women and cutting off their clothing with scissors. This routine call to P4W's segregation unit would have gone unnoticed by anyone in the outside world if they had not videotaped the whole thing, a standard procedure that is still in place today. Why wouldn't they record everything? They had done this sort of thing many times before, as any lifer in P4W could testify. At least every other month there would be some "incident" in segregation that would call for the male IERT to come over and pacify whatever prisoner had reached her last straw. Unfortunately for the CSC, this particular videotaped incident was leaked to *The Fifth Estate*, a popular Canadian investigative television program. If this video had been aired ten years later, it would have gone viral, but in the mid-nineties it just got traction and leaked out all over the place, to newspapers, radio shows, and Parliament.

The public and politicians were shocked to see a grainy, porn-like reality show on primetime showing women being handcuffed and leg shackled after having their clothes cut off with scissors by men in intimidating regalia in the darkness of the women's segregation unit of P4W. At this point the women were either screaming, pleading, or crying, which would be the response of any normal human. But taking into consideration the historically consistent statistic that 80 percent of all women prisoners have been physically or sexually abused, or both, this experience would have resonated traumatically into the very depths of these women's psyches. Off camera, they were subjected to involuntary "cavity" searches, aka vaginal and anal searches, by a female nurse.

In light of the airing of this incident on *The Fifth Estate*, the government felt compelled to set up a public inquiry through which the public could vicariously and officially vent some of their anger. Public inquiries had become the government's go-to method to deal with outrageous human rights abuses that had escaped from the shadows into the public light of day. They appointed Louise Arbour to chair the Commission of Inquiry into Certain Events at the Prison for Women in Kingston. The inquiry would focus on the events surrounding the stripping and shackling of the women prisoners by male guards, the extended and illegal segregation of the women, their involuntary transfer to Kingston Penitentiary, as well as the practical implications of these events in light of the last government inquiry, the 1990 Task Force on Federally Sentenced Women and the ensuing report, *Creating Choices*.

It is at this point in the Canadian history of women's imprisonment that the official narrative usually jumps from the "segregation riot" in 1994, to the 1996 recommendations of the Louise Arbour Inquiry, to the construction of the five regional prisons and the "healing lodge," culminating in the closing of P4W in 2000. The "healing lodge," aka Okimaw Ohci, was built on the Nekaneet First Nation's land in Saskatchewan to address the needs of the vastly overrepresented Indigenous people in the prison system.

This narrative follows the classic story arc of conflict between good and evil, leading to a resolution, and finally culminating in redemption. However, reality is usually much messier, and rarely follows classic story arcs. In the case of Canadian women's imprisonment, the resolution and redemption phases never actually occurred.

Even before Louise Arbour had finished her inquiry and officially reported her recommendations in 1996, the CSC had already embarked on the project of building five new regional prisons for women as well as a "healing lodge" for Indigenous women. The blueprint for these new regional prisons was based on the progressive *Creating Choices* document. The women would live in a minimum-security dynamic environment in bungalows within a static medium-security perimeter. Other than segregation cells, there would be no maximum-security units.

The evidence upon which the CSC based this decision was numerous studies of women's violence. "In the past twenty years," a CSC literature review stated, "violent crimes committed by women have increased slightly relative to violent crimes committed by men, but the disparity between the percentage of violent crimes committed by men and women, is still so significant, that it is safe to say that women prisoners do not pose a serious threat to the public."[39]

The new prisons would stress women-centred programming and vocational training that would address what prison reformers considered the root causes of their criminality—that is, a lack of job skills and education, as well as all the collateral damage experienced by those with histories of sexual and physical abuse. Only time would reveal what prison abolitionists continued to warn reformers: that unemployment and class-based educational standards are systemic features of capitalism that cannot be eliminated without abolishing capitalism itself.

Louise Arbour's recommendations reinforced her belief in the necessity for a paradigm shift in penal philosophy. She mused bitterly over the fact that serious human rights violations had taken place four years after the CSC had decided to implement the reforms listed in the *Creating Choices* document in 1990. She slammed the fact that women in segregation had no access to lawyers in the week following the so-called "riot," and did not have any exercise for a month. Six of the women from segregation were involuntarily taken over to Kingston Penitentiary's treatment centre, but the remaining women spent eight months in segregation without bedding, clothing, writing materials, exercise, or family contact. She concluded that "once again, it seems that even if the law is known, there is a general perception that it can always be departed from for a valid reason, and that, in any event compliance with prisoners' rights is not a priority. At best, denial of exercise can be attributed here to inadequate staffing. More realistically, it was part of a general punitive attitude which required inmates to earn entitlements to everything perceived as a privilege, rather than a right."[40] Arbour also pointed out that in the hours and days after the initial "segregation riot," staff had access to counselling, time off from work, and debriefing sessions with other staff, while the prisoners involved had no way of dealing with the stress and consequences of the same events, other than screaming and throwing things at the guards.

In the end, Louise Arbour recommended many of the same policies and actions that were already being implemented after the *Creating Choices* document was submitted to Parliament in 1990. Her 1996 recommendations validated and gave justification for the new architecture, programming, and philosophy upon which the new regional prisons for women were being built.

The Arbour Inquiry was the final death knell for P4W. It was scheduled to close in 2000. Meanwhile, some of the new regional prisons for women had opened in Edmonton and Nova Scotia in 1995. A few months later, Okimaw Ohci, the "healing lodge," was also opened. All three prisons opened a year before Arbour's recommendations were made public.

Nova and Okimaw Ohci opened without incident. But when the first group of federally sentenced women was moved into the new Edmonton regional prison in 1995, the perimeter wall was not completely finished. Predictably, seven women escaped over the low, uncompleted wall. At the same time, the warden's unwavering enforcement of the new protective custody integration model led to the unprecedented murder of one prisoner by another. During the murder trial, it was revealed that this murder could easily have been avoided had the administration heeded the warnings of both the perpetrator and the victim. The perpetrator's motive for murder became apparent to the public during her trial, when her victim's lawyer revealed that his now-deceased client had testified against the accused in another case before they were imprisoned together in the same living area of the Edmonton prison.

Anyone who works or has lived in a prison, including the warden, knows article one of the prisoner code: a person who testifies against another in court is considered "a rat." This code is not unique to prisoners. However, the warden would not budge on implementing the new protective custody integration policy and refused to follow the previous custody standard, under which the two women would have been placed in separate living areas.

The escapes and murder in the Edmonton prison, as well as the 1994 P4W "segregation riot," were used to mythologize the violence of female prisoners in order to justify the construction of separate maximum-security units inside the compound of each new regional federal prison for women. For approximately $25 million more, the CSC quickly drew up plans for small, self-contained maximum-security units in each prison compound with the capacity to hold a total of approximately twenty women in three pods, plus a separate segregation unit. The maximum-security units ran counter to, and had never been part of, any of the recommendations made by either the *Creating Choices* document or Louise Arbour's 1996 Inquiry.

If a man is convicted of murder in Ontario, he will do his first two years in the Millhaven maximum-security penitentiary, where he will have access to apprenticeship programs in the trades, his own cell in a general population of roughly four hundred other men, access to a large outdoor exercise yard with a track and basketball courts, weight room, and various sports teams, a school that offers upgrading and university courses through correspondence, and a variety of spiritual services. The government stopped providing free university correspondence courses to prisoners during the 1980s.

For the same crime, a woman must spend the first two years of her sentence as a maximum-security prisoner in the maximum-security units, without contact with any other prisoners than the other four women in her pod, regardless of the circumstances or how much risk she poses to society. Most of the women lifers were doing time for murdering a family member or husband or boyfriend who had a well-documented history of abusing them.

In 1990, a landmark decision by the Supreme Court of Canada, *R. v. Lavallee*, allowed women who had been physically and emotionally abused for long periods of time to use self-defence as a mitigating factor in cases where they had murdered their spouse or in sentencing. This became known as the battered wife defence. A few of the women in P4W serving time for having murdered their abusive spouses had their sentences reduced on appeal using the Lavallee precedent.[41] Despite the Lavallee precedent, there are still many women doing life sentences for what most people would consider acts of self-defence.

There are six maximum-security prisons for men, much like Millhaven, across Canada, whereas there are no maximum-security prisons for women.[42] Today every federal prison for women, except the Okimaw Ohci "healing lodge," is a multi-security prison with a tiny, isolated, maximum-security unit inside each compound. These women's maximum-security units resemble the only men's special handling unit (SHU) more than they do any of the many male maximum-security prisons across the country. The ninety-bed SHU for men at Sainte-Anne-des-Plaines is a super-max, as are the women's units in everything except name.

However, until these maximum-security units could be completed, the CSC had quietly transferred a small group of women into four maximum-security isolation units inside four men's federal prisons starting in 1994, shortly after the airing of the video footage of the riot squad cutting off the clothes of the segregated women prisoners in P4W. Most of these women were Indigenous.

These isolation units were essentially a section of a men's range that had been segregated from the rest of the prison. The women had no programming and were basically being held in long-term segregation conditions. Whenever women had to be moved outside the isolation units to the visiting area, to exercise in the gym or yard, or to the health unit, the men in general population would be locked.

The conditions inside these isolation units were reminiscent of the infirmary and the north block inside the Kingston Prison for men, where the first Canadian women prisoners were held for ninety years, from 1844 until the Prison for Women was completed in 1934. In a case of back to the future, women in the isolation units had more in common with their counterparts during the nineteenth century than they did their contemporaries in the twenty-first century.

They remained largely invisible to the Canadian public until the Elizabeth Fry Society in Saskatchewan filed a complaint regarding discriminatory prison conditions for federally sentenced women with the Canadian Human Rights Commission in 2001. This complaint was filed on behalf of all the women in the isolation units, but concentrated on the case of an Indigenous woman who had already been in P4W's segregation unit for over a year before the IERT "incident" on April 27, 1994. This woman went on to spend nine more years segregated in men's prisons in Saskatchewan until 2003, but still remains in a federal prison to this day, November 2017.

By 2002, CAEFS had enlisted sixteen national equality-seeking women's organizations to add their voices to their human rights complaint that Canada and the CSC were guilty of systemic discrimination against female prisoners.

In February 2003, three Indigenous women prisoners being held in the isolation unit inside Springhill, the men's federal prison in Nova Scotia, initiated a hunger strike in order to be allowed to attend sweat lodge ceremonies and to have access to programming to have their security levels dropped so they could be transferred back to a women's prison. Springhill, as well as other Canadian prisons, had transformed the right of Indigenous prisoners to engage in their spiritual practices into a privilege that had to be earned through good behaviour. By linking Indigenous prisoners' right to participate in their traditional spiritual practices with good behaviour, the CSC was denying them their Charter right to freedom of religion. Even though most Indigenous peoples do not describe their traditional spiritual practices as a "religion," the "Canadian Charter of Rights and Freedoms and the United Declaration of the Rights of Indigenous Peoples include legal protections for the fundamental right of Indigenous peoples to freely practice their religious and spiritual traditions and to be treated equally and with dignity."[43]

By May 2003, the human rights complainant—the Indigenous woman who had already endured fifteen years under some form of segregated maximum-security imprisonment—was transferred from the Psychiatric Treatment Centre in Saskatoon to the completed maximum-security unit in the Edmonton regional prison for women. Unfortunately, her story of long-term segregation would not be unusual.

In December 2003, the Canadian Human Rights Commission published their report *Protecting Their Rights*, which listed a number of human rights violations and made numerous recommendations to eliminate discriminatory prison conditions for federally sentenced women. These included recommendations to rescind the CSC policy of condemning all lifers with first- and second-degree murder sentences to a mandatory minimum two years in a maximum-security setting; that the CSC should implement a pilot needle exchange program for women by June 2004; that an independent adjudicator should oversee decisions regarding long-term segregation; and too many more recommendations to list here.

Conveniently, the CSC was almost finished constructing the maximum-security units in the four regional women's prisons, Nova, Joliette, Grand Valley, and Edmonton, by the time the CHRC report was published. The regional prison for women in BC, the Fraser Valley Institute for Women, was not yet completed, but would also eventually have a maximum-security unit. The Okimaw Ohci "healing lodge" was the only federal prison for women not to get a maximum-security unit. The women imprisoned in the isolation units in the men's prisons were transferred into the various maximum-security units across the country.

Despite the recommendations from the *Creating Choices* document, the Arbour Inquiry, and the CHRC, the CSC continued to follow the beat of its own drum. Women continued to be imprisoned in maximum-security settings that were much more restrictive, with less movement and programming opportunities, than their male counterparts. A needle exchange pilot project was never implemented. Male guards continued to patrol the women's living units, and long-term segregation continued unabated. In its characteristic manner, the CSC would pay homage to the various recommendations made by outside inquiring bodies but would carry on with the same policies and actions that had sparked the inquiries in the first place, much like a snake sheds its skin only to emerge as the same snake in a new skin.

I was reminded of this pattern in 2003, when I was working with a collective of ex-prisoners from P4W, Womyn4justice, who were asked by CAEFS to testify before the CHRC about our "lived experiences" in prison. This political engagement was exciting because it signalled the first time I began working with other prisoners in an open activist capacity. In prison, the vast majority of women were not overtly political, probably because the repercussions were so extreme—dynamics that reflected those outside the walls. The few activists I did encounter tended to be reformist. The longer I remained in prison, the more I witnessed the results of reform disappearing before our very eyes as the CSC quickly transformed whatever progressive reform had been adopted back into its repressive default position, once again reflecting the dynamics of reform outside the walls.

In the years since I had first been arrested, my political identity had not been altered or destroyed, but rather had assumed a backstage role to my prisoner identity in order to adapt to the concrete social conditions in the various prisons I found myself. It's not always possible to assume the same political tactics and strategy in each social situation in which a person finds themselves over the years. There are also times a person will go through personal transitions, but neither of these situations imply that a person has lost their political identity.

There are many paths leading to the mountaintop, and so when a person is confronted with an insurmountable obstacle blocking their way, it might be necessary to take a different path, or sometimes a person must stop and rest before they can go on. But as long as they never lose sight of the mountaintop, it will remain their guiding beacon no matter what kind of adverse conditions or detours they may face along the way.

Twenty One

I became increasingly aware that my life was following a circular, or perhaps more accurately, a circuitous path—the same path that the cycles of reform and repression were taking in the larger political landscape. Even before I had been transferred to the minimum-security "house" in 1990, political events outside the prison walls were causing a seismic shift in the prison landscape.

During the 1980s, the neoliberalism that had started with the presidency of Ronald Reagan had not yet had an impact on the Canadian prison landscape. But for those who believed you could see the future by looking to the South as though into a crystal ball, it was clear that the prison industrial complex would eventually hit Canada. Canada had a history of trailing along behind the United States in terms of political and economic developments, like a small boat riding every dip and swell in the wake of the mother ship.

By 2003, the changes brought on by the advent of neoliberalism were becoming apparent within the Canadian women's prison system. Even the term "prison industrial complex," which had seemed so uniquely American, could now be used to describe the prison system throughout North America.

My political activism was coming full circle. I had first become politically active when I helped organize Prisoners' Justice Day in Toronto in 1980. Twenty-three years later, I was out of prison on full parole and had begun a personal catharsis by helping to organize Prisoners' Justice Day in 2002 with Womyn4justice. We organized a screening of the iconic film *P4W*, the same film that had dispelled my fears of what prisoners and prison would be like so many years ago.

I was fortunate in having spent my seven years of federal imprisonment in P4W in the aftermath of the prison reform movement of the

1970s, before the Harper Conservatives began its inevitable dismantlement in the new millennium. I had learned enough skills in the industrial woodworking shop to get a job at a commercial cabinet shop in Kingston almost immediately upon my release on day parole. I had been able to update those skills at the Freedom Farm during my daily work releases from the minimum-security house, and had earned enough money to buy a used car. Without this car, it would have been difficult to work in Kingston Township, which was very poorly serviced by public transportation in the early nineties. The six months I lived in the Kingston Elizabeth Fry halfway house also gave me the opportunity to save up enough money for a rent deposit on an apartment, which I moved into in the spring of 1991 after I was released on full parole.

My release coincided with a sea change within the Canadian women's prison system. In the same year that I was released on full parole, P4W's B range was transformed into an isolated maximum-security unit. An area that had been an orientation range was now a repressive control unit. Since 1991, this pattern of isolating women in long-term maximum-security settings has continued unabated right up until today. If the original point of isolating women who are supposedly dangerous was to create a safer environment, then this practice is a failure. This pattern of long-term isolation in small maximum-security units has coincided with a growing number of violent incidents involving prisoners attacking staff, other prisoners, and even themselves.[44] There is no evidence to support the view that isolating people in maximum-security conditions makes them kinder, gentler, or better equipped to be reintegrated back into society.

Even though I had benefited from the prison reforms of the seventies and early eighties, my life did not follow the uplifting trajectory that would make telling this story much simpler. I have never felt that I personally suffered in prison. I was shielded from so many abusive situations by my privileged position. But despite this privileged shield, I was still afflicted with the dark shadows and angst that I believe every prisoner carries around within them even after their release.

All these situations led me to a point where I was not surprised to find the morphine a friend in the halfway house offered me incredibly seductive. But I don't think my seduction was simply a matter of the morphine obliterating my psychic pain, because I don't think I was experiencing any more pain than so many others experience. My attraction to opiates stemmed from a combination of morphine's renowned pain-relieving qualities with the fact that opiates simply made me feel extraordinarily good.

In my case, the opiate family of drugs seemed to counteract perfectly the negative aspects of my natural brain chemistry, at least in the beginning. I was normally a very hyperactive and tense person who felt a little stressed around other people. Opiates took just enough of the edge off my anxiety and stress levels to make me feel like a confident, relaxed, yet energetic superhero who viewed the world through rose-tinted glasses. To put it simply, I could have lived contentedly in a Dumpster if I had enough opiates. But as any addict knows, once the honeymoon phase ends—and it always does—the superhero with the rose-tinted glasses always deserts you. All you are left with is the struggle to feel normal every day. I became an addict.

Becoming an addict does not happen overnight. Everyone has their own unique pattern of addiction. Some people can accelerate from using their drug of choice for the first time to using every day within a twenty-four-hour period. It took me a couple of years to become a full-blown, three-times-a-day user. I discovered heroin was even better than morphine, and at the time, easier to get. For several years I lived in a delusional world in which I justified using heroin with the argument that it was no worse than drinking beer on a Friday or Saturday night. Some people drank … I preferred junk.

For the first few years I managed to maintain a normal life. I met my partner at my first job in the kitchen cabinetry business in Kingston Township. A year later we teamed up to start our own commercial cabinetry business. It didn't take long before we were able to buy a small farm with some horses, dogs, and chickens. Even though I appeared to be living in my own personal nirvana on a farm, I was using three times a day, a habit I financed through working long hours and weekends in our shop. I could barely stop myself from driving straight into those concrete overpass supports on the 401 as I drove into work every morning.

I can testify from this experience that reality exists inside the mind, not outside it. I was actually living the most hellish experience I could imagine. I could not make it through the day without three shots of heroin. Despite waking up every morning to the singing of birds and the sight of intense lime and hunter green sunlight filtering through the maple trees, all I could see were shades of grey, and all I could hear were voices whispering to me that I should just kill myself, and everybody would be the better off for it.

For many years, I tried everything in the book to quit. I went to several treatment centres, thinking they would cure me like a miracle. But within days I was using again. I took counselling and learned the techniques involved in cognitive behavioural therapy. I tried tapering at a beautiful provincial park, but as soon as the drugs wore off I went speeding home to get some relief from the nausea, anxiety, and sickness.

I am convinced that I would have died from my addiction if methadone maintenance programs had not become widely available in 1996, when Ontario embraced the harm reduction model of dealing with addictions. Essentially methadone takes away the symptoms of withdrawal and the craving for opiates, but it still takes a lot of hard work to completely overcome an addiction. In my experience, the methadone program combined with counselling is the most effective treatment program available for opiate addiction, and the closest thing to a miracle I had ever experienced.

Once I was stabilized on the methadone program, I felt much happier, but I still felt like I was white-knuckling it through my daily life, grasping the steering wheel in a desperate attempt just to stay on track and avoid being sucked back into that black hole of addiction and depression. In a less metaphorical expression, I needed to find meaning and purpose in my life again.

Part two of my recovery started when I got together with Womyn-4justice to organize our first Prisoners' Justice Day in 2002. Working with my comrades from P4W on a political project created an opening for my repressed political identity to re-emerge and take centre stage in my life again. We continued to organize film nights and public-awareness campaigns, and embarked on a long-term project of raising money to start a Transition House for women just getting out of prison.

As long as I can remember, I have always had a strong political identity. Embracing my political identity helped me find meaning and purpose in life again. I felt less vulnerable to that soul-destroying depression that I could still feel lurking just under the surface.

I began to see parallels between using the strategy of harm reduction in the struggle to overcome addiction and the strategy of using political reforms to abolish prisons. Old-school addiction activists argue that there are only two options: to be or not to be an addict. They argue that harm reduction programs such as needle exchanges and methadone programs only facilitate addiction. They argue that addiction should be treated as a lifestyle choice and should be criminalized and punished. The criminal justice system, they believe, is the only effective deterrent and cure for addiction.

The one thing harm reduction activists share with their old-school counterparts is the goal of eradicating addiction from society. But instead of treating addiction as a lifestyle choice that should be criminalized, harm reduction activists argue that addiction should be treated as a chronic health issue that will involve a long road to recovery. The role of harm reduction activists is to make that road less debilitating so recovering addicts can lead meaningful and socially useful lives, even while in recovery.

For many addiction activists, years of working on the frontlines in the war on drugs had proven that punishing addicts was a failed policy. It is impossible to talk about harm reduction policies and the war on drugs without mentioning the election of Ronald Reagan during the 1980s, and the fallout from his war on drugs. Reagan's election represented a paradigm shift in economic and political policy that became known as neoliberalism, or more colloquially, Reaganomics.

One of the major policy platforms of neoliberalism is the implementation of law-and-order policies to deal with crime: mandatory minimum sentencing laws, three-strike laws, and laws reducing parole and early release time. One of the consequences of these policies was the quadrupling of the prison population in the US between 1980 and 2003.[45] Even though many studies have proven that increased prison sentences do not reduce crime rates, politicians championed these policies because appealing to the public's fear of criminals is a tried and true method for getting elected.

Ironically, since 1980, three quarters of new admissions to prison are not the violent prisoners who are the object of the politicians' fear mongering, but rather non-violent criminals convicted of drug offences. The number of people imprisoned for drug offences has increased twelve times since 1980, until they now make up half the prison population.[46] Not only has the war on drugs had a dramatic impact on the prison population, it has also given a huge boost to the expenditures of the criminal justice system. From 1982 to 2006, police expenditures increased 420 percent, corrections expenditures increased 660 percent, and judiciary expenditures increased 503 percent.[47] The costs of the criminal justice system have spiked until many cities in California and Texas have had no choice but to declare bankruptcy and rethink their law-and-order agendas. The war on drugs may not have put a dent in the distribution of illegal drugs, but it sure has been good for the expansion of the prison industrial complex.

There has been a steady drop in Canada's crime rate since 1991.[48] There are many theorists trying to take credit for this phenomenon, including everyone from tough-on-crime advocates to demographers. Of course, the cause of any phenomenon as complicated as dropping crime rates is not singular, but the argument coming from the methadone maintenance advocates is the strongest considering the leading role that opiate addiction has historically played in criminal activity. The synchronicity between the slow downward slide of crime rates and the legalization of and popular access to methadone maintenance programs during the nineties is not a coincidence. Thousands of addicts no longer had to do B&E's or robberies, turn tricks, or take part in some other risky business to support their habit. Embracing harm reduction policies has contributed to the reduction in crime rates and in the cost of the criminal justice system, as well as in the spread of sexually transmitted diseases, AIDS, HIV, and hepatitis C.[49]

Using the harm reduction model as a metaphor, I began to see that the struggle to abolish prisons did not have to be an either-or proposition. Prison reforms could contribute toward revolutionary change as long as the activists kept their "eyes on the prize," and as long as the "prize" remained creating revolutionary change, not just prisons that are nicer places to live.

The concept of applying the harm reduction model to seemingly reformist political projects is not new. In the late sixties, the health clinics and breakfast programs that the Black Panthers ran in the ghettos were referred to as "survival pending revolution."[50]

Throughout my political activist career I had witnessed the traditional conflict between prison reformists and abolitionists. Both abolitionists and reformists believe prisons are a social control mechanism for capitalism, but abolitionists typically view capitalism and prisons as systemically destructive, and therefore can only be abolished through revolutionary change. Prison reformists believe capitalism and prisons are essential but need to be improved, something that can be accomplished through the existing parliamentary process.

This conflict is presented as a dichotomy between two contradictory arguments. Prison abolitionists are often portrayed as revolutionary anti-capitalists, while prison reformists are portrayed as liberal parliamentarians. I had always remained steadfastly in the prison abolition camp until I experienced the harm reduction model of coping with addictions and began to see the argument for revolutionary versus reformist change in a less black-and-white perspective. Without getting into a long drawn-out analysis of capitalism, revolution, and the state of modern democracy, I realized that this conflict between abolishing and reforming prisons is rooted in a false dichotomy.

Like the harm reduction struggle to eliminate addiction, the struggle to abolish prisons and capitalism is a long-term struggle. Prisons are a social control mechanism for capitalism, and as such capitalism could not exist without them. If you flip the equation around, capitalism is an economic system based on systemic inequality, injustice, and racism, and as such prisons would not be needed if capitalism did not exist. Unfortunately, throughout history many other political economic systems have also institutionalized inequality, injustice, and racism, and hence the history of prisons across the globe both in time and space.

Like harm reduction activists, prison abolitionists can campaign for concrete reforms that can improve prison conditions to alleviate the suffering of real people now. As long as these campaigns are focused on ultimately abolishing prisons, as opposed to simply making them nicer places to be confined, they will contribute to revolutionary change.

I continued to work with Womyn4justice from 2002 to 2006. Our mission was to empower women prisoners and show society through consciousness-raising events that the vast majority of prisoners were the scapegoats for so much of what is wrong with our society.

Our long-term project was to establish a Transition House for women getting out of prison that would be run by ex-prisoners. We had to have a constitution in order to apply for funding. One of the main principles embedded in our constitution was the stipulation that the Board of Directors and employees of the Transition House must always be composed of a majority of women ex-prisoners. The premise for our plan was that ex-prisoners would be the experts in creating housing, work, and treatment programs for other prisoners.

On the main floor of the Transition House there would be a bookstore/café where the women could work, and on the other floors would be apartments for the women getting out of prison who did not qualify for halfway houses or other housing. We wanted to create a safe place where women who had fallen through the cracks could live.

It was a good plan, until it was derailed by a sharp turn in the road that took me back to prison again.

PART IV
TAKE THE LONG WAY HOME, 2006

"The Panopticon is a type of prison building designed by English philosopher Jeremy Bentham in 1785. The concept of the design is to allow an observer to observe (opticon) all (pan) prisoners without the prisoners being able to tell whether they are being watched, thereby conveying what one architect has called the 'sentiment of an invisible omniscience.'"

Silke Berit Lang, *The Impact of Video Systems on Architecture* (dissertation, Swiss Federal Institute of Technology, 2004).

Twenty Two

In the fifteen years since I had been officially released on full parole, life's journey had taken me down many roads, both good and bad. But none had been as sharp and dangerous as the one my friend Henry and I turned down just before midnight on June 21, 2006.

We were on our way home after visiting some friends when a spectacular light show of silent heat lightning began flashing across the eastern sky. Between trying to watch this spectacle and trying to avoid running over any little critters crossing the road, we were already travelling at a snail's pace when we came to a ninety-degree turn just before reaching the only intersection in the small town of Yarker. As we executed this turn, we noticed a man standing in the middle of the intersection waving a red light back and forth. We were past the point of no return when we realized he was a cop.

The sight of the cop triggered a series of red flags in my mind. Suddenly the innocent bag of garbage in the back of the van that our friends had asked us to dispose of was no longer so innocent. I could smell the decaying marijuana leaves that they had warned us were interspersed among the fluffy dog hair and dust balls. I was also reminded of my life sentence and parole status, which made even a minor offense major.

Why was I so careless? Our friends were paranoid about throwing out their marijuana garbage in their neighbourhood, even in the country, so I had volunteered to throw it out on the way home. My only real concern had been whether it was organic!

"Start smoking!" I hissed at Henry, as I fumbled for a cigarette in a desperate bid to camouflage the odour.

It's amazing how many thoughts can pass through one's mind in a matter of seconds. I had always assumed that the cops would never pull you over if your car was in perfect working order and you weren't breaking any rules of the road. How could I have overlooked the RIDE programs so popular these days? RIDE (Reduce Impaired Driving Everywhere) was essentially a roadblock set up by the cops to catch unsuspecting intoxicated drivers. Tuesday night in the middle of an isolated two-horse town was not the usual focus of RIDE programs. But now that I thought of it, a friend of ours had run into just such a RIDE program not so long ago, in the middle of the afternoon down an isolated gravel road a few hundred yards from a rural golf tournament. I should have known better.

Another possibility for this improbable road check also crossed my mind. Only a week earlier my parole officer had warned me not to go to a fundraising dinner being organized by a local group fighting the use of "Security Certificates," which were used to detain and deport immigrants. Apparently the Canadian Security and Intelligence Service (CSIS) had this group under surveillance because the main targets of the "Security Certificates" were Muslim Arabs. Ever since 9/11 and the war in Iraq, Muslim Arabs had become the modern-day counterpart of the communist bogeymen of the fifties.

In an infamous statement made during a press conference with French president Jacques Chirac in November 2001, US president George W. Bush had said, "You're either with us or against us in the fight against terror." I took it that the "us" was meant to refer to all those who valued American capitalism. I would be considered "against us" in light of my anti-capitalist and anti-imperialist views. I found myself more often than not being viewed by the authorities as the leopard that will never lose its spots. It seemed all too possible that this roadblock had been set up as a ruse by CSIS to search my vehicle in case I was involved with "those Muslim terrorists" in some way.

Unfortunately, the billowing clouds of tobacco smoke did not win out over the pungent odour of pot. "Smells like pot in there," said the cop, after motioning for me to roll down my driver's side window.

Now that he had the smell as evidence, he asked me to step out and open the back of the van, where a large plastic Tupperware container sat suspiciously alone. It contained two garbage bags, which he asked me to open. After I had opened the one filled with miscellaneous car fluids, I acted as though we should both be satisfied, and was about to shut the van door again when he pointed at the other garbage bag. "And what about that one?" Looking a little irritably at him, I untied the knot on the other bag, and a handful of dry marijuana stalks popped up as though they had just been waiting for someone to liberate them from their hunched-over position inside the bag. I could practically hear the keys clanging as my cell door shut.

He smiled at me with a look of satisfaction and reassured me that he knew exactly what those plants were because he had just been transferred over from the drug squad. Even though I was still feeling relatively calm, he warned me not to "get too excited because this really isn't a big deal." Obviously he didn't know about my record yet. In no time a couple of other cop cars arrived, and we were taken in separate vehicles to the Napanee police station. All the way I clung to the naive hope that once we got there I would be released.

As soon as we were inside the police station, I was strip searched in a manner that would become routine over the next few months, and fingerprinted. Then I was given an asbestos gown, known as a "baby doll" in prison slang, and a blanket, and locked up in a freshly painted cell with a cement slab, stainless steel toilet, and thin mattress. I was surprisingly relaxed, which I attributed to a rather fatalistic attitude. Obviously they had run our IDs through the Canadian Police Information Centre.

A couple of hours passed before a female cop escorted me out to the front, where they handed me a charge sheet for possession of over thirty grams of pot. At this point feelings of outrage began to well up in me, because our friends had reassured us that the garbage bag only contained some old marijuana debris that they were paranoid about throwing out in their neighbourhood. I found out later that the charge sheet stated we were in possession of two pounds of pot based on the weight of the entire garbage bag of debris, which also contained some dried-up marijuana stalks. Apparently the cops phoned Parole Services in the wee hours of the morning, and once they heard that I had been in possession of "two pounds of marijuana," they decided I should be detained in the Quinte Detention Centre. Henry was released a few hours later and personally driven home by the cop who had arrested us.

On our drive to Quinte, I resigned myself to going the long way home. Just how long was another question. Coincidentally, my parole officer had just recently reminded me that any lifer who is convicted of a crime while on parole will have their parole revoked until they have gone through many years of the protracted release procedure. This means applying to the parole board for escorted passes, then unescorted passes, then day parole, and finally full parole. Since each application can take at least a year, going through the whole release procedure could take anywhere up to five years, depending on the seriousness of the crime.

The eastern sky was still black when we pulled off the 401 into the industrial "park" area where the Quinte Detention Centre is situated. The only aspect of the drab brick one-storey complex that differentiated it from the rest of the area architecture was an eight-metre chain-link fence topped with coils of razor wire and bright floodlights illuminating every nook and cranny. The nondescript building could just as easily have been an old slaughterhouse.

Quinte is a provincial prison both figuratively and literally speaking. It is a stagnant backwater of mainstream society, on the margins of a small town. The province uses the small number of women in Quinte as an excuse for not allocating any money for programming or education, creating a perfect specimen of human warehousing. It has remained invisible since it was built in 1971, overlooked even by the major prison reform movements of today, like so many small-town detention centres. Thirty-five years of invisibility and lack of oversight have had their trickle-down effect on Quinte, resulting in a prison population in a constant state of conflict and tension. Increasingly in the twenty-first century, these relatively small provincial prisons are becoming extinct as they are amalgamated into super-jails housing well over a thousand prisoners.

We waited in front of an electronically controlled chain-link gate until a sound like a broken buzzer warned us the gate was opening. There was no sign of life other than a black cat running across the lane in front of us toward some Dumpsters silhouetted against the floodlit parking lot in the back of the building. This dark omen left me with a sense of dread, despite my usual dismissive attitude toward superstitions.

The back entrance led into the admittance and discharge area, where a female guard took control over me. She strip searched me and gave me a one-size-fits-all dark green sweatsuit and a pair of shoelace-free running shoes that all the female prisoners wore, then left me in a segregation cell for the rest of the night. I positioned myself carefully on the thin plastic mattress so as not to touch the grimy cinderblock wall decorated with grim graffiti messages etched into the paint. Oddly, I felt nothing.

I woke up dead tired to the sound of a voice asking me through the meal slot if I wanted to go out to yard and have a shower. At the same time, a pair of latex-gloved hands slid a tray with two hardboiled eggs, a container of orange juice, and a coffee through the slot in my door. I declined the offer of exercise and a shower, but forced myself to eat the eggs in the hope that they might pick up my spirits.

A few hours later a female guard unlocked my door and took me to the women's unit. We walked through a maze of old corridors constructed of cinderblock walls and poured concrete floors. The walls and floors were covered in different shades of washed-out green and grey paint. There were no windows, photographs, plants, or furniture to break up the visual monotony or to absorb the sounds of voices that seemed to echo down the corridors from what sounded like miles away.

I guessed by the age of the coffee stains on the floors and the grime and dirt everywhere that Quinte did not employ prisoners or staff as institutional janitors. Along the way, we passed a number of men dressed in orange jumpsuits accompanied by guards. Some of the men walked stiffly, like junkyard dogs, bristling with anger and generating machismo like electricity, while others shuffled lazily past with indolent expressions on their faces, baiting the guards with their lackadaisical attitude. Sometimes the men would catch my eye with fleeting glances, but the guards looked through me as though I were invisible.

To get into the women's unit, we had to ring a buzzer and wait for another female guard to escort me. We passed through a warren of segregation and protective custody cells, and then a short corridor with a so-called "women's dorm," laundry room, tiny library, legal visiting room, and guard's office. The guard's office was separated from the women's common room by a Plexiglas wall, through which they could watch the women like chimpanzees in a zoo.

At ten square metres, the common room was surprisingly small for a place where twenty-five women were supposed to spend most of their days and evenings. Like the rest of the prison, it was constructed of cinderblock walls and poured concrete floors, with two metal picnic tables bolted into the floor and a small television hanging from the ceiling. If there wasn't enough room for the women to sit around the picnic tables, they could walk around in small circles.

There were six cells opening up onto a corridor that ran off the common room. I learned that the place is almost always filled beyond capacity, so most cells house three women at any given time. In order to accommodate this number of women, half the population gets out into the common room for an hour, while the rest stay locked in their cells. So the population alternates in hourly shifts between staying locked in their cells and then hanging around in the common room. The whole women's population is only together when the yard is open for the daily hour exercise period.

In every prison a person's reputation precedes them, but in Quinte this was truer than most. As I walked through the electronic barrier into the common room, most of the women in the room already knew the facts in my file that were relevant to them—that is, I was a federal prisoner, in on a parole suspension. This information is either gleaned through the prisoners' grapevine or from the guards. They had even learned that my file had me tagged as a "terrorist." Some people might think these facts would be negative, but within the prison subculture they gave me a certain amount of respectability. They meant I had done time, and could quite possibly be violent and dangerous. Although that would have been to my advantage, I'm sure my attitude and demeanour made that possibility questionable.

Almost immediately a Kingston woman offered me some shampoo and conditioner from her canteen as a token of friendship. I accepted her offer, and then we hunkered down at one of the picnic tables to exchange notes on the street. Once she had established that I knew many of the same people she did, she gave me the green light with her friends on the unit. Not everyone is so lucky. As time went on, I saw women walk through those same doors for the first time and immediately be shut down as "PCs," or protective custody cases, "goofs," "rats," or some other untouchable class of prisoner. It all depended on your reputation on the street. If you didn't have one, then you would generally be left alone until you had proven yourself one way or another.

An hour after I had arrived on the unit, a guard emerged from the office and locked us all in our cells for lunch. Inside my cell I was surprised to see a bunk bed with two women already in it and a thin plastic mattress underneath, which I assumed was my "bed." It was a typical three-by-four-metre cell, with three women crammed inside like sardines in a can. Besides the bunk bed, there was a stainless steel toilet and a small sink, and a long metal table to which were bolted two metal swivel seats.

When the metal meal cart arrived with two latex-gloved guards to slide the food trays through the meal slot, one prisoner got off the top bunk in order to get her tray by using the toilet bowl as a stepladder. And when the toilet was being used for its real purpose, the only thing separating it from the prying eyes of the guards was a metre-high "privacy wall." This wouldn't have been so bad if there hadn't been male guards doing rounds. This took me by surprise as, back in the day in P4W, male guards had only been used in emergencies and in areas outside the so-called living units.

I took my plastic meal tray and forced myself, once again, to eat the food. This time it was fried baloney with mysterious embedded black sediment from the grill and instant potatoes, with a rotting orange for desert. The other women reassured me that this was good food, as prison fare goes, because in the other provincial prisons the food was prepared at the Maplehurst super-jail in Milton, then frozen and shipped out to the other provincial super-jails, where it was reheated and served. Quinte was the only provincial prison left in which the food was "homemade," prepared the same day by the minimum-security men in the kitchen. After lunch I shimmied down onto my mattress under the bunk bed, and prayed that no matter what happened I wouldn't be spending more than a month in this place.

Twenty Three

By 2006 both the provincial and federal prison systems had implemented methadone programs for opiate addicts. In Quinte there were usually about 25 prisoners on methadone out of a prison population of roughly 225. Since we had to be escorted to the nursing station in small groups by the medical escort, it took all day for this process to be completed. For twenty-four hours methadone keeps you feeling normal, but after that you begin to feel progressively more tired, edgy, and depressed: the typical early symptoms of drug sickness. For this reason, most addicts on the street pick up their methadone every day at the same time, but in Quinte, our escort could arrive anytime of the day, keeping us in a constant state of low-level anxiety.

I first met Kelly a few days after she arrived at Quinte during our daily journey to the nursing station. I was feeling that mixture of relief, anticipation, and excitement I always experienced when our medical escort—we called him the methadone man—arrived in the guard's office.

When he saw me through the Plexiglas wall, he smiled and winked, and I got up slowly, trying not to reveal my feelings to those around me. It was never a good idea to wear your emotions on your sleeve in prison, but this was particularly true in regards to anything drug related. Other drug addicts not on "the program" would inevitably feel some kind of resentment toward those getting their daily dose of opiates. Kelly, on the other hand, had obviously never been to prison before, because as soon as the guard came out of the office and called her over to go for her methadone, she began smiling and jumping up and down, like a little kid who can't wait for her ice cream cone. Out of the corner of my eye, I caught a few of the other women staring at her with open hostility, or, in prison slang, gunning her off.

I was already standing casually by the barrier, waiting for it to open, when she came running over, asking me a million questions. Her exuberance and openness made me nervous enough that I stepped back a little.

The guard unlocked the big iron barrier, and we stepped through and began walking down the corridor of the women's unit with the methadone man. It hadn't taken long to discover he was a kind-hearted soul, probably known as a "con lover" by the rest of the guards. In the short time I had been there he had already passed on the regards of a male prisoner I had known on the street, who was also on the methadone program.

The methadone man had spoken quite freely of his long history at the prison, beginning when he was a young man working in the youth offender's wing before it had been transformed into the women's unit. He had taken the "kids," as he called them, on outings, swimming, camping, and hiking, and made it quite clear to me that he didn't approve of the modern warehousing techniques of the current prison regimes. He was looking forward to retiring in a few years. I did not trust his loyalties, so I limited my communication to listening while he did the talking, but as soon as we were in the presence of other guards or prisoners, he would keep his distance and disregard me completely, both for his sake and mine. He understood the code.

In the short time it took for Kelly and I to reach the barrier at the end of the women's unit, she had revealed that one night a couple of cops had arrived at her apartment door with a warrant for her arrest. Apparently she had not paid a fine for driving while under suspension, so they had arrested her and told her to pack her kid's bag because they were dropping him off with her relatives, friends, or Children's Aid. Kelly explained tearfully that she was a single mother on social assistance and didn't know many people in Kingston, so she had nowhere to leave her son on such short notice. On their way to Quinte they dropped her son off at Children's Aid.

She did not appear to be in great shape, and she shuffled down the corridor in a pair of oversized running shoes that she had stuffed her toes into like a pair of sandals. These combined factors left Kelly huffing and puffing by the time we reached the end of the unit.

"I hope they give me an inhaler. I can hardly breathe," she gasped. "I have felt like shit since I got here. I haven't had a smoke in two days, and I don't even have the energy to comb my hair."

In 2006 the Ontario government had banned smoking in provincial prisons. The federal government had decided to gradually implement a complete ban on smoking in federal prisons until 2008, when smoking would become illegal inside and outside every prison across the country.

During the walk to the nursing station and the thirty-minute methadone ritual, Kelly kept up a friendly banter with me, whether I reciprocated or not. She seemed a little desperate for friends.

Although there are few addicts who wouldn't congratulate the government for implementing the methadone program inside the prison system, it is administered with a degree of security that borders on the absurd, as though it were a highly volatile, explosive substance.

Every day, as soon as we passed through the last electronic barrier into the nursing station, we had to sit in a row on a bench and not move about, change seats, or touch one another. We couldn't bring anything other than the clothes on our backs and our shoes. Books, combs, paper, pencils, an extra sweatshirt—these were all prohibited, in case we were able to somehow figure out a way of vomiting the methadone into these items for another prisoner to consume later without being noticed by the guard. It would have been difficult for the guard not to notice, since they sat on a chair facing us behind a barred barrier with the express purpose of surveying our every move without distraction.

Once we were seated, the nurse would arrive and pour a large glass of water for the first methadone "patient." From this moment on, the nurse would observe the patient so intently that I have seen some crane their necks, eyes bulging, as though this would somehow help them to see better. We were constantly treated with the utmost of suspicion.

After drinking the first large glass of water, the nurse would ask us to give our names and methadone dose, to verify that we were the people in the photos with the prescription that was propped up beside each bottle. Next, we had to open our mouths for inspection. The nurse would usually ask to see under our tongue and lips if we didn't voluntarily expose those areas ourselves. Finally, the big moment arrived. We would take the methadone and a second big glass of water. By this time, prisoners who were drug sick would often have to fight the urge to puke from drinking so much fluid. Once the entire group had finished this ritual, we would have to sit quietly with the guard staring at us for exactly twenty minutes while our methadone digested.

The minute we stepped back into the common area, the bond between Kelly and me evaporated and we went our separate ways, invisible to each other even though we were circulating around the same ten-square-metre area. I often caught Kelly's eye, but carefully avoided making contact. I was in no hurry to make friends with anyone.

When we got back, the rest of the women's unit was milling about the common area waiting for yard to open. A few women sat on the edge of the metal picnic tables, staring at the tiny television suspended from the ceiling. The volume was on high, but the sounds reverberated unintelligibly off the cinderblock walls. It was impossible to follow any show involving dialogue or a storyline. Despite these obstacles, the game shows and tabloid-like talk shows that featured the misfortunes of various social misfits attracted a dedicated following. I suppose a fascination with the misfortune of others made sense, since the only thing that kept some women going was the knowledge that other people had even worse lives than theirs.

On this particular morning, the show featured a woman whose baby's DNA had been tested against no less than seventeen men she had slept with, and yet not one of them was the father. The women on the picnic tables, along with the studio audience, were swearing at and threatening the woman with the baby.

Across the room a couple of women were yelling into the phone while holding their other hand over their ear. Still others congregated in small packs, whispering and giggling over some bad scoop they had on another. The best way to survive in this environment was to take everything in while appearing to be focusing on no one in particular.

There was a very thin, young woman, with hair that was bleached as white as her pale skin, sitting across from me. Her hair was cut short, yet by using some kind of powerful hair gel she had managed to stick it back into a miniscule ponytail. She suddenly turned to me and asked my opinion regarding her chances of getting out on bail. After listening to her story, I told her I would be surprised if she didn't get bail. Just as suddenly, she got up and went into the shower stall. No sooner did she leave than another woman at the picnic table, who had been eavesdropping, leaned over and explained to me that this woman was driving them crazy in the dorm, barfing up every meal in the communal washroom.

"She's a loon, and if she doesn't quit with the barfing we're going to give her a few shots in the head so she'll move back into one of the cells."

"She's probably bulimic," I said.

"Ya think?" She rolled her eyes.

Thankfully our conversation was interrupted by a guard announcing, "Yard." The yard was surrounded on three sides by the walls of the building, and on the fourth side there was an eight-metre-high chain-link fence topped with one-metre coils of razor wire. This fence faced a large, unused field that was overrun with wildflowers and weeds. Almost every day a rabbit or groundhog would wander by, and a flock of seagulls would arrive on cue for leftover bread from our lunch. There were also stray cats that lived around the prison grounds, feeding off table scraps from the prisoners and the overflowing Dumpster. Just past the field, the reflection of the sun on glass and metal from the cars would flash through the trees bordering the four-lane freeway that passed by a few hundred metres from the prison. It was a tantalizing setting for escape dreams for those so inclined.

There was a story about a guy who had scaled a similar fence in the men's yard on the other side of the building adjacent to ours. He had managed to escape over the fence to his girlfriend's apartment in Kingston, an hour's drive from the prison, but not without injuries. By the time the cops arrived, they had to call an ambulance. The razor wire coils along the top of the fence had cut into his flesh like a thousand stab wounds. He just barely survived from the loss of blood that took over three hundred stitches to contain. This was one of the many prison stories that were both entertaining and a cautionary tale, intended to discourage escapes. I wondered if they were authentic or planted by the administration.

In the yard most of the women aligned themselves with a group or an individual, hoping that this would bring them some security, but I had taken the position of a lone wolf, gambling that my reputation as a fed and my physique would act as a deterrent to those who did not wish me well.

Women who had spent time in federal prison always had this reputation to their advantage. With it comes the mystique that we had survived longer sentences and tougher prisoners, and thus were tougher people as well. Most prisoners considered provincial prisons the training grounds for the more prestigious federal penitentiary system. The history of the notorious federal penitentiaries would cling to us like another layer of skin.

Every afternoon I would spend my hour of yard time walking around and around in circles, hundreds of times, no matter how tired and dizzy I felt. I made a conscious decision to carry myself tall, with a carefully cultivated attitude of fearlessness. I gave off just enough of the machismo vibe to deter anyone looking for easy prey from thinking I was their ticket to advancement up the ladder. At the same time, I took care not to attract the attention of those at the top who might feel threatened. It was a fine line.

At any given time, a prison will have a distinct personality made up of the sum total of its parts. Sometimes it will actually be friendly and relaxed, but more often than not remand prisons like Quinte are like a sadistic bully. There is no time for a group of prisoners to establish a stable pecking order, or even a collective order made up of a group of strong-minded people.

It was an oppressively hot afternoon. The guard on yard duty pulled her chair into the shadows of the portables just off to one side of the yard. Inside the prison, the air conditioning was blowing on high so the guards who were active wouldn't melt in their uniforms. But the minute anyone stepped outside, it was like stepping from a meat freezer into the Sahara Desert. The walls that surrounded the yard on three sides protected us from the slightest breeze, and at high noon there wasn't an inch of shade.

A few women lay down on their sweatshirts, protecting them from the heat waves rising out of the asphalt, and rolled their T-shirts into bandanas to cover their breasts. Then they would take turns spreading cheap institutional deodorant all over their bodies, hoping that the oil would protect them from the sun.

The women split up into their different little groups, circling around the various alpha women. The followers moved freely back and forth between one group and another, depending on which alpha female was on top that day. Loyalty and solidarity were nonexistent in this ruthless environment. One day a woman would be on top, and the next day she would be free falling down to the bottom, all depending on the most superficial criteria.

Some of the regulars had learned to turn a one-size-fits-all prison uniform into a fashion statement, like high school girls in school uniforms all over the country. They turned their green sweatpants and T-shirt inside out and rolled the elastic waist band down so they hung just above their pubic hairline like the low-rider pants that were all the fashion on the street at the time. Some women had branded their butts in gold nail polish with names like "NIKE" or "JUICY."

I stopped my circling by the fence for a moment to watch one of the wild rabbits sitting under the shade of a willow tree in a little dried-up pond area of the field. I was startled when Jay, one of the alpha women, sidled up beside me and placed a little wad of toilet paper in the palm of my hand, "just a little somethin' for later." I thanked her, not knowing exactly what she had given me. When I got a chance I opened the packet discreetly and found three pills and enough tobacco for a cigarette. I had seen enough drugs to know they weren't from the opiate or benzodiazepine family, so they were probably what were commonly known as "sleepers." I pocketed them for later.

After an hour I thought I was going to faint from the heat when finally they closed the yard. As soon as we were back in our cells and the guards had come by for count, my cellmates used a piece of paper tampon wrapper to roll a cigarette and blew the smoke down the toilet bowl. It seemed I was not the only recipient of a care package.

"Hey, you want these sleepers?" I said. I was a fussy drug addict. The only type of drug I liked was opiates. "With the amount of methadone I'm on, I wouldn't even feel them. It'd be a waste, and I may as well quit smoking since I've gone this long."

The two of them looked truly amazed that I would give up three sleeping pills and a cigarette and not even want something in exchange. They stayed up for hours, talking in low droning voices about the various major crimes they had committed and how many abusive men they had tolerated.

I drifted off to sleep reading the pulp fiction graffiti on the ceiling above my bunk. Some young boy, I assumed, had written about his lover, or rapist, in pencil: "fucked little boys up the butt for drug money and I know cause I was one of them." The graffiti explained that "mr. bum-fucker fucks around on his women and actually thinks he gets away with it. He ain't the sharpest pencil in the box, but then again, neither am I, I went back twice. I'm done now." I wondered if the author was a boy from the days when the unit was a youth offender wing. I also wondered why no one had cleaned this off the ceiling, since it could be done if one stood on the bunk, although I didn't have the urge to clean it off either. Perhaps it was a universal story that touched a chord others did not want to forget.

As it turns out, the source of the sleepers and tobacco was a woman I'll call Gypsy. She had just gotten out of seg and was making a move to consolidate her power on the unit by gifting everyone with a taste of the future. There were a lot more drugs where those came from, so Jay, who could always tell what direction the wind was blowing, immediately buddied up with Gypsy as soon as she got out of seg. It was unusual for two alpha females to bunk together, but in this case they would both benefit from the relationship. Gypsy could get drugs in, and Jay could make sure she kept them.

They fit together like pieces of a puzzle. Gypsy was a born-again Christian, a calling Jay had been attracted to for some time. From the day Gypsy got out of seg they were inseparable, praying before meals, conducting their own Bible study, and prophesizing on world events as well as those behind the fences of Quinte.

Gypsy had been in Quinte longer than anyone else at the time: nine months. She was built like a professional weightlifter, thick from neck to toe, a wall of muscle covered in a layer of hard flesh. Gypsy had two distinct features: her intimidating physique and her one-inch-long, pointed, manicured, and fluorescent-coloured fingernails.

There was no programming or educational courses in Quinte, other than church on Sunday, and the "nailpolish lady," on Tuesdays. She came in every week with a large supply of colored nailpolish, removers, and coatings, which I believe she supplied herself. She was a wonderful person who always drew every single woman in the unit to the picnic table, where she would spread out her polishes and sit quietly listening to the women, without judgment or comment, for the entire hour. By the time I left Quinte, I was sporting some eye-popping bright fluorescent-green fingernails.

Once Gypsy got out of seg, she would park herself every morning on the edge of the picnic table closest to the TV, like some stone Buddha, in complete command of the channels. She often complained of back problems, which could have been the reason she would sit ramrod straight and only move her pupils if she had to make visual contact with you. Regardless of the reason, it gave the impression that when you were trying to talk to her, you weren't important enough for her to make the effort of turning her head to make direct eye contact.

"Have you noticed that the signs of the apocalypse are happening all around us?" Gypsy commented to me one day as the daily news on the war in Iraq echoed off the cinderblock walls. Her eyes remained fixed on the screen. "It's all about a Christian crusade against the barbaric forces of Islam, and God is going to punish them." I figured it would be a hopeless cause to even begin to argue with her. "And if we folks in America don't stop with our drugs, sex, and rock and roll, God is going to take us all down along with those barbarians. The fires, pestilence, floods and disease are already upon us."

The Bible appeared to be a good influence on Jay, because within forty-eight hours of bunking with Gypsy, she saved Kelly from a bullying cellmate by inviting her to move in with them. After weeks of moping around in a depressed state, Kelly became buoyant. Finally she had people who accepted her and to whom she belonged, although I think she was fairly resistant to religious indoctrination.

Once the drugs ran out, Gypsy and Jay let everyone know they were committed to a program of Bible study and abstinence from drugs and alcohol, at least until someone said they were coming back from court with some crack. At the time, there was only one lighter on the unit. It belonged to an aging hippie woman named Misty, who got the odd joint sent over by her "old man" from the men's unit. This was her only card. People tolerated her hanging around their group because whenever she did get a joint, she would share a few tokes with whomever she was hanging around with that day. But other than the lighter and the joints, she didn't have anything going for her. She was old, small, and unconnected. In fact, she was probably no older than I was, but the constant disparaging comments about people over forty were taking a toll on my conception of age, as well as my own self-image.

The problem, as Gypsy and Jay saw it, was that Misty wouldn't up her lighter. She wasn't stupid; she knew the lighter was all she had in Quinte. The joints would be no good to her without that lighter, and if she let that lighter out of her cell, the odds of getting it back were zero to none. So she wasn't going to give it up without a fight.

For the moment, Gypsy and Jay's shared craving for crack trumped their religious beliefs. On the afternoon the crack was supposed to come in, Misty went for a shower, as was her custom, just before yard was called. As soon as the sound of the shower spray could be heard coming from the shower stall in the common room, Gypsy and Jay slipped in behind her while Kelly distracted the guards with some phony medical emergency. But they underestimated Misty's fight, and soon everybody could hear her screaming and the sound of flesh on flesh. Ignoring Kelly, the guards came rushing through as fast as they could, which wasn't very fast considering they had to open two barriers, one electronically and one with a key. By the time they got to the shower room, Gypsy and Jay were mingling with everyone else, and Misty was escorted out without ceremony, wearing a pair of broken eyeglasses, a blackening eye, facial scratches, and a soaking wet towel wrapped around her private parts.

After all that, the guards got the lighter, and the crack never came in. Misty was nonetheless condemned as a "goof" and "PC" for screaming and upping the lighter to the screws. It seemed to me that it would take a lot more than Jesus to keep Gypsy and Jay away from drugs in the real world.

Gypsy and Jay's honeymoon with Kelly was short lived. Perhaps in the aftermath of their failure at abstinence and peace, all their projects of salvation felt like frauds. I don't know, but they were more frequently overheard telling Kelly to shut up and get her "ugly mug" out of their faces.

One evening, after the usual day of avoiding being sucked into some negative vortex, I fell into some good fortune. Not just one but both of my cellmates were released from court, leaving me completely alone in my cell. It is hard to imagine the joy. Unless you have been locked up for nineteen hours a day for weeks on end in a small washroom without a bathtub with two complete strangers who are coming down off crack, you don't truly know the joy of solitude.

When the guard confirmed during supper count that they really had been released, I decided to celebrate by staying in my cell all evening. I lay there appreciating the fact I could read without trying to muffle out the sounds of other women talking endlessly.

Miraculously, I had come upon a book, Frantz Fanon's *The Wretched of the Earth*,[51] that had somehow made its way into Quinte. I gobbled it up like a starving person. Fanon's analysis catapulted me back to reflect on ideas I had read in another groundbreaking book, Paulo Freire's *Pedagogy of the Oppressed*.[52] The analyses in these books, which were first published in the sixties, were truly revolutionary in describing the psychology of oppressed people living under colonial regimes in so-called "third-world countries." The conditions and social dynamics in Quinte inspired me to use their analyses to understand the psychological coping mechanisms so familiar to prisoners in modern prison regimes across the globe.

Prisoners, like the colonized subjects of these books, both internalize the values of the dominant society and internalize the negative identity that is imposed upon them by their colonial oppressor, or in this case, the prison regime. Most prisoners have internalized the capitalist values of the dominant society—that is, competition, hierarchy, materialism, and violence. Many ambitious prisoner capitalists have built profitable underground "black" market ventures, such as drug and contraband trafficking networks, gambling rings, and extortion schemes. They have learned to adapt their own capitalist ventures in order to be successful despite the watchful eyes of the quasi-military prison regime. Black market ventures thrive not only because capitalist values are alive and well, but also because it is almost impossible for most prisoners to make enough money in their official prison jobs to afford phone calls, toiletries, stamps, clothes, and many other necessities.

Just like in the dominant society, the prisoners who run these black-market enterprises must have a way of enforcing the rules of the marketplace—rules such as not stealing and paying your debts. The prisoners who run these enterprises, much like successful businesspeople outside the walls, have the power and material clout to enforce these rules using a combination of fear and respect. A prisoner who does not pay her debt or collaborates with the enemy must be subjected to some kind of punishment. Since the prison subculture does not have the financial means to develop the more sophisticated methods of social control familiar to the dominant society, punishment is usually ruthless, violent, and corporal, much like that of the Middle Ages.

The prison regime is aware of this phenomenon and uses it to their advantage. It is common knowledge within the prison subculture that prison administrators and guards will extend favours to prison leaders in exchange for their influence in pacifying the prison population in times of conflict. As long as the prison population remains passive, guards and administrators will turn a blind eye to all kinds of infractions, particularly infractions by the segment of the prison population that has power. That is one of the reasons so many of those who languish in isolation for years on end are not the ruthless and powerful, but the mentally ill and unpopular.

While prisoners generally internalize the capitalist value system, they also embrace the lazy, sneaky, predator-like stereotype the dominant society imposes upon them. This conflicting identity may seem irrational to an outsider, but this negative stereotype is actually an essential coping mechanism for survival in prison.

Let's look at the lazy stereotype. It's amazing how the slothful prisoner shuffling down the range at a snail's pace with an indolent yet defiant expression on their face transforms into an industrious, clear-headed capitalist when engaged in their own underground economies. The reasons for this transformation have more to do with logic than psychology. Why would a prisoner bust their ass working for next to nothing as a prison labourer if we are being treated like slaves? Not only is there nothing in it for us, but our fellow prisoners would treat us like an occupied population would collaborators and traitors during wartime.

What's with the sneaky stereotype? In our presentation to the prison regime, and even within our own subculture, prisoners universally wear a mask: a blank facial expression with glazed, hooded eyes that camouflage our true feelings. Prisoners learn very quickly that everything we say can and will be used against us, not just in court but in our daily lives. It doesn't take long before prisoners begin to speak only when spoken to, and even then to provide only the essential and barest of information. Like the old saying goes, "Loose lips sink ships." Ditto for other prisoners. Damaging gossip passed on to the wrong person can destroy another person's reputation, and in a world without other social yardsticks, a person's reputation is the most important possession we have.

A prisoner's reputation is based on their ability to maintain their principles regardless of the consequences. It doesn't matter whether their principles are the same as everyone else's, but rather whether they will stick to them no matter what. This quality gives others confidence that they can trust this person to do what they say they will. In a world where the authorities put tremendous pressure on individuals to capitulate in order to gain some freedom or some other advantage, a person's reputation is worth more than money or any status their career or social standing may have bestowed upon them outside the walls.

It is never safe to let others know exactly how one feels or thinks. It is in everyone's best interests to conceal your true feelings, whether they are rage, fear, anger, happiness, love, or despair. To let others know how one feels and what one is thinking is to become vulnerable and lose what little power and control a person has over any given situation.

The cold, ruthless predator is not just a stereotype, but a necessary survival mechanism in a world defined by constant injustice and punishment. Any prisoner who becomes too attached to any one person or thing is destined to truly suffer. One of the first methods used by prison regimes to punish or break up prisoner collectives is to separate prisoners with strong relationships through involuntary transfers to other prisons, segregation, or special handling units, or even through granting parole or statutory release.

Any prisoner who is doing a significant amount of time learns the danger of powerful emotional attachments to other people. Most rounders learned this lesson as foster children or as juvenile prisoners. It is not safe to invest too much emotional energy into anyone, because the extreme angst, loneliness, depression, and anxiety that comes with the inevitable separation is just not worth it. The ability to detach from both physical and emotional pain is recognized by prisoners as an important coping mechanism in a world where injustice and punishment are the norm, and this ability to detach is rewarded by a higher status and respect within the prisoner hierarchy.

The same can be said of attachment to things. The expression "nothing left to lose" has special significance in prison. Most prisoners realize that the most powerful weapons the prison regime has are the ability to take away their so-called "privileges," which turn out to be everything, even life itself. Passes, parole, release from segregation, radios, televisions, visits with friends and loved ones, personal letters, clothing, religious relics, books, participation in spiritual ceremonies—anything can be taken away as punishment or used as a threat to leverage more control over prisoner behaviour. The best emotional armour is, ironically, no emotions at all—a cold, unemotional detachment to everything, to expect nothing, want nothing and no one, until there is literally "nothing left to lose."

The logic behind the predator stereotype is easy to understand. There are no police to defend prisoners from physical threats, and asking for help from the guards is "ratting out," treason, a betrayal of the prisoner code. In the dominant society, an elaborate system has been designed through the use of police forces to protect the citizen from defending themselves. Prisoners do not have this luxury, and have no choice but to defend themselves from danger. To people outside the prison subculture, this act of defending oneself is seen as acting like a predator or an animal, but that is exactly what a prisoner must do: defend themselves from threats, just as an animal would defend itself from another predator. A well-adjusted prisoner is able to defend themselves physically, or at least align themselves with those who can.

. . .

As with all things Quinte, the joy was short lived. The next morning Kelly and Gypsy shanghaied me on the way to get our methadone, putting an end to any plans I might have had for a day of solitude. As we stood waiting for the barrier to the nursing station to open, a pale, skeletal woman in a "baby doll" made of asbestos was being escorted down the corridor by a guard. She was the unfortunate bulimic woman I had given legal counsel to when I had first arrived. She had two black eyes, and her arms were bandaged at the wrists. I wouldn't have recognized her if she hadn't worn her short white hair greased back into a miniscule ponytail. Apparently, neither did Kelly and Gypsy, because they continued talking to me as though she were invisible.

"Do you think I could move in to your cell?" Kelly asked me sheepishly. "They'll probably put someone else in with you anyway later on today, so I was hoping I could move in." I was distracted by the thin, white woman, who looked right through us as she passed by.

"Yeah," Gypsy backed her up. "Me and Jay need some privacy for our Bible studies. We are really in the serious stages of planning our Bible camp, and it's hard on Kelly listening to us all night. It's not 'cause we don't like her, we just think she'd be happier with you." How selfless of them to be thinking only of Kelly's happiness.

I surrendered, knowing a hopeless cause when faced with one. I should just be happy I got the one night. I put on my best happy face and asked Gypsy how we could arrange it.

"I got connections," she smiled. Sure enough, she did, because within the hour Kelly was standing in my cell with all her worldly possessions stuffed into a pillowcase, looking like a hand-shy dog waiting for a slap in the head.

I mustered together all the enthusiasm I could and heard myself tell her how happy I was that she was bunking with me. Slowly her tail came out from between her legs and began wagging while she fawningly tried to win my approval. I hated her and myself for this degrading dynamic we found ourselves in.

"Look, Kelly. You don't have to be thankful I said you could come in here. The guards would have just put someone in here anyway, like you said, so don't worry." We smiled. I changed the topic. "Hey, did you see that young girl being escorted down the corridor today when we went for methadone?"

"Yeah. They PC'd her, 'cause she kept barfing in the dorm, and the girls said she was a rat. I heard she's been banging her head against the wall and trying to kill herself, so they got her in the rubber room now." It seemed that PCs were no longer sex offenders, child abusers, and rats, but were more frequently people that someone powerful in the prison population didn't like for whatever reason.

"Oh." I felt my stomach turn like when I saw a cat lying beside the road that had just been hit by a car.

We were out in the common room for the last hour before supper, so I found a spot on the picnic table and pretended to be interested in one of the late-afternoon talk shows. There was really nothing to do in the common room. Like most of the women, I spent a lot of my time figuring out how to avoid problems. It was a draining pastime. With twelve women in the room, we were stacked like plates on the two picnic tables, and there was nowhere else to go but the phone or the shower stall. The sound of the laugh track and the TV dialogue reverberating off the cinderblock walls, and the two women yelling into the phones, made for a wall of sound that was impenetrable for any train of thought.

I fell asleep that night listening to Kelly's riff on a familiar prison theme. The number of times I had heard the expanded version of the same story reflected just how traumatized she felt. After a number of accidents while driving under the influence, she had lost her license, got a suspension, was later fined, and then arrested when she didn't pay the fine. The final blow had been the Children's Aid Society taking temporary custody of her son.

I wondered just how much money the government spent imprisoning women on welfare who hadn't paid fines for one thing or another. I dozed off thinking that nothing had really changed. Quinte was like a modern-day debtors' prison, poor house, and insane asylum all conveniently rolled into one, like in a Charles Dickens novel.

I woke up the next morning to the sound of the medication cart rolling down the corridor. At first I thought it was the breakfast cart and almost fell off the top bunk in my panic to get our coffee cups to the shelf before it passed us by. But even in my panic, I managed to slow myself down in order to avoid accidentally dropping the cups off the twelve-inch-by-four-inch shelf. I had heard enough legends about the group punishment meted out in response to those who dropped their coffee cups too often, or worse still, intentionally dropped empty meal trays. One story I had heard more than once claimed that the whole unit had been locked down for three days when some women had pushed their meal trays off the shelf in an act of resistance. The spectacle of three empty meal trays crashing and bouncing down the corridor, leaving leftovers behind, always flashed before my eyes whenever I was balancing three empty meal trays that were six inches square onto a shelf that was four inches deep. I marvelled at how effective a deterrent group punishment could be.

The nurse's face appeared in the slot. "Medication."

"Kelly!" I yelled at her, still snoring under her blanket. She got up quickly and downed her medication.

"Aren't you going to court today?" Kelly asked groggily through her long bangs.

"Yes! I forgot." I felt a surge of adrenalin course through my veins. Great! Any change of scenery would be an improvement over Quinte. We struggled through our breakfast of two fried eggs on toast with our plastic spoon, the only piece of cutlery allowed. After eating Sunday "roast beast" dinner with a spoon, fried eggs were a breeze. Apparently plastic knives and forks could be used as weapons. Even the plastic spoons had to be counted after every meal.

I brushed my teeth quickly, taking care not to swallow any of the toothpaste. The brand name, Dawn Mist, was deceptive considering the warning on the label: "If you swallow more than used for brushing teeth, contact the poison control centre immediately." I wondered why the plastic spoons were treated as dangerous weapons when the real danger appeared to be in the toothpaste.

Down in the admissions and discharge area, I stripped down for the guard at her command.

"Hair." I leaned over and flipped my hair over my head so she could see that nothing was hidden underneath.

"Mouth." I opened my mouth and stuck out my tongue.

"Ears." I flipped each earlobe forward so she could see behind them.

"Turn around. Feet." I lifted each foot and wiggled my toes to show her that nothing was hidden between them.

"Bend over and touch your toes without bending your knees." I did this, knowing she was looking up my genitals as much as possible.

"Squat and cough." This was done with the hope that anything stuffed up your vagina or ass would pop out through the force of coughing. To my knowledge, nothing that has been suitcased properly has ever popped out of a vagina or anus from squatting and coughing, but it sure was humiliating.

"Okay. Turn around and lift each breast up." Done. I was used to this by now, but once when I had gone through the list of motions like a trick pony, the guard had lectured me on the finer points of following her orders. I was truly amazed at the number of problems that could arise if an "inmate" were to start stripping down at their own speed and convenience.

I shuffled out of the prison behind the sheriff and stood ready to get into the van, pondering how I was going to get my foot from the ground to the top of the step, which was about three inches higher than the length of chain between my leg irons. It didn't help that I was handcuffed as well. Eventually I visualized how I could jump up on the step without falling—something like the visualization techniques Olympic athletes use before their event.

Outside there was a record-breaking heatwave, but after sitting on the cold steel mesh seats in the sheriff's van, followed by several hours more in the air-conditioned holding cell, I felt like a piece of meat in the deep freezer. All my body heat had drained from my flesh into the cold steel seats. The unseen advantages of the huge green prison sweats slowly revealed themselves to me. I regretted not wearing them even more when it became obvious that I wouldn't actually make a court appearance; my lawyer was working out a deal with the judge and Crown for my co-accused to take the rap.

Henry didn't have a record, so, in legalese, they would "stay the proceedings" for him. If he stayed charge free for one year, he would remain record free. He would not go to prison at all. A stay of proceedings is effectively the same as if he had been acquitted, but if he is charged with another offence during the following year, the charge can be reactivated. In contrast, because I was a lifer, I would not get bail, and if convicted I would have to do at least five years regardless of my sentence because I would have to go through the whole slow-release program of escorted and unescorted passes, followed by day parole, and finally I would have to reapply for full parole. It was a no-brainer.

So Henry got a stay of proceedings, and I was acquitted. However, this did not mean I was being released from prison. Any lifer who has their parole suspended for any reason has to be returned to a federal prison, where they will wait for the next sitting of the parole board at that prison. Their wait is limited by law to three months from the day their parole was suspended. Predictably, most federal parolees will wait close to the full three months before they see the board. So any parole suspension results in a three-month prison sentence, regardless of the innocence or guilt of the parolee. There is also no guarantee that the parole board will release you, innocent or not. That is the nature of the beast.

Twenty Four

The next morning began like any other. When I felt a sharp pang in my gut, I slid easily off the bed onto the toilet. I had just settled down to the task at hand when the keys jangled in the door. Before I could pull my pants back up, a hulk of a man was in my doorway, with one of the female guards standing right behind him. She couldn't have been an inch over five feet, with long, thick brown hair that she kept immaculately groomed. They looked just like Barbie and Ken. She had an hourglass figure, finely tweezed eyebrows, and as much makeup as she could apply without it dripping off her face. Her perennial smile appeared detached from her emotions.

He must have represented the maximum physical requirements for the job, filling the doorway with what I would have guessed was a six-foot-four frame and 240 pounds of flesh. His appearance was accentuated by the bright white shirt that all lieutenants were required to wear in order to distinguish them from the rest of the staff. For this reason, they were known as "white shirts" by prisoners and staff alike. During the day shift, there was a lieutenant in charge of every unit at Quinte: one each for the maximum and minimum men's units, and one for the women's unit. The superintendent was the only person in Quinte with higher seniority than the lieutenants.

"Ken" caught my eye, smirked, and walked right back out again. I could hear them jangling their keys in the next cell. My blood went from its normal slow simmer to instant boil. I pulled up my sweatpants and crawled back up onto the top bunk, trying to concentrate on the soothing narrative of my book, but found my eyes wandering to the ceiling, where the young boy had written his short pulp-fiction graffiti about his drug-addicted lover or rapist.

Sure enough, they came back. As soon as he stepped into my cell, my mouth went into autoplay. "Why don't you call 'man on the range' before coming in here?"

Barbie was standing in the doorway while he began rapping different fixed objects in my cell with a large rubber mallet like the kind they use in cartoons. He hit a few bars on my window and the stainless-steel sink. This was a preventative security ritual the white shirts reenacted every few days, just in case anyone had ideas of escaping through the bars or making a weapon out of the plumbing.

"If you clean off all that graffiti on the ceiling, maybe we will." He glared at me.

I had spent too many years in prison biting my tongue whenever guards baited me. Over time most prisoners realize that talking back to a guard isn't worth the punishment. Better to pick your battles. Retorts, arguments, and acts of vengeance against Barbie and Ken played out like a violent cartoon in my head. He couldn't be serious about the graffiti. It was signed and dated "1997," I thought foolishly, as though evidence of my innocence was relevant.

Since my arrest in 1983 until I went to the halfway house in 1990, there were no male staff allowed in the living areas of women's prisons, either federally or provincially, unless they were there for emergencies or building repairs. Even then, the policy demanded that the women prisoners be notified when a man was entering the area. The same held true in the men's prisons in regard to female staff. This policy had been developed in response to a long history of documented cases of sexual abuse by male staff. As with so many things penal, these policies had been reversed, and all those hard-fought-for prisoners' rights vanquished.

In 2003, just three years before I arrived at Quinte, Womyn4Justice had testified before the Canadian Human Rights Commission (CHRC) about our experiences in P4W as part of their investigation into human rights violations in federal women's prisons. As part of this investigation, they were reviewing the CSC's "gender-neutral" hiring practices, or the Cross-Gender Staffing Policy.

Some of the women who had been sexually or physically abused, or both, as children explained how they would feel about having male guards working in the living areas where they were using washrooms, undressing, and sleeping. The CSC acknowledged that "more than 80% of federally sentenced women (fsw) have such histories (abuse), and more than half are survivors of sexual abuse," and we naively thought that would be a good enough reason to have male guards restricted from entering the women's living areas except for emergencies and repair work.[53] But we were sadly mistaken.

The CHRC upheld the CSC Cross-Gender Staffing Policy on the basis of a 1989 decision by the Public Service Commission Appeal Board, as well as a Supreme Court of Canada ruling. The Supreme Court had ruled that it would be discriminatory to restrict men's and women's rights to work in all areas of the prisons, regardless of their gender. The CHRC ruled that this right superseded the rights to privacy of federally sentenced women or men in custody. The CHRC ruling was made despite our testimony and that of the CSC's own appointed Cross-Gender Monitor's recommendation that "men not be employed as front-line primary care workers."[54] The CSC Cross-Gender Monitor made its recommendation because there was evidence of "extensive violations of protocol" by "front-line male staff." In a small nod to the Monitor's evidence, the CHRC added a caveat recommending more stringent monitoring and training programs. With no means of enforcing this caveat, it was unlikely these programs would actually be implemented.

Although I was disappointed in the CHRC's final decision, I was not surprised. I was already very cynical about the possibility of any government-appointed body supporting prisoners' rights. However, my cynicism toward my fellow prisoners reached new depths when I read the final results of the 1999/2000 survey by the same Cross-Gender Monitor, which concluded that "82% of federally sentenced women and 78% of staff supported the use of male guards."[55] This final statistic only served to verify my view that the modern prisoner was more than ever internalizing the values of their oppressor, and as a result would experience more self-loathing and internalized rage than ever before. No wonder the women in Quinte were in a constant state of war against one another. There was no solidarity, no politicization.

I was still mulling over these paradoxes when my new cellmates, Dee and Annie, came in from their hour in the common room. Kelly had been moved out of my cell while I was in court so these two could be bunked together. Kelly was not connected, while these two obviously were. They had arrived twenty-four hours ago and this was the first time they had left the cell. Since arriving, Dee had remained in a fetal position under the blankets, sleeping like a dead person, while Annie had been reading incessantly on the floor under Dee's bunk. That suited me just fine. At this point I preferred my own company anyway.

Against my better judgment, I began to vent about the incident with the male guard. It never occurred to me that they would not share my feelings until Dee looked at me like I was from another planet. At least this was a change from her permanent scowl. I had deduced from the few words they had exchanged that she was coming down off a hard crack habit. She was a small, thin woman with white, sallow skin. Hostility oozed off her, like a junkyard dog on the end of a short chain.

"This ain't P ... 4 ... W," she said, lingering on each letter of P4W for emphasis. "A prison is a prison is a prison."

She skulked over to her bunk in a hunched posture, like life had beaten her down. On her way, she picked up a candy and threw the wrapper on the floor. "You got an attitude problem, girl," she spat in my direction, and crawled under her blanket. Her reaction, combined with my lingering rage at the male guard issue, took me by surprise and left me in a state I rarely found myself ... speechless.

Twenty Five

Yard came up soon enough. Dee and Annie stayed behind, sleeping off the street. As I waited for the yard to open, I sat down and watched the news for the first time since I had arrived at Quinte. As usual the audio was unintelligible, but despite this, it dawned on me that I hadn't given a thought to what was going on in the world outside. I knew the war in Iraq was raging on, but from the newsreels on the screen, it seemed the Israelis were about to invade Lebanon. The Israeli military had given the civilians of Beirut a window of opportunity to evacuate before the bombing began. The commentators speculated the Israeli army wanted to isolate the "insurgents" inside Beirut. I had come to translate the use of the word *insurgent* by the mass media when referring to the Middle East as meaning any able-bodied Arab. Normally this kind of news would never fail to horrify me and capture my attention, but it occurred to me that world events were no longer part of my consciousness since arriving in the very demanding world of Quinte.

It could only mean that these seemingly superficial daily events, like a male guard entering my cell unannounced, the constant conflict between the women, and wondering if everyone hated me, had begun to absorb all my attention. Perhaps these events seemed harmless, but under the surface the constant stream of injustices and calamities erupting around me kept my attention focused on the here and now, like someone walking gingerly around fissures of molten lava on an active volcano. I suppose that explains why so many truly poor people on the streets do not usually dominate the local political activist groups. They are probably too busy trying to survive daily life. The people with the most time and privilege to attend meetings in the evenings and take risks at demonstrations are too often the students and intellectuals with middle-class backgrounds.

"Yard up." We filed out into the stifling heat of July. A lone guard sat on a wooden chair in the shadows. She had been working at Quinte for twenty years. Twenty years of eight- to twelve-hour shifts, sitting under banks of fluorescent lights, staring at a room crammed with women prisoners who hated her guts. Twenty years of serving food trays, opening and locking cell doors dozens of times a day, bringing bad news 95 percent of the time, gossiping day in and day out about the prisoners and the other guards, dreary institutional cinderblock walls painted shades of grey, windowless rooms, dirty concrete floors, counting people over and over again in a fortress-like building without plants, pictures, or adornments. In many ways the life of the guard and the life of the prisoner were flip sides of the same coin, except that the guards had all the power and were paid for their time.

I had just walked halfway around the yard when a small group of women from the dorm flagged me down. The dorm is considered a privileged area because it is twice the size of a cell, with two bunk beds instead of one, a TV, a card table, and a washroom. The dorm is the carrot, the cells down the corridor the stick. Women who were charge free and no longer considered security risks were moved to the dorm. I had vowed never to move there, even if offered the spot, because I was opposed to the carrot on principle. Besides, I figured the odds of getting along with four women in the dorm would be a lot lower than three in the single cells.

Their leader, a young woman not a day over twenty, eyed me up and down, assessing my worthiness as an opponent. "Hey, Hansen," she said, using my last name as a form of putdown usually reserved for the guards. She was a young alpha female looking for a step up the ladder. "Hear you don't like men." I stared at her blankly.

"I don't have any problem with men. I do have a problem with male guards coming in my cell unannounced when I'm on the can."

"Well, we heard you were complaining, and we don't got no problems with men around here."

"I've never been in a prison where men are in the living areas and just waltz in and out of cells without warning. I don't like it."

"Well, this ain't P4W, you know," she said. By this time I thought I would have to agree with her. I turned around and kept on walking, feeling their stares against my back. It was too coincidental that this woman would use the same expression as Dee, yet Dee hadn't left our cell since the incident with the male guard.

Every time I paced by the fence overlooking the meadow, I felt tears welling up in my eyes. The beauty of the wildflowers, the gentle green grasses, and the long weeping willow boughs bending in the breeze broke my heart. I inhaled the smell of buttercup flowers every time I passed through a cloud of their scent as though it were a refreshing drink of water. The inaccessibility of nature made its beauty so much more intense. To visitors passing by it was an acre of undeveloped land, but to us it was an oasis of wilderness.

When we went back into the common room, the recycled, cold, institutional air hit us like a wave of cold water. I felt as though my world was penetrated by spies. Nothing in this room alleviated my anxiety. The dry, dirty air smelled of bleach and cleansers.

The only thing I looked forward to was supper. Annie and Dee were still sleeping when I heard the rattle of the meal cart. I slid off the top bunk like an otter down a riverbank. I carefully aligned the cups on the narrow shelf for the meal trays, but not carefully enough. To my horror, my thick plastic cup went bouncing down the concrete floor. I could see the guard stepping over to pick it up just as Barbie came into view.

"Don't pick that up!" Barbie ordered. I could almost see the guard calculating which would be more humiliating, to obey Barbie or pick up a prisoner's cup against her orders. Of course she chose the latter. Her face was red as I pleaded hopelessly for her to pick it up. In a heartbeat, I dumped the packets of sugar out of an empty cup and placed it on the shelf.

"Don't use that cup, I need it," Dee growled from under the covers. Like the good cop in the good cop/bad cop routine, Annie picked her steaming coffee cup off the shelf and handed it to me.

"I don't drink coffee," she explained, but I suspected she could sense the numbers of straws on the camel's back were dangerously high.

"You got a problem with Barbie?" asked Dee, giving me no time to answer. "She's the best one of the bunch. You got real attitude problems. I come in here and treat this place like a vacation. I eat, sleep, get some sun, read. You're just fucking yourself with your attitude."

She wasn't the only one who saw prison as a time to fatten up and get away from the drugs for a while. In fact, stints in prison had saved many seriously addicted women from death, but I didn't see this as a reason to praise its merits. If a society is judged on how it treats its poor, then ours would be on death row. Condemning people with addictions and mental health issues to prison was a policy of neither compassion nor wisdom. Unfortunately, our personal conflict obscured my ability to see her life within the context of the big picture.

"A screw is a screw is a screw," I retorted, throwing her rhetoric back at her. As I brushed past her to pick up my tray, I consciously bumped her leg. She leapt to her feet as though I had electrocuted her.

"What the fuck! What the fuck!" she hissed, jumping up and down as though the jolt was still passing through her. A rush of pleasurable adrenalin coursed through my veins as I edged dangerously close to a physical confrontation. I knew the bump had been like waving a red flag in front of a bull, but she was obviously still a little intimidated by my superior height, weight, and fitness. However, what she lacked in these categories she more than made up for in wit, street smarts, and rage. For a split second she stared at me, weighing the odds of beating me up. The calculation came up in my favour. She jumped under the covers.

"Sorry about that. I didn't mean it," I said in a barely audible voice, giving her a small concession. I knew that my level of restraint was dwindling, like a rope frayed down to a string.

At seven in the morning, like always, the dim nightlight suddenly became a bank of bright, imperceptibly shimmering fluorescence, illuminating the old toothpaste, graffiti, and dirt smudged on the grey cinderblock walls. The cold air conditioning disguised the simmering July heatwave. Muffled women's voices and the clanging of the medication cart echoed down the corridor.

The hours drag by in Quinte time. The only clock in the office has read 8:50 for at least two years, according to the other women. I often see the clock drooping off its nail on the wall, defying the laws of physics like a Salvador Dali painting. Time is measured in hourly intervals: one hour locked, one hour unlocked. The Maury Povich poor-bashing hour, the Price is Right consumer hour, walking up and down and up and down the corridor, feet slapping the hard cement in rhythmical beats, then around and around and around the yard. The only disruptions to this hourly rhythm are the random lockdowns for cell and strip searches.

I could smell the legendary macaroni and cheese coming before I could see it. I'd been hearing about it all morning. I lifted the plastic lid off my tray and my mouth started to salivate like the wolf waiting for Red Riding Hood. But when I put a heaping spoon of the stuff into my mouth, I got the same sensation you get when you take a big sip of coffee and realize too late that instead of sugar you put in salt. Phew! Dee and Annie were wolfing it down like starving people.

Quinte's claim to fame among provincial prisons is its reputation for serving "home-cooked meals." But after several weeks, I learned from the other women that the main ingredient in these so-called home-cooked meals was water. If it was technically possible, the food in the kitchen arrived dried in packets to which you just add water, no chef required.

Gone were the good old days when women and men worked together in the kitchen preparing food from scratch. Apparently this practice ended when one too many women ended up with more than just bread in the oven. I also suspect the same culprit that was eroding away all government services was involved: cutbacks.

When I was released, I was able to get a breakdown of Quinte's 2005–2006 budget under the *Freedom of Information and Protection of Privacy Act*. The total annual budget, including staff salaries, prisoners' food, maintenance, and other budgetary items totaled $11,467,157.00. Eighty-four percent of this budget was allocated for staff salaries, at a cost of $9,646,189.00, while 3 percent was allocated for the prisoners' food and beverages. This amounted to a daily food and beverage expenditure of $3.75 a day per prisoner, or $1.25 per meal, assuming there are roughly 250 prisoners in Quinte on any given day.[56] At least the Ontario taxpayers couldn't complain about the amount of money spent on food in the "country club" conditions of their provincial prisons.

About half an hour after the guards had collected our carefully stacked trays and plastic spoons from our food slots, the familiar code green blared out through the intercom, indicating that all the spoons were safely back in custody. Once again the worn-out legends would be dragged out, reminding me and anyone else interested of the dreaded lockdowns and cell and strip searches that would inevitably follow a dropped tray or lost spoon. Good behaviour in Quinte came from a whispering guard living inside most prisoners, breathing fear into anyone who dared to break rank with the group.

We had just settled down on our bunks when a code blue rang out over the intercom system. We heard the guards who had been doing count racing down the corridor in their soft-soled shoes. Code blue meant there was some kind of emergency in the building, and a code green would be called out when it was over. As soon as a code blue was announced, every staff in the building, other than the classification staff, would drop whatever they were doing and race to the scene of the "crime." It could be anything from a couple of prisoners yelling at each other to a bloody stabbing or hostage-taking. But the staff seemed to enjoy it; they always came back excited and satiated, seeming to feel as though maybe their job of counting, feeding, and locking up a bunch of poor people might not be boring, but might even be dangerous. Certainly it made all the special codes, fancy military uniforms, and titles seem somewhat justified, at least to them. To us, it was a joke.

I was feeling somewhat down from my conflict with Dee and the fact that I wouldn't be getting my methadone until after the code blue. But when they finally called code green, the keys jangled in our door. *Thank God*, I thought with relief, fighting the urge to smile. But instead of a methadone escort, a white shirt loomed in the door.

"Okay, girls, you know the routine," he said, watching us carefully. I had nothing to fear from a strip search because I had no drugs or tobacco to hide. We were each taken to a separate area to be strip searched.

I walked into the shower stall and took my clothes off in front of the female guard standing in front of me, who just happened to be Barbie. She took them with her latex-gloved hands and began barking orders. I had the distinct impression that she harboured a serious personal grudge towards me.

"Hair." I flicked my hair over my face so she could see there was nothing hidden underneath it. She went through her list, ears, mouth, breasts, and so on.

After I had submitted to her command, she looked at me like I was a piece of faulty merchandise and swept her arm toward the door, as though it was too much effort to tell me to leave. Dee and Annie were waiting with another guard outside the room and rolled their eyes as I walked past.

We were herded down to the holding cell behind the A&D area. Once they locked the door behind us, I could see that it was a windowless room without a ventilation system, just the quarter-inch space under the door. It was a claustrophobic's hell. The pungent air was a nauseating mix of sweat, urine, and what I imagined to be blood. There was a thick layer of grime on the walls, floor, and benches. The cinderblock room was a perfect square, with nothing to stimulate the eye other than someone's raw attempts to scrape paint off the walls to create graffiti messages crying out for help. The room had the feng shui of a torture chamber.

Slowly, the room filled until there was about twelve of us. After a while the alpha girls started telling their stories while the rest of us sat around the perimeter on the benches and floor, trying to remain invisible. A feeling of paranoia swept over the group. What if your personal defects became the brunt of someone's jokes? People started to laugh to keep the fear and anger at bay.

"Back in the day," Jay began. She was standing on top of a bench. "When I was just a young pup straight out of juvie, I was a bad player with a bad attitude." Some chuckles went around the room. "So one day, I can't remember why, but I know I deserved it." More giggles and a few snorts. "Shipley, you know the man. He's still here." Some of the women said, "Yeah."

"He comes out of the cold blue and picks me up by the collar. I'm about a hundred pounds soaking wet, and he carries me back down here to this holding cell. He throws me in so hard I hit my head on the other side of the room." A few women burst out laughing. "I thought I was out cold until he starts beating me so bad I shit myself. I lay there puking and shitting. No toilet, no toilet paper, no blanket, no water, no food, and I'm coming down on top of it all." There were howls of laughter. "Finally, after twenty-four hours, they let me out. Them were the days, let me tell you." A few women chuckled.

After a couple of other short stories highlighting the pain tolerance theme, the keys clanged in the door and the white shirt motioned for us to follow him. We walked in single file, women yelling out at guards or male prisoners they recognized along the way, until we reached the barrier to the women's unit. A couple of female guards were there to escort us the rest of the way, but the white shirt singled me out to go with him to get my methadone in the nursing station.

Retracing our steps back through A&D, he started to get chatty. He was not the same one who had done the cell search the other day.

"So you're the terrorist, eh?" He smiled, oozing a false charm and warmth.

"No, I'm not a terrorist."

"That's not what I hear."

"So you've been reading my file?"

"I fought in Vietnam, so I know a thing or two about fighting with guns, except we weren't looking for attention. From what I've learned, people like you are attention seekers."

"That's bullshit!" I explained hotly, making a quick decision to talk politics with him since I figured my political views were already part of the public record. "I'm not going to get into it here, but I'll give you this … we wanted the destruction of the earth to stop, and justice for the poor. We were acting as genuinely as any soldier in the army, except that we weren't fighting on behalf of a bunch of old, rich, white men." I hoped that last comment would not be construed as a backhanded racist comment, considering that he was Black.

"No," he retorted, "I enlisted because I believe it's very important to fight for freedom and democracy."

"You mean like what they're doing in Iraq?"

"Yeah, kinda like what they're doing in Iraq."

"You mean like fighting for American oil interests in the Middle East?"

I was relieved when we arrived at the nursing station. He made himself comfortable in a chair with his feet up on the bars, facing my direction, but not exactly looking at me. I drank my glass of water, my methadone, and my second glass of water, then settled down to read, for the hundredth time, the laminated plaque on the wall explaining that "inmates" could write letters of complaint to the Ontario ombudsman once they had exhausted the internal avenues of redress. I had memorized the address and instructions on the plaque, not because I intended to write the ombudsman, but out of sheer boredom.

After his failed attempt to spark up a conversation on terrorism and global politics, he apparently decided to zero in on home.

"So I hear you're very concerned about injustice in Quinte."

The word "injustice" jumped out at me like a beast in the dark, sparking a memory of a letter I had been writing the night before in which I had tried to explain why most women in prison were so angry. A cloak of paranoia enveloped me. I decided now was a good time to keep my mouth shut. But after a quick internal debate weighing the risks and benefits of continuing the conversation, I weighed in on the side of bene-fits, deciding that there could be no harm if I could get more information from him than he could from me. In retrospect, this was a very dangerous justification for engaging with any authority figure, because it can lead down the slippery slope of unintended consequences. I didn't give him any sensitive information, but talking to him was wrong, period.

"So you've been reading my letters?"

"You mean your journal," he replied.

"Those are letters," I said emphatically.

"Fifty pages! That's no letter."

"What can I say? I like to write. Besides, we can only send two free letters a week. So I like to write long letters."

"It looks like a journal to me." After that I retreated like a turtle into its shell, and there was nothing he could do to get me back out again. On the walk back to the unit I went over everything I had written since I got there. There was nothing of consequence in my letters. If I was guilty of anything, it would be long-winded political rants against the prison system and capitalism. But then again, why was I so paranoid? Nothing that I had written was illegal. It all came back to the feeling of lawlessness in Quinte, a feeling that anything could happen. As soon as we got back I tracked Jay down and asked her about this particular white shirt.

"Oh yeah, Rick. He's an okay guy. I remember when he first got here years ago. They gave him a rough time of it 'cause he's a nigger and everything, but he stuck with it and now he's a white shirt. He's probably one of the best of them. Why?"

"Oh, he's just nosy. He took me down for my meth after the strip search and was asking me a bunch of questions."

"Yeah. He's friendly," Jay said.

When I was locked back in my cell again, I noticed a faint whiff of tobacco in the air, and Barbie glanced in through my window. I started picking up the pages that were strewn all over the table and floor.

"You better watch what you're saying. Nobody likes people who keep journals," Dee warned me. I stopped what I was doing and turned to stare at her.

"It's not a *journal*," I said.

She retreated under her blanket. But then I started thinking. Why did she call those pages a "journal?" Even if she had read my letters, she wouldn't call them a "journal," and the white shirt had no opportunity to talk to her.

"So, I guess Barbie has been complaining to you guys about my letters, eh?" I speculated.

Dee sat up, and Annie stared at me like I had lost my mind.

"Why have you got it in for her? She's the best screw they got here."

"You have a funny way of judging screws," I said bitterly.

Later that day I parked myself on the picnic table beside Gypsy, who was sitting ramrod straight watching a soap.

"Gypsy?" She stared at the screen as though I hadn't spoken. Maybe she didn't realize I was talking to her. "Gypsy, why does everyone like that screw Barbie so much?" I ventured, even though I knew my lack of discretion would probably warrant silence. She smiled along with the canned laughter on the screen. I settled in to watch the soap with her, pretending I hadn't said a thing. After about ten minutes the show went into commercial. Without moving, she said, "Are you stupid?" For a moment, I thought she was talking to the TV. When the show came back on, I glanced up at her face. There was nothing to indicate she had been talking to me.

Dee and Annie surfaced for showers during the last hour out of our cells. Every time someone came out of the shower stall, a faint whiff of tobacco followed in their wake. I started pacing up and down the corridor, feeling more boxed in than ever. Everyone seemed to be glancing over at me when they didn't think I was looking, whispering about what an asshole I was, making enemies with the only "good" screw, although I still couldn't figure out what was so good about her. They were probably going to band together to get me PC'd. Nobody trusts a prisoner who keeps a journal. But I hadn't been writing a journal. How could they know I wasn't keeping tabs on all the contraband action going on? I had gone to great pains to avoid mentioning anything that could get other prisoners in trouble. I should have shredded all those letters, or better still, not have written anything at all.

Dee and Annie were on the other side of the barrier, whispering to Barbie and openly pointing at me and laughing. I could feel myself sinking. If I didn't get it together soon, the other women would smell blood and really go for the jugular. In no time I would be in administrative seg, simply driven there by my own fear. I'd seen it a million times. Like they say, there is nothing to fear but fear itself. I held my head up high and straightened my back. At least I wouldn't look afraid. But did I look like a crazy person, walking stiffly up and down the corridor, avoiding everyone's eyes?

At lockup I breezed past Barbie into the cell, but instead of Dee and Annie, Smokey's broad silhouette filled the doorway for a few seconds, just long enough to convey the message that Barbie was willing to lock her in with me to teach me a lesson if need be. I had barely had time to digest this when Smokey stepped aside to let Dee and Annie slip in past her.

Smokey was the only woman higher in the pecking order than Gypsy or Jay. Her legendary rage was the first thing anyone learned about her. She had spent her entire last bit in segregation because she had beat up a woman who had insulted her. After Smokey was in seg and the woman in the hospital, her cellmate had to clean up the huge puddle of coagulated blood, which she described as having the same consistency as raspberry Jell-O.

Smokey was doing time for an aggravated assault charge from the street involving multiple stab wounds. Anyone talking about her outside charge never failed to mention that the final thrust had left just the handle of the shank sticking out of the person's body. Luckily for Smokey her victim had survived, but she was definitely facing pen time. The possibility of going to the pen was referred to in the same way most people would talk about going to university.

As Barbie was about to lock the cell door behind us for the night, she smiled broadly at me. "Hansen, pack your stuff. You're moving." The door clanged shut. All my fear sank in a storm of rage. I turned on Dee. "So you asked her to move me out of my cell?"

"I wouldn't do that," she said disingenuously. Her features were a series of slits. For a few seconds I debated slugging her, but I wasn't prepared. The fear had exhausted me. I knew that I would have to strengthen my resolve and find the right time to put a stop to this, or I would end up at the wrong end of the unit.

True to her word, Barbie was back in five minutes. My pillowcase was stuffed with my letters, toiletries, and clothes. I followed her down the corridor as closely as I could without touching her, breathing down her neck. She was so short I could see the top of her head. She was not just small, but petite and feminine. Probably couldn't defend herself without a fully automatic weapon and a jump start.

When she opened the cell door, I couldn't believe it. There was a bunk bed with no mattress on the floor and no sign of anyone else: a cell of my own. At that moment I couldn't have been closer to heaven. I made the bed on the top bunk and lay down, staring at the tiny cell around me. It seemed so warm and cozy and inviting. I pulled a book out of the pillowcase and began to go through the motions of reading, although I was much too happy to read. Reality was so much more pleasant. I didn't want to miss a minute of this delicious solitude, knowing that it could never last.

Dee and Annie stayed hunkered down in their cell the next afternoon. Even though I was thrilled to be in a cell of my own, the way it had happened was humiliating. I felt contaminated. Everyone must know that I had been kicked out of my own cell and had not resisted, like a coward. I avoided talking, sitting near, or contacting anyone for fear of being shunned.

After spending the evening locked in solitude, I ventured out again for the final hour. Dee and Annie had also chosen to come out and were playing cards with the alpha girls, Gypsy and Smokey. Once again I found refuge in pacing up and down the corridor, never stopping, so I wouldn't have to sit beside or talk to anyone. But there was no escape. Every time I had to turn around in the common room to make my next round down the corridor, I heard them whispering and chuckling. A few key words jumped out at me: "journal," "writing," and "man on the range." This was as low as I would sink. Something inside me clicked and I knew the time was right. I waited, stalking the moment when Dee would get up and away from the Plexiglas windows of the guards' office.

She must have felt my challenge like a magnetic pull. Our rendezvous was inevitable. She got up with Smokey and headed down the corridor toward me. I took the centre of the corridor, forcing Dee to squeeze up against Smokey to avoid physical contact. When I turned around at the bottom they were heading straight toward me, well away from the prying eyes of the screws.

"Dee!" I said in a firm but quiet voice. She lifted her head and our eyes met. She knew what was coming. Although I couldn't count on a one-on-one, Smokey did the honourable thing and backed off.

"You've been riding me and riding me. What's your problem?" I asked, barely able to contain myself, and then, without waiting for an answer, I called her out. "Let's go." But Dee had been bluffing all along. Instead of trying to deck me, she smiled.

"I was just joking around. There's no problem," she said softly. In that instant, she surrendered. Her surrender was rather anticlimactic. It took me a few seconds to stop myself from decking her anyway. It was like slamming on the brakes just before a collision, but then still skidding for a few more yards.

At lockup, Dee managed to run down the corridor to my cell and pushed an offering, a pad of paper that she had bought from canteen, under the door. She peered through the tiny Plexiglas window and smiled.

The next day Jay caught up with me circling around the yard. She was a multitasker, having no trouble keeping up with me while maintaining a running dialogue with the other women sunbathing on the hot asphalt.

"Look!" she cried, stopping beside the high-wire mesh fence. A flock of seagulls were raucously fighting for bits of bread that some women had squeezed through the fence. She took a handful of white bread and gummed it up into a ball, leaned back like a ball player, and pitched the wad over the coils of razor wire at the top of the eight-metre fence. She had the type of athletic body needed for Olympic shotputters, although I suspected much of her fitness was from living life on double time, fuelled by speed-induced adrenalin. The evidence was in the thick band of scar tissue that ran like burn marks down the inside of her arm. She wore her scar tissue shamelessly, like a tattoo.

"Hey, Barbie wants to know if you're going to drop it," Jay said cheerfully.

"Drop what?"

"The journal you're writing, the complaints, whatever."

"I don't know how many times I have to tell you I'm not writing a journal. They're just letters."

"All I know is I ain't gettin' no kites from my old man 'cause she says you're writing complaints about them. And no smokes either. She's the best one we got, so I don't know what went down between you and her, but I hope you're going to let it drop. This ain't P4W, and it ain't ever going to be. So can I tell her it's over?" I could not believe what I was hearing. If anything, this was going to raise the bar, but I wasn't about to tell Jay that.

Now Barbie had crossed the line. Not only was she spreading vicious rumours that my letters were a tell-all journal, but now she was reaching out to the alpha girls, hoping they would muscle me into submission. Obviously the guards' concept of someone fighting for justice was someone who would report corruption. They did not have the analysis to understand that we weren't interested in reporting a little corruption. We were interested in pulling back the screen and exposing the Wizard, and dismantling the whole damn Oz.

After the yard closed we sat around the picnic tables for a little while, waiting for the guards to lock us up for supper. When Barbie and another screw came shuffling in, I took my time going toward my cell. By the time I got there, the other screw had disappeared back into the office. At the end of the corridor, Barbie was just finishing locking up Gypsy. For a split second I saw something pass between them, just before she turned in my direction, winked, and closed her fist, leaving her finger pointing at my face, as though it was a handgun.

. . .

A few weeks later Kelly was back in my cell again, and we were talking about all the tension and violence that comes from imprisoning three women in a cell designed for one for nineteen hours a day. We became very enthusiastic about the idea of writing a letter about the conditions in Quinte to the editor of the local paper, the Kingston *Whig-Standard*. Not only would we explain why we thought this was an inhumane practice, but we would also suggest that prisoners be credited with three days for every day they served in Quinte as compensation by the sentencing judge. It was already a common practice for judges to credit prisoners two days for every day they were awaiting sentencing in overcrowded remand prisons like Quinte.

Our discussion inevitably led to the possibility of getting this archaic prison shut down, or building an extension so there would be room for more cells. But then we remembered what had happened when they closed down the Prison for Women. They had opened six new regional prisons for women under the pretense that the prisoners would be closer to their families and communities and have access to more programming and better facilities.

When the recommendations from the Arbour Inquiry into Certain Events at the Prison for Women first came out in 1996, the capacity for P4W was 142 prisoners.[57] By 2006, ten years later, after the new regional prisons were operational, the number of women in federal prisons had jumped by 44 percent, to over 400.[58] Within six years the population of Grand Valley, the Ontario federal prison for women, had surpassed that of P4W when it closed in 2000! Certainly this dramatic population explosion could not be explained by a similar increase in the general population of women in Canada or even the crime rate for women. Yet in 2013, "Statistics Canada said the overall police-reported crime rate decreased 3 percent, reaching the lowest point since 1972."[59] The expression "If you build it, they will come" could not have been more prophetic.

"You know what would be a good idea?" said Kelly. "I should have been given a community service option, 'cause I'm no threat to the community just because I was driving under suspension. They got my kid in foster care and me in here. What good is that goin' to do? If they absolutely got to, they should give us sentences that will get us out quicker, 'cause we're no threat to anybody. That way the girls that are in here can do time in a cell of their own. Less stress. No way do we want a bigger, better Quinte." The suggestions in our letter were far from revolutionary, but at least they would be a voice from Quinte, no matter how small.

After lockup we sat huddled over our article on the bottom bunk. It was a collective effort that buoyed our spirits. We had distilled our personal problems into a clear solution. The experience of taking our snapshots of experience and quilting them together into a mosaic not only channelled our negative energies into something positive, but also contributed a concrete solution to the problem.

I crawled up onto my top bunk and looked down at Kelly, translating her illegible scrawl in the dim nightlight. In the morning I would put our letter into a sealed envelope for my lawyer so she could mail it to the *Whig*.

A few hours later the unit was quiet, a rare moment. The only sounds were the soft snores of Kelly on the bunk below. I rolled over and peered out the barred window through the yellow lights illuminating the grounds outside. Just through the line of dark trees silhouetted on the horizon, I could see the odd set of headlights whizzing past on the freeway. It must have been very late.

What would happen when the article appeared in the letters-to-the-editor section of the *Whig*? We were going to sign it, but even if we didn't, I would be their first suspect. How would the other prisoners react? There would be consequences. There always were. Perhaps they would take away our two free letters a week, or maybe they would do more strip and cell searches. There was a real possibility that the other women would blame me for this. Of course the administration would believe that I had pressured Kelly into signing the letter. Of course they would initiate some new repressive measures as group punishment for the letter.

Barbie would go scrambling around from one prisoner to the next, blaming me for everything going on in the institution, egging them on to punish me. It would be a blessing if all I would have to deal with was the wrath of the administration and guards, but no, it would be the prisoners who would mete out the worst punishment of all … me, me, me, me. At least that's how I saw things when dark thoughts reigned supreme in the early hours of the morning. I tried my best to refocus with a more revolutionary, big-picture lens, rather than the small, selfish snapshots preoccupying me at the suicide hour of four in the morning.

I slid down quietly onto the toilet bowl, trying not to wake Kelly. The letter lay on the desk, with Kelly's neat, bold printing visible even in the dim nightlight. I thought of ripping it in two and then shredding it again, and again, and again, until the pieces were small enough to disappear down the toilet. Kelly rolled over and grumbled. Then I climbed back up and went to sleep.

Fate intervened. Early the next morning I was transferred. I don't know if Kelly posted the letter, which the guards would no doubt censor, or if she had second thoughts like I had. All I do know is that our letter to the *Whig* never saw the light of day.

Twenty Six

On August 3 I was surprised to be woken up by a couple of guards, who told me to put all my belongings in a pillowcase because I was being transferred. I remember the date because it was Henry's birthday. I was escorted to the legal visiting room, where I had breakfast and waited. After breakfast the guards began one of their weekly strip and cell searches, which I assumed they would claim was related to my transfer. The guards were constantly scapegoating federal prisoners as the source of all trouble. No doubt the women would think that my "journal" had revealed their secrets.

As I watched the guards systematically trashing each cell, I remembered hearing stories from the women in P4W about the 1981 human rights investigation into discrimination against federally sentenced women. The guards constantly tried to sabotage this investigation by reminding the prisoners that if they cooperated, they would lose the "privilege" of wearing their own street clothes and the freedom to decorate their cells. They were warned, in the name of gender equality, that they would be wearing institutional prison sweats and living in barren cells with the most minimalist of decor, just like the guys in Millhaven. In time these warnings would live on as the whispering guard in the women's heads.

Yes, I was quite confident that this whispering guard would be blaming me for this early morning cell and strip search. As the women were shuffled one by one into the shower stall to be strip searched, I could hear them complaining about the phones being shut off—a routine procedure every time a prisoner was transferred. Apparently this measure would prevent prisoners from being able to coordinate escape plans with anyone from the outside.

Finally I was shuffled out to a waiting Econoline van in my leg irons and handcuffs. I had anticipated being transported in the usual cubbyhole in the back of a custom prison van, so I was pleasantly surprised to be sitting facing forward in the backseat of a regular van with windows and two provincial cops. I was given the most minimal explanation of where I was going, but no answer as to why. Otherwise they acted as though I didn't exist, which suited me just fine. For some unknown reason I was being transported to the new Central East Correctional Centre, more commonly referred to as either CECC or Lindsay, the town near where it is located.

CECC and its twin, the Central North Correctional Centre (CNCC), are typical of the new architectural prototype of the twenty-first century super-prison, with its pods, bubbles, and high-tech surveillance. They are described as super-prisons because they were built for economies of scale by amalgamating a number of smaller regional prisons. CECC and CNCC were designed to each hold 1,200 remand and provincial prisoners. "Lindsay" was constructed along with the CNCC as an experiment in Ontario Conservative premier Mike Harris's "common sense revolution" to determine which would be more effective and efficient: a government-run or a privately run prison. They were identical in every way except that the CNCC, which is near Penetanguishene, was to be managed by a private American-based firm, the Management and Training Corporation, while the CECC in Lindsay would be managed by the provincial correctional services. I could just picture Harris's Minister of Provincial Corrections making sure that none of the staff had put scenic posters on the walls to soften the atmosphere before he proudly took Harris on his first tour of the CNCC. After five years, the government of the day would decide which type of management had proven best.

The decision to build provincial super-jails, with a design that emphasized security and cost-efficient human warehousing features, was another example of the trickle-down effect of neoliberalism. The expression "trickle-down effect" was first popularized in the eighties and used by neoliberal economists to justify maintaining an uber-wealthy elite at the top of the social order. They argued that the economic policies that favour the wealthy would inevitably create positive spinoffs for the working and middle class. In other words, they believed that policies such as deregulation and low income and corporate taxes would benefit the wealthy, who in turn would hire more people, expand their businesses, and invest their wealth, resulting in more jobs, money, and security for the working and middle class.[60]

Time has proven this theory to have the exact opposite effect. It's really more like the wealth generated from the majority "trickles up" to the already wealthy, creating a situation in which a small percentage of the global population get even richer at the expense of the vast majority. In fact, the effects that are "trickling down" to people in the middle and working classes are the *negative* effects from the growing concentration of wealth among the already uber-wealthy, such as poverty, crime, addiction and homelessness, the growing crisis of climate change, and growing political instability on a global scale.[61]

At first, the small, rural town of Penetanguishene was thrilled to have all the much-needed employment and capital expenditures they were promised a new prison would bring. However, after their community was selected, the townspeople began to feel betrayed when they learned the prison was to be privately run, with all the many pitfalls associated with privately run prisons in the United States. They learned that the guards would be hired from the private sector and thus would not have the relatively high wages, nor the training and expertise, of unionized guards. They also learned that privately run prisons scrimp on programming and education, translating into higher recidivism rates than publicly run prisons. The fear of violent escaped and paroled prisoners sent a chill down the spines of the good citizens in Penetanguishene and motivated them to organize against the privately run prison in their backyard. Unfortunately their efforts failed, and CNCC was built and then run by the American management company.

Five years later, in 2006, the newly elected Liberal premier of Ontario, Dalton McGuinty, announced that the competition was over and the government-run prison had won the race; according to the Ministry of Corrections, there had been "no appreciable benefit from the private operation," and the publicly run prison, CECC, performed better in key areas such as security, health care, and reducing recidivism rates. In what would become a pattern, the public sector had won, but the private sector was sneaking into the prison system through the back door. Food services for three super-jails in Ontario would be centralized via a private contract awarded to Eurest Dining Services, a member of Compass Group Canada. This private company would run a cook-chill food preparation centre on the site of another super-jail, Maplehurst, where meals would be prepared and then frozen for short-term storage until they could be shipped to the other super-jails, where they would be reheated for service.

I spent the next few hours enjoying the pastoral countryside through the windows of the van until we pulled up under the sally port of "Lindsay." From my van window, all I could see was a sprawling complex of low brick buildings surrounded by high-wire mesh fences topped by the usual coils of concertina wire. At some point during my research for Womyn-4Justice projects, I had seen aerial photographs of CECC and its twin sister, CNCC. Architecturally they resembled other members of the super-prison family, which can be spotted from the air in poverty-stricken rural areas bordering small towns across North America, looking like huge spiders with their legs splayed out across the barren landscape. The spider's body is the administrative hub of the building, where the main bubble is situated, and the legs are the pods, where the mini-bubbles and "living units" of the prisoners are located. The 1,200 prisoners are imprisoned in six self-contained octagonal pods, each able to hold 192 prisoners. The main bubble is the brain of the building, a glass-walled surveillance hub manned by at least one guard who monitors banks of CCTVs and, with the flip of a switch, the corresponding audio feed, 24/7. The barren landscape is typical because new prisons are usually located near economically depressed small towns in rural areas, far from the families of the prisoners.

Once I had been shuffled inside, I realized that the only thing that distinguished this Admissions and Discharge area from that in Quinte was a fresh coat of paint. The feng shui was Kafkaesque. There were no pictures or adornments of any kind, nothing to distinguish this area from another except the colour of the paint. I was struck by the fact that everything was either numbered or caged, including the lightbulbs and the people. I still can't get my Federally Sentenced Prisoner number, FPS532914B, out of my head.

As soon as my handlers and I stepped through the doors, we were greeted by two guards with clipboards who started asking the cops my vital statistics. With the first question, my name, I instinctively began to answer when one of the cops cut me off. I realized that I was a hologram, and the only real, reliable people were my OPP handlers, so I took on the usual generic expressionless, silent prisoner persona.

I began to understand why so many poor people are willing to appear on television shows like *Jerry Springer* and *Dr. Phil*. Why would anyone voluntarily humiliate themselves on live television in front of millions of people? Those who are invisible, irrelevant, and useless in this society will often do anything, no matter how degrading, to be recognized for once as alive, relevant, and useful.

Despite having been strip searched in Quinte just before leaving, and having had no contact with anyone since, I was strip searched again and given a pair of dark green prison sweats, the colour code of provincial prisoners. Grey was for federally sentenced women, and purple was for prisoners being transported. If they had put our prisoner number on the front of our coloured prison sweats, we could have been considered labelled and branded for scanning just like groceries on the checkout counter. If I could only snuff out my political conscience, I would trademark that idea.

The purple transfer sweats were euphemistically called "Barney" suits, after the iconic purple dinosaur in a popular children's TV show at the time. The purple was supposed to deter prisoners from successfully executing a "switch," a scheme in which one prisoner successfully assumes another prisoner's identity who is supposed to be released, and then feigns surprise when the authorities discover the error.

Once admitted, I was left alone in a holding cell, where the architectural lines made by the poured concrete benches and privacy walls were round, leaving no sharp edges, the architectural enemy of prison construction. Even the profiles of the stainless-steel toilet/sink module conformed to this roundedness. I assumed a hole in the floor was where the water would drain after they had spray-cleaned the room with a high-pressure hose, like a bloody abattoir.

I realized I was not alone when I heard the voice of a woman with a Jamaican accent in another holding cell yelling into the phone. She was probably yelling to avoid wasting any time or money on repeating words, since the Millennium phone system is very expensive. Even local calls are collect. This is a new, computerized phone system designed explicitly for the prison system. Once admitted, a prisoner submits a limited list of phone numbers for approval. All calls are automatically recorded, and cost more than the same calls would outside prison.

I couldn't help eavesdropping and thinking about how difficult it was for some people with a dialect from certain regions to get housing or a job. Many people from Toronto's social housing projects in the Jane-Finch neighbourhood develop a dialect that is often associated with rap or poor Black people. Like so many other people from economically depressed neighbourhoods in Canada, regardless of their colour, they find it hard to get a job because prospective employers will judge them sight unseen based on their dialect. This is the case not only for those growing up in the Jane-Finch neighbourhood in Toronto, but social housing projects in general, Indigenous reserves, the East Coast, Quebec, rural areas—any place where a person's dialect brands them as poor and uneducated. Of course, a person's dialect is not an accurate indicator of their education or competence, but it can be an indicator of a person's class, even in a so-called classless society like Canada.

In prison, where the social yardsticks outside the walls are irrelevant, I have noticed that many educated, middle-class prisoners will avoid speaking in their native middle-class, educated dialect. Instead, they will embrace the dialects associated with illiteracy and outlaw neighbourhoods: dialects that will reinforce their otherness, distinct from the enemy, the prison regime and the outside society.

Finally, all this eavesdropping and reflection were interrupted when one of the clone-like guards came to escort me to my pod. They were wearing all-season, unisex clothing to match the all-season, gender-neutral atmosphere of the place. The building was either air-conditioned or heated to an optimal temperature for a working guard, and considering that there were no windows or clocks, it was impossible to know what time of day or season it was. A constant subtle hum emanated from the building, contributing to the impression that the building was alive and controlled the people. Whether the hum came from the heating/cooling system, the fluorescent lights, the all-pervasive electronic surveillance system, or all of the above doesn't really matter. The hum was a constant reminder of the building's presence, unlike the guards, who walked silently around in soft-soled shoes and disappeared into bubbles surrounded by one-way black glass. Most of the time the only human sound, other than the prisoners, was a robotic-sounding voice periodically echoing down the corridors from the two-way intercom systems.

We walked silently down a series of identical corridors, distinguished only by the walls painted in different bright colours as we passed from one pod into the next, until we came to a huge bubble. This seemed to be the centre from which all the pods emanated. Throughout the building, on the ceiling of every corridor, there were these round, bluish-black, luminous yet expressionless eyes watching like the eyes of a cow, but never blinking. These were the 360-degree lenses of the 24/7 CCTV monitoring system inside the bubbles that keep track of everything going on everywhere except inside the cells. Not only could reality be monitored in real time, but the past could be rewound and reviewed with the press of a button. It was the ultimate in reality TV, with hours of mind-numbing content interspersed with the occasional blood-and-guts sequence of a crime drama or the laugh-out-loud humour of a sitcom. The one-way black glass walls, the doors that could only be opened from the inside, and the enclosed toilet made the security inside these bubbles more impressive than the cockpit of a 747. At this point I was struck by how much everything about Lindsay was like a cheap Star Trek set.

I would have been quite comfortable to see Captain Kirk or Captain Picard, wearing their unisex jumpsuits, disappearing into a black bubble.

Then we turned down a corridor, where the sounds of women's voices echoing against the cinderblock walls led us to a barred barrier. Someone somewhere inside a mini-bubble must have detected our presence because the door clicked open. The women's pod consisted of two living units with one adjoining floor-to-ceiling Plexiglas wall facing a raised platform where a mini-bubble was located. Inside you could very faintly see the dull glow of TV monitors, but otherwise it was just a black glass–walled room where an unknown number of guards resided. It felt a bit like looking at the glass wall of a police interrogation room, where you know a number of detectives are watching you, sight unseen. The guards led me up to the glass entrance door of one of the units, which automatically clicked open, and then disappeared into the mini-bubble.

The two women's living units were identical, mirror images separated by a cinderblock wall. Each living unit was designed for sixteen women and contained eight double-occupancy cells and a common room with exactly four plastic picnic tables bolted to the poured cement floor, with four swivel seats attached to each table, providing one seat for each woman. Hanging from the ceiling, just beyond reach, was a small television screen blasting out the laugh track from some sitcom. The television's soundtrack reverberated unintelligibly off the cinderblock walls, mingling with the yelling and laughter of the real women's voices. Hanging from the walls were three Millennium phones with no corresponding chair or stool, no doubt to discourage long conversations. Otherwise there was nothing on the walls but the coloured paint of this particular pod. On the opposite side of the common room were a series of small rooms that I later learned were the laundry room, bath and shower room, and toilet stall. The entire unit was constantly being monitored by a number of CCTV cameras and grilled intercom devices scattered about the two-storey ceiling.

Even the exercise yard was impeccably secure and sterile, surrounded by three brick walls, one Plexiglas wall, and a Plexiglas ceiling, so we could go out for our one hour of daily exercise rain or shine. There was not a speck of gravel, grass, or any living thing in that yard, just asphalt. When I did eventually go out for our daily hour of exercise, I would pretend the prison was a module on the moon. We were completely contained inside concrete without another plant or living organism, other than the guards and other prisoners. Not even spiders and mice could survive here. Although I was always vigilant, I never saw even a trace of a spider's web, dead fly, dried-up leaf, or mouse turd. The only contact we had with the natural world was by looking up at the sky through the Plexiglas ceiling in the yard to watch a cloud or occasional bird fly silently by.

The only other windows I encountered were these four-foot-high-by-six-inch-wide windows in each cell that would be impossible to escape through even if the glass was broken, unless you were a new superhero, "Rubber Woman." The vista these windows faced was the wall of the next arm of the building, separated by a swath of grass.

I had to admit the pod was a marvel of human warehousing design. Just one guard inside the mini-bubble could effectively control the daily lives of thirty-two women without ever stepping foot outside the bubble, no latex gloves required. By constructing the bubble a few feet above the floor level of the rest of the pod, the guards could survey all the activities taking place inside the two separate living areas, plus two separate activity rooms, the exercise yard, the segregation area, and the health care unit, without ever leaving their swivel chairs.

The pod was also a marvel of technological security. One guard could control the entire pod: their arms were the electronically controlled doors; their eyes, ears and mouth, the audio/visual equipment; their brain, the computer. I imagine these expensive technological gadgets save the government untold millions by eliminating the even more expensive, yet less predictable—as well as less competent—human beings.

Anytime a prisoner needed to interact with the guards, they would put in a paper request and arrange to rendezvous at the sliding glass window in the Plexiglas wall, the same portal used by the nurse to dispense medication. At meal times, a prisoner trusty for each living unit would deliver meal trays to a slot in our cell doors, then sit in the common room by herself, ready to respond to any requests, and then pick up the finished meal trays. Throughout the day she was the go-between the guards and us, delivering cleaning supplies or anything else we might need that was outside our living unit.

The only time the guards really needed to enter the living units was when there was a disturbance or to carry out a cell or strip search. In the future they'll just use robots. In the short time I was there, the only disturbance involved a table of four women raising their voices in a dis-agreement over what TV channel to watch. The guards simply threat-ened, through the intercom system, to lock us down if everyone didn't quiet down. The women did quiet down, but not quickly enough, so within the hour backup arrived, followed by a cell and strip search. These searches were used both as punishment and a deterrent to future "disturbances" that might be interpreted as a threat to the "good order" of the institution. Security in the twenty-first century is all about deterrence. The guards were conveniently and securely situated inside their own self-contained bubble, from which they could orchestrate their own Machiavellian horror show if they were bored. Without ever setting foot inside the common room, they could charge us, order us locked down, or do anything else that might stir up the pot. Then they could just sit back and watch while we began imploding and exploding on each other. The sinister beauty of it all was that, in the end, we would only hold grudges against each other, because the real source of our anger was so out of reach. Like when someone driving down the highway becomes consumed by road rage after learning over their cellphone that their loved one is having an affair. The next person that cuts them off gets his head blown off.

Through my prison abolition work, I had heard about the classic prison architecture, the Panopticon, first designed in 1785 by Jeremy Bentham, a British philosopher who described his design best: "A new mode of obtaining power of mind over mind, in a quantity hitherto without example."[62] The now-defunct Kingston Penitentiary was a textbook example of Panopticon architecture when it was built in 1835. Inside a high rotunda, tier upon tier of cells constructed against a circular outer wall encircled a central guard tower in such a way that the guards could watch the prisoners without being seen. A singular prisoner among hundreds could never see if a guard was actually observing him, but was aware that he could be observed at any time. The cumulative psychological effect was that prisoners would regulate their own behaviour, knowing that they could never be sure whether or not they were actually under surveillance. In this way, the few could guard the many.

The architectural design of P4W and Quinte strayed from the original principles of the Panopticon, particularly in terms of surveillance. Other than actually patrolling past the cells, the guards relied heavily on creating stories of legendary consequences for bad behaviour that were passed down from prisoner to prisoner—the old-school notion of deterrence through example. But the prison architecture of the twenty-first century, in the form of podular prison design and high-tech surveillance techniques, has remained true to the inspiration of Jeremy Bentham, creating the illusion that one is always under surveillance.

The feng shui is not the only Kafkaesque aspect of the CECC. So too is the bureaucracy, in that the rules and procedures are based on the universal principle that what is good for one is good for all. The result is an oppressive bureaucracy bordering on the absurd. Washing your hair with your own shampoo is legal, whereas sharing some with a newcomer who has none is not. Regardless of how reasonable an explanation you offer a guard for being one minute late entering your cell at lockup, you can still be charged with refusing to obey a direct order. The boundaries defining the legality or illegality of the endless list of rules that control the minutiae of daily life are fluid.

I arrived during the lunch hour, when everyone was locked down. At least Lindsay was not so overpopulated that the prisoners were triple-bunked, as they had been in Quinte. But then, Lindsay had only been operational for about five years. My cellmate was also on methadone, so I naturally asked her when we normally got our methadone. She explained that I probably wouldn't have to see the doctor since I was only going to be there for a few days before I would be transferred to Grand Valley.

To my surprise, she mentioned the name of the same shrink, Dr. Duncan Scott, who had renewed my methadone prescription in Quinte. He was the same shrink who "treated" the 250 prisoners in Quinte, as well as the 1,200 prisoners in CECC! This was no small feat, because a disproportionate number of prisoners would need to see the shrink compared to a similar population from the outside world. The shrink would be responsible not only for renewing prescriptions but also for "treatment," which is synonymous with medication in prison. This explained why, during my doctor's appointment in Quinte, there had been a guard in the background impatiently shuffling about as though the three minutes I was actually seated talking to the shrink were three hours.

The other surprise associated with Dr. Duncan Scott was the fact that his father, Dr. George Scott, was the infamous psychiatrist who had worked for the CSC during the sixties and seventies, running a notorious LSD program in P4W. He was the same doctor who had subjected seventeen-year-old Dorothy Proctor, the woman I had met many years earlier in P4W, to his LSD program.[63] Dorothy was one of twenty-four women who had successfully sued Dr. George Scott in the late nineties for subjecting them to LSD, sensory deprivation, and electroshock "treatments" during their imprisonment in P4W.

Twenty Seven

A few days after arriving at CECC, I was once again strip searched and loaded into a prison van, but this time for the Grand Valley Institution for Women (GVI). I wondered if GVI would be as much a counterpoint to P4W as the CECC had been to Quinte. Once again, I was strip searched upon my arrival at GVI. I had been strip searched so often during the past month that I was considering suggesting to the CSC that they could save some serious money if they scrapped strip searches altogether and just declared all prisons nudist colonies.

GVI, located on the outskirts of Kitchener, is the only federal prison for women in Ontario. When the newly constructed maximum-security unit was completed in 2005, GVI had a capacity for 130 federally sentenced women. Before P4W began shipping out its prisoners in 1997, it had a capacity for 142 women, only 12 more than GVI just a decade later. In other words, by 2005 the CSC had close to the same number of women in prison in Ontario alone as they had previously had in the whole of Canada in 1997.[64]

After being admitted and decked out in my grey federal sweatsuit, I was sent over to the health care unit, which was in another area of the administration building. Even in the short walk from the A&D office to the health care unit, I could feel a weight lifting off my shoulders. I followed a long corridor with a huge plate-glass window spanning the length and depth of the building. After Quinte and CECC, I couldn't quite believe what I saw. Since there was no one escorting me, I dared to stop and survey the prison compound, if you want to call it that.

I saw a large, park-like setting in which nine clapboard bungalows sat picturesquely on their own little lots around a small paved road circling a grassy commons. Each house had a few lawn chairs scattered about a front porch with a railing and overhanging roof. Each house also had a smattering of evergreens and the odd deciduous tree growing in its front yard, with a small vegetable plot separating it from the next house. The houses on the circular drive faced a small open park with a large wooden gazebo as its heart.

I watched a couple of women I assumed were prisoners strolling around the paved road arm in arm, looking more like they were in love than just a couple of friends. Another small group of women was sitting around one of many picnic tables, playing cards, and on the porches of the bungalows other women were chatting and smoking cigarettes. Everyone was wearing civilian clothes. A short ancillary road diverged from the main circular drive toward the back of the prison compound, where it disappeared into a large, open, undeveloped field. Two bungalows sat picturesquely at the end of this road: not a guard, bar, wall, or roll of razor wire in sight.

My attention was drawn away from this scene by a young woman, also in civvies, coming toward me with a purposeful gaze.

"You must be Hansen," she said, and I thought, *And you must be staff*. Despite the fact she was not wearing a uniform, her dominant bearing, as well as her knowledge and disrespectful use of my last name, smelled of staff. There is something intangible about authority figures. They approach you like a tomcat would a younger rival, with a slightly stiff-legged swagger, head held high, and direct eye contact, and they give off some odourless yet aggressive pheromones that hit your subconscious like a club to the head.

"They told me in A&D to make sure you made it to the health care office." She smiled at me disarmingly, but I still felt a wall go up around me and my eyes glaze over protectively. She opened the glass door into the health care office and held it for me so I could walk in ahead of her, which I did.

As soon as we were in the office, a couple of women I figured must be prisoners started to pepper her with questions. "Hey, Foxie! When are you gonna get me my parcel?" I could feel the attention of the other women sitting around the office fixating on me, even though no one looked at me directly. If I was to compare the group dynamics of a prison to anywhere, it would be high school, which isn't saying much for high school.

Foxie ignored the other women and instructed me to "just go in there and they'll give you your methadone and check your vitals, then I bet Jordie will take you to your house." She smiled at me again, and then looked pointedly at an Indigenous woman my age who was giving me a big smile just outside the office window. I recognized her immediately from P4W. She was also a lifer who had been in P4W when I had first arrived in 1984 and had only been out on a few passes since, one of which had not gone well. Being Indigenous played a significant role in the length of time she had spent in federal prisons. To my knowledge she had been in prison for close to twenty-five years, with only a few passes on the street. She was one of a handful of lifers in GVI that I would recognize from my P4W days.

After I drank my methadone, the nurse did a basic physical, which took up the twenty-minute methadone digestive time. All the while I couldn't help noticing the parade of women prisoners hounding Foxie for one thing or another. If it wasn't for the intangibles mentioned earlier, I would have assumed Foxie was another prisoner, and a hot one at that. She looked like a thirty-something and was dressed in a form-fitting tank top and tight blue jeans. She interacted fearlessly with the other women, giving as good as she got in a game of witty putdowns that went on the whole time I was there.

Even though the women vying for her attention obviously liked her as though she were the popular girl in high school, I found the whole dynamic unsettling. What kind of prison and prisoners were these? I had never seen a guard being treated like one of the gang. The wall of silence was down, the code unenforced. Even the non-custodial staff in P4W had never been treated with the same degree of openness as another prisoner. There was always the unspoken prison code that every staff, whether in uniform or not, was an informant who could use anything you said against you. Even the rats and protective custody cases would only talk openly to staff in secret, in places where they could not be observed. For one, I figured these particular prisoners were not hardcore, and secondly, that times were a-changin'.

When I was finished in the health care office, Jordie and I hugged, and she handed me a little care package consisting of her own personal shampoo, conditioner, and some snacks from canteen. It felt so good to be with a kindred spirit. She walked me across the compound to one of the bungalows, the orientation house where everyone stayed until the administration had decided what to do with you. On our short walk across the compound, I noticed Foxie again, but this time with some young guy, also in civies. If she hadn't been walking so purposefully with a man, both carrying crackling walkie-talkies, I would never have pinned them as guards.

Jordie gave me a quick rundown of the place. We were locked for count three times a day, during lunch, supper, and overnight. Otherwise, from eight in the morning until ten at night, we had free range of the entire prison compound, including the administration building. The only exception was the administrative/custody offices in one section of the building. At night we could go out and stroll around the "park," looking up at the stars. I could play the piano in the nondenominational "spiritual" room whenever it wasn't being used for "spiritual" purposes. There was a gym and weight room that we could access any time of the day or night when we weren't locked. Once again, not a bar, wall, or coil of razor wire in sight.

Jordie left me on the porch of the orientation house, since that was one place we also couldn't go—into any other house than "our own." I had never been in a prison where everything seemed so much better than I had expected, and believe me, when it comes to prisons in particular, my expectations are not cushioned by a positive attitude. It was just like any regular house, with a fully equipped kitchen, dining room, living room with a sofa and chairs facing a large TV, and five small bedrooms off the main floor and four bedrooms upstairs, one of which was a double. I found out later that the double was usually occupied by a power couple—a couple who had the respect of the population, but weren't into rocking the administration's boat.

I took the key to my room and opened the door, which had a little window with a curtain that could be pulled open from the outside for the guards to peek in during counts. Once again, I felt the last of whatever stress had been building up inside me leave my body in a deep sigh. I flopped fully clothed down on my bed and fell asleep instantly. I don't know how long I slept, but I was finally awoken by the sound of birds chirping away in some bushes right outside my window. For a few minutes I lay on my back, listening to their sweet singing, and wondered if this is how people felt who had just risen from a bed of nails. They couldn't have felt more euphoric than I did in those minutes. If this prison was the fruition of the Louise Arbour Commission, then I was a convert. I was now officially a reformist, a liberal, someone who could believe that reform was still possible within the capitalist framework! After Quinte and CECC, this was nirvana! Bring it on!

I spent the rest of that day wandering around the compound, hanging with Jordie and learning more about this so-called prison. At one point I was called to A&D to receive a whole wardrobe of regular street clothes to wear until I could get a parcel sent in, toiletries, and even a loan so I could buy some stuff on canteen. I found myself pencilling in with my imagination chicken coops, goats, and wood shops, creating this idealistic women's community right here at GVI. Of course I also used an eraser to obliterate segregation, the max, and the guards. Instead, the administrative offices would be converted into social services offices and other strictly administrative functions necessary for a community of roughly one hundred women. For a few days I wandered around the real-life prison complex, but in my mind, the features of an anarchist women's kibbutz were pencilled in all around me.

I floated around in this nirvana, wondering when this bubble would burst. How could anyone call this place a prison? Each house had one woman who was paid to budget, order food, and cook meals. For supper that night we had pizza and brownies with fudge icing to die for.

After supper count I met up with Jordie again, and we wandered around under the night sky, smoking and gossiping. She warned me that smoking was only allowed outdoors. There was a 360-degree security camera, nicknamed the "eye in the sky," located high up on a pole that recorded everything going on all over the compound. According to Jordie, it had been known to film women inside the house smoking if the windows were not obstructed. This sounded to me like another one of those legends that could have been planted by the administration as deterrence.

In 2006, the federal government had instituted a partial ban on smoking in federal prisons, making it illegal to smoke indoors, including in the cells. The immediate impact of the ban was to make cigarettes a highly sought-after black-market item, since they could no longer be purchased on canteen. It would just be a matter of time before smoking anywhere on the property of any prison in Canada would become illegal.

I asked Jordie about security. How would the guards know if someone was trying to escape? She explained that even though the guards only patrolled through the houses hourly, the windows were outfitted with some kind of electronic security system that would trigger alarms in the security offices in the main administrative building if anyone tried to open or tamper with them or exit through the door after the last count was completed at eleven. There was also a four-metre wire mesh fence around the perimeter of the complex that was outfitted with motion detectors and cameras. And of course, the "eye in the sky."

Unfortunately, all good things must come to an end. Within twenty-four hours, reality began to prick my bubble of prison delusions. After the house doors were locked at nine, I went into the kitchen, looking for a bedtime snack. A lean young woman with black eyes was just closing the doors to the fridge as I homed in on it. She was a stunning, dark-haired woman who exuded a defiant wildness like a powerful perfume. Hurling a hostile glance at me, she spun around to leave the kitchen, but not before snapping, "Don't take any of those brownies with the decorations on top, or they'll be your last!"

I have had a tendency for as long as I can remember to develop crushes on women who are rebels. Even in public school, I remember spending way too much time staring at this confident, yellow curly-haired girl at recess who was as tough as any boy. I wanted my mother to buy clothes like hers from the Sears catalogue, but she refused. I was left wearing my mother's homemade dresses, which I am ashamed to admit were a source of embarrassment for me at the time.

Anyway, this woman happened to be the cook for the house, and a good one at that. Ironically, at least so I thought, her name was Angel. I opened the fridge door and immediately zeroed in on the brownies with icing sugar guns and roses ornaments piped on top. These decorations only piqued my interest in Angel.

The other thing I noticed was that there was almost nothing else in the fridge but a little milk. I rummaged around in the cupboards and found a half-empty (or half-full, depending on how you look at things) box of Rice Krispies. I helped myself to a heaping bowl of cereal and went to my room for the night. Over the next few days, this situation remained the same. Angel would always provide us with an excellent supper, but otherwise there was literally nothing left in the fridge or cupboards but cereal, and even that was becoming dangerously scarce. Since I hadn't had any money sent in to me yet, I had only purchased the necessities at canteen, things like shampoo, stamps, and envelopes. I began to think that I could seriously starve to death in here if I could not afford to buy extra food on canteen.

Every time I saw Angel, I would watch her out of the corner of my eye like she was a celebrity from Hollywood. She could have been French Canadian, Native, Métis, Arabian, or any other combination of nationalities. Her default facial expression of surliness and fast-motion body movements reinforced the impression that she was always being pursued by enemy combatants.

Probably around day three, we ran into each other in the kitchen again. With her eyes like slits, she stopped long enough to watch me pour a cup of coffee from the percolator, then warned me to "slow down" because the coffee and cereal were for everyone. I got the distinct impression that we did not share the same feeling of awe for one another.

I was never one to keep my mouth shut. I began to explain in my long-winded way that I hadn't received any money yet until she cut me off. "I don't give a fuck. Just quit with the coffee and Rice Krispies."

Once I got my first paycheque of $2.50 a day for the unemployed, I got Jordie's drift. I couldn't imagine how any prisoner could survive on $2.50 a day until I realized what a windfall this must seem to those on welfare, who got only $1.00 a day. These sums seem particularly brutal when you consider how few women get any outside financial assistance.

I also discovered that the pay for prisoners had not changed since I had first entered the federal prison system over twenty years ago, but the prices of necessities certainly had. The maximum wage a prisoner could make, whether man or woman and regardless of the job, was $6.90 a day. This money had to cover phone bills, postage stamps, personal hygiene products, snacks at canteen, and any clothes a person wanted to purchase through the catalogue.

It didn't take long before the food issue came to a boil. I don't think a week had passed before someone yelled into my room to say there was a house meeting just starting. I figured this would only involve the women living in the orientation house, but of course I was wrong. By the time I came out of my room, all the other women were spread around the living and dining room, sitting quietly as though they were extras in a movie, facing the stars of the show: Foxie and her male counterpart, still in their civvies.

Obviously things had changed dramatically since I had left the half-way house in 1990. I could see that the CSC was using every trick in the book to break down the code of silence. Were we so stupid as to think that just because these guards were wearing the same clothes as us, we shared the same power, values, and class?

The answer to this question became clear as the women waved their arms in the air, vying for the guards' attention to be the first to complain about the fact we had no food. To her credit, Angel sat ramrod straight on a chair, as close to the exit as possible. Her black eyes were like laser beams penetrating whatever Crown witness was testifying. I figured Angel was recording their testimony in her memory banks for future retribution. The gist of their testimony simply involved the fact that supper was served each night, but otherwise there was no food in the fridge, and that even prime supper items, like roast beef, seemed to disappear from the menu once it arrived in the locked house freezer.

"How come there's no lunch meat or yogurt even though we ordered it?" asked one young woman defiantly. "Besides, twenty-eight dollars a week ain't enough to feed a person anyhow." All the questions were directed to Foxie and her sidekick, who nodded their heads up and down and back and forth like a couple of bobbleheads. At no point did any of the women actually state the obvious, nor did they ever attempt to put the problem into its wider political context. There were no connections made between our impossibly low wages, or no wages, and the disappearance of the food. The closest anyone came to laying the blame on prison policy were statements condemning the amount of money the cook was allotted on a weekly basis, which was $28.00 per head per week.

That night Jordie and I discussed the food issue and agreed that the cafeteria set up at P4W had been less vulnerable to corruption, but ultimately the amount of money that the women earned was not enough to survive on, even in prison. The black-market prison economy thrived on poverty. Of course women were going to devise ways to supplement their income if they didn't have enough to eat, couldn't afford to keep in touch with their family and friends, and couldn't save up money for passes if they were ever granted. Yes, the trickle-down effect of starvation wages was a thriving black-market economy, and the violence involved in enforcing it.

The next morning I headed over to the administration building to see if there were any jobs. Unlike P4W, where the corridors and ranges had been deserted during working hours, I noticed that there were women sitting around on their porches, strolling around the circular drive, and hanging out in the administrative building. I was not instilled with a mindless Protestant working ethic, so at first I didn't read much significance into this. In the background, the noise of lawnmowers and the sight of a couple of women zooming around on a cool mini-tractor unloading garbage bags from the cans in front of each bungalow indicated that there was a yard crew. Inside the administration building I passed small groups of women congregated here and there outside the gym and health clinic, laughing and chatting, giving the place the atmosphere, once again, of a high school. Although no one ever caught my eye or said a word to me, I could feel them assessing me as the "newbie" that I was.

I decided to head up to the school and stopped along the way to read a job bulletin board hanging outside the Inmate Committee office. There were some interesting postings for an Inmate Newsletter editor and apprentices for the beauty parlour, but otherwise there was nothing. I passed by a few empty rooms before I found a regular classroom-sized room filled to capacity with women sitting at computers. Great! A large man sitting at a desk chatting with a couple of women looked up at me when I came in, but then resumed his conversation. I waited patiently for him to finish, but I got the distinct impression he was hoping I would disappear.

I wandered around the room, killing time. The women were not working on assignments, but were writing letters on these ancient five-inch floppy disks, the only kind that would work in the outdated computers. When he realized I wasn't going away, he shouted over to me if there was anything he could do. I thought of a few things, but decided to go the safe route.

"Are there any jobs or chances of going to school here?"

"School's out for summer," he sang, mimicking Alice Cooper. "I'm just here for a few months so the girls can use the computers." I took that to mean he was babysitting so a few women could at least get out of their house and write a few letters. Prisoners across Canada of all stripe and colour had no Internet access.

"What about the job postings? You know, for the Inmate Newsletter."

"That's coming down the pike. For now, that's there for visiting luminaries," he chuckled. At least he had a sense of humour.

"What about the BP?" I asked desperately, BP being the acronym for "beauty parlour."

"No instructor. It'll probably reopen in the fall," he said, looking over my head at a young woman who was yelling a question at him. "Look it. There's not much right now, but in the fall things should pick up. They should have the CORCAN house done by then."[65] In case I hadn't got the message, he lurched out of his seat and lumbered over to the woman yelling for him.

I guess I could come up here and just write letters, and make do on the one-dollar-a-day welfare wages. But if my parole was revoked I'd have to come up with some creative way to make a living. If the CORCAN work at the now-defunct women's minimum prison was a clue as to the type of work to expect at the new GVI CORCAN building, I was not eager to spend my days sewing men's prisoners' underwear for $6.90 a day.

After supper that night I spent some time strolling around and around the little paved road, asking Jordie about jobs and prison programming. Another one of my prison delusion bubbles was popped when I learned that there were no jobs for anyone under parole suspension, and very few for anyone else. The blueprint for the new prisons was supposed to be based on two of the main recommendations of the Arbour Commission and the 1990 *Creating Choices* document: to provide meaningful job skills training and having access to women- and Indigenous-centred programming. It was becoming increasingly obvious that these recommendations were being sacrificed on the altar of security. In sharp contrast to the original visions of both the Arbour Commission and the

Creating Choices document, in midstream the CSC had decided to con-struct a maximum-security unit at every federal women's prison across the country, except the Okimaw Ohci "healing lodge" in Saskatchewan. As an indication of their cost, the max at GVI had just been completed in 2004 with a maximum capacity for twenty women at a cost of $6.3 million.[66] Imagine if this money had been spent on women- and Indige-nous-centred programming instead.

Early the next morning, I was headed back over to the school when a young woman with a slight speech impediment pulled me over on the road.

"You a friend of Jordie?" she asked, looking up at me shyly. She was quite short, and all things considered seemed almost childlike. I nodded.

"I got an essay to write for my teacher. Would you do it for me if I bought you some stuff off canteen?" I was taken aback; people wouldn't normally approach a new person to do something like this.

"Um, I just got here, and I don't think I'm ready to do anything yet," I said, making a snap decision.

Later that same morning, I was completely devastated when I over-heard a couple of women in the kitchen talking about this same young woman being rushed to the outside hospital after they found her slashing and covered in blood in her room. I stopped looking for a morsel of food in the fridge and went out to the compound, looking for Jordie.

She was parked in a lawn chair, absorbing the morning sun in front of her house on the curb of the circular road. I sat down on the curb beside her and told her my story. Jordie laughed.

"That's got nothing to do with you or her homework. Someone in her house told her she stinks and should take a shower or get out. I guess she couldn't take the criticism."

Although I was relieved, I felt sorry for this woman, who had fallen prey to the collateral damage of society's brutal mores. All too often in my prison career, I had witnessed women, particularly the lowest in the peck-ing order, being victimized by a hygienic witch hunt. There was an expec-tation that these lesser players should be absolutely sterile. No doubt their accusers had also been stigmatized as dirty and smelly at some time by the outside society.

The universal fallout from this stigma is that prisoners place an extremely high value on cleanliness. There are always certain women who make it their business to keep tabs on whether other women have show-ered and shaved or have body odour. I have seen women who scrub their cells with toothbrushes and wash everything, including their sheets, every day. You get the impression they truly believe that society would accept them if only they were clean enough.

It didn't take more than a week to realize that the job training and education that could help "wash their troubles away," as the old laundry ad proclaims, didn't exist. Ironically, P4W actually had more job training and educational opportunities than these new regional federal prisons.

I hadn't even been in GVI one week before Prisoners' Justice Day (PJD), August 10, dawned. I was really hoping that my Prisoners' Justice Day expectation bubble would not be popped. In P4W the administration had given anyone who refused to work on PJD a minor charge, adding one more day of time to their sentence before they could apply for parole or be released on mandatory supervision. The vast majority of women fasted and refused to work anyway, and wore PJD T-shirts if they had one. In the men's federal prisons, PJD was honoured universally, if not through respect then through force. The administrations even allowed the men to silkscreen special T-shirts, which were mailed out to prison support groups that sold them to raise money for the various inmate committees. In general, the CSC did not play hardball when it came to outlawing Prisoners' Justice Day.

I was surprised to discover that the GVI administration was not just tacitly approving the honouring of this day, but was actively supporting it. The Inmate Committee had ordered a PJD film produced by the Lifer Committee from the men's medium prison, Joyceville, which was being screened in one of the activity rooms in the administration building.

I remember sitting outside in the yard on a blanket with a group of women, reminiscing about the lives of the many women we had known who had died in prison, to the backdrop of Indigenous women drummers. The pounding of the deerskin drum sounded like their hearts beating across the compound.

Kim Pate, the executive director of the Canadian Association of Elizabeth Fry Societies (CAEFS), was coming in to participate in a ceremony in the middle of the yard. There was to be an opening prayer by an Indigenous elder who worked at GVI with the Indigenous women, followed by speakers from the population, and then Kim Pate. No one had to work.

I had the greatest admiration for Kim at the time. She was a fearless advocate for prisoners' rights. She was the first white person I heard who always began each speech with a statement of thanks and recognition to Indigenous people for permitting us settlers the use of their land. She also described herself as a revolutionary prison abolitionist, which was very courageous considering that the long arm of the law, in the form of the Solicitor General's office, fed her. She represented a coalition of Elizabeth Fry chapters from across the country that could be described as anything from conservative to radical. The genuine passion, hard work, and competence with which she executed her mandate was the glue that bound all these politically disparate chapters to support her as their representative in the umbrella organization of CAEFS. I hadn't seen Kim since she had invited me, as a representative of Womyn4justice, to travel with her to Kitchener in order to visit a woman in the max who was interested in the Human Rights in Action project. In the aftermath of the 2003 Canadian Human Rights Commission recommendations, CAEFS, in conjunction with some federal prisoners, was putting together a pamphlet detailing the Charter rights of prisoners that would be available in all the living units of federally sentenced women.

I was just beginning to settle in nicely when I got a call from my institutional parole officer, excitedly explaining that they had managed to fit me into the August 30 parole hearings. Admittedly, a part of me was relieved, but another part of me felt almost embarrassed to tell the other women. It was too soon. I felt as though I was betraying them because I had done nothing to deserve this shot at freedom—no suffering, no severe punishment, and no real time. I believe in other contexts these feelings have been labelled "survivor's guilt."

With all this baggage weighing me down, I had no inclination to share my feelings about my impending parole hearing date with anyone. Rationally I knew that it wasn't my fault I was probably going to get out soon. Being a white woman didn't help matters either. If I had been Indigenous I wouldn't be burdened in this way. I would definitely *not* be getting out anytime soon. Even with my "terrorist" label, my odds of being released were better than those of an Indigenous woman with a far lesser criminal record.

Soon enough, August 30 arrived. I wasn't nervous; I was quite confident my parole would not be revoked. I had a great lawyer, my parole officer was supporting me, and I had done well on the street for fifteen years. Despite all my feelings of guilt, betrayal, and embarrassment, the bottom line was I wanted out.

My parole hearing went well. After the obligatory questions regarding whether I had accrued any institutional charges or positive urinalysis samples, and the interrogation regarding whether I was still involved in "terrorist" activities, they announced I was free to go. They were not going to revoke my parole.

Now that I knew I was going to be released I began to let myself think about how lucky I was, but I still didn't run around the complex celebrating my imminent release like some women did. I went back to my house, thinking I'd have a little snooze, when someone called me to the phone. It was from the administration offices, and they wanted me up there as soon as possible so they could have me out by the end of the business day. I quickly began divvying up my personal possessions amongst my friends, a sacred ritual for anyone leaving prison.

I wished I could tiptoe out of there or that I could leave during lockup so that I could disappear without anyone even noticing, but it was not to be. I took little piles of my clothes and walked around the yard, handing them out to the women escaping the heat in the dark shadows of the late August afternoon sun.

In a couple of hours I was pulling up in a cab at the bus station, wearing the same clothes in which I had been arrested only seventy days earlier. I still felt as though I was just taking the long way home. The familiar noise of the city, the busy travellers, and the suffocating heat reflecting off the sidewalks made it feel like I had just been in prison overnight. I wondered why I didn't feel like I should have. In movies, people being released from any kind of confinement are always pictured floating through the air, with everyone around them moving in slow motion. The soundtrack is playing a jubilant version of Beethoven's "Ode to Joy." Instead I felt "postal."

In the bus terminal, everyone was rushing to and from the ticket booth with glum faces and flaccid bodies. It was both suppertime and rush hour, so people were trying to stuff their faces with artificial food while talking on cellphones, reading newspapers, and rushing and rushing and rushing. Everything was covered in grime, and there wasn't a natural object around. I stepped out onto the bus platform into a cloud of diesel fuel smoke and thought, *Why bother trying to quit smoking?* I bought a pack and took a drag off my first smoke in months. I felt nauseous and slightly faint.

On the bus ride home to Kingston, I stared out the window at the pastoral countryside, now being invaded by urban sprawl from the outskirts of every town and city. I found myself feeling a mixture of anger and despair that I hoped would disappear after a good night's sleep. But it didn't.

In the weeks and months that followed, I rarely felt a sense of peace and contentment. I quarrelled with my partner and Henry and gave in to my desire to remain isolated and reclusive, not answering phone calls or emails. I felt so much anxiety over the thought of being around people that I didn't even visit some of the women who had arranged for my lawyer and visited me in Quinte. Once again I was plagued with guilt, but never enough to break out of my self-imposed exile.

When I look back and psychoanalyze myself, I think I had been repressing all my anger and resentment at being imprisoned for essentially nothing. At least as far as I was concerned it was nothing. Like so many prisoners have proclaimed, the real source of anger and violence in prison stems from a sense of injustice. And I felt it deep inside myself, not necessarily for my own personal circumstances but for the whole damn thing.

PART V
CANADA, THE US MINI-ME, 2006–2012

"The smart way to keep people passive and obedient is to strictly limit the spectrum of acceptable opinion, but allow very lively debate within that spectrum—even encourage the more critical and dissident views. That gives people the sense that there's free thinking going on, while all the time the presuppositions of the system are being reinforced by the limits put on the range of the debate."

Noam Chomsky, *The Common Good*

Twenty Eight

Reclusiveness and anxiety plagued me for years after my release in 2006. Perhaps I would have been plagued by these symptoms in my old age regardless of my life circumstances. Maybe they are not symptoms but traits. But for almost five years after my release from GVI, I lived a reclusive albeit idealistic lifestyle in the country, trying to live as self-sufficiently as possible with my partner and my dear friend Henry. But, just as I had discovered after originally being released from P4W in 1991, there was still a darkness lying under my consciousness, where a tiny black hole was trying to suck me into its depressive universe. I didn't need to learn again that I was never going to be a truly happy, balanced person unless I was in my natural default position as a political activist. And so I cultivated a relationship with a local collective of prison abolitionists known as End the Prison Industrial Complex (EPIC). I began to feel nourished and rejuvenated from my work with EPIC.

EPIC is an anarchist collective made up of a group of loosely knit individuals, each working to varying degrees on different projects. EPIC is more like a stream with many fish swimming in the same direction but in different currents than a freeway where all the cars are driving in single file. I was mainly involved in a Books to Prisoners project and in organizing a local prisoners' art show. Unfortunately, as is the case for so many prisoners on parole, no good deed goes unpunished.

I was invited to screen a film about Prisoners' Justice Day on the evening of August 2, 2012, at a workshop organized by EPIC and the Cataraqui Resistance School in preparation for the leafletting and a one-hour blockade of Collins Bay penitentiary on August 10, Prisoners' Justice Day. This was one part of an ongoing campaign to stop the Frontenac prison farm from closing, and the construction of a super-prison on the Collins Bay/Frontenac prison compound. The screening of the PJD film would be a prelude to a "direct action" 101 workshop by a local lawyer that would follow a similar format to other workshops being held globally before any large protest. They teach people how to participate in large consensus decision-making processes, how to interact with the media, what to do if you are arrested, and a host of other skills that are necessary for engaging successfully in large-scale protests.

In retrospect, the billing of the event as a "Direct Action Tactical Training Workshop" should have given me a clue that the cops would view this event with great suspicion, at the least. I should have known that they wouldn't understand the nuances of the word "direct action"— that it could apply to any action, legal or illegal, in which people initiate political change themselves as opposed to going through an intermediary such as the government or a nongovernmental organization. I should have known that the fact it was openly advertised and was being held at the main public library would not calm their jittery nerves.

When I first arrived at the library, there was a middle-aged man dressed in normal clothes lounging on the front steps. I had to carry in this old-school TV and a box of leaflets up from my car to the third-floor meeting room, so I made a few trips. I don't know exactly what it was about this man that caught my attention, but the fact that he kept lounging around for the entire time it took to unload my car played a small role.

Then there was another guy who suddenly jumped out at me from the elevator as it stopped on the third floor. He stuck his foot in the elevator door so it couldn't close while he peppered me with inappropriate questions about the event. "Do the guys in Collins Bay know about the blockade? Are you in charge of this event?" Like the loiterer outside the library, this guy was not dressed like any radical I knew. But it wasn't just his clothes, it was the intangibles: his demeanour, his smell, his vibe. They just reeked of cop. I had not come to this event thinking about or expecting undercover cops, but their presence invaded my consciousness like a bad acid trip. He must have smelled my suspicion because he suddenly aborted his line of questioning by inexplicably stating that he was a teacher and "couldn't stick around for the event." Weird! Why come here at all then? And what's with the questions? But I knew the answers.

By the time we had everything set up, it was fifteen minutes after the event was scheduled to begin. Then a strange woman came in late, causing heads to turn. Strange because everyone else in the room, and I mean everyone, was involved in some way or another with the groups that had organized this event.

When another strange woman came in and sat at the exact opposite side of the room as the first strange woman, everyone just stared at the two of them like they were two geese in the chicken coop. After the film and workshop, during the question-and-answer period, they began to ask a stream of questions. The grand finale to their incognito performance was their decision to exit separately but before anyone else. I don't think anyone was fooled.

After they left, the room was filled with a deafening quiet as everyone realized the event had been a flop, and noticeably infiltrated by the cops. I figured the cops were drawn to this event for the same reasons that no one but the organizers were drawn to it. A blockade of the entranceway to Collins Bay penitentiary was bound to involve varying degrees of civil disobedience, trouble, and possible jail time. The demographic that would normally come out to this kind of protest was probably just too burnt out after just having been involved in the trials and fundraising events surrounding the prison farm protests, and the trials in the aftermath of the 2010 G8/G20 Summit in Toronto.

Later in the evening, Henry and I were sitting in lawn chairs in our front yard when I saw something that sent a surge of panic through my body. One of my recurring fears was becoming a reality. A convoy consisting of three large, black SUVs sped from the corner of my eye into our driveway. The first two slammed on their brakes, parking at strange angles in order to block any other vehicles from leaving or entering our driveway, while the third parked up on the road. Four cops dressed in full Darth Vader gear, with the Ontario Provincial Police acronym on their uniforms, jumped out and began brandishing their automatic rifles for full dramatic effect. Up on the road two other cops paced around, cradling their rifles, looking for action. They really looked hopeful that maybe a dozen terrorists in black ski masks might come flying off the roof so they could pick them off like they were skeet shooting. After a disappointing wait, they realized that their fantasies weren't going to materialize, so they walked briskly over to where I was waiting and handcuffed me. By now I could see the large yellow acronym ROPE (Re-offenders and Parole Enforcement) on their bulletproof vests.

"So what's this all about?" I asked in an unnaturally calm voice. Everything seemed to be unfolding in slow motion.

"Parole suspension. We've already done sixteen this week," offered one cop, glancing around. I felt a little relieved because I knew I hadn't done anything illegal. Once this cop seemed to realize that there probably wasn't going to be any more excitement, he asked me how much land we owned and to point out the boundaries, as though he were sizing it up for purchase in one of those proceeds-of-crime sales.

After a brief stay at the local OPP detachment in Odessa, I was transferred over to the Quinte remand centre. For those who find comfort in "no surprise" accommodations such as those advertised by the Holiday Inn, Quinte would fit the bill nicely. It was as though I had left that horrible place yesterday. The faces of some of the prisoners and guards had changed, but not the food, physical setting, or routine. The only upside to having stayed there in 2006 was that I felt somewhat relaxed about it. My anxiety was focused more on questions related to why I was being suspended.

Almost a week later, on August 9, I was called into the interview room to speak to my parole officer. I was a little surprised to see not my parole officer, whom I had known for over twenty years, but a woman I had never seen before. She introduced herself as a CSC parole officer who was taking over my file since my own parole officer was on vacation. At that point, I remembered that my regular Elizabeth Fry parole officer had mentioned a few months before that the Kingston Elizabeth Fry chapter had lost their contract with the CSC to do parole supervision, and so I would be getting a new CSC parole officer soon. From that day on, the trickle-down effect from Harper's Conservative government winning a majority in the May 2011 election had a great impact on my life, as it did every prisoner's life, whether it was through changes in parole regulations, sentencing rules, or prison conditions. If anything, Harper's election could be compared to Reagan's Republican election victory in 1980, and the ensuing law-and-order campaign that followed.

This mystery parole officer had just begun interrogating me when a strange man came in unannounced to the legal interview room. He turned out to be the CSC's intelligence security officer for the region. These two grilled me in a bad cop/badder cop routine for what felt like hours. Essentially, they tried to scare me into giving them the names of people involved in the blockade, information about future plans, and a written consent form to search my computer in exchange for my freedom. When they realized their threats were going nowhere, they left with a commitment to see my parole revoked and to see me do at least another five years in prison. I eventually got a formal eleven-page parole suspension paper outlining their many reasons for a "strong recommendation for revocation" of my full parole to the Parole Board.[67]

Over the years I had often felt critical of the Kingston Elizabeth Fry Chapter, particularly their decision to do parole supervision, but after three years of CSC parole supervision, I can testify to the difference shades of grey make in a parolee's life. The Elizabeth Fry and John Howard Society's mandate is rooted in a history of advocating on behalf of prisoners' rights, whereas the CSC's roots are firmly embedded in the role of protecting society from "criminals." Any parolee can testify to what a difference these nuances make in a prisoner's life.

In 2012, after twenty-two years, the CSC did not renew its contract with the Kingston Elizabeth Fry Society to supervise female federal parolees. As a result, I had the good fortune of being able to compare the supervision provided by the Elizabeth Fry Society with that provided by the CSC. I stand by my assertion that a parole officer is a parole officer no matter what hand feeds them; however, in the real world with its messy shades of grey, there are significant differences in how they administer said contract. These differences are reflected in their mission statements. The CSC, "as part of the criminal justice system … contributes to public safety by … assisting offenders to become law-abiding citizens,"[68] but "with the protection of society as the paramount consideration."[69] The Elizabeth Fry Society "works with and for women and girls in the justice system … to ensure substantive equality in the delivery and development of services and programs."[70] If justice really could be represented by a scale in which the ideal balance would be achieved by protecting law and order on the one side while protecting prisoners' rights on the other, then the Elizabeth Fry Society would tip the scale in the direction of protecting prisoners' rights, whereas the CSC would tip the scale in the direction of maintaining law and order.

A concrete example of how these differences would play out can be illustrated through a common situation in which a parole officer has to decide whether or not to suspend a prisoner's parole based on gossip from a sketchy informant claiming the prisoner is dealing drugs. The CSC parole officer would probably suspend the prisoner immediately, based on her overriding concern for maintaining law and order, whereas the Elizabeth Fry parole officer would probably not suspend the prisoner until more concrete evidence became available based on her concern for the prisoner's rights. Having experienced parole supervision from both Elizabeth Fry and the CSC, I can say unequivocally that I would rather be supervised by Elizabeth Fry. I say this not because they are more lenient but because they have more respect for prisoners' civil rights, which ultimately leads to prisoners having more stable, healthy lives, which contributes to a more stable, healthy society.

At first I was outraged over my suspension. Theoretically at least, prisoners are supposed to have the same Charter rights as any other Canadian citizen, so why was my parole being suspended for essentially exercising my right to free speech and assembly? Surely screening a PJD film during a civil rights workshop by a lawyer must be protected by Canada's Charter of Rights and Freedoms? But once I started to analyze the international context in which Canadian political events had unfolded over the last few years, everything started to make sense. The key to unlocking this puzzle was the expression "pre-emptive security."

Ever since 9/11, international politics have been marked by pre-emptive war and its trickle-down effects: pre-emptive security, pre-emptive arrests, and even pre-emptive behaviour modification. The United States had led this paradigm-shifting change when it decided to bomb Afghanistan and invade Iraq in the years following 9/11. This was the first era of war launched under George W. Bush's new pre-emptive war doctrine, which justified attacking countries or organizations the US administration believed posed a security threat before they had actually attacked the US in any way. Establishing a foreign policy based on pre-emptive strikes was easy, since the only superpower that could seriously contest US foreign policy, the Soviet Union, had collapsed in 1990. Thus, the US could invade Iraq and Afghanistan on the flimsiest of pretexts without the backing of NATO or fear of reprisals from any other nation.

George W. Bush's pre-emptive war doctrine began to trickle down from foreign policy into American domestic policy, and inevitably into the policies of its neocolonial subjects, such as Canada. It is within this context of pre-emptive security that we can understand the imprisonment of Canadian activists during the Harper era. I was only one of many activists arrested between 2008 and 2012 in typical pre-emptive style. In the days leading up to the 2010 G8/G20 Summit, seventeen activists were arrested for an alleged conspiracy and became known as the Toronto G20 Main Conspiracy Group.

Even the political paradigm shifts after 9/11 would probably not have resulted in my 2012 suspension had it not been for the 2011 election of a Conservative majority government. This majority came on the heels of Stephen Harper's first term as prime minister of a Conservative government, characterized by a strong neoliberal ideology.

Not long after the election, the government released its *Roadmap to Strengthening Public Safety*,[71] a plan to build regional super-prisons in Canada modelled after the multi-security, no-frills, high-tech prison compounds that had become the signature brand of the post-Reagan era's prison industrial complex. Never mind that twenty-five years later Reagan's law-and-order policies were considered a failure even by Republican Texans and the governor of California, who were trying to find alternatives to mass imprisonment in order to save their states from bankruptcy.[72]

Two years after rolling out their roadmap, the Conservatives announced their plans to close six prison farms across Canada, a move that was strongly opposed by a wide coalition of diverse people, including prison guards, prisoners, farmers, local food activists, progressive Christian organizations, and prisoners' rights and abolition groups. Nowhere was this opposition stronger than in Kingston, the prison capital of Canada, with nine federal prisons in the area.

The closure of the prison farms didn't seem to make sense; they supplied food at a reasonable cost to the local prisons, and the prison farm program was considered one of the few rehabilitative programs left in the CSC portfolio. However, from the Conservatives' perspective, the closure of the prison farms would free up valuable land and budgets to help offset the costs of the massive prison expansion they had in mind. Not to mention the ideological importance the prison expansion played in satisfying the Conservatives' right-wing base.

In the Harper Conservatives' 2010 budget, they unveiled plans for a $155.5 million prison expansion.[73] In order to implement their new law-and-order legislation, they would have to expand the prison system with an estimated 2,700 new cells—a project whose costs have now ballooned to at least $2 billion over five years.[74] The Parliamentary Budget Officer would later complain that for the fiscal year 2011–12, the total criminal justice system expenditures of $20.3 billion were comparable to the $22.8 billion budget of the Department of Defence.[75]

Yes, everything would have been just fine if it weren't for the greed and arrogance of the Wall Street financiers and their international cronies. The 2008 financial meltdown and the ensuing plans for global "austerity measures" were an untimely roadblock for the Conservatives' roadmap.

Internationally, governments were hammering out a plan to bail out the largest corporations from massive debts they had accumulated as a result of the sketchy stock market transactions that had resulted in the 2008 meltdown. Of course, once these corporations had been bailed out of debt, governments all over the world would be saddled with crippling deficits, which would be paid down by taxpayers' dollars that would normally have been used for the social programs making up the social safety net. The biggest stumbling block for the smooth implementation of these "austerity" plans was that ordinary people everywhere knew it was unfair for government deficits to be paid back by slashing the social safety net, rather than by the greedy financial sector that had caused the financial meltdown in the first place. But, in Canada as elsewhere, the government went ahead with its "austerity measures" despite the vocal opposition of organized labour, the poor, and even large segments of the middle class.

By the time the Conservatives unveiled their 2012 "austerity" budget, their original prison expansion plans had become increasingly unpopular. However, implementing law-and-order legislation was part of the Conservative brand, so instead they decided to go ahead with plan B, which would mean sliding in their prison expansion plans through the back door. By 2011 they had already closed the prison farms, but instead of building new regional super-prisons across Canada, they would just expand existing prison compounds to accommodate the 2,700 new prison beds they would need for the influx of prisoners as a result of their Omnibus Bill C-10. This bill mandated minimum sentences for some crimes, tightened up parole regulations, and made changes to the *Corrections and Conditional Release Act*, resulting in longer prison sentences for many.

In Kingston, a group called Save Our Prison Farm (SOPF) had been actively organizing to prevent the closure of the local prison farm since it had first been announced in 2009. By 2010, the SOPF campaign had really gained momentum, attracting a thousand people to a meeting at which Margaret Atwood was speaking. The campaign culminated in a blockade of the Collins Bay/Frontenac prison farm entrance in August 2010, with the goal of stopping the CSC from transporting its heritage herd of cattle to an auction house. Hundreds of demonstrators showed up prepared to be arrested, taking the Kingston cops by surprise and overwhelming them so they couldn't transport the cows off the property. Unfortunately, the cops were able to convince the organizers to go home that night with a promise that they would leave the entrance open until the next morning, as though they were leaving mid-chess game. The SOPF organizers had not prepared for the very real possibility that the cops would not play fair, so they were a little surprised when they arrived the next morning to find a large contingent of OPP who had been brought in overnight from Toronto to arrest anyone obstructing the entrance to the prison farm. In the end, fifteen people were arrested, which is impressive considering that many of the SOPF people were not from the usual radical demographic. This was the backdrop to the 2012 Prisoners' Justice Day film and civil rights workshop that took place at the main library just days before a one-hour blockade of the prison farm entranceway was scheduled to take place.

Looking at my own predicament within the larger scheme of things, I realize that my suspension was all about the authorities wanting to take me out of circulation in order to minimize whatever influence I had over the local prison abolition movement, and to use me as an example of what happens to people who rebel. I believe they had blown my significance out of all proportion.

On August 13, after only a week, I was called to the barrier along with three others and told we were leaving Quinte. In the Admissions and Discharge area we were strip searched and changed into our "Barney suits." The other women were dropped off at the Maplehurst complex in Milton, while I went directly on to Grand Valley Institution for Women, where I would wait to see the National Parole Board.

PART VI
GVI, 2012

"Big Brother Is Watching You."

George Orwell, *1984*

Twenty Nine

As we pulled into GVI, I tried to suppress feelings of excitement as I anticipated being back in a house with a room of my own, writing and playing the piano in the spiritual centre. I knew these feelings were wrong, but my experience in GVI in 2006 had been so positive that in light of my experiences in Quinte, I couldn't help anticipating my arrival at GVI like a drowning person finally being able to breathe again.

I considered being shipped out of Quinte a mere seven days after being suspended nothing short of good luck. My luck continued to hold even after we arrived at GVI. Struggling out of the van with my legs shackled and my hands cuffed, I managed to stick the landing and shuffle awkwardly up to the front entrance of GVI, feeling a sense of relief with each step. My anticipation was rewarded when the door opened and I was confronted by a normal office, with real plants, photos, knick-knacks, and a friendly old A&D staffer who looked somewhat familiar.

She smiled at me warmly. After the transportation guards had removed my chains and left, I leaned up against the reception desk and was considering expressing my gratitude for the normality of this office when a dark shadow obliterated the lightness of the moment.

A young guard came beetling into the room, wearing a sharply pressed guard's uniform. At first I thought she must be with the transportation crew that had brought me here, but she quickly ordered me to sit in one of the plastic chairs up against the wall. Her order was a sharp reminder not to forget myself, that I was a subhuman, her prisoner. As I slumped into the chair, I stole a glance over at the kindly old staffer out of my peripheral vision, hoping for a sign of support. Instead she kept her eyes averted—a sign, I imagined, that she was ashamed of the young guard's behaviour, but didn't have the courage to defy her. Without even this imaginary support, I felt like crumbling.

Despite being subjected to a thorough strip search just before leaving Quinte, and then being transported directly to GVI without any human contact, I still had to be subjected to another thorough strip search by this cold-eyed young protégé.

After I had changed into my institutional grey sweats, the young guard ordered me to kneel on a wooden bench, where she proceeded to deftly snap on a pair of leg shackles and handcuffs.

"Why?" I asked, using as few words as possible.

"'Cause you are going over to the max," she said without further explanation.

I looked over hopelessly to the A&D staffer for support again. She shuffled some papers around and briefly explained that my paperwork indicated I was maximum security, and since it was after office hours, they couldn't confirm my security designation until the administrative staff arrived in the morning. I went against my usual protocol of never letting staff know that I was pissed off and began ranting.

"This is bullshit. Last time I was here I came in as a minimum. This time I come in with no charges, no violations of conditions, and I'm classified as a max!? All I did was screen a bloody film on Prisoners' Justice Day, and I get leg shackled just to be escorted to the max!" My voice was cracking because I was fighting off the urge to cry.

It occurred to me that the fact I hadn't taken my methadone yet, and it was well past five o'clock, could be contributing to my overwhelming emotional state. But then again, there was no reason for all this high-security bullshit. I had been out of prison too long, and had forgotten just how mind-numbingly pervasive injustice is in prison.

"Let's go," the young guard said in her militaristic voice, cocking her head toward the door, as though I was a prisoner of war.

She marched along beside me as I shuffled down the long, glass-walled corridor of the administrative building toward the maximum-security unit. I took the opportunity to look out the windows hopefully at the prison compound. What I saw sucked out the last little bit of hope I had harboured for my future stay at GVI. In the six short years since I had last been there, the nine neat wooden bungalows facing the little paved road that had circled the once pleasant open prison yard, with its mature trees and picnic tables, had been completely transformed into a construction site—an industrial "park." The bungalows were obscured by two portables, like the ones used at overcrowded high schools, parked in the middle of the once grassy yard.

Between March 2010 and March 2012, the population of federally sentenced women in prison topped 600 for the first time: a 21 percent increase in just two years.[76] A construction crane and bulldozers sat waiting for the morning beside the segregation area of the maximum-security unit. The entire compound was littered with construction equipment, the grass torn out, and trees razed to the ground. There were more bungalows in various stages of construction, and the once virgin field behind the bungalows where the Native Sisterhood had held sweats had been ransacked and pillaged. I am sure that if I could have seen the sweat lodge, it would have cried out to me.

Nothing is more humiliating than allowing the prison staff to see your sorrow, so I kept my face toward the window, fighting back tears. A familiar female guard strode purposefully between the portables with a male guard at her side. I recognized her face instantly. Foxie! Even from a distance I could tell that she had transformed into a wolf. Instead of her 2006 black fashionista leather jacket, she wore her 2012 dark blue coat with the CSC ensign on each shoulder. Gone was the loose swagger that used to separate her from the rest of the pack, replaced by a purposeful march from building to building, a grim expression on her face. The fact that the prisoners passed through her like she was a hologram only confirmed my suspicions.

I knew the uniform couldn't be responsible for her literal transformation, but it was no doubt a contributing factor. In 1997, when GVI first opened, the CSC decided the guards should wear civilian clothes instead of uniforms. By 2012, this policy had been thrown out to make room for the new "tough on crime" policies that the Harper Conservative government had introduced.

The policy of guards wearing civilian clothes had turned out to be a double-edged sword for the CSC. On the one edge, it facilitated a more "normal" relationship between prisoners and guards, which the CSC hoped would help to break down the prison code of silence that was the invisible wall between the guards and prisoners. On the other, as the population of GVI ballooned, there was a real danger of a guard being mistaken for a prisoner and consequently being tasered or pepper-sprayed. By 2013, the population at GVI would reach 180, three times the number of women the prison was originally designed to accommodate.[77]

When we reached the solid metal security/fire door of the maximum-security unit, the guard pushed the buzzer. Then we waited until an invisible guard monitoring the overhead camera had confirmed our identity and opened the door with a mechanical click. Normally the absurdity of the situation would have touched my funny bone—being shackled and handcuffed just to walk a hundred metres inside a building inside a prison complex for the crime of screening a Prisoners' Justice Day film—but I was too shocked to feel it.

After a nurse from the health unit brought my methadone, I was left in a small room for twenty minutes until my methadone had digested. Right across from where I sat was a large, black, one-way, glass-walled enclosure that the ignorant observer might think was just another room. But this was not any old room. This was the brain, the bubble, where at least one guard controlled the entire max unit, sitting in front of a bank of CCTV screens streaming live feed 24/7 from every pod, room, corridor, and yard of the max. Personal computers were not allowed in the bubble ever since a guard had failed to notice a stabbing on one of the pods because he was too busy surfing the 'net. Luckily for him, the guards doing count had noticed that one of the prisoners had a lot of blood coming out of a hole in her forehead, so they just played back the film from her pod and watched the reenact-ment of a stabbing from the night before. Not so luckily for the perpetrator, she was charged and sent to segregation. I imagine working in the bubble was like watching grim reality TV shows all day long.

The maximum-security unit consisted of three pods with five cells, in each of which only one was a single occupancy for prisoners with phys-ical disabilities. The other four cells were double-bunked, so each pod had a maximum capacity of nine prisoners. The max unit had a total capacity for thirty-three prisoners, once the four-cell segregation unit was included. There were also two small activity rooms and a few even smaller interview rooms, including a closed visiting room with a Plexiglas screen and grill. The pods and rooms were scattered over two floors with the bubble overlooking the entire area. A tiny exercise yard like a modern version of Quinte's yard, the size of a doubles tennis court, butted up against the building, with walls on three sides, and on the fourth side a high-wire mesh fence topped with concertina wire.

After my methadone was digested, the guard escorted me to pod 1, where I was left to my own devices. There were no guards around, only the round eyes of the two surveillance cameras and two intercom systems at each end of the pod. Much like Lindsay, it felt like the building was alive and could function without human supervision. I believe the day will come when the building will supervise itself, and only call on the guards to execute its orders.

I was only in my cell for a few minutes before they unlocked the doors for supper, but even in that short time I got myself in trouble by pushing the emergency button, which was conveniently located right beside the toilet. I mistook the button for the one that flushes the toilet, so I was quite embarrassed when a couple of guards arrived at my door, breathless but not surprised that I was not in an emergency. They warned me not to let it happen again, since they were obligated to drop everything and go running to whatever cell from which the emergency was coming.

Supper had arrived in an insulated meal cart filled with pre-prepared hot supper trays, which the other women gravitated to as soon as we got out of our cells. There were only five of us. I lingered behind, respectfully following the usual protocol for new arrivals: watch and learn. The fact that I had done time in P4W did not amount to much. There were risks and benefits to my history. The benefit was that the others had to proceed with caution, especially with my "terrorist" designation, but this was paradoxically also the risk; anyone who aspired to be at the top of the pecking order would see me as a threat.

The pod was an approximately forty-by-twenty-metre rectangular arm of the building, connected via the video cameras and two-way intercoms to the bubble. The only regular direct contact we had with the guards was during the hourly counts. The five cells, a bath/shower room, and a washing machine and dryer consumed one side of the pod, while a kitchenette, metal picnic table, two sofas, the TV, and a stationary exercise bike took up the other side. There was a very slim corridor, perhaps a metre wide, running the length of the pod, where prisoners could move back and forth.

I purposely took my time getting my tray until I could see that everyone else had taken their seat at the picnic table. There were three young Indigenous women and one other white woman, demographics typical of maximum-security units. Nobody said much because silence is usually golden in this type of setting. Chitchat all too often degenerates into a covert way of sniping and hurling vicious curveballs at one another. After everyone had just about finished their meal, a young woman dressed in baggy sweats, a hip logoed sweatshirt, and a ball cap suddenly turned to one of the other women and began summarizing what they had learned in their DBT, or dialectical behavioural therapy, class that afternoon. No one's head raised or gave any indication they were paying attention to her comments. I followed suit, but actually listened with great interest, since I was very curious about DBT.

I had learned through my prison abolition work that the CSC classified DBT as their "dynamic security model" in the max units, meaning it was their default treatment program.[78] The "static security model" was historically your stereotypical walls and fences, but in these maximum-security units, static security was augmented with surveillance technology.

"So the reason us fuckups are in here is because we don't follow the norms of society." She smiled defiantly, glancing around the picnic table at the top of each bent-over head still finishing up their meals, daring anyone to challenge her newfound knowledge.

"What are the norms of society?" I asked, foolishly taking up the challenge. I was still in outsider mode, oblivious to the possible danger I was treading into by even asking a question. It was immediately obvious that I had crossed a line. I could tell by the look on her face, but I couldn't suck the words back into my mouth. Nobody questioned the Q, a name I soon found out was her handle.

"The norms of society are the normal way things are done in society. Things like doin' drugs, stealin', beatin', killin,' 'n' burnin' down houses, all that kind of antisocial stuff, are *not* the norms of society," she said, enunciating each word with dripping sarcasm. "The clue is the word 'norm' that sounds a lot like normal."

Nobody needed to tell me that she was the boss on this pod. She didn't look a day over twenty, but she had the audacity to look me directly in the eye and talk down to me as though I were two. A million subtle gestures and interactions with the others indicated her rank, but she appeared genderless and difficult to define. She cultivated the stereotypical "butchy" features, such as a short, masculine hairstyle and a manner of talking and walking that was very male, features that complimented her naturally broad back and stocky build. But then she wore bright blue eyeshadow with glitter, mascara, and nailpolish topped with an extremely intricate hand-painted face on each fingernail. She was definitely one of those millennials who refuse to be defined by either gender or stereotypes. I admired her audacity and courage and could see how these qualities made her leadership material, despite her youth.

Even though she exuded signals that my physical well-being would benefit from keeping my mouth shut, I just couldn't. "I don't think most people are here for not following the norms of society. I'd say it has more to do with being poor and being forced to sell drugs, or doing whatever it takes to make money," I said in my normal tone of voice, looking her directly in the eyes.

I was shocked at just how angry she became instantly. She spat out her words. "It ain't got nothin' to do with drugs. I can't stand people who do hard drugs! You don't know fuck all! Don't talk to me!" Her position on hard drugs also threw me off. She was unpredictable, and did not conform to any familiar stereotypes. She stood up, defying me to respond, which I did.

"Well, then, don't talk to me either," I said in a calm, even voice, despite my feelings of complete confusion over what had transpired. She stormed off in the direction of her cell. I instinctively knew that was the direction I should head as well, at least until the tension had dissipated. During our brief encounter no one else had said a thing. They just kept eating as though nothing was going on. No one indicated they had any position on this surprisingly contentious topic.

I had first heard of DBT during Womyn4justice's testimony before the Human Rights Commission in 2003, almost ten years earlier, when one of the women had testified about the early use of DBT as a treatment program by the CSC. DBT is a prolonged treatment program involving "dialectical thinking," in which the "patient" learns to adapt to stressful or emotionally triggering situations by changing their "undesirable thoughts and behavior."[79] The goal of this treatment is to increase the "patient's" ability to adapt to their environment by teaching them how to regulate their emotions, rationalize difficulties, and learn adaptive behaviours. The treatment was originally devised to teach patients with bipolar disorder how to live a happy, functioning life without necessarily curing their disorder.

DBT is not a bad treatment program for everyone in every situation, but as a treatment program for prisoners, it has a lot of problems. DBT does not take into account the systemic injustices that are proven preconditions for the vast majority of crimes. A book co-authored by one of the leading clinicians in DBT, Marsha Lineman, admits, "The most likely reason for recidivism, however, is not the fact incarceration occurred but that afterward these individuals return to the same criminogenic conditions, including high poverty and crime neighborhoods, with the same risk factors as when they entered the system."[80] Even when DBT therapists do recognize the role systemic injustices play in crime, the treatment does not encourage the "patient" to become actively engaged in social change.

DBT is also fundamentally rooted in neoliberal ideology: the individual is ultimately responsible for their own behaviour and thoughts. Neoliberalism has always placed a huge responsibility on the shoulders of the individual in society. In idealistic terms, neoliberals see the individual as standing alone in a competitive world armed with their inalienable rights and freedoms, responsible ultimately for only themselves. If the individual thought they could turn to society for help in a pinch, they are sadly mistaken because, in this neoliberal paradise, society has been stripped of its collective rights and freedoms. A society fully loaded with its rights and freedoms is the enemy who would choke and cripple the individual from realizing their true potential in this competitive world where "may the best man win!"

In this neoliberal paradise of the twenty-first century, have mercy on those who end up in prison. No longer can they blame childhood incest or rape for their difficulties later in life. No longer can they blame racist social conditions for their lack of education, housing, or employment. No longer can they blame fate for their predicament. They can only blame themselves. Paradoxically, even if they do manage to pin some of the blame for their predicament on social injustices, they will soon discover that it is very difficult to change their social circumstances because, in reality, all those individual liberal rights and freedoms are nothing but a hologram for anyone who is not a white middle-class male. They are left standing alone, a "criminal" stripped bare of their social context, responsible for all the circumstances of their life that led up to that defining moment: the crime.

Even if DBT is an effective treatment for some disorders, there are many practical problems involved in administering this kind of behaviour modification program in prison, not the least of which is coerced participation. Those who advocate the use of DBT acknowledge that it won't work unless the "patient" is participating voluntarily. Even though the CSC claims that a "behavior contract is a negotiated, explicit and written agreement between 2 or more individuals (staff and inmate)," they acknowledge a few paragraphs later in the same document that "it is also important to remember that women are not necessarily participating in the Secure Unit on a voluntary basis."[81] In the case of women in the maximum-security units, aka the "Secure Unit," their participation can hardly be described as voluntary when, for example, their security level reduction, release from segregation, or maximum-security conditions are predicated on their participation in DBT.

Another problem related to the involuntary aspect of the treatment is the "inter-disciplinary team approach" used by the CSC. This means the therapy is implemented through the interaction between psychologists, guards, and behavioural counsellors working in the "living units" with the prisoners. Needless to say, there is a huge conflict of interest between the roles of guards and other staff who, on the one hand, have the power to punish and deny freedom to a prisoner, while on the other hand are supposed to be trusted and respected by the same prisoner in their roles as therapists. It goes without saying that these conflicting roles will only create great distrust and anxiety among the prisoners.

Since psychologists, guards, and counsellors can't work in the pods with the prisoners who live in the maximum-security units, most intensive DBT is done in the Structured Living Environment (SLE). This is a separate "house" in the compound designed especially for DBT. Many women in the maximum-security units are pressured into DBT through the offer of being released into the compound if they agree to live in the SLE and participate in the intensive DBT program. If they initially refuse, the notion eventually sinks in that it might be better to participate in therapy in the SLE than stay in the maximum-security unit indefinitely. This is the kind of offer that is difficult to refuse.

The CSC has another lever at its disposal: money. If there are no jobs available, prisoners can apply for incentive pay, $5.80 a day. "Only inmates who participate in program assignments related to their correctional plan are eligible for incentive pay."[82]

Incentive pay became even more attractive in 2012 for prisoners who earned more than $1.00 a day when the Conservatives began docking 30 percent off their pay for room and board.[83] This was considered double jeopardy by many critics because a 30 percent room and board deduction was already factored in when the original pay increase to a maximum of $6.90 a day was first instituted in 1981.

In thirty years, wages for prisoners have never been adjusted for inflation. More necessities have to be purchased on canteen, and there is a 10 percent profit margin added on all canteen sales. The canteen profits go into the Inmate Welfare Fund to pay for recreational, cultural, and educational activities, prisoner publications, and CSC-approved legal fees for legal actions. In other words, none of these items are paid for by the CSC. Not to mention that funds are also deducted from prisoners' weekly pay and then deposited into the Inmate Welfare Fund to pay for things such as cable. Jobs are scarce in general, but particularly in the max, so when prisoners are offered incentive pay to see the psychologist or participate in DBT, it is another offer that is hard to refuse.

In retrospect, I can say with confidence that after the Q left the picnic table, she was not contemplating how to use DBT to resolve our conflict. Ditto for me. I sat in my cell after supper, shaking with a mixture of fear, anger, and apprehension. When I heard a guard yelling down the pod that the yard was open, I got up immediately and headed for the barrier. Despite my fear that the Q might at any time decide to sucker punch me or worse, I instinctively felt that the best way to deter her was to show no fear. Keep her guessing. I sensed that she was the kind of person who would not start a fight impulsively, but only if she knew she would win.

Nobody came out of their cell except for a young Indigenous woman who was already standing by the barrier, ready to go out. After the guard had patted us down I followed her out into the yard. The only difference between this yard and those at Quinte and Lindsay was a small gardening space that skirted the building, where someone had planted tomatoes, basil, herbs, and many different flowers.

I started pacing quickly around the perimeter of this small space. I felt desperately in need of an outlet for the accumulated stress of the last twenty-four hours. After a few rounds, the young Indigenous woman, who I later learned was named Rosie, sidled up beside me and kept pace wordlessly. Although I was the type who usually filled up any void with words, in this case I instinctively respected her silence. After about half an hour of this dizzying circling, we began to slow down. Without any prelude, she suddenly gave me a soft-spoken warning.

"You're best off just to keep your opinions to yourself around the Q, 'cause whether you're right or not, she is going to get pissed if you question her, and she is always lookin' to fight." She kept her head down for a few seconds before briefly summarizing a few of the Q's fights. One involved punching "the nose of a woman right off the side of her face." She glanced up at the building as though checking to see if anyone was watching us. Considering the carpet surveillance, I figured she wasn't concerned about the guards. Even out in the yard, she was probably worried that one of the Q's many minions would see her talking to me and inform on her. Despite the danger to her reputation, she continued to walk with me. I admired her gumption.

After we had circled around a few more times, I finally broke the silence by pointing out, "It's not that hard to wipe someone's nose off the side of their face 'cause it's only attached by cartilage. It's not like she punched her head off her neck or something." We laughed. Even though I was trying to be cool, her stories had shaken me up a bit. I usually finished off my walking with a few pushups. I struggled to complete ten, but my young friend commented, "Hey, that's pretty good for an old broad."

When our hour was up, a couple of guards showed up at the door and escorted us back to the pod. I decided to spend the last few hours before lockup in my cell. There were two small sofas, a coffee table, and a television, all bolted into the concrete floor right outside my cell. The sofas were diabolically designed to discourage lounging, with their square, solid wooden arms and five-foot length of no-nonsense, spring-less padding that resembled a futon more than a conventional sofa. There was not quite enough room for five people to sit together on these two small sofas, let alone nine people if the pod was completely full.

Not long after I settled down in my cell for the night, I distinctly heard the Q telling a story to a couple of other women watching TV with her. She didn't seem concerned about having her story recorded by the bubble. She was reenacting the different fight stories that I had just heard in the yard. She described each move in great detail, even repeating the most dramatic bits slowly so that the listener could see the action in slow motion in her mind's eye. Over the next few days I heard these stories in an instant replay loop, over and over again. I started to get the impression that this was her claim to fame. The constant reenactment of these stories also acted as her preventative security model for deterring others from standing up to her. I must admit it was an effective technique. I did find these reenactments unnerving despite my self-assurances that at fifty-eight, I was still in better shape than a lot of twenty-somethings. But when it came right down to it, most prisoners who felt unsure of their ability to win in hand-to-hand combat would not hesitate to use an equalizer or a surprise attack to secure the advantage. Even though the morality in prison was medieval, the morals around warfare were not. They were nonexistent. The only objectives were to win and not get caught.

In my dreams that night I kept visualizing in slow motion this old woman being sucker punched into a brick wall; her body, with the physical properties of Jell-O, would then slide slowly down. The bystanders in the background all had their hands up against their ears, with the whites of their eyes showing and their mouths in perfect ovals, silently screaming, like the iconic Edward Munsch painting. Just before she drips to the ground, her unseen assailant grabs her around the throat and pushes her back up into a standing position again, and repeats the sucker punch. This scene played over and over in my head until I woke up in the morning feeling as though I had actually witnessed it.

I started to suspect my little confidant from the yard was secretly on my side when at dinner the next night, she nonchalantly mentioned to another prisoner that I could do ten pushups without effort. I thought this was pathetic—the pushups, I mean—but apparently the women were not in good shape. How could they stay in shape walking around in circles in that tiny yard, with no access to the gym?

My main preoccupation during this time was avoiding a serious fight. Back in the day I probably would have initiated a fight, just to be able to control it and therefore have the advantage, but having my parole and freedom merely suspended, dangling by a thread in front of me all the time, changed everything. In P4W I had nothing to lose but my reputation. Now I had an idyllic farm, my partner, my old friend Henry, and many dependent animals. Not to mention the fact that I had no charges and no parole conditions to violate, so I would have to give them a reason to revoke my parole. Certainly a fight would be reason enough for the parole board to revoke me for at least five more years, the time it would take to go through the long, laborious release program for lifers.

I was surprised one afternoon when a guard at the barrier yelled, "Library." Surprised because I clearly remembered the GVI library in 2006, which was located in the administration building just outside the max unit. It had been relatively large, with a librarian and a really good selection of books. Were they actually going to take us out of the max to the library?

I practically ran up to the barrier. The guard took me up a flight of stairs to a small activity room on the second floor and left me in the room with a friendly young woman in street clothes who I assumed must be the librarian. In light of the fact she was staff, her incredibly warm manner and open smile completely threw me off. But then she introduced herself as Nyki Kish, and slowly I began to remember stories I had heard on the street about this young woman. She was definitely not staff, but a prisoner, just like me.

She explained that her job was the max librarian, and then with an ironic smile swept her arm in the direction of a four-by-six shelving unit filled with books. I went over and began looking over the books, and realized that she had actually filled this tiny shelf with a wide assortment of popular fiction, some classic literary books, and a surprising variety of radical books and zines. It was miraculous that she had managed to fill such a tiny shelving unit with such a good sample, like a modern-day Jesus making a few fish and loaves of bread go a long way. Then she showed me a zine of prison poetry from GVI that she had compiled. If I had to deduce from this shelf of books what kind of person she was, I would say she was an intelligent free thinker. She was a breath of fresh air.

From that day on, every time the library was open I would go up there, and we would talk excitedly in hushed tones, using coded language to speak about our lives, prison, and our big ideas. The library was monitored by a two-way intercom, so even though our conversations did not cover anything illegal, we had to be careful of what we said. On our first meeting, she explained that when I first arrived she had requested I be moved to her pod, where she had volunteered to double-bunk with me, a huge sacrifice and gamble considering that she had never met me before.

But the max manager at the time had immediately nixed this idea on the grounds that the administration was convinced we had known each other on the street, and that I had been involved in the infamous noise demo of 2011. I am ashamed to admit that I had not heard of this demo, and had never had contact with Nyki until our first meeting in the max. Other than the library, we were never able to see each other because each pod is isolated from the others, and even have separate yard times.

Nyki is another in a long line of falsely convicted prisoners in Canada. She was convicted in March 2011 of second-degree murder and was sentenced to life without parole for twelve years. This was astounding considering there were no witnesses, and the only hard evidence, two video recordings from surveillance cameras facing the scene of the crime from two different directions, were either "lost" or recorded over while in the possession of the police. Nyki's lawyer had recommended they choose a trial by judge as opposed to judge and jury, thinking a judge would be better able to objectively consider the lack of hard evidence. Even though the judge acknowledged that the loss of the video evidence was a breach of Nyki's Charter rights due to "unacceptable negligence" on behalf of the police, he did not take this egregious situation into account, but simply shrugged it off as a consequence of the "frailties of human nature." With no eyewitnesses and no evidence, the judge decided to convict Nyki because, as he saw it, "in this case, we are not dealing with direct identification but rather with circumstantial evidence," and "there is an irresistible inference" that Nyki killed the man.[84]

Many people, including the Innocence Project, believed the "irresistible inference" was that Nyki was convicted on the basis of the circumstantial evidence created by the media and the proponents of the controversial *Safe Streets Act*. When the *Safe Streets Act* was first legislated in 1999, its critics denounced it as a means of criminalizing and targeting mainly the visible poor, such as "panhandlers" and "squeegee kids."[85] The media had dubbed Nyki the "panhandler killer" even before she went to trial. She became a convenient scapegoat, used to vilify the panhandlers and squeegee kids that the *Safe Streets Act* had been designed to eradicate.

Now that I was finally with a kindred spirit, I began peppering Nyki with questions about life in the max. I told her why I was in the max, and she nodded her head knowingly. She was more up to speed on the politics of Prisoners' Justice Day than I was. Sometimes I underestimated how threatened the government of the day was to what I considered passive resistance.

On June 14, 1974, a lifer in Millhaven, Eddie Nalon, was given a thirty-day stint in segregation for refusing to work. Eddie was no stranger to segregation. A little over a month later, the segregation review board recommended that he be released from segregation, but only after he had submitted a note requesting his release. But when he hadn't been released by August 10, he became upset and slashed his inner elbow, severing veins and arteries. The other prisoners in segregation began calling for the guards and pushing their emergency buttons until finally one guard arrived. But he did not open Eddie's cell door. Later, the guard explained that he was not authorized to open Eddie's cell door when he was alone, despite the fact Eddie was obviously bleeding out. Finally other guards arrived, but they did not try to stop the bleeding either, even though there was blood everywhere. Eddie bled to death in his segregation cell.

During the inquest into his death, it was revealed that psychiatrists and doctors had recommended that Eddie *not* be placed in segregation. It was also revealed that the emergency buttons in the prisoners' cells were not working, and that the guards had disconnected the receiving mechanism in the control towers.

One year later, on August 10, 1975, prisoners in Millhaven refused to work and went on a one-day hunger strike to commemorate the death of Eddie Nalon and all the other prisoners who had died in prison. Many of the alleged leaders of this peaceful protest were still in segregation one year later. Refusing to eat or work is considered a disciplinary offence.

A year after the first official August 10 Prisoners' Justice Day, another prisoner in segregation at Millhaven died under similar circumstances as Eddie Nalon. Bobby Landers had been an activist for prisoners' rights as a member of the Inmate Committee in Archambault prison in Quebec before he was involuntarily transferred to Millhaven and placed in segregation. Just before his transfer, Bobby had been organizing a prisoner strike to improve conditions inside. While in segregation at Millhaven, Bobby began experiencing chest pain and tried to get medical help, but the emergency buttons were still not fixed. Three other prisoners testified later that they could hear the nurse and guards laughing at the end of the range, but the staff did not respond. Bobby wrote a note describing his symptoms, which later indicated a heart problem. By the morning of May 21, 1976, he was dead of a heart attack. At his inquest, a heart specialist confirmed this diagnosis.[86]

No government since 1975 has taken Prisoners' Justice Day more seriously than Stephen Harper's federal Conservative Party. So when they were elected with a majority government in 2011 on a law-and-order platform, promising to close the prison farms and announcing a massive prison expansion, they also began to quietly and systematically eliminate programs and employees who were facilitating prisoners' rights. The Elizabeth Fry Society lost their contract to supervise parole, and wardens were ordered to stop honouring Prisoners' Justice Day. PJD T-shirts could no longer be silkscreened on CSC soil; there would be no more commemorative services like the one I had experienced in GVI in 2006; and prisoners refusing to work would be penalized.

Ironically, the PJD film I had seen in GVI in 2006 was the same powerful film I had wanted to show in the Kingston library in 2012. This film had been the last of a trilogy of films produced and distributed by the Lifers Group in Joyceville, a medium men's prison. But after an exhaustive but unsuccessful search, I eventually succumbed to showing another film from a Prisoners' Justice Day event in 2003. When I contacted the Social Development officer in Joyceville prison, she explained that there had been a riot on Easter Sunday in 2011 in which there had been a fire in the area of the prison where the Lifers Group met. Triumphantly, she told me how the staff had destroyed all the materials left in the Lifers Group office that the fire had not destroyed, so there was no copy of the film. She was right; there was no copy to be found, which gave me a case of conspiracy theory.

When I learned the historical context in which this film had disappeared, my conspiracy theory gained some weight. The year before the fire, in August 2010, a PJD T-shirt was printed and mailed back inside Joyceville for distribution among prisoners and outsiders. Up until this point, the CSC had allowed PJD T-shirts to be distributed and sold in order to raise money for the various inmate committees across the country. However, prisoners would still lose one day of remission off their sentence if they refused to work. The 2010 PJD T-shirt depicted a pair of prisoner's hands grasping the bars on either side of an upside-down maple leaf, similar to that on the Canadian flag, a symbol, the prisoners explained, of Canada's state of "political and social distress."[87] Vic Toews, the federal Public Safety Minister, promptly banned this T-shirt and condemned the "misuse of Canada's national symbol."[88] The prisoners responded by launching a $1.25 million class-action lawsuit against the Attorney General. At the heart of the lawsuit was the notion that prisoners' Charter rights must be protected, and that the T-shirt ban violated the prisoners' right to freedom of expression.

In 2011, some prisoners in GVI produced a similar hand-painted T-shirt with an upside-down flag in solidarity with the Joyceville prisoners. With the blessing of staff, another small group of prisoners in GVI criticized this T-shirt, which resulted in a split in the prisoner population.

With a divided population, the T-shirts were not mass produced. From secondhand accounts, I heard that some prisoners opposing the upside-down flag argued that "prisoners should be grateful to live in a country like Canada, where prison conditions are 'soft.'"

On July 9, 2011, about thirty people gathered just outside the fenced perimeter of GVI for a "noise demo" to express solidarity with the hunger strikers in the special handling units at Pelican Bay prison in California, and the prisoners in GVI. Noise demonstrations were a relatively new form of protest in which prison abolitionists swarm the prison and try to get as close to the prisoners as possible to demonstrate both their solidarity with the prisoners and the vulnerability of the prison regime. In this case the protesters carried placards and balloons, read out statements of support for the Pelican Bay hunger strikers, and chanted, "Free Nyki Kish!"

It took longer for the guards to notice the demonstrators than it did the prisoners. By the time the guards were organized, the prisoners were heading toward the crowd at the fence. The climax of the "noise demo" was a fireworks display, which was well received by the prisoners but not so much the administration. They ordered a lockdown, followed by the arrival of five cop cruisers. For the prisoners, this experience was liberating and exciting. The sheer audacity of the demonstrators was thrilling, especially since for once the people protesting outside the walls weren't protesting in support of more money for the guards or more time for crime. The demo ended peacefully, with the protesters making their getaway without any charges, and ditto for the prisoners. The CSC did not know who had organized the protest, so they decided to use Nyki Kish as their scapegoat, since she was the most politicized prisoner in GVI at the time. She is probably the bravest activist I know, because the consequences in prison for resisting are many times more severe than they are on the street.

When a guard called me to the barrier a few days after this first meeting with Nyki in the library and told me to pack up my things because I was being moved upstairs, I practically high-fived her. I thought I was being moved up to Nyki's pod, but it turned out to be pod 2—still an improvement over pod 1. On my way back to my cell I noticed Rosie was packing her stuff. We were both being moved. My first thought was that they were moving me because perhaps they had surmised that there was trouble brewing between myself and the Q and that moving my friend with me would completely eliminate the problem, but then on second thought I realized that people were moved around in the max on a weekly basis for no apparent rhyme or reason. I had wasted a lot of time trying to understand the logic behind these moves, but 90 percent of them defied all logic.

One night I phoned a friend of mine and explained my curiosity surrounding these apparently random moves, particularly in light of the fact that I had been left in the same cell in P4W for almost the entire time I was there, and I had not been a perfect "inmate." This had not been unusual in P4W. It seemed obvious that life would be easier for everyone, staff included, if the prisoners were stabilized in the same cell in the same milieu for long periods of time. This friend told me they did the same thing in the army, constantly moving guys around, but he had been told it was to keep solidarity among the soldiers unstable and weak. The army did not want the bonds between soldiers becoming stronger than their will to obey orders. It was counterintuitive, but I figured the prison regime also felt that having strong bonds and solidarity among small groups of prisoners in the pods could become a threat to the "good order of the institution." Having prisoners off kilter and squabbling among themselves was better than a small group of prisoners whose loyalty to one another trumped their own personal interests, which were usually tied to their willingness to obey orders. Now it all made sense to me. Everything the prison regime did was for a reason. They didn't pay all those administrators just to organize recreation and rehabilitation.

So we hauled our pillowcases full of stuff up the stairs and began the process of reintegrating into this new pod. Cleaning didn't take me very long, but Rosie was meticulous and scrubbed her cell from ceiling to floor. Like most of the other women, she blocked the space between the floor and her door with a towel to prevent dust and lint from wafting into her cell and parked a pair of slippers right inside the door so she didn't have to wear her "dirty" regular sneakers in her cell.

A few days later, a phalanx of guards came marching through with two prisoners who were going to be temporarily held in our pod due to overcrowding in segregation. We were warned not to communicate with them and that they would be getting out for their one-hour exercise period in the yard and their daily shower when the guards had time to supervise them. At the same time, I was told that Rosie would be moving into my cell temporarily to make room for these segregation prisoners. With the exception of Quinte and a few days in P4W's segregation unit, I had never been double-bunked before, although double-bunking was rapidly becoming the norm.

It was clear that one of the consequences of Bill C-10, namely stiffer prison sentences and tighter parole restrictions, was an exploding prison population that couldn't even be contained by the new prisons being built. The only place for many of these prisoners would be dou-ble-bunked cells. "The percentage of inmates sharing cells built for one has more than tripled since 2004. Incidents of prison violence have also risen. More than 2,600 federal inmates, about 18.5% of the prison pop-ulation, are double-bunked. That's a 300-person increase in 4 months."[89] As the new prisons were being built, the Conservatives tried to placate their critics by reassuring them that double-bunking would only be a temporary measure, but the architectural blueprints for the new prison at Collins Bay penitentiary indicated otherwise. They clearly showed stan-dard cells with provisions for a "future upper bed."[90]

I made a quick calculation and decided it would be easier for me to move in with Rosie, since she had a lot more stuff and was much fuss-ier than me, having literally cleaned parts of her cell with a toothbrush. When I told her the good news that I would move into her cell instead of vice versa, she did not seem to appreciate my self-sacrifice; instead, she quickly laid out the rules, since I would be the visitor in her cell. I was increasingly finding my bourgeois tendency to be nice a handicap. I longed for the ability to snap back at people with my cutting wit or act out in righteous indignation instead of always trying to be liked for my accommodating, self-controlled nature.

I moved into her cell that afternoon, reassuring myself it would only be for a few days, or at least that's what the guard had told us. I lay down on the top bunk and looked around at the shiny cell, where everything had an exact place. I knew this cell would not be a shelter from the storm for me, but at least we got along. Ever since she had warned me about the Q, I had felt a certain gratitude toward her. In little, subtle ways she had demonstrated some loyalty toward me, and an unspoken resistance to the dominance of the Q. When she came in at lockup I was already curled up in my bunk, reading a book by Naomi Klein, *The Shock Doctrine*.

"I can't wait for the weekend!" She laughed and twirled around like a ballerina.

"Why?" I asked, propping myself up on my elbow to face her.

"Don't you remember life on pod 1?" She turned up her boom box quite loud and started dancing, and then I remembered. She had been in the handicapped cell by herself, even though she wasn't handicapped, and was notorious for having her own private heavy metal dance party every Saturday night, when the guards let us make noise as long as we wanted. Luckily for me, my cell had been at the other end of the pod, so I had been able to sleep by simply putting a pillow over my ears to muffle the sound. It was bad protocol to tell other prisoners to turn down their volume. That was the job of the screws.

"I can't wait for the weekend so I can dance and dance to my heavy metal as loud as I like!" She squealed with delight. I knew I was getting too old for this because the thought of lying there listening to heavy metal pounding off the walls all night long was like torture to me. I smiled weakly at her and prayed that for once the guards would be true to their word and return me to my own cell before the dreaded weekend. I reminded myself that this scenario was a typical "white people" problem until I came across a section in Naomi's book that described the torture inflicted on Iraqi prisoners as involving blasting them with strobe lights and heavy metal music at high volumes for long periods of time.[91] I could relate. I felt vindicated.

I don't know what all the subtle nourishments are that help dreaded situations to grow and flourish in a person's head, but I do know I had a healthy garden of these things by this point. In one, the Q's long cartoon arm pulled me quickly into her cell and began stabbing me in a constant stream to the soundtrack of "Psycho," followed by a night of Ozzy Osbourne's song "Crazy Train" blasting away as I suffocated my one and only friend under her pillow.

I was on the verge of requesting a vacation in segregation when an unknowing guard saved me from my own demons. "You're going back to your old cell, Hansen," she said gruffly. Once again suppressing a high five, I coolly went back to my friend's cell and told her the good news. She yelled, "Yeah," unafraid of expressing her relief that we wouldn't have to share a heavy metal all-nighter.

Thirty

As I moved my stuff back to my old cell, I noticed that one of the visiting segregation prisoners had been moved back to seg, but the other still remained. Her large face with a big smile filled her small cell door window. I smiled back. I had noticed that the other women all seemed to know who she was and were familiar with her backstory, yet rarely stopped to chat with her. Rosie explained that this new prisoner, Norma, had been in now for about fifteen years, even though her original six-year sentence for manslaughter had expired long ago.

"How did she rack up so much more time? Did she murder someone else or something?"

Rosie laughed at me as she always did. "No. She just keeps racking up institutional charges. They take her to outside court and add more time to her original sentence. So here she is fifteen years later." Norma's Indigenous status was probably a key factor in the outrageous growth of her original sentence from six years to fifteen without ever being released from prison, I thought.

"Wow!" I exclaimed. "Back in the day they would only charge people in outside court for serious shit like murder. I don't even think they took them to outside court for stabbing someone if it wasn't life threatening. There was always at least one person doing years in seg for a ton of institutional charges, but I can't remember anyone going to outside court while I was there. It seems like double jeopardy to take a person to outside court and get more time added on to their sentence, plus be put in segregation. In the olden days a person would just be put in segregation for institutional charges, and believe me, that is punishment enough."

"Eh, Norma has all kinds of outside charges, mainly for property damage, stuff like trashing her cell or the pod or something."

"How come no one talks to her?"

"'Cause she can be an asshole. She just trashed pod 3 and destroyed lots of stuff that people like—TV, coffee percolators. You know." Flashbacks of the hot dog fiasco in BC danced through my head.

"How old was she when she was first sentenced?" I asked.

"Oh … I heard she was eighteen when she first went to jail and got her six years for manslaughter," said Rosie. Thoughts of Ashley Smith flashed through my mind.

Ashley Smith had first entered the prison system as a juvenile in 2003 after throwing crabapples at a postal worker, who she believed was withholding a neighbour's welfare checks. Four years later she finally left the prison system, in a box.

As a juvenile she spent over three years at the New Brunswick Youth Centre, where she racked up more than eight hundred documented incident reports.[92] By 2005, at the age of seventeen, she was placed in adult prison. Over the next two years she was repeatedly transferred and held in segregation. By the last year of her life, she had been transferred seventeen times.

On October 19, 2007, Ashley Smith choked to death with a ligature around her neck in a segregation cell between her bed and a wall in GVI. She repeatedly managed to hide shards of glass in her body that she could use later to cut pieces of material that could be used as ligatures. Before her death she had been tying ligatures around her neck daily, and choking herself until the guards rushed in just before she stopped breathing.

A coroner's inquest into her death pulled back the curtains, giving the public a rare glimpse into how the invisible administrators behind government desks in Ottawa manipulate our reality through quiet phone calls and text messages. The inquest revealed that four guards had stood outside Ashley's cell for ten minutes, watching and videotaping her strangling and eventual death. It also revealed that a prison manager had been told by the administration to falsify reports on procedures. Guards testified that the administration had ordered them to intervene when Ashley Smith tied ligatures around her neck, but only when they believed she was going to die, or they would be subjected to disciplinary action. Eventually documents surfaced to support this testimony. It was also revealed that the administration called national headquarters about Ashley Smith daily. In fact, the direct orders regarding her supervision were coming from national headquarters.[93] In the end, three guards were acquitted of criminal negligence causing death, but fired, while the other four were suspended without pay for three months. A warden and deputy warden at GVI were also fired. No one from the administration or national headquarters was ever charged.

The days dragged by. I spent most of my time writing long letters about my possible parole strategy to the various people supporting me. Unlike 99 percent of the other women in prison, I had a bourgeois white person's privilege of community support, lawyers, and family support, even though I was from a working-class background. I also cared about getting out this time, unlike in P4W, where I was just thankful to be alive and had completely accepted and adapted to prison life. This time I was older, had a life outside prison that I loved, and did not want to do any more time than I had to.

I had to pass by Norma's cell many times a day and often tried to see her through my peripheral vision. She was almost always slumped over her TV watching cable, very expensive cable, I might add. I didn't have a TV, but had noticed that $7.00 was automatically taken out of everyone's account every two weeks to pay for cable service, whether or not they had a TV. With 177 women in GVI during 2012, that meant $2,478 a month was being allotted to pay for cable—an awful lot of money in my world. Pretty much everyone bought a TV as soon as they had a couple hundred bucks in their account. Television is probably the cheapest and most seductive pacification tool at the administration's disposal. I'm surprised they don't give them out for free and make them mandatory viewing.

Even through the small window in her cell door, I could tell Norma was a big woman. She had the classic long-term segregation physique that inevitably develops from lack of exercise, a steady diet of sugary, starchy foods, and a concoction of behaviour modification drugs such as sedatives, sleeping pills, anti-anxiety drugs, anti-depressants, and anti-psychotics. Sadly, if you were to line up a series of photos of women who had spent two or more consecutive years in seg, you would swear they were related. Many women developed round faces and soft, round body profiles, a description meant not as body shaming but rather as an indictment of long-term segregation. Norma was no exception to this profile.

Other than watching TV or sleeping, she would sometimes just stand there and peer out her cell window, as though she was looking out her living room window down the street. If she was, I would always smile at her or say hi. Sometimes she would respond with her big smile; other times her eyes were dead, and her face completely expressionless. Who knows what was going on in her head? It was as though she sometimes thought I was mocking her and imagined everyone was laughing just out of her sight. Other times she seemed to accept my greeting as genuine, and would return it with a large smile that spanned the entire width of her face.

I was saying goodnight to Norma before lockup when Rosie hissed at me, "What the fuck are you doing that for? You don't even know her." This was true, but I felt sorry for her because everyone ignored her, and she seemed so lonely. But I didn't explain myself to Rosie. I already knew it was never good protocol to be friendly with someone unless you knew them quite well.

One afternoon Norma whispered, "Get me a peanut butter sandwich," through the crack in her door. I had already seen women making sandwiches for the other segregated woman, so I decided to honour her wish. I made the sandwich by smearing peanut butter on two pieces of white, spongy Wonder Bread, then flattened the whole thing until it was about a quarter of an inch thick and stuck it in a plastic bread bag. I flashed it discreetly in front of two women at the picnic table, who obligingly went and opened their cell doors for a minute, blocking the camera, while I quickly pushed the pancake sandwich under Norma's door. She picked it up and gave me two thumbs up.

The day finally came when I returned from a lawyer's visit and there was Norma, sitting on the sofa, her big smile spanning her face. As soon as I walked onto the pod, she patted the sofa seat and motioned for me to come over. She was wearing what looked like brand-new black sweats and a T-shirt with an Indigenous logo, feathers and an eagle head. Another couple of women sitting at the picnic table seemed oblivious to us, but I could feel them observing every minutia of communication that passed between us.

With no introduction, Norma handed me an essay she had written on Cleopatra. I was definitely taken aback; it wasn't the first topic I would have suspected she would write about. I couldn't really concentrate, but after a superficial reading I was impressed.

"It's a paper for a university course I'm taking," she said with great pride. "You can keep it and give it back to me later."

"Do they have free university courses here?" I asked, wondering if they had resurrected the free university courses for prisoners that had been an important program during the prison reform movement of the seventies.

"No, a university professor that visits me arranged for me to take some courses by correspondence." Then her eyes lit up. "I have something else for you to read."

She pulled out a long poem from a file folder and leaned over so she could hold her hand over the title as I began reading. Perhaps frustrated with the effort of hiding the title, she suddenly took it back and scribbled it out. The poem was a long, emotional declaration of love for a man she described in great detail without revealing his name. Even though I had not been there very long, I immediately recognized him through her description as one of the managers of the max unit. I later learned that he had been working at GVI since Norma first arrived and frequently played backgammon with her in the activity room.

The poem did not have any sexual overtones, but it was filled with terms of endearment and affection that clearly crossed the professional line that was supposed to separate prisoners from guards. I doubted he was aware of the poem, but as time went on I couldn't help noticing how her eyes lit up every time he was on the pod. I wondered why this manager paid special attention to her. Cynically, I wondered if it was because he was genuinely concerned about her isolation, or if it was because the administration had approved these games to reduce the probability of her mutilating or even killing herself. The coroner's inquest into the death of Ashley Smith was coming up, and I suspected the administration was well aware that Norma's imprisonment was following the same trajectory as Ashley's.

Norma watched my face intently as I read her poem, which I found profoundly sad, because I could not imagine her feelings being reciprocated by this man. Understandably, she had completely misinterpreted his attention to her as an expression of genuine love. I felt so overwhelmed I was afraid I was going to start crying and be unable to explain myself.

"This is a really good poem," I said pathetically, and then excused myself to go to the washroom. I fled to my cell. Norma spent the rest of the day doing her laundry and changing her wardrobe every few hours. It was almost as though she was an actress who had to change her wardrobe for each scene change, although in Norma's film, the scene change only involved the clock. I figured she was rarely out of seg for very long, so she had to cram everything she could into every day, including wearing all her clothes.

Later that day the max manager came on the unit and went directly to Norma's cell, where she was folding her wardrobe. I wondered if he was going to play backgammon with her in her cell, which would be highly unusual, but he did not. Naturally after reading her poem, I was looking for some kind of inappropriate behaviour on his part, but he just stood outside her cell until she had her coffee cup ready and then escorted her to one of the activity rooms, which were under constant twenty-four-hour audio/visual surveillance by the bubble.

At the time Norma did not seem to have too many close relationships with other prisoners, but she was particularly fond of two male staff.

One, of course, was the male manager mentioned in her poem, and the other was a young male guard she often joked around with. Some of the women, especially those with mental health issues, would develop very strong emotional attachments to a guard who paid attention to them. I am sure that some of these guards genuinely cared about these prisoners, but if they didn't keep their emotions in check, they would be without a job. I thought of the guards who showed some compassion and empathy as "guards," and the ones who enjoyed their power and used it to make our lives miserable as "screws." Ultimately, however, the qualities that make a person either a "guard" or a "screw" disappear whenever they are given a direct order, because at that point they either obey or lose their job.

"Hey, pussy face. Why don't you get a Brazilian?" Norma called out to the young male guard as he came through during count.

He chuckled a little and shot back, "One more comment like that and we'll have you locked up in the stockade right out on Homer Watson so people can throw pies at you! If you're lucky, maybe the real Homer will come by with a pie—you know, Homer Simpson, before he started using his alias." Homer Watson Boulevard was the main highway that ran right in front of GVI.

"Put a sign up, 'Lemon Meringue pies only.'" She laughed hysterically.

Sometimes she'd pass little scraps of paper under her door that he would read out loudly so the other guard at the barrier and the rest of us could hear him. It was usually a rap song or joke.

I had been assigned a job as the activity room cleaner but had never been called out to do that job because they did not have the staff to supervise me. Being jobless was not unusual, but I decided to clean the pod voluntarily once in a while, since they didn't have a pod cleaner at the time.

When I was cleaning, Norma would come out of her cell and sit on the sofa, chit chat, and watch me, but as time went on she dropped the chit chat and concentrated solely on supervising my work. I would sweep the floor first, then go over it with soapy hot water and finish off with a quick clean-water rinse. It was not rocket science, but Norma became increasingly critical of my work. In general, the more comfortable she was with me, the more critical she became.

"Hey, don't sweep so close to my door. You're just going to sweep all that dust under it. Keep away from it," she'd yell from her post on the sofa. I'd make a large arc away from her door.

"You put so much soap in the water, you're going to have to rinse it twice or we'll stick to the floor," she said, pretending her feet were stuck. The litany of flaws she found in my cleaning techniques were endless. I found myself fighting back the urge to just chuck the whole bucket of water at her, but I knew she was flirting with the idea of going back to seg anyway and would retaliate.

The legend of her beef with another woman on pod 1 replayed in my mind. Someone had goaded Norma into sneaking up from behind her nemesis, who was sitting on the sofa watching TV, and stabbing her in the forehead with a ballpoint pen. There were so many morals I could take from the ballpoint pen legend, but I chose the one that was relevant to my safety at the time—that is, watch your back if Norma has a grudge. Watching my back meant pinpointing my focus on the little things instead of opening my eyes to the big picture. Once again I wished that I had nothing to lose, because the more I let her walk all over me the bolder she became. She respected people she feared more than those who were kind and forgiving. She clearly felt that people who did not stand up to her bad behaviour were suckers and had it coming—a feeling she shared with the vast majority of prisoners.

I was not afraid of her, but I was afraid of not being able to stop myself from fighting over some insignificant straw that just so happened to be the one that would break my proverbial back. I was painfully aware that if my parole was revoked I would have to go through the mandatory five-year release program of escorted and then unescorted passes for lifers. Yet if I didn't stand up for myself, I would be abused by people who needed an easy outlet for their rage at the world, or who saw me as just another rung up the ladder of social advancement. The collective personality of this pod was that of a bully who gained respect through fear rather than compassion or good deeds. Bullying was particularly rampant in prisons where the population was transient, like in Quinte or this max unit, creating a constant power vacuum that people were always trying to fill as they came and went.

My musings were suddenly interrupted by a voice from the intercom. "Hey, Norma! I've got Winnipeg's Most on my playlist. Want to hear it?" It was the young male guard Norma exchanged rap lyrics with.

She dropped me like a hot potato and jumped to her feet. "Yeah!"

"Well, then, hop on that bike down there and get moving." Norma struggled onto the stationary bike and started pedalling to the rap music of Winnipeg's Most booming out of the intercom. He was definitely taking a risk; guards were not supposed to use the intercom for anything other than official communication.

For the next hour Norma pedalled away to nowhere on the bike, breathing heavily and struggling at times, but never stopping. The guard kept up a running commentary on her progress as well as the music, as though he was a DJ on some local rap radio show. I managed to finish cleaning the pod without hassle. I felt a sense of gratitude toward this guard, daring to think that he was doing this to keep me from getting into a situation that would have dire consequences for my future. But in reality, he was probably just playing tunes for his own amusement and to humour Norma.

One day our pod was called out to go to a "bullying sensitivity workshop" in one of the small activity rooms. A woman from the outside lectured us for an hour on the ins and outs and intricacies of bullying, but managed to skillfully avoid ever digging below the surface to get at the root of the problem. Worse still was the fact that this room full of impoverished women, of whom the majority had little education and were not white, were the ultimate victims of systemic bullying. How could she not see that putting these women, who had been born into social circumstances that put them at such a disadvantage in society, for making a living in the black market or defending themselves by whatever means necessary or self-medicating was the ultimate act of a bullying society?

Chapter 31

Norma kept me on an emotional rollercoaster ride. If I ignored her, she would kick at my door until I came out. Like Sammy, life had dealt her a very bad hand. In the snapshots of our daily lives, I felt like the victim, but in the big picture, she was definitely the victim.

One day she asked me discreetly if she could borrow some of my shampoo. I went into my cell and got it, then was about to hand it to her when she rolled her eyes in the direction of the cameras. I had almost forgotten that we had to open our doors simultaneously to block the view of the camera before exchanging the shampoo, because it was illegal to share or give anyone anything.

After her shower, she was struggling to put nail polish on her toenails, so I offered to do them for her by making use of the skills I had developed through the Quinte "nailpolish lady program." I had just begun painting her "dogs," which she had parked on my knees, when a voice over the intercom warned us, "No physical contact."

"What?" I looked up at the ceiling. She explained to me that horseplay, affection, or any kind of physical contact was completely illegal in the max. This, of course, led to "the talk"—a detailed explanation of how women in the max have sexual contact, which inevitably was intense but brief.

In every prison, including the compound of GVI in 2006, consensual sex between women was handled with a "don't ask, don't tell" policy. As long as gay women did not openly flaunt their homosexuality, the authorities would not ask or punish them for their sexual orientation. But these relationships were still exploited as a social control mechanism. Often couples were assigned to the same bungalows, giving the administration a carrot they could give or take away, depending on how compliant the couple was. This dynamic was particularly useful to the administration with power couples, who were often assigned the one double bedroom that had been designed into each house. If the power couple were not compliant, they could be punished or manipulated back into compliance through separating them into different houses, putting one in the max, or even transferring one of the women to another prison.

Here in the max, not only sex but any kind of physical contact, whether affectionate, neutral, or hostile, was prohibited. Sex took place after carefully sneaking into a cell or shower room together without being noticed by the cameras.

I had noticed that women were no longer calling the bungalows "houses," but rather "units." This change in terminology reflected a more accurate and critical consciousness regarding this prison complex. The women were no longer being taken in by the mirage created by the physical structures of the prison. Just because a building had been constructed into the shape of a clapboard bungalow with a kitchen, living room, bathrooms, and bedrooms for which we each had our own key did not mean it was a "house." A house cat shares the same features—claws and fangs—as another feline, the lion, but ask a gazelle if that means they are same kind of animal.

I began asking Norma to go out to the yard with me. She was in terrible shape, huffing and puffing after fifteen minutes of circling as though she had jogged ten kilometres. So instead we would pick cherry tomatoes, basil, and lettuce from the tiny garden to make salads when we got back in. Sometimes we would pick flowers and fill up every empty shampoo bottle, pop can, and container with stunning floral arrangements.

One evening Foxie came through, doing count in her usual brisk manner. We had all agreed that the place looked like a floral shop or wedding chapel, but Foxie took one look around and said, "Looks like a funeral parlour to me." She had been on duty the night they had watched Ashley Smith strangle herself to death.

Norma's cell was right beside mine, so our bunk beds butted up against our shared wall. Many mornings before we were unlocked she would push her emergency button. I would wake up to the sound of gum shoes shuffling down the pod toward her cell. "What's the problem now?" the guards would ask in an exasperated tone, as though they had been interrupted from some important task. Most of the time she would want a drink of juice or something to eat because she was diabetic, or she would complain of chronic stomach problems. They were never sympathetic, treating her as though she was playing malicious jokes on them.

One morning she began banging on the wall separating us until I woke up. I could hear her muffled voice through the cinderblock walls.

"Hey, can you push your emergency button? I'm too sick to get up." I knew the guards would not respond kindly to my emergency button, but I did what she requested. This time I heard their gum shoes running down the pod. But when I explained to them that I had pushed my button because Norma was too sick to do it herself, they gave me a venomous glare, locked my door again, and asked Norma what was wrong in their most what-is-it-now voice.

"I can't get up," she mumbled. "My stomach hurts too much. Can you get me some water?" Wordlessly they brought her a glass of water, and left grumbling.

A few hours later I was sitting in the activity room with Foxie, who was supervising my twenty-minute methadone digestion period. Almost immediately she chastised me for pushing my emergency button "needlessly," and suggested that if it happened again I should just pretend to push it because, in her opinion, Norma was just seeking attention.

"But what if she's not?" I countered, a little surprised she would ask me to conspire with her.

"Oh, trust me. She's just looking for attention." Of course I would push my button again if asked, but the situation did not arise. Later that evening, when Foxie was doing count on a double shift, Norma asked her for something, and Foxie just lost it. In a loud voice that we could all clearly hear she spat out, "You're thirty-five years old! When are you going to stop acting like a little kid and grow up?" She stormed off the pod, ignoring Norma's request.

Norma had taken to muttering that she wanted to go back to seg, not an uncommon feeling among women who had spent many years in isolation. I assumed it would be very difficult to adjust to all the noise and the complicated social dynamics that develop when you live in a small pod with absolutely no control over your life. Life in segregation, where everything is relatively predictable and quiet, could seem like an attractive escape from the never-ending tension and stress of the soap-opera world of the pods. I considered myself relatively stable, and yet I struggled to reign in paranoid feelings if people didn't make eye contact or seemed to be whispering behind my back, even though I was aware that seeing without looking, and speaking without talking, and hearing without listening, were the norm.

One evening I was trying to make my way back to my cell without being noticed when one of the women asked me to sit down and watch a sitcom with them. All four of the women were already sitting squished together on the two small sofas, so I declined, using the excuse that there were no more seats.

I was the only white woman on this pod. Rosie and Norma were Indigenous, and the other two women, Paula and Lateesha, were Black. This disproportionate number of non-white people on our pod reflected the racist population percentages in prison—that is, the higher the security level, the higher the proportion of non-white people in that population.[94] Even though Aboriginal people make up only 4 percent of the Canadian population, they account for 32.6 percent of the total number of women in federal prisons.[95] Yet Aboriginal women made up 45 percent of the women classified as maximum security.[96] By 2013, the number of Aboriginal women in prison had increased by 80 percent over the past decade. This increase was described by the federal Correctional Investigator in his 2013 Annual Report as "critical" for Black and Aboriginal women.

"Pull up a chair," said Rosie, referring to the plastic telephone chair. I was always trying to understand the motives behind everything, so I dragged the chair over to the TV area and wondered where I should park. I was confronted with the dilemma of either sitting beside Norma on one sofa or beside Rosie on the other. I decided on Norma, since I figured she would be the most likely to feel rejected if I didn't choose to sit beside her.

Wrong. The minute I settled into my chair beside her, she ordered me to move over beside Rosie, because apparently she thought I was blocking her exit. I debated holding my ground, but decided I didn't want to have an argument with Norma. The second I started sliding my chair over, Rosie looked at me, astonished, and said, "What the fuck are you doing that for? You're not blocking her route. Don't let her push you around like that!" Then Rosie glared at Norma. "Don't talk to her like that."

Norma got up in a huff and stormed off into her cell, slamming the door behind her. I stayed in my seat, eyes glued to the Black sitcom on the TV, one of a series that Paula and Lateesha watched every night.

"I would never in my life go out with a guy that black," laughed Lateesha. Paula agreed. They continued commenting and chuckling over the darkness of the various male characters, whom they were assessing as future imaginary partners. I was taken aback and found myself expressing my opinion again, a trait that was not making my life any easier in these little cubicles of insanity.

"How can you make choices about who you would go out with based on the colour of their skin?" I asked, stating the obvious. They just looked at me like I was a dumb child and then burst out laughing, refusing to dignify my question with an answer. I started second-guessing myself, wondering if maybe they had just been parodying racists, or the hypocrisy of some Black people judging others as "too dark."

While this was going on, I noticed Norma peeking out of her cell door and then heading toward the refrigerator. During a commercial break Paula and Lateesha started whispering the latest gossip from the compound regarding women putting shit and piss in the food of women who had killed or abused their children. The CSC had abolished protective custody units in all prisons except the men's maximum-security units, where men doing life with no chance for parole had nothing to lose. But regardless of their official label, these former PC women were still branded as pariah and abused whenever the opportunity arose.

I tried to ignore their whispering; I knew it was the only way to converse without sharing your conversations with the bubble. But I couldn't ignore the sudden shattering of cups and food containers as they rained down on the cement floor or smashed into smithereens against the cinderblock walls. Everyone's head swivelled around to see what the hell was going on.

"Put shit in my food?! I don't think so, you pack of rats and goofs," yelled Norma, throwing all precaution to the wind.

"We weren't talking about you," yelled Rosie, who perhaps had the most sway over Norma. "If I had something to say to you, I'd say it to your face!" Her retort had no impact on Norma, who continued her rampage, throwing the Plexiglas coffee pot on the floor. When it bounced around instead of breaking, she started kicking it furiously.

"Get back in your cells, girls," a voice boomed out over the intercom system. I don't think we had even left our seats before a small team of guards appeared at the barrier. Norma positioned herself in the middle of the pod and refused to go to her cell. The rest of us were not motivated to sacrifice everything in some kind of suicide mission for someone who had just called us all "rats and goofs." We trudged to our cells and took up our positions as spectators, peeking through the slits in our curtains that the guards had immediately closed from outside our cell door windows. The max manager for this shift stood back, just out of Norma's throwing range, while the other guards stationed themselves in a little pack behind him. It looked to me like they were familiar with Norma's MO and were going to use the strategy of waiting for her to exhaust herself.

I had already witnessed a takedown in the short time I had been there, but it had been according to the book. In that case, the "offending" woman had already been locked in her cell, while everyone waited for the institutional emergency response team to arrive from their homes. Even then, they still had to get suited up, so it was several hours at best before everyone was in their plastic Darth Vader outfits, which at this point in history had been downgraded to the quality of Halloween costumes. Then they had gone through a series of textbook manoeuvres that had nothing to do with the unfolding reality. Screaming through the door, they threatened to use pepper spray and force if she didn't pass any weapons out under the door, quoting sections from the regulations that authorized this level of force. By this time she had smashed everything in her cell into tiny pieces of wood, plastic, and metal that couldn't fit under the door, but could easily be secreted in any number of places on her body. She burst out laughing at the absurdity of it all, even though she had already been doused with pepper spray several times. All the while a guard was crouched outside her cell with her video camera, ready to record everything once the door opened. It was impossible for them to see what was going on inside the cell, since she had covered the tiny window in the door with paper from the inside.

Back to Norma, who seemed to have a game plan of her own that had been worked out well in advance, which involved targeting as much stuff that the rest of us might cherish as possible. After destroying all the food in the fridge and freezer and unsuccessfully attempting to destroy the coffee pot, she headed over toward the coffee table in the TV area, which we had all noticed weeks before was no longer bolted to the floor.

To her own soundtrack of "you goofs and rats," she picked up the coffee table and began trying to smash the TV screen. I was right across from the TV and expected it to explode any minute, which would have damaged Norma more than anyone, but she didn't seem to care. It did not explode. Later I found out that it was covered in a smash-proof Plexiglas screen that was bolted to the TV. They had done a good job, because I had never noticed this before. The coffee table bounced off the TV screen as though it were made of rubber. When she had exhausted this tactic, she narrowed her focus to the little buttons just under the screen that could be manually used to change channels should the remote be unavailable.

By now I could hear Norma breathing so heavily I was afraid she might have a heart attack. As she became progressively less able to pick up the coffee table with its thick, steel legs, the manager began to approach and tried to calm her with soothing words he would repeat hypnotically over and over again. "Come on, Norma. Just put it down and we'll take you to seg."

She made a few more half-hearted attempts to throw the coffee table in his direction, but her strength was definitely waning. Eventually he was standing only a few feet away from the coffee table's farthest trajectory, just close enough to reach over and pick it up once it had landed. Norma surrendered.

The manager talked to her like a hypnotist in a soft, soothing tone, repeating reassuring phrases over and over again. I knew this was not a textbook takedown, but it sure looked like he was familiar with Norma and had done this before.

"Come on, Norma, just kneel on the sofa there, 'cause you know we have to shackle you, and we'll take you to seg and get you a nice, cool drink. That a girl," he purred, standing just out of her reach. For a few more minutes Norma stood there like a boxer in the ninth round. But soon enough his hypnotic speech seemed to hit its mark in her exhausted mind. She dropped her head, kneeled on the sofa, and let them shackle her ankles together. The rest of the guards continued to stay in the background, moving quietly out of the pod behind Norma as she shuffled out. Soon enough a pair of guards returned, unlocked us, and ordered us to "clean up this mess, girls." The buttons on the TV were mangled beyond repair. We milled about the TV, mourning its passing as though it was kin. To most of the women, it was the most precious item on the pod.

"We'll never see Norma's face on this pod again. I'll make sure of it!" Lateesha spat out. She could not afford her own TV, so she spent an hour after lockup every night staring out her cell window at the one on the pod until the guards finally turned it off.

A few days later, after a visit with my lawyer, I was waiting outside the bubble for an "escort" to take me back to our pod when I noticed Norma sitting in the closed visiting room. She caught my eye at the same moment and yelled, "Tell the rest of those goofs and rats that I hope they miss their fucking TV!"

There were a few things for which I would jeopardize my parole hearing: to defend someone from serious harm, to participate in any righteous resistance, and to defend my own life. The latter would include reacting to anyone who would dare to call me either a goof or a rat. I struggled with this dilemma. Normally I would react to these words, but in this case, I knew that Norma was struggling with mental illness, and even if she had been perfectly sane, there were walls and thick glass between us. There was nothing to be done but ignore her. I didn't share her words with the other women on the pod.

Paula had the job of cleaning the segregation area every day. Although there was no guard actually standing in the corridor watching her, the cameras feeding into the bubble were always watching. As she explained to us later, she was mopping the floor when Norma yelled through the crack in her door, "You don't even know how to clean, nigger!" She then continued along this vein, repeating the slur as much as possible. Within a few minutes a guard appeared, went straight to Norma's cell, and asked her to repeat what she had just said. She remained silent.

He ordered Paula to carry on and left the area, slamming the door as he left, but then very quietly opened it again just enough so that he could see and hear what was going on. Within minutes Norma began her tirade again. He pushed the door open and stormed up to her cell. "What did you say?" he roared, and once again she remained silent. He told Paula to go back to the pod.

When Paula got back up, she immediately broke down in sobs as she reenacted the whole scene for us.

"She's dead meat!" declared Lateesha, facing the camera defiantly.

A few weeks passed by, and then, during one of his weekly sitdowns, the max manager warned us that they were going to have to release Norma from seg, and there was nowhere to put her but back with us in pod 2. He explained that she had just been sentenced in outside court for having trashed pod 3, and another woman on pod 1 was an "incompatible." I had noticed that this particular manager always sat down right in the middle of the picnic table. Most of us would end up standing around him, but at a distance, because no one liked the optics of sitting right down beside him. I figured he did this for a reason.

The purpose of these informal meetings was supposedly to discuss solutions to problems we were having on the pod. No one ever brought up interpersonal problems or even issues with a particular guard because that was the same thing as informing, so people would bring up things like running out of laundry soap or the lack of employment. He always acted humble, and his position sitting down in the middle while we stood up around him gave the impression decisions were being made collectively, which in reality they decidedly were not. The only problems these meetings ever resolved were the most superficial. Systemic problems were never addressed. We never got more or better jobs, or faster resolutions to official grievances, for instance.

This particular meeting was more serious than most. This was obvious from his decision to stand up beside the disabled TV at the end of the pod, so we had to face him, sitting down at the picnic table or on the sofas if we didn't want to stand. This time he had taken a commanding, offensive position, like the coach of a football team or a general giving his troops orders.

He didn't start off the meeting with his customary pleasantries and questions regarding our well-being, but went straight to the heart of the matter. "Listen. You girls are familiar with our problems with Norma. We can't leave her in segregation indefinitely, and there are people on the other pods who don't want her with them either. We're stuck between a rock and a hard place. So we have decided that this pod would be the best place for her under the circumstances. You will have to learn to live with that decision or learn to live with the consequences."

Right away Lateesha stood up to confront him. "Would you invite Norma to come and live in your house with your wife and kids?" He didn't answer. "Would you live with her if you were Black, and she called you a nigger all the time in front of your wife and kids?" He stared at Lateesha for a minute before responding.

"Listen. You have committed crimes and acted in antisocial ways, and yet you expect to be treated fairly despite these facts. Why should Norma be treated any differently than yourself?" he said curtly. He hadn't exactly answered her. He had slid sideways with a rhetorical question, just like a seasoned politician.

I could see Lateesha struggling to contain herself, because she knew that anything she said would be used against her. Then he walked off the pod, knowing he didn't have to answer to any to us. A few days later we heard that Norma had been released to pod 1, while her "incompatible" was released into the compound. Under the circumstances it was definitely the best solution, and everyone breathed a sigh of relief.

I was finding myself increasingly conflicted over my feelings and actions in the max unit. It seemed that the more stress and pressure I was under, the harder it was to make decisions that were either ideological or ethical. The consequences in the maximum were more immediate and dangerous than they had been in the compound in 2006, or in P4W. The pressure to make practical decisions was much more intense because the consequences for each decision involved an immediate loss of freedom or a physical threat.

At least a third of the women in the max had serious mental health issues. Some were clinically depressed, paranoid, schizophrenic, psychopathic, or simply very violent. Indigenous prisoners, like Norma, were affected by the collective fallout from colonization: living on reserves in which Indigenous peoples' traditional culture had been under constant assault; their spiritual practices made illegal; their sense of self systemically under attack through the residential school system, leading to astronomical suicide rates, addictions, interpersonal violence, imprisonment, and mental illness. But no amount of awareness of this history could save me from becoming the focus of some random prisoner's rage when her emotions were sublimated to such an extent that I became the stand-in for anyone who had fucked with her in her past. In that moment I would have to deal with the possibility of being the one with the ballpoint pen sticking out of the side of my head, and whatever historical abuses a prisoner had suffered would seem irrelevant.

After lockup I lay back on my bunk and once again thought about the iconic book I had read in the seventies, *The Wretched of the Earth* by Frantz Fanon. He was a native Algerian who had written extensively about the power dynamics between the French colonizers and the Algerians during the revolution of the 1960s. I saw how his analysis of the psychological effects of colonization on his native Algerians could be applied not only to Indigenous people, but also prisoners. It was easy to replace the words "native Algerians" with "Indigenous people" or "prisoners" in general.

The native Algerians had no real power. If they resisted the French colonialists, even using legal methods, they would be arrested, often tortured, and sometimes killed. As a result, many Algerians would take out their unresolved rage and frustration on each other. "While the settler or policeman has the right the livelong day to strike the native, to insult him and to make him crawl to him, you will see the native reaching for his knife at the slightest hostile or aggressive glance cast on him by another native, for the last resort of the native is to defend his personality vis-à-vis his brother."[97] As a psychiatrist, Fanon argued that the strategic violence of the resistance movement against the French colonialists in Algeria was actually therapeutic for the native Algerian revolutionaries, because then they would be directing their anger at the real source of their suffering.

This counterintuitive dynamic helped me to understand why prisoners, including myself, would sometimes find ourselves feeling somewhat ingratiated to a guard or administrator who seemed to be kind or who had given us some ridiculous reward for our "good behaviour." This dynamic was even more pronounced and dangerous in those who were mentally ill or naive. In our day-to-day lives, the source of the violence and racism of the prison regime is often invisible and inaccessible, like the Wizard sitting behind his screen, manipulating the citizens of Oz for his own benefit. In every prison compound, racial groups band together, believing that the other prisoners of a different colour are the enemy, not the racist political economic system and its prison regime. It is so much easier to control another prisoner lower down the pecking order than it is to control the decisions of the administration. It is so much easier to pull a knife on a prisoner who is darker or weaker than yourself than it is to change the racist history of this country that got you here in the first place.

I thought about Norma's racist assault on the segregation cleaner. Racism in prisons was rampant right from the top to the bottom. Once again, this phenomenon is best understood by turning the "trickle-down effect" on its head. When the trickle-down effect is turned upside down, it explains how systemic racism trickles down into the prison regime, where the numbers of Black and Brown people increase disproportionately as the security levels rise. In other words, it isn't wealth from the tiny 1 percent of the uber-wealthy power elite that trickles down to the rest of us, but rather the racism, the poverty, and all the other injustices inherent in the capitalist economic system. Freedom, rights, and wealth stay at the top, leaving all the other detritus to trickle down to the bottom.

Thirty Two

The events of the evening and its aftermath consumed me. I lay on my cot for a long time, mulling over prison dynamics, until I felt this magnetic pull from an object in my peripheral vision. As I turned my head, it stood out from the other mundane items on my shelf by its soft glow. My mouth began to water, and I felt a cozy, warm feeling envelop me. It was my breakfast muffin.

I don't know what it was about some prison food, but it could be indescribably delicious. Every night our breakfast would come up with our supper trays so the kitchen staff did not have to make and deliver breakfast early the next day. Most of the time it would be little cereal boxes, or a boiled egg, toast and fruit, or some other plain food. But once in a while they would drop in something delicious like, in this case, a ginger bran muffin, or sometimes a granola bar. When this happened, I would heat up my muffin right before lockup, take some peanut butter packages, and after lockup, sit down to savour this special treat. I can't describe how content I would feel sitting on my bunk, listening to the radio in the soft, yellow glow of the nightlight, savouring the delicious blend of ginger, peanut butter, and bran.

When I got out I tried to replicate these muffins with many different recipes, but could never get that indescribable taste. Without all the stress and general bullshit going on all day, the muffin did not take on the same soothing, comforting, mouthwatering taste. I eventually realized that the missing ingredient was adversity.

A few days later I was sitting on the sofa, waiting impatiently for the methadone call, when I couldn't help but overhear the other four women gossiping loudly about "the bust" during the night of a guard who had been caught, again, in a compromising situation with one of the prisoners. I guess no one cared about the bubble overhearing, since their relationship was common knowledge among the administration already. His wife had an administrative job at GVI.

Sexual relationships between guards and prisoners have been going on since the first prison was built. Prisoners are infantilized, with no power to make even the most trivial decisions. Even their morality is determined by these prison authority figures, and if they resist, their punishment has no boundaries. Like children, there is no escape, and even complaints to the outside world are met with skepticism and silence. Even though most of these relationships are consensual, the unequal power dynamic and the prison setting make these relationships about as consensual as that between a priest and an altar boy.

Rosie was cutting up apples that no one had eaten from their meal trays. "So, I guess she had a solo visit booked, and they planned to meet up in the trailer," she said, smiling. "How they thought they could get away with it, I'll never know."

"Do you want these in the microwave?" asked Paula, pointing at a bowl already full of cut and peeled apple pieces. Rosie nodded her head.

"You know how it is when you're horned out. You'll do anything to get it. Their brains were fucked up," said Rosie. Everybody laughed loudly. "Anyway, the administration probably thought that with the wife working there and all, it would seem just too outrageous for those two to carry on!"

The microwave dinged, and Paula took the apples out and slid in another bowl. She carried the cooked apples over to Rosie, who topped them with crushed-up granola bar to make a mouthwatering apple crumble. She slid the bowl over to Paula. Like the breakfast muffins, these prison recipes were a hundred times better than any equivalent dish on the street.

"I guess they organized some kind of sting operation, so as soon as the guard was in the trailer with her and doing who knows what, the guards came in and busted them. She ain't talkin' cause she's in looooove," cooed Rosie. "Hey, you want an apple crumble?" she yelled over to me.

"Sure," I said, coming over to the picnic table. I was thinking about a delicious birthday ice cream cake I had eaten on pod 1 that someone had made from canteen ingredients like ice cream bars, chocolate bars, and jam. Sometimes I think the limitations imposed in these pods brought out the creativity in people. Necessity is the mother of invention, as they say.

"Anyhow," continued Rosie, "everybody knows about it now, so they're going to have to get rid of him."

As it turned out, everybody did know about it, but GVI did not do anything about it. There were probably a lot of factors involved in this decision, such as not wanting to reinforce the optics of male guards on the frontlines sexually abusing women prisoners; the guard having strong union protection; the woman prisoner refusing to cooperate; and GVI maintaining its default position of invisibility and unaccountability. However, an issue like this is like trying to hide water under a rubber mat; it just keeps leaking out all over the place. At least three prisoners contacted the media, at which point their stories were confirmed by the Canadian Association of Elizabeth Fry Societies. The CBC later revealed that Norma had been one of several sources claiming a male guard had given drugs or tobacco to a female prisoner in exchange for sex. Norma had requested anonymity for fear of "staff reprisals." She had also admitted she was struggling with self-harm issues and "other interpersonal problems," which contributed to her agreeing to a voluntary transfer to the psychiatric treatment centre in Saskatoon, as "a reprieve from her isolation" at GVI.[98] Norma was transferred one week after the CBC went public with the "sex for drugs" allegations. Like a rat caught in a corner with a very bright light illuminating its every move, the CSC finally contacted the Waterloo Regional Police. After a two-month investigation, the police concluded the "allegations were unfounded."[99] No surprise there.

I had been feeling increasingly nervous about my parole hearing, and yet relieved, because knowing my fate would be an improvement over my present state of limbo. If they revoked me, at least I wouldn't have this "freedom" carrot constantly dangling around in front of me. There was something very relaxing and comforting about having no choices, even if it is prison. Most people can adjust to anything if they have no options.

On October 31, 2012, my parole was reinstated. My "freedom" did not come cheap financially, even though my progressive lawyers did 80 percent of their work pro bono. Once again, I was privileged to even have a lawyer, thanks to support from the political community. The vast majority of prisoners do not have legal assistance for parole hearings, or for that matter, any issues of injustice that arise during their time in prison. As a study into Legal Aid access concluded, "even clients who were able to obtain a certificate for legal aid services … were often unable to find a lawyer who would take a certificate case."[100]

"Freedom" did not come cheap in terms of conditions, either. Despite having been suspended without charges and having violated no conditions, the parole board members seemed to feel compelled to tack on two new conditions in order to satisfy Kingston Parole Services. First,

I was not permitted "to knowingly associate with any person you know or have reason to believe is involved in criminal activity," and I was required to "notify your parole supervisor, in advance, of any politically motivated event you will attend or participate in, including but not limited to, speaking engagements, meetings, and protest/pickets."[101]

I accepted these conditions, planning to contest them at a later date. The goal of these new conditions was clear: to prevent me from participating in political activities, even if they were legal. The Harper Conservatives' Bill C-10 made changes to the *Corrections and Conditional Release Act* that shifted the emphasis on parole to ensuring "public safety and offender accountability," at the expense of human rights for prisoners.[102] In practical terms, this meant that Parole Services could revoke any prisoner's parole for any activity that they claimed was a threat to public safety, regardless of their Charter rights. Before Bill C-10, at least according to the law, prisoners had the same Charter rights as any other citizen. Not anymore. It might seem like a small thing, but it's like thinking that putting a tiny nail hole in the hull of a row boat will have virtually no impact on your upcoming journey across the lake. It won't take long to discover just how wrong you were.

I had vowed that if I got my parole back, I would not allow myself to fall back into the reclusive lifestyle I had experienced in 2006, when I had not been able to answer a phone, email, or knock at the door. But despite my best intentions, I found myself once again irritable, angry, and unable to engage with other people outside my own home. I did appreciate the beauty of nature and the animals all around me. They seemed even more beautiful and sacred than ever before. Colours took on a physical aspect. I could feel the oranges and yellows of the autumn leaves. I could spend hours gardening or talking to the horses, chickens, and birds in the sky, but I could not drag myself downtown to get involved in political events. It didn't help that the few times I tried to get involved in perfectly legal political activities, I was denied permission.

I cannot say that I had suffered in prison, like so many people. In fact, I have not *really* suffered at any time in my life. As I said earlier, I was buffered from tragedy by being born a white woman into a happy working-class family in the Western world. I certainly could not compare my experiences to those of so many women in prison or to those of a soldier at war, yet the more I heard stories about soldiers suffering from PTSD, the more I wondered if my symptoms of reclusiveness, anger, and irritability, and my generalized feelings of social anxiety, could be considered a form of PTSD light.

I did not fit the stereotype of those suffering from PTSD, but the more I heard about the effects of PTSD on soldiers coming back from Afghanistan, the more I began to see the parallels between most prisoners' life experiences and those of a soldier in a war zone. "The vast majority, 84% of [federally sentenced] women had a history of being abused physically, sexually or emotionally, most frequently by parents, step-parents or common-law or marital husbands."[103] A disproportionate number of Indigenous women in prison grew up among the violence, addictions, and poverty that are the collateral damage from colonization. Yet the authorities seemed loath to put the PTSD label on anyone who does not have a respectable profession. Soldiers, cops, first responders, yes, but not prisoners.

The following example is dated, but it illustrates very clearly the double standard in diagnosing PTSD that still exists today. In 1975, a group of lifers in the BC Penitentiary who had just been released from long-term segregation took some hostages in order to bring attention to the issue of isolation. During the three-day hostage-taking, guards accidently killed one of the hostages, Mary Steinhauser, a prison classification officer. A former ambulance paramedic who accompanied Steinhauser to the hospital in an ambulance and administered emergency treatment was diagnosed with accumulative post-traumatic stress disorder in 1998, over twenty-three years after the hostage-taking. Andy Reekie, a BC spokesperson for the Union of Canadian Correctional Officers, said the "Steinhauser case" had a heavy impact on many of those involved. "There are people who are suffering through post-traumatic stress disorder" over the hostage-taking and subsequent shooting, said Reekie.[104] However, the class-biased nature of the PTSD diagnosis left all the prisoners involved in this same tragic event untreated and undiagnosed, but more criminalized than ever.

It's unlikely the government would want to recognize that many prisoners suffer from PTSD, because the consequences would be too much like surrendering to the idea that the vast majority of prisoners really are the scapegoats for all the systemic injustices and inequalities in society. If the government were to recognize the many PTSD sufferers in prison, they would have to treat them as suffering from mental health issues, and would also have to take a look at the conditions that caused their "disorders" in the first place: the racism, inequality, addictions, and abuse that so many prisoners have suffered.

On January 20, 2013, I learned that Norma had died of an apparent heart attack after repeatedly pushing the emergency button in her cell at the Regional Psychiatric Treatment Centre in Saskatoon, Saskatchewan.

I was saddened but not surprised by the news. "[She] entered the corrections system when she was 18. At the time, her sentence was 6 years, but she accumulated a string of other charges that increased it to more than 15 years. Her charges included manslaughter, assault, uttering threats, arson, and obstruction of justice."[105]

On the evening of Norma's death, she had repeatedly pushed her emergency button in her cell, complaining of stomach pain. When the guards failed to respond, the women in the adjacent cells also began to push their cell emergency buttons. The guards finally responded, but it took over an hour for someone from health care to arrive, and by that time there had been no sounds coming from Norma's cell for at least an hour, leading her fellow prisoners to conclude that she was either already dead or unconscious.

Norma had spent fifteen years in segregation, broken up only by short stints in maximum-security units or psychiatric prisons … shades of Ashley Smith. The silent response of the guards to Norma's emergency button and the screams of her fellow prisoners … shades of Eddie Nalon. She died while waiting for over an hour for a nurse to arrive … shades of Bobby Landers. They died the death of a million little cuts, as have so many others before them.

Epilogue

"And Aaron shall place lots upon the two goats: one lot 'For the Lord,' and the other lot, 'For Azazel (for absolute removal).'"

Leviticus 16:8

"Country-boys ... are patient, too, and bear their fate as scape-goats, (for all sins whatsoever are laid as matter of course to their door...) with amazing resignation."

Mary Russell Mitford, 1824, *Our Village*

Scapegoating is as universal as prisons. The ancient Hebrews, Syrians, Greeks, and Christians shared similar rituals in which a goat or some other living substitute became the vehicle for the sins or evils of the community and was banished, thereby purging the community of its problems.

In today's world, instead of symbolically banishing a goat, real people are blamed for society's problems and isolated in prisons. These are the scapegoats: the people whom society is unwilling or unable to accommodate. As a result, prisons are the most important social control mechanism a society has, short of execution. Prisons are also an integral part of almost every society on this planet, whether capitalist, socialist, or theocratic, and so they reflect the society they serve.

Since capitalism is the dominant economic system on the planet, it is important to have a basic understanding of how it functions if we are to understand prisons. Capitalism for dummies, as they say.

Capitalism is based on a market economy in which some individuals have become owners of land, tools, and technology. This private ownership has made it possible for a relatively small percentage of the population to profit from the labour of the majority. With the advent of corporate capitalism, large numbers of citizens, with no vested interest in a company other than purchasing shares, are also able to profit from the labour of others. These profits have been kept artificially high through the collusion of corporations controlling the purchase and selling prices of similar products, thus eliminating the kind of competitive pricing that keeps profits down. In order to keep the cost of labour down as well, corporations have also campaigned relentlessly to systematically strip labour unions of any real power. Most importantly, they have learned that labour is cheaper when there is a surplus.

The conditions of capitalism, as simplified above, create material inequality, in that a few wealthy owners and shareholders can exploit and profit from the labour of the majority, with devastating results. "A 2006 study by the World Institute for Developmental Economics Research at United Nations University reports that the richest 1% of adults alone owned 40% of global assets in the year 2000, and that the richest 10% of adults accounted for 85% of the world total. The bottom half of the world adult population owned barely 1% of global wealth."[106] This economic disparity has only worsened over time.

Since capitalism first began to dominate the Western world, it has relentlessly pushed the idea of humans as "homo economicus," a term coined by the famous critic of capitalist theory John Stuart Mill. As Mill explained, "the political economy is concerned with [man] … solely as a being who desires to possess wealth, and who is capable of judging comparative efficacy of obtaining that end."[107] Since 1836, Mill's "homo economicus" has evolved into the perfect specimen, the neoliberal individual who views life without economic value as having no value at all. Even though we may not believe that humans are primarily motivated by economic needs, the successful subliminal effects of corporate culture's multibillion-dollar marketing campaigns have made "homo economicus" a self-fulfilling prophecy in the twenty-first century.

In the world of "homo economicus," the environment is a resource to be developed for farming, housing, mining, energy, lumber, and so on. Animals are on this earth for our use as pets, entertainment, clothing, food, and sport. If humans cannot produce or consume products, they are considered "a burden." If these "burdens" learn to survive through an illegal or "black" market, as outlaws, they will be criminalized and imprisoned. But if the outlaws become revolutionaries, conscientiously rejecting capitalism, becoming organized, effectively fighting back, and inspiring more and more of the "consumers" and "producers" to defect from the capitalist system, they will be branded "terrorists." In the world of "homo economicus" the first two categories, the "burdens" and the "outlaws," are consciously transformed through political campaigns by the ruling elite into the scapegoats for all that is wrong with the system.

In a world in which public policy aspires to be based on evidence, it would be safe to say that prisoners are society's scapegoats, based on statistical facts that have remained consistent over time. As Canadian prison demographics reveal, Indigenous prisoners and prisoners of colour are grossly overrepresented. According to the government's own prison watchdog, the Correctional Investigator of Canada, "while Aboriginal people make up about 4% of the Canadian population, as of Feb 2013, 23.2% of the federal inmate population is Aboriginal (First Nation, Metis, Inuit).[108] There are approximately 3,400 Aboriginal offenders in federal penitentiaries, approximately 71% are First Nations, 24% Metis and 5% Inuit.... The incarceration rate for Aboriginal adults in Canada is estimated to be 10 times higher than the incarceration rate of non-Aboriginal adults...In 2010/2011, 41% of females (and 25% of males) in sentenced custody (provincially, territorially and federally) were Aboriginal."[109]

Over the past ten years, the Black prison population has increased by 50 percent. In Ontario, 20 percent of the federal prison population is Black, even though Black people make up only 2.5 percent of the general population.[110]

The fastest-growing prison demographic is not seasoned violent psychopaths or serial killers, but youth, women, Indigenous people, and Black people. Yet 75 percent of the population of federally sentenced women are in for non-violent crimes such as shoplifting, drug-related crimes, and fraud.[111] "Sex differences in rates of violence by men and women are consistent, with men outnumbering women by a very large margin. This is so across countries, over time, at all ages, and in relation to different types of violence.... Overall, women are more likely to be charged with minor assaults than men. Very few are charged with robbery and fewer still, sexual assault (a pattern which is similar in the USA)."[112] Just as Indigenous and Black women are overrepresented in prison, so too are they overrepresented in the maximum-security units.[113] We could go on and on.

Unless one believes that there is a correlation between genetics and crime, the only explanation for these statistics is that social conditions are responsible for uneducated people, poor people, unemployed people, youth, Indigenous people, people of colour, and those with mental illnesses committing "crimes" at a far greater rate than others. In some cases these conditions have damaged the person, leaving them vulnerable to self-medicating and struggling with deep-rooted rage.

While crime rates for women, children, and non-white populations are increasing, crime rates for white men are decreasing. The key to understanding this paradox lies in the position of women, children, and non-white populations at the very bottom of the economic food chain. Women are the first group forced to step out of the legal boundaries to provide food and shelter for their families.

The following statistics have not changed significantly since 2011. Crime rates in Canada reached a twenty-five-year low in 2006, yet the numbers of women being imprisoned are increasing.

> The escalating numbers of women in prison is plainly linked to the evisceration of health, education and social services.... While more than 80% of women in Canada have progressed beyond grade nine, for women prisoners the figure is closer to 50% ... 80% of the women serving time in a federal facility were unemployed at the time of admission, compared to 54% of men.... More than half of all charges for which federally sentenced women are convicted are non-violent property and drug offences. Prop-

erty offences account for around 32% of all court cases
and 47% of all charges against women.... In many cases in
which federally sentenced women are charged with causing
death, their actions were defensive or otherwise reactive to
violence directed at them, their children or another third
party. They pose little risk to the public.[114]

Yet despite these statistics, the percentage of women, particularly Indigenous women, classified and treated as maximum security is much greater
than that of male prisoners. "Aboriginal women were 38% of the population of the maximum-security units in the 2 establishments [Nova
and GVI], and 40% of the population in maximum security units in the
overall federal system."[115]

When you connect the dots created by the statistics describing
impoverished women and those describing women in federal prisons, you
get a very clear snapshot of women with no place to go to provide their
children with food and shelter other than small-time drug dealing, fraud,
and shoplifting. One of the common features of these snapshots is that
there is a growing pile of them.

Exponential growth in the women's prison population is typical
of prison population growth across North America. Three months after
Kingston Penitentiary was first opened for men in 1835, the first three
federal women prisoners were sentenced to serve their time inside its
infirmary, as there was no federal prison for women. By 1934, almost one
hundred years later, the first forty federal women prisoners were transferred to the newly built Prison for Women. By 1980, fifty years later, the
number of federally sentenced women (fsw) in Canada had more than tripled, to approximately two hundred women. Over the next twenty years,
from 1980 to 2000, the population of fsw increased by 75 percent, to
350.[116] By the time P4W closed in 2000, the CSC had built six regional
prisons for women; Grand Valley in Ontario, Joliette in Quebec, Nova in
Nova Scotia, Edmonton in Alberta, Fraser Valley in BC, and the Okimaw
Ohci "healing lodge" in Saskatchewan. In the ten years after P4W closed,
the population of fsw almost tripled again, increasing from 350 to 850.
Even the CSC admits the prisoner population is expected to triple once
more over the next five years, when they add another 144 beds to the
women's federal prisons.[117]

If there is a parallel universe to be found in relation to North American exponential prison growth, it will be found in the growth of the

1 percent's wealth and power—not in crime rates, general population growth, GDP, or the overall tax base. "This generation of rich Canadians is staking claim to a larger share of economic growth than any generation that has preceded it. Since the late 1970's, the richest 1% has almost doubled its share of total income; the richest .1% has almost tripled its share of total income; and the richest .01% has more than quadrupled its share of income."[118]

While the percentage of people amassing most of society's wealth is shrinking, the percentage of people who are under- or unemployed has been growing.

This economic trend began in the early 1980s, during the Reagan era, with the advent of neoliberalism as the dominant economic model of the Western world. In practical terms, neoliberal policies advocate free-trade agreements that result in the exodus of the manufacturing sector from "developed" countries to "underdeveloped" countries, where products can be produced more cheaply due to the nonexistence of labour unions, environmental laws, and protective tariffs. Neoliberal policies also encourage the privatization of the traditional public sector, thereby opening up even more vistas for the insatiable appetite of corporate profiteers. And last, neoliberal policies encourage transforming the human collateral damage from the first two policies into "criminals" who can be managed through tough-on-crime, law-and-order legislation.

This ongoing neoliberal economic agenda is largely responsible for growing economic disparity as more and more industries relocate to "underdeveloped" parts of the world. More and more of the public sector is being sold off to the private sector or replaced by technology, and more and more people are being forced to commit crimes of survival because the social safety net is shrinking and full of holes. If they don't land in the social safety net, the only place left is prison.

The meaning of the expression "contradictions in a capitalist economy" can be found in the contradiction people experience between their lived reality and the illusions of democracy, freedom, equality, and rights they are being sold. In a capitalist economy, these contradictions grow as the rich get richer and the poor get poorer. In order to maintain the illusion that we live in a true democracy, the corporate and political elite market another illusion: that everyone has the same fundamental rights and freedoms. Unfortunately for the wealthy, the day-to-day reality of millions of Black, Indigenous, gay, female, poor white, and immigrant people is in stark contrast to the illusions they are being sold. It takes a multibillion-dollar marketing machine to counteract the obvious contradictions between the hard, cold reality of peoples' daily lives and the virtual reality that people experience through their TVs, movies, and computer screens.

In North America there would be no contradictions if capitalists laid their cards on the table and stated unequivocally that the American Constitution and the Canadian Charter of Rights and Freedoms are mainly applicable to the wealthy, white, male minority, with the exception of a few token representatives from all the other segments of society. If human rights could actually be realized by the poor, women, and people of colour, capitalism would slowly wither away and die. How has a tiny percentage of the population become insanely wealthy if not at the expense of the vast majority of the planet's people? One person cannot accumulate billions of dollars through their own labour, nor can they protect it by themselves. To possess billions of dollars, they need to exploit the labour of millions of people, and they need millions more to protect it. The rights of the poorest, people of colour, women, children, animals, the environment, and just about every living thing must be sacrificed in order for this tiny percentage of people to accumulate this massive wealth.

It would be nice to think that these contradictions could be eliminated by levelling up the playing field through better education, more job training, and more affordable housing for non-white and poor segments of the population, but unfortunately racism, sexism, inequality, and injustice are systemic symptoms of capitalism, just as fever, coughing, respiratory infection, and nausea are symptoms of pneumonia. Even if some marginalized people could get meaningful employment through better education and job training, capitalists need that pool of poor and unemployed people from which to hire fruit pickers, waitresses, and factory workers at unbelievably low wages, and those that are left over in the pool become the disposable demographic that must commit crimes in order to survive. In other words, as long as there are systemic inequalities and injustices, there will always be people who must commit crimes to survive.

Why are prison populations increasing while crime rates are decreasing? The root causes of this paradox are embedded in the law-and-order legislation that defines the neoliberal economies of our times. The greater the global economic disparity, the more laws and prisons are needed by the ruling elites to control the poverty-stricken masses. Harper's 2012 Omnibus Bill C-10 is a good example of this "tough on crime" legislation, which increases prison sentences and creates tougher parole regulations and more mandatory minimum sentences, contributing to the paradox of a burgeoning prison population despite lower crime rates.

There are many of us who have come to the conclusion that a just and equitable society can never exist within a capitalist framework. And so, we struggle to abolish capitalism and its social control mechanism ... prisons. But can prison reform play a role in a revolutionary campaign to abolish prisons and capitalism?

First, let's see what happens when well-meaning prison reformers' projects are embraced by the Canadian government and the CSC. Even more specifically, what happens when the government decides to close an old prison and replace it with what they claim will be a new, progressive prison with more treatment-oriented programming, education, and job skills training?

After the recommendations from the Arbour Inquiry into Certain Events at P4W were published in 1996, the federal government decided to close P4W and use these recommendations to create a blueprint for six new regional federal prisons for women. The heart and soul of the Arbour recommendations was the idea that the new prisons would have women-centred programming and Native-specific cultural programming. This would translate more concretely into better access to sexual abuse counselling, job skills training and education, a well-equipped library, escorts so women could gain access to professionals and jobs in the community, a Native elder on staff, a sweat lodge, and a strong Native Sisterhood.

What the new regional prisons would *not* have were maximum-security units, guards in uniforms, tiers, barred cells, ranges, pods, bubbles, or long periods during which women would be locked in their cells. The centrepiece for the CSC's new prison paradigm would be the Okimaw Ohci "healing lodge" in Saskatchewan, a prison where "corrections" would be infused with Indigenous spirituality and culture. Okimaw Ohci even had horses to help rehabilitate the prisoners—a prison where captive horses would whisper universal truths to their fellow human captives.

Unfortunately, this new reformist paradigm began to melt like McArthur Park in the rain, even before P4W was closed. The CSC used the 1995 prison escape of a few women over the unfinished perimeter wall of the new Edmonton Institution for Women, and the confrontation between the guards and prisoners that precipitated the 1994 IERT intervention in P4W's segregation unit, to justify building multimillion-dollar maximum-security units in each women's federal prison compound. Security and repression are such integral features of the CSC that, like two starving dinner guests, they quickly began eating up all the money originally allotted for progressive programming and education.

Between my two short stints in GVI during 2006 and then again in 2012, I witnessed the devolution of GVI from a prison compound where women cooked and lived collectively in bungalows perched neatly in grassy, tree-lined yards, where vegetables were grown in kitchen gardens and the women moved about freely from eight in the morning until ten at night throughout the compound … to a multi-security prison complex with few jobs or programming and with double-bunking everywhere, including maximum-security units and segregation. This devolution unfolded in all six regional federal prisons for women during the fifteen years after P4W closed in 2000. This feat is surpassed only by the fact that the entire federal prisoner population for women actually in prison had increased by 40 percent, to 550 women, in the ten years after the closure of P4W.[119] This in a country where the crime rates have been on a steady decline over the past two decades.

This is a pattern all too familiar to those who study the history of prison reform. The glaring contradiction between the branding of the soon-to-be-opened Millhaven Institution in 1972, as a showcase for the CSC's rehabilitative programming, job skills training, and education, and its actual opening became painfully obvious in a 1976 report by a sub-committee of the Commons Justice Committee: "Dogs were let loose on prisoners in the yard and in their cells. Gas was used to punish prisoners frequently … in March 1973, as often as three or four times a week, prisoners who were first shackled, sometimes hands and feet together, were beaten with clubs, made to crawl on the floor and finally gassed."[120]

Millhaven had opened prematurely in 1971, after six hundred prisoners in Kingston Penitentiary (KP) rioted, at least in part because they had heard rumours that their every move would be recorded by cameras and every whisper by microphone once they were transferred over to the new penitentiary, Millhaven. Life was breathed into these rumours when the CSC began reassuring the public that security would be maintained using the latest in modern surveillance technology and new long-term isolation units, known as special handling units.

Instead of guards patrolling the tiers, like they had in KP, guards in Millhaven would sit inside Plexiglas consoles, where they would open or shut cell doors electronically with the push of a button while simultaneously watching movement on the ranges and hallways via 24/7 live feed streaming through CCTV monitors. And there would be call buttons attached to two-way intercoms in each cell block so the guards didn't have to go anywhere to communicate with prisoners. The fanfare surrounding

Millhaven's new security system provided a stark counterpoint to the that surrounding progressive programming.

Few rounders were surprised when the four hundred prisoners who were supposedly involved in the KP riot were shipped off to Millhaven, where they were stripped and forced to run a gauntlet of guards with riot sticks, and then left locked down for months at a time. KP did not close for another forty years, until September 2013.

The closure of the British Columbia Penitentiary (BC Pen), followed by the opening of Kent Institution, is Exhibit C in the metaphorical CSC display case of prison reforms gone bad. A few years after the opening of Millhaven on June 9, 1975, three prisoners were about to be returned to solitary confinement at the BC Pen when they took fifteen hostages and held them for forty-one hours. The three prisoners involved were lifers who had just recently been released into general population after having already spent considerable time in solitary. The hostage-taking ended when the hostages decided to attack one of the prisoners while he was sleeping. In the ensuing chaos, the guards, who were just outside the hostage-taking zone, began firing at the prisoners, who were interspersed amongst the hostages. When all was said and done, one of the hostages, Mary Steinhauser, a classification officer, was dead, and Andy Bruce, a prisoner, was injured. In the ensuing inquiry it was determined that Steinhauser had been killed by a bullet from an unknown guard, since the prisoners were only armed with knives.[121]

After the BC Pen riot in 1975, a prisoner, Jack McCann, who had spent 1,471 uninterrupted days in "the hole," launched a court case involving seven prisoners who had collectively spent eleven and a half years in solitary confinement. The court case was meant to challenge the use of solitary confinement. In 1975 institutional charges were dealt with in Warden's Court. The following facts were essentially the same for any federal prison in Canada. The prisoners were not allowed to defend themselves against institutional charges with lawyers or witnesses. Once convicted they could spend weeks, months, or even years in solitary, locked up twenty-three hours a day with one hour of exercise per day, if they were lucky. Solitary cells vary according to the prison in which they are located. In the BC Pen, the cells were six and a half by eleven feet and consisted of three concrete walls and a steel door with a five-inch-square window. There was a steel slab covered with a foam mattress for a bed and light twenty-four hours a day from a 100-watt bulb, and a 25-watt bulb at night. Exercise involved walking up and down the corridor outside their cells for an hour a day. In *McCann v. the Queen*, Mr. Justice D. V.

Heald of the Federal Court of Canada ruled that solitary confinement, as used in the BC Pen, consisted of "cruel and unusual punishment."[122] In today's world, prisoners can have a lawyer and call witnesses, but otherwise the conditions in segregation have not changed much since the ruling of *McCann v. the Queen* in 1975.

As this book goes into print, the Canadian Civil Liberties Association is challenging and attempting to have the practice of solitary confinement abolished by the Supreme Court of Canada as a violation of our Charter Rights and Freedoms.[123] The use of solitary confinement has long been considered a form of torture by the United Nations Committee on Torture.[124] However, most prisoners, myself included, are cynical at best that any legal challenges or lofty ideals as expressed in various Charters will actually eliminate this support beam of prison regimes. As long as there are prisons, capitalism, or any other economic system based on inequalities, the odds are in favour of solitary confinement in one form or another.

In 1979, just four years after the infamous BC Penitentiary riot, the BC Pen was replaced by a new, modern prison, Kent Institution. Within two months of its opening, prisoners lit fires, took hostages, and rioted over demands to end unnecessary body searches, the denial of visiting privileges, and the excessive use of solitary confinement for the slightest infraction. There was also a month-long prisoner strike over the postponement of the promised "rehabilitative programs."

By 1981, the Kent Lifers Organization was so concerned about the ongoing use of solitary confinement that they issued a fifty-four-page statement, of which the following are excerpts: "… placing prisoners in a cell, hand-cuffed and shackled for days at a time and taking away all clothes, bedding, personal effects and food … unnecessary beatings upon hand-cuffed prisoners … 10 minutes for showers every 5 days … only 20 minutes exercise every 2 days … locked up sometimes for 24 hours a day for weeks at a time."[125]

These three examples represent a pattern that has become predictable not only in Canada, but globally. New prisons come wrapped in progressive packaging, decorated with pictures of rehabilitation and programming, but once they are opened, out comes a shiny new prison filled with all kinds of technological gadgets designed for enhanced surveillance and security that cost so much, the prison regime claims it can no longer afford all the progressive programming promised on the packaging.

In 1982, Canada enacted the Canadian Charter of Rights and Freedoms, which was intended to apply to all Canadian citizens, whether they were prisoners or not. Many prisoners are aware of their rights, but as soon as they try to exercise them, they disappear like a mirage in the desert. These theoretical rights are often treated as privileges or programs that prisoners must earn.

In 2012, with the advent of Bill C-10, changes to the purpose and principles of the *Corrections and Conditional Release Act* (CCRA) emphasized the power of the parole board or a judge to restrict prisoners' Charter rights. The revised CCRA states "that all offenders keep all the rights of all members of society except those that are a consequence of their sentence lawfully and necessarily removed."[126]

Prisons ultimately serve as a social control mechanism, so when there is a conflict between prisoners' rights and maintaining "the good order of the institution," or society, the "good order" will always win. This supremacy is written into the amended principles and purpose of the CSC as stated in the CCRA: "The protection of society is the paramount consideration for the Service in the correctional process."[127] If this were not the case, the very capacity of prison regimes to control prisoners would be in jeopardy. Prison reforms are doomed to be like the disappearing bunnies in the magician's hat—an illusion.

My personal situation illustrates these changes and the effect they have on a parolee's ability to exercise their Charter rights and freedoms. In 2013, a few months after my release, I was called in to the parole office and reprimanded because I had not notified my parole supervisor about a speaking engagement that was posted on the Internet, scheduled to take place during an International Women's Day event. Even though this Internet posting occurred without my knowledge, a little less than three weeks before the event, I was still warned that, had I not been able to prove that this posting was an error by an inexperienced volunteer, I could have been suspended.

Late in the afternoon of August 9, 2013, I received an email from my parole officer saying that my case management team were recommending that I not attend a Prisoners' Justice Day (PJD) event that was scheduled for the next day, even as a spectator, because I had not identified and notified them that the organizers were End the Prison Industrial Complex, a local prison abolition group, and the local Idle No More group, an Indigenous activist group. I had given them the time, date, and location of this event weeks in advance, but had not researched who the organizers were. I did not read this email until the following week, but didn't go to PJD due to a sudden but serendipitous case of sciatica. My parole was not suspended.

In the fall of 2013, my book publisher, Between the Lines, asked if I would read a manuscript by Steven D'Arcy, *Languages of the Unheard: Why Militant Protest is Good for Democracy*, and then write a two- or three-sentence blurb if I liked it. A blurb is a technical term used to describe those short reviews you see on book jackets. This was essentially an academic book, written by an associate professor and chair in the department of philosophy at Huron University College in London, Ontario.

I notified my parole officer (PO) of my intentions to write a blurb, but explained that the book was still in manuscript form so I was not authorized to share it. I gave her a short synopsis of the book's theme. After several requests by my PO to read some of the manuscript, Between the Lines made a generous exception and emailed her a copy of the introduction to this book. Just days before the deadline for the blurb, I was called into the office and given notification by Parole Services that I could not write a blurb for this book.

I eventually used the official grievance procedure to complain about my parole condition being applied in such a manner that I had to seek permission to participate in perfectly legal political events. In the end, my grievance was rejected because the CSC believed that my participation in the events listed previously could have jeopardized "public safety." The amendments in Bill C-10 are equivalent to giving Parole Services deep-sea drag nets to catch and destroy everything in their path. The prisoners, like the fish, have no rights to protect themselves from being hauled out of the water willy-nilly.

My case is not unique. Common catchphrases used to suspend some parolees' legal activities are accusations by Parole Services that parolees are exhibiting a "lack of transparency" or "deteriorating behaviour." These experiences have a chilling effect on parolees and even their acquaintances.

When Justin Trudeau's Liberals became the governing party in Canada after a landslide victory over Harper's Conservatives in the 2015 federal election, many prison reformers rejoiced, believing that the election of Trudeau was the secular version of the second coming of Christ. But to prison abolitionists and revolutionaries, Trudeau's election is a real-life demonstration of how the ruling elite are masters in the use of illusion and doublespeak to create the impression that they will implement real change while not really changing anything at all.

Even if the Liberals enact legislation that appears more progressive than the Conservatives, if history is to be our guide, the way the legislation will be implemented will be virtually identical, because all three federal parties share the same capitalist values and paradigm. After the 2015 election, the Liberal minister of justice and attorney-general Jody Wilson-Raybould was mandated to increase the use of "restorative justice amongst Indigenous Canadians." Instead, in February 2017, "56.6 million in infrastructure funding was allocated towards the new $75.8 million 112-bed Qikiqtani Correctional Healing Centre that is slated to replace the notoriously decrepit and crowded 68-bed Baffin Correctional Centre despite the fact that the Liberals critiqued prison expansion in the Harper years while in opposition.... This 'healing center' will be built in Nunavut, whose prison system has the highest rate of imprisonment in the country (534 per 100,000) in 2014/15 with 100% indigenous prisoners."[128]

After two years in power, the Trudeau Liberals have not rescinded any of Harper's law-and-order legislation, despite promises to do so during the 2015 campaign. Despite the Kingston and the Islands riding electing a Liberal, they have not made any promises to reopen the two prison farms in the area. Typically, they have engaged in harmless exercises that may create the illusion that they are going to, but have not actually done anything concrete. They have even been careful enough not to make any promises to reopen the prison farms. After several months of "consulting with citizens in Town Hall forums" and an online feasibility study, CSC spokesperson Sara Parkes said there is no timeline or decision whether the prison farms in Kingston will be reopened.[129]

Prison reformers address the existential problems of prisons and prisoners by advocating for better education, vocational skills training, and addictions counselling. If only prisoners were better educated with more job skills and did not have to struggle with addictions, then there would be no need for prisons. If only pigs could fly.

The problem with these types of reform is that they imply that the prisoners are the problem. If prisons could be improved to address the inadequacies of the prisoners, then there would be less crime. Victim blaming. But no matter how many prisoners are educated, acquire job skills, and overcome their addictions, there will still be a growing mass of disenfranchised, disillusioned, and dysfunctional post-citizens in the twenty-first century who will be compelled to commit crimes of economic survival, and who will feel outraged at injustice.

The problem does not lie in the uneducated, unskilled, and addicted people; the problem lies in the political/economic system, in this case, capitalism and its values. No matter how many prisoners become educated and employed and overcome their addictions, there will continue to be an endless supply of more uneducated, unemployed, and addicted people to fill the void, because without them capitalism could not support the uber-wealthy 1 percent.

Prison reforms also fail in part because it costs a lot of money to build even the most no-frills prison complexes. But it is cheaper to warehouse prisoners in these no-frills, high-tech prison complexes than it is to educate and train prisoners to be reintegrated into a society where there are already too many people to fill even the role of surplus labour. As the computerization and technological takeover of labor escalates, more and more people are becoming obsolete. Without a social safety net, many of these obsolete people end up dealing with their angst through addictions, committing crimes of economic survival, or both.

The root cause of prisons and prisoners lies in the perceived right of the few to accumulate wealth and power at the expense of the many. Believing that educating and training and counselling prisoners is a means of abolishing prisons is like suggesting that cough syrups, aspirin, and thermometers will cure the flu. Treating the symptoms of a disease may alleviate the suffering somewhat, but the only way to cure the patient is to treat the root cause—which brings us face to face with this enigma. Even though we know that treating the symptoms will not cure the disease, shouldn't we at least make life bearable for the patient until we can cure the disease? Is treating the symptoms of a disease a waste of time, a distraction from the real work of finding a cure?

Prison reforms are doomed to eventual failure, but that does not mean that we cannot use the fight for reform within a revolutionary context as a means of raising awareness. Real people are suffering in prisons now. If any one of us were stuck in solitary confinement for years at a time, would we want to wait for the revolution before anyone tried to help us? The answer lies in the murky grey zone between struggling for reform and struggling for revolutionary change. These struggles are a false dichotomy in which the murky grey zone can be bridged. As long as concrete campaigns for reform are framed within a revolutionary context and are guided by revolutionary principles, then they can play a role in the campaign to abolish both capitalism and its social control mechanism, prisons.

There is always a lot of pressure to have a story arc in a prison memoir that goes something like this: Good girl goes bad. Then through suffering she redeems herself and comes to the revelation that the status quo was right all along. Bad girl ends up good. I'm afraid that is not the story arc in this memoir. I still stand by my core beliefs and values that capitalism and its core values of materialism, competition, and hierarchy are the root cause of the Sixth Extinction; that prisons are an essential social control mechanism for capitalism; that reforms are useless, other than as a fleeting relief from suffering, unless they are rooted in a revolutionary analysis and practice; and finally, that the roads to revolution include many paths, not the least of which is militant resistance. As the Black Panthers put it in the sixties, when questioned about the purpose of their breakfast and health care programs in the ghettoes: "Survival pending revolution."[130]

Acknowledgments

I would like to thank Craig for quietly supporting my time spent writing. Anyone who writes knows that there is someone who has taken up the slack by food shopping, washing dishes, answering phone calls, and the many other life-sustaining daily chores.

Ed, for patiently listening to my ideas and political rants, and taking up the slack after Craig was gone.

I would also like to thank Johny for lighting up the darkness, always laughing during the funeral, and making the prison her carnival. An old soul surrounded by youthful energy, passion, and determination.

All the women I did time with in prison, and those I continue to work with in this minimum-security setting we call society. I will honour their anonymity.

To the many mentors I have looked to for guidance and who have paved the way for the next generation of prison abolitionists … Jill Bend, Filis Iverson and Elaine Stef, Pam Cross and Peter Dundas, Jim Campbell, Claire Culhane, Peter Collins, Joan Ruzsa, Kim Pate, Brent Taylor, Doug Stewart, Gerry Hannah, Julie Belmas, Aric McBay and Emily Dowling, Cedar, Devyn, and Amile, and the collective End the Prison Industrial Complex.

I would also like to acknowledge Maureen Garvey for planting a tiny seed of hope that I could write. I think most people who aspire to make a dream reality can trace their determination back to someone who gave them their first simple statement of encouragement.

I would also like to thank Between the Lines for publishing this book. In particular, Amanda Crocker, Tilman Lewis, and Jessie Hale, editors who could miraculously separate the chaff from the wheat, turning a 1,000-page manuscript into one digestible book.

And lawyers like Stan Guenther, Sean Ellacott, and Paul Quick, who fought the good fight in the legal arena, not for money, but for their principles.

And last but not least, my family, who visited and loved me throughout my prison years and after. They have remained supportive and non-judgmental, even when the path of least resistance was headed in the opposite direction.

Notes

1   Howard Sapers, *2013–2014 Annual Report of the Office of the Correctional Investigator*, report prepared for the Minister of Public Safety of the Government of Canada.

2   Noam Chomsky, *Syntactic Structures* (The Hague: Mouton and Co., 1957).

3   *The Oxford Modern English Dictionary* (New York/Oxford: Oxford University Press, 1996).

4   Benjamin N. Cardozo, "Eyewitness Misidentification," The Innocence Project, accessed June 6, 2012, https://www.innocenceproject.org/causes/eyewitness-misidentification/.

5   Harvey J. Krahn, Graham S. Lowe, and Karen D. Hughes, *Work, Industry and Canadian Society*, 6th ed. (Toronto: Nelson, 2014), 26–27.

6   Erika Simpson, *NATO and the Bomb: Canada's Defenders Confront Critics* (Montreal: McGill-Queen's University Press, 2001).

7   Simon Rosenblum, *Misguided Missiles: Canada, the Cruise, and Star Wars* (Toronto: Lorimer, 1985).

8   Milton Friedman, "Neo-Liberalism and its Prospects," *Human Events* (February 17, 1951) 89–93.

9   Eryk Martin, "Burn it Down: Anarchism, Activism and the Vancouver Five, 1967–1985." PhD diss., Simon Fraser University, Burnaby, BC, 2016.

10 Ann Hansen, *Direct Action: Memoirs of an Urban Guerrilla* (Toronto: Between the Lines, 2001), 476.

11 Ibid.

12 Beverley's story is paraphrased from Bonny Walford, *Lifers: The Stories of Eleven Women Serving Life Sentences For Murder* (Fountain Valley, CA: Eden Press, 1987), 69–78.

13 Howard Sapers, "Backgrounder: Aboriginal Offenders—A Critical Situation," September 17, 2013, Office of the Correctional Investigator, Correctional Service of Canada.

14 Statistics Canada. 1996. *Juristat*. Statistics Canada Catalogue no. 85002X1E, vol. 19, no. 5.

15 Ibid.

16 Government of Canada, *Report of the Royal Commission on Aboriginal Peoples* (Ottawa: Government of Canada, 1996).

17 *A Vision for Publicly Funded Legal Aid in British Columbia,"* by the Law Society of British Columbia, March 3, 2017, p. 3.

18 Laura Fraser, "Middle Class Injustice; Too Wealthy for Legal Aid, Too Pinched For 'Average' Lawyers' Fees," *CBC News*, March 7, 2016, http://www.cbc.ca/news/canada/legal-aid-middle-class-1.3476870.

19 "Native Spirituality in Prisons," *Wii'nimkiikaa*, Issue 2 (2005), https://wiinimkiikaa.wordpress.com/native-spirituality-in-prisons/.

20 Canadian Human Rights Commission, *Protecting Their Rights: A Systemic Review of Human Rights in the Correctional Services for Federally Sentenced Women* (Ottawa: Human Rights Commission, 2003), 7.

21 George Caron, *Mouse on a String: At the Prison for Women* (Renfrew, ON: General Store Publishing House, 2009).

22 Bronwyn Chester, "Report on LSD Raises Hackles," *McGill Reporter*, November 5, 1998, http://reporter-archive.mcgill.ca/Rep/r3105/lsd.html.

23 Tom Lyons, "Debate Rages over Safety of ECT Used on the Elderly," *Canadian Press*, September 28, 2002.

24 Karlene Faith and Anne Near, *13 Women: Parables from Prison* (Vancouver: Douglas & McIntyre, 2006), 321.

25 Ibid., 328.

26 Ibid., 329.

27 "Prison Double-Bunking Used in Segregation Cells," *CBC News*, November 22, 2011.

28 Faith and Near, *13 Women*, 330.

29 Ibid., 331.

30 Centre for Infectious Disease Prevention and Control, Health Canada, and CSC, *Infectious Disease Prevention and Control in Canadian Federal Penitentiaries 2000-01* (Ottawa: CSC, 2001), 6.

31 L. Calzavara et al., "Prevalence of HIV and Hepatitis C Virus Infections Among Inmates of Ontario Remand Facilities," *Canadian Medical Association Journal* 177.3 (2007), 257–61.

32 *Kingston Whig-Standard*, December 5, 1988, and December 6, 1988.

33 Solicitor General of Canada, *Commission of Inquiry into Certain Events at the Prison for Women*, commissioner Hon. Louise Arbour (Ottawa: Minister of Public Works and Government Services Canada, 1996), 4.1.2.

34 Jan Heney, "Dying on the Inside: Suicide and Suicidal Feelings Among Federally Sentenced Women," Jan Heney (doctoral thesis, Carleton University, Ottawa, April 1996).

35 Gayle K. Horii, "Addead Punishment," *The Insider* (Matsqui's prison newspaper), August 1990, 12–14.

36 Anne Kershaw and Mary Lasovich, *Rock-a-Bye Baby: A Death Behind Bars* (Toronto: Oxford University Press, 1991).

37 Correctional Service Canada, Bonnie Diamond, and James A. Phelps, *Creating Choices: The Report of the Task Force on Federally Sentenced Women* (Ottawa: The Task Force, 1990). http://www.csc-scc.gc.ca/women/toce-eng.shtml

38 Kim Pate, "The CSC and the 2 Percent Solution: The P4W Inquiry," *The Journal of Prisoners on Prisons* 6, no. 2. (1995): 41–61.

39 Margaret Shaw and Sheryl Dubois, "Understanding Violence by Women: A Review of the Literature," *Women Offender Programs and Issues* (Ottawa: Correctional Service of Canada, February 1995).

40 Michael Jackson and Graham Stewart, "A Flawed Compass: A Human Rights Analysis of the Roadmap to Strengthening Public Safety," in *Justice Behind the Walls: Human Rights in Canadian Prisons*, ed. Michael Jackson (Vancouver: Douglas & McIntyre, 2003).

41 Parliamentary Research Branch, Law and Government Division, *The Battered Wife Defence: The Lavallee Case*, prepared by Christopher Morris and Marilyn Pilon (Ottawa: Parliamentary Research Branch, May 11, 1990).

42 Correctional Service of Canada, "Classification of Institutions," amendment to the *Corrections and Conditional Release Act* (Ottawa: Correctional Service Canada, June 9, 2014). http://www.csc-scc.gc.ca/lois-et-reglements/706-cd-eng.shtml

43 Ontario Human Rights Commission, "Indigenous Spiritual Practices," in *Policy on Preventing Discrimination Based on Creed* (Toronto: OHRC, September 17, 2015), 103–119.

44 Correctional Service Canada, Office of the Correctional Investigator, *Risky Business: An Investigation of the Treatment and Management of Chronic Self-Injury among Federally Sentenced Women—Final Report* (Ottawa: Correctional Service Canada, November 10, 2013).

45 Human Rights Watch, *Incarcerated America: Backgrounder* (New York: Human Rights Watch, April 2003). https://www.hrw.org/legacy/backgrounder/usa/incarceration/

46 Ibid.

47 U.S. Bureau of Justice Statistics, *Direct Expenditures by Criminal Justice Function 1982–2006* (Washington: U.S. Bureau of Justice Statistics, December 29, 2007).

48 "Interactive: Statistics on Canada's Crime Rate," *Globe and Mail*, July 25, 2013.

49 Neil Hunt et al., *A Review of the Evidence-Base for Harm Reduction Approaches to Drug Use* (London: Forward Thinking on Drugs, 2003).

50 Mumia Abu-Jamal, *We Want Freedom: A Life in the Black Panther Party* (Cambridge: South End Press, 2004).

51 Frantz Fanon, *The Wretched of the Earth* (New York: Grove Press, 1968).

52 Paulo Freire, *The Pedagogy of the Oppressed* (New York/London: Continuum, 1970).

53 Canada, Canadian Human Rights Commission (CHRC), *Protecting Their Rights: A Systemic Review of Human Rights in Correctional Services for Federally Sentenced Women* (Ottawa: CHRC, December 2003), 41.

54 Ibid., 42.

55 Ibid.

56 Request no. CSCS-2007-00531 and CSCS-2007-00532, Freedom of Information and Protection of Privacy Services, Ministry of Community

Safety and Correctional Services, March 5, 2007.

57   Solicitor General of Canada, *Commission of Inquiry into Certain Events*, 28.

58   Correctional Service Canada, *Ten-Year Status Report on Women's Corrections 1996–2006* (Ottawa: CSC, April 2006). http://www.csc-scc.gc.ca/publications/fsw/wos24/index-eng.shtml

59   Jim Mahoney, "Crime Rate Hits Four Decade Low, Toronto Leads Trend," *Globe and Mail*, July 25, 2013.

60   Alanna Petroff, "The 'Trickle-Down Theory' Is Dead Wrong," *CNN Money*, June 15, 2015.

61   Era Dabla et al., *Causes and Consequences of Income Inequality: A Global Perspective* (Washington: International Monetary Fund, June 25, 2015).

62   Jeremy Bentham, "Panopticon (Preface)," in *The Panopticon Writings*, edited by Miran Bozovic (London: Verso, 1995), 29–95.

63   Mike Blanchfield and Jim Bronskill, "Experiments in Pain: Prison Doctor Sheds No Tears," *Ottawa Citizen*, September 27, 1998.

64   Solicitor General of Canada, *Commission of Inquiry into Certain Events*.

65   CORCAN is acronym for Corrections Canada, the department responsible for employing prisoners.

66   *Correctional News*, "Closer to Home," December 9, 2005. http://correctionalnews.com/2005/12/09/closer-home/

67   Parole Officer Christina M. Iamundo and Parole Supervisor Deb J. Chase, personal communication.

68   Correctional Service Canada, *The Mandate, Mission and Priorities of the Correctional Service of Canada* (Ottawa: CSC, March 2010), http://www.csc-scc.gc.ca/text/pblct/sb-go/pdf/2-eng.pdf.

69   Correctional Service of Canada, "Correctional Interventions," amendment to the *Corrections and Conditional Release Act* (Ottawa: Correctional Service Canada, June 9, 2014), http://www.csc-scc.gc.ca/lois-et-reglements/700-cd-eng.shtml.

70   "Mission Statement," Canadian Association of Elizabeth Fry Societies, accessed November 26, 2017, http://www.caefs.ca.

71   Jackson and Stewart, "A Flawed Compass."

72   Vauhini Vara, "Will California Again Lead the Way on Prison Reform?" *The New Yorker*, November 7, 2014.

73   "Tories Announce $155.5M Prison Expansion," *CBC News*, October 6, 2010.

74   Jim Bronskill, "Critics Say Harper Government Throwing Prison Expansion Money Away," *Toronto Star*, January 11, 2011.

75   Aaron Wherry, "The PBO Tallies the Cost of Crime Policy," *Maclean's*, March 20, 2013.

76   Sinead Mulhern, "Crime and Punishment," *This*, August 21, 2014.

77   Ibid.

78   Correctional Service of Canada, "Part 3, C: Secure Unit Operational Plan," in *Women Offenders, Programs, and Issues* (Ottawa: CSC, 2003).

79   Gretchen Lemmon, *Impact of a Modified Dialectical Behavior Therapy Treatment on Coping Methods and Impulsiveness in Female Inmates* (doctoral dissertation, Pacific University, 2008), http://commons.pacificu.edu/spp/115.

80 Linda A. Dimeff, Kelly Koerner, and Marsha M. Linehan, *Dialectical Behavior Therapy in Clinical Practice* (New York: Guilford, 2007), 113.

81 Correctional Service of Canada, "Part 3, C: Secure Unit Operational Plan."

82 Tonda MacCharles, "Mental Health Problems Treated as Security Issue in Federal Prisons, Report Says," *Toronto Star*, October 23, 2012.

83 Meagan Fitzpatrick, "Inmates to Pay More for Room and Board," *CBC News*, May 9, 2012.

84 Eugene Ochs, "Convicted by the Media, Sentenced by the Courts," *Dominion: News from the Grassroots*, June 17, 2011.

85 "Squeegee kids" is slang for people who offer to clean car windows at intersections in exchange for money.

86 "History of Prisoners' Justice Day," accessed November 26, 2017, http://www.wcn.bc.ca/august10/politics/1014.history.html.

87 Curtis Rush, "Canadian Inmates Sue Government over T-shirt Ban," *Toronto Star*, August 30, 2012.

88 Ibid.

89 Anna Mehler Paperny, "Double Bunking in Crowded Prison Cells is Not a Problem for Toews," *Globe and Mail*, July 11, 2012.

90 Anita Grace, "Double Bunking Part of Prison Expansion Plan," *Critical Social Justice*, May 9, 2012.

91 Naomi Klein, *The Shock Doctrine: The Rise of Disaster Capitalism* (Toronto: Vintage Canada, 2008), 448.

92 *The Fifth Estate*, "Out of Control," CBC, January 8, 2013.

93 Christie Blatchford, "Senior Managers More Interested in Careers than Inmates: Ashley Smith Inquest," *National Post*, January 29, 2013.

94 Maureen Brosnahan, "Canada's Prison Population at All-Time High," *CBC News*, November 27, 2013.

95 Howard Sapers, Correctional Investigator, *Annual Report of the Office of the Correctional Investigator 2009–2010* (Ottawa: Office of the Correctional Investigator, June 30, 2010).

96 Ibid.

97 Fanon, *Wretched of the Earth*, 51.

98 Dave Seglins and Brigitte Noël, "Prisoner Death Sparks New Allegations of Guard Neglect," *CBC News*, January 23, 2013.

99 Ibid.

100 Canada, Department of Justice, Legal Aid Research Services, *Study of the Legal Services Provided by Penitentiary Inmates by Legal Aid Plans and Clinics in Canada* (Ottawa: Department of Justice, October 4, 2002).

101 Regional Grievance V40R0000976 3.

102 Canadian Bar Association, *Submission on Bill C-10, the Safe Streets and Communities Act* (Ottawa: CBA, October 2011).

103 "FORUM on Corrections Research," Correctional Service Canada, accessed March 5, 2015, http://www.csc-scc.gc.ca/research/forum/e092/e092e-eng.shtml.

104 "Who Killed Mary Steinhauser?" *The Province*, Pacific News, reprinted in the Union of Canadian Correctional Officers newsletter, August 2013.

105 Kim MacKrael, "Corrections Canada Changes Rules for Medical Emergencies after Inmate's Death," *Globe and Mail*, April 11, 2013.

106 "Richest 2% Own Half the World's Wealth: Study," newsletter of United Nations University, Issue 44, December 2006–February 2007, http://archive.unu.edu/update/issue44_22.htm.

107 John Stuart Mill, "On the Definition of Political Economy, and on the Method of Investigation Proper to It," in *Essays on Some Unsettled Questions of Political Economy* (London: Longmans, Green, Reader, and Dyer, 1874).

108 Office of the Correctional Investigator, Government, of Canada, *Aboriginal Offenders: A Critical Situation* (Ottawa: Office of the Correctional Investigator, September 16, 2013).

109 Statistics Canada. 1996. *Juristat*. Statistics Canada Catalogue no. 85002X1E, vol. 19, no. 5.

110 Brian Judge, "A 'Slip of the Tongue' May Reveal Greater Truths," *Kingston Whig Standard*, March 28, 2013.

111 Laura Stone, "On the Winding Road to Redemption in Canada's Women's Prison System," *Calgary Herald*, May 25, 2012.

112 Margaret Shaw and Sheryl Dubois, "Understanding Violence by Women: A Review of the Literature," in *Women Offender Programs and Issues* (Ottawa: Correctional Service of Canada, February 1995, updated December 18, 2012).

113 Ibid.

114 Donald MacPherson, *Mandatory Minimum Penalties: Their Effects on Crime, Sentencing Disparities, and Justice System Expenditures* (Ottawa: Research and Statistics Division of the Department of Justice, Canada, 2011).

115 Inspector for Her Majesty's Inspectorate of Prisons (HMIP), investigating the CSC's response to the recommendations from the Canadian Human Rights Commission Inquiry in 2005.

116 Melanie Kowalski and Tullio Caputo, "Recidivism in Youth Court: An Examination of the Impact of Age, Gender, and Prior Record," *Canadian Journal of Criminology* 41, no. 1 (1999), 58–59.

117 Laura Stone, "On the Winding Road to Redemption in Canada's Women's Prison System," *Calgary Herald*, May 25, 2012.

118 Armine Yainizyan, "The Rise of Canada's Richest 1%," *Canadian Centre for Policy Alternatives*, December 2010.

119 Stone, "On the Winding Road to Redemption."

120 "History of Prisoners' Justice Day."

121 "This Day in History: June 11th, 1975," *Vancouver Sun*, June 11, 2013.

122 "History of Prisoners' Justice Day."

123 Miriam Katawazi, "Harm 'Very Real' for Inmates in Solitary Confinement, Court Told," *Toronto Star*, September 11, 2017.

124 Sridevi Namblar, "UN Committee on Torture Says U.S. Must Reform Its Use of Solitary Confinement," *Solitary Watch*, December 5, 2014.

125 "History of Prisoners' Justice Day."

126 Correctional Service of Canada, "Discipline of Inmates," amendment to the *Corrections and Conditional Release Act* (Ottawa: Correctional Service

Canada, October 26, 2015), http://www.csc-scc.gc.ca/lois-et-reglements/580-cd-eng.shtml

127 Ibid., section 3.1.

128 Justin Piché, "The Liberals Promised Prison Reform, So Why are They Funding Prison Expansion?" *Ottawa Citizen*, March 16, 2017.

129 Madelaine Bielski, "A Herd and a Hope: The Fight to Reopen Canada's Prison Farms," *Pulitzer Center*, March 15, 2017.

130 Abu-Jamal, *We Want Freedom*.